The Evolution of D

The Stanford Series on Education and Public Policy

General Editor: Professor Henry M. Levin, School of Education, Stanford University

---

The purpose of this series is to address major issues of educational policy as they affect and are affected by political, social and economic issues. It focuses on both the consequences of education for economic, political and social outcomes as well as the influences of the economic, political and social climate on education. It is particularly concerned with addressing major educational issues and challenges within this framework, and a special effort is made to evaluate the various educational alternatives on the policy agenda or to develop new ones that might address the educational challenges before us. All of the volumes are to be based upon original research and/or competent syntheses of the available research on a topic.

The Stanford Series on Education and Public Policy

The Evolution of Deficit Thinking:
Educational Thought and Practice

Edited by

Richard R. Valencia

RoutledgeFalmer
Taylor & Francis Group

LONDON AND NEW YORK

First published in 1997
By RoutledgeFalmer
2 Park Square, Milton Park, Abingdon, Oxon, OX14 4RN

Transferred to Digital Printing 2006

A Catalogue record for this book is available from the British Library

Library of Congress Cataloging-in-Publication Data are available on request

ISBN 0 7507 0664 3 cased
ISBN 0 7507 0665 1 paper

Jacket design by Caroline Archer

Typeset in 10/12pt Times by
Graphicraft Typesetters Ltd., Hong Kong.

Publisher's Note
The publisher has gone to great lengths to ensure the quality of this reprint but points out that some imperfections in the original may be apparent

Contents

Acknowledgments

Sincere appreciation is extended to the Center for Mexican American Studies at The University of Texas at Austin who provided me with a 1995 summer Faculty Research Award to undertake work on this book.

To my colleagues — Marta, Doug, Art and Danny — who contributed to this volume, *muchísimas gracias* for your fine work and for putting up with my deadlines.

Special thanks goes to Vera Lopez, graduate student at University of Texas, Austin, who served as my research assistant in tracking down invaluable primary and secondary sources.

Finally, my affection and gratitude are extended to my wife, Marta, who gave me strength and well received intellectual insights while bringing this project to fruition. And, of course, my loving appreciation goes to Carlos and Juan, my twin boys, who were so patient while Daddy was working on his book. *Mijos*, I owe you a lot.

Richard R. Valencia

Introduction

Several years ago I purchased a pair of prescription eyeglasses, a routine of upgrading my lenses for a long-standing, commonplace vision problem. The new frames looked attractive, the stronger lenses provided better acuity, and all seemed well. A week later, however, problems with the glasses arose. Upon taking the glasses off my face and gently placing them on my desk, the right lens popped out (in the absence of any external force). I took the glasses back to the place of purchase, and upon close inspection, the salesperson from whom I initially purchased the glasses informed me that the lens had been cut too small for the frame, and thus a poor structural fit was the problem.

After receiving the repaired glasses a couple of days later, I wore the glasses and went on with my daily schedule. Lo and behold, a week later, the right side lens popped out again — as if it had an energy source of its own! Again, I returned to the optometrist and spoke to the same salesperson about the obstinate little lens that was refusing to stay put. Having been employed in retail business many years ago while I worked my way through college, I was well aware of the business maxim, 'The customer is always right.' Thus, I was expecting an honest and complete resolution to the problem at hand. Apparently, the salesperson with whom I had been dealing did not embrace the above code of business conduct. Much to my amazement and disappointment, she, in a hostile tone, *blamed me* for causing the problem! She more than suggested that I was being too rough with my glasses by placing excessive pressure on the lens during my regular handling of the glasses, causing it to become displaced. She also informed me that the glasses, since repaired, were structurally fit (a point she underscored the optometrist would confirm, if need be). After denying her ludicrous accusations — and seeing I was not going to receive satisfaction — I stormed out, stuck with defective eyeglasses. Suffice it to say, for the next pair of prescription glasses I went to a reputable business.

There is a related account I wish to share with the reader. In early December 1995 I viewed the weekly news program, *Dateline*. The program contained an interesting segment on the dangers of escalators (Grassie, 1995), those power-driven moving stairs that make our travel less arduous in large, spread-out buildings. To my surprise, I learned from the *Dateline* story that approximately 16,000 people, most of whom are children, get injured on escalators each year. The injuries, which involve mangled toes and ankles, typically occur when the space between the side of the escalator wall and the moving belt of steps gradually widens over time due to normal wear and tear, and thus limbs (caught by clothes) can enter and get entrapped. The gist of the *Dateline* segment was to examine two opposing perspectives on the cause of the injuries — one view representing escalator manufacturers, the other representing people who were injured.

The position of the manufacturers was that they were exculpatory, claiming that those injured were at fault because they stood too close to the side of the escalator wall or they wore shoes or leg clothing that placed them at risk for entanglement. The injured, on the other hand, vociferously voiced that they were not at fault, pointing to the disrepair of the escalators as the cause of the bodily injury. Based on my analysis of the evidence provided — especially that of an expert on escalators — it appears that the cause of thousands of injuries was due to the gradual and normal wearing down of the escalator belt and the subsequent failure of the manufacturers or owners to repair the mechanical defects.

So, what do a defective pair of eyeglasses and an escalator in disrepair have in common, and what do they have to do with 'deficit thinking' — the construct under study in this book? Well, a lot. In both instances, the blame for the problem or injury is located — by the more powerful party — in the individual person, the victim — rather than in the structural problems of the unit. In both cases above, *there is a shift of blame from structural defects* (i.e., a poor fit between lens and frame of the eyeglasses; worn, moving parts in disrepair in the escalator) *to the alleged disregard, faults and carelessness of the parties, who claim exculpation.* Although the units of analysis described in the two examples are inorganic (i.e., the eyeglasses) and mechanical (i.e., the escalator), I trust they provide mundane and commonsense illustrations of the notion of deficit thinking to the reader who may be unfamiliar with the idea. If I were to compress the construct of deficit thinking into its most condensed meaning, it would be this: *Deficit thinking is tantamount to the process of 'blaming the victim'. It is a model founded on imputation, not documentation.*

The present book examines the evolution of deficit thinking in the context of education — both in 1) the academic discourse as to what constitutes deficit thinking and 2) the schooling practices resultant of this social thought. Regarding the term itself, 'deficit thinking', it is difficult to pin down precisely when it was first coined. It appears that this brilliant two-word phrase was invented by a small cadre of scholars in the early 1960s who launched an assault on the orthodoxy that asserted the poor and people of color caused their own social, economic and educational problems (A. Pearl, personal communication, August 8, 1991). Thus, the term deficit thinking appears to have its origin as a social construction stemming from the heterodoxic thought of the 1960s, a period in which deficit thinking discourse had its own socially constructed terms, such as, the 'culturally disadvantaged child' (Black, 1966); 'socialization of apathy and underachievement' (Hess, 1970); 'cultural deprivation' (Edwards, 1967); and 'accumulated environmental deficits' (Hess and Shipman, 1965).

In reference to deficit thinking models, scholars typically use related terms. For example, Boykin (1986) uses the term 'deficiency approach', Nieto (1996) uses 'deficit theories', and Swadener (1995) refers to the term 'deficit model'. It is our preference in the present book to employ the term deficit thinking because it comes closest to what we believe constitutes the notion, that is: 1) a mind-set molded by the fusion of ideology and science; 2) a dynamic form of social thought allegedly accounting for between-group behaviors; 3) an actual way of thinking to combat problems (for example, imputational; top-down approach; paternalistic).

Our focus in the present book is on how the deficit thinking model has been advanced to explain school failure, particularly among economically disadvantaged racial/ethnic minority students (such as African American; Mexican American; Puerto Rican). These students have been and continue to be substantially over-represented among those who experience academic problems and school failure (for example, reading below grade level; dropping out of high school), and they are prime targets of the deficit thinking intellectual discourse and schooling interventions.

Of the various conceptual frameworks that have been advanced to explain school failure among low-income minority groups, the deficit thinking theory has held the longest currency among scholars, educators and policymakers. Although there are several explanatory variants of this model, the deficit thinking paradigm, as a whole, posits that students who fail in school do so because of alleged internal deficiencies (such as cognitive and/or motivational limitations) or shortcomings socially linked to the youngster — such as familial deficits and dysfunctions. Given the endogenous nature of deficit thinking, systemic factors (for example, school segregation; inequalities in school financing; curriculum differentiation) are held blameless in explaining why some students fail in school. It must be underscored, however, that students who are failing in school must — along with their parents — muster every effort they can in achieving school success (the development of good study habits; parental involvement in education; political involvement and action). Of course such endeavors are difficult to mount in alienating, inequitable learning environments. In short, although deficit thinking overwhelmingly locates school failure causes in students and their families, failing students and their significant others must be assertive in their quest for school success, in that deficit thinking theory and practice will not work for their best interests. As Arthur Pearl discusses in Chapter 7, connecting political action and education can result in workable school reform.

Although the deficit thinking model is held in disrepute by many contemporary behavioral and social scientists, there is mounting evidence that deficit thinking is experiencing a resurgence in current educational thought and practice. The 1994 publication of the disputatious *The Bell Curve* by Herrnstein and Murray — which is an atavistic treatise similar to 1920s hereditarian thought in which racial/ethnic differences in intelligence were believed to be genetically based — is the latest offering of the growing neohereditarianism. The popular 'at-risk' construct, now entrenched in educational circles, views poor and working-class children and their families (typically of color) as being predominantly responsible for school failure, while frequently holding structural inequality blameless. Present anti-deficit thinking discourse, on the other hand, sees the 'at-risk' child as a retooled construct of the 'culturally disadvantaged' child notion from the 1960s when deficit thinking held orthodoxic currency (see Swadener and Lubeck, 1995).

Notwithstanding the historical and contemporary influences of deficit thinking in educational thought and practice, no sustained analysis of this theory appears in the literature. We find this remarkable given the long-standing history and ubiquitous nature of deficit thinking. There are bits and pieces of discussion (e.g., Boykin, 1986; Neisser, 1986; Nieto, 1996), but what is clearly absent is a comprehensive and integrated analysis of the general deficit model and its several variants. This book attempts to fill this lacuna. Particular focus will be on how the deficit model has evolved over the decades. Our analysis will cover the time frame from the early 1600s to the mid-1990s. We will strive to seek out, describe and discuss the implications and linkages between the educational theory and practice of deficit thinking. In that the model is rooted in ignorance, classism, racism, sexism, pseudoscience and methodologically flawed research, we will provide critiques of deficit thinking discourse and research, and when necessary, offer rival explanatory models for school failure.

Our general plan in the present book involves the examination of numerous primary and secondary sources in order to investigate how ideological and scientific thinking merged over the decades *vis-à-vis* the education of the poor and specific racial/ethnic minority groups, such as African American; Mexican American. Historically, the confluence of ideology and science made a volatile union in understanding the educational problems and needs of economically disadvantaged and socially segregated groups. In our analysis, the major goal is to provide a fuller understanding of the evolution of both educational thought and practice of deficit thinking. Given the anticipated breadth and depth of such coverage, the proposed book, for the most part, uses a periodization scheme to examine the evolution of deficit thinking.

Richard Valencia's task in Chapter 1, Conceptualizing the Notion of Deficit Thinking, is to unpack the characteristics and complexities of deficit thinking. Valencia does so by discussing six aspects that describe the construct of deficit thinking. To wit, he asserts deficit thinking is: 1) a process of blaming the victim; 2) a form of oppression; 3) pseudoscientific in its pursuit of knowledge; 4) a dynamic model, changing according to the temporal period in which it finds itself; 5) a model of educability; that is, it contains suggestions or actual prescriptions for educational practice; 6) a model so controversial that dissent, and in some cases, heterodoxic discourse is inevitable.

Martha Menchaca presents Chapter 2, Early Racist Discourses: The Roots of Deficit Thinking, in which she examines the foundation of deficit thinking in the United States and delineates how racist discourses impacted the schooling practices towards racial minorities. The historical periods examined range from the early 1600s to the late 1800s. American racist discourses centered on the assumptions that people of color were either biologically or culturally inferior to Caucasians.[1] One of Menchaca's main conclusions is that early racial discourses were independent from, but strongly interconnected to, white economic interests. Between 1620 to 1870, whites enslaved or maintained racial minorities in positions of servitude because it economically benefited them. They were able to do this by passing discriminatory racial legislation. Whites rationalized their actions, however, by claiming the moral right to govern racial minorities in that the latter were either animals or were culturally inferior. By 1870, the reasons for subordinating racial minorities became more complicated, yet for many whites, economics continued to be a motivating factor. In the area of American education, Menchaca shows that racist beliefs and economic interests were clearly intertwined. In most communities of the United States, racial minorities were prohibited from being schooled and when public education became available to whites in the United States, denying schooling to racial minorities continued to be strongly motivated by economic interests. After whites were extended public education, nearly a century passed until racial minorities were given the same privilege. Yet, such schooling for students of color typically was segregated and inferior — thus demonstrating the pernicious impact of deficit thinking on schooling practices.

In Chapter 3, Richard Valencia offers his analysis of The Genetic Pathology Model of Deficit Thinking. This theory, which contends that inferiority is transmitted by the genetic code, was very popular from about 1890 to 1930. Valencia's focus, however, is on the 1920s when hereditarian thought was at its zenith. With the advent of the intelligence test in 1905 in France and the subsequent importation, cultural appropriation, and standardization of the test by US scholars, an intelligence testing movement rapidly swept the decade of the 20s. Based on numerous race psychology studies of this era, the lower intellectual performance of certain groups (such as poor and working-class black and Mexican American students) was deemed to be genetically based. From such research, specific deficit thinking schooling practices emerged (e.g., outright segregation; dead-end classes for the 'mentally retarded'; low-level vocational education). Valencia's analysis of the genetic pathology era covers: 1) the nature vs. nurture debate; 2) ideological and measurement foundations of the genetic pathology model; 3) cross-racial research on intelligence testing and actual use of tests in curriculum differentiation; 4) heterodoxic, anti-deficit thinking views raised by white scholars, and that which is frequently overlooked by historians, dissent launched by African American and Mexican American scholars of the 1920s and 1930s.

Chapter 4, entitled Deficit Thinking Models Based on Culture: The Anthropological Protest, is written by Douglas Foley. He portrays how cultural deficit thinkers replaced their early genetic models of deficit with a highly selective concept of culture, appropriated from anthropologist Oscar Lewis' 'culture of poverty' theory. After presenting Lewis' theory, Foley illustrates how the culture of poverty perspective was fused with narrower, more technical deficit studies of language and parenting into a 'poverty discourse'. As the poverty discourse became fashionable in public policy circles, anthropologists, especially ethnic minority scholars, produced a host of empirical studies that replaced cultural deficit models with cultural difference models of language, family and community. Ultimately, anthropologists also dismantled the culture of poverty theory with new paradigms of culture revised with theories of class, class cultures and power. Taken together, Foley shows how the studies thoroughly discredit the culture of poverty/cultural deficit thesis.

In Chapter 5, Arthur Pearl analyzes the Cultural and Accumulated Environmental Deficit Models. In the 1960s, the conservative genetic deficit theories were replaced by liberal *'cultural deficit'* theories. These theories took many forms and drew upon different branches of social science, particularly psychology. The three that had the greatest influence were 'cultural deprivation', 'inadequate socialization' and 'accumulated environmental deficits'. Pearl shows that all were 'cultural' because all contacted to the particular styles of parenting. Cultural deprivation drew upon anthropology and postulated the existence of an anti-intellectual culture of poverty that perpetuated itself. Inadequate socialization drew upon psychoanalysis; it was predicated on the proposition that failure to provide proper nurturance produced character defects in the ego and superego. In the former case, the deficit resulted in an inability to delay gratification; in the latter case, the deficit was a flawed social conscious and the inability to distinguish right from wrong. Accumulated environmental deficit theorizing was spawned from the emerging cognitive science. The lack of intellectual stimulation in poor homes was postulated to lead to irreversible cognitive deficiencies. Pearl contends that the accumulated environmental deficit argument became the official policy of the Kennedy–Johnson administrations and underpinned the Head Start early intervention program and the Elementary and Secondary Education compensatory education act. Both of these 1960s interventions continued to be supported, and even grew under the Reagan and Bush administrations, as Pearl examines how deficit thinking grew and proliferated in the past three decades. Deficit models now have conservative tinges. The major difference in treatment of deficits in conservative and liberal administrations is that conservatives are more likely to treat deficits with punishment and threats of punishment, whereas liberals institute remedial programs.

In Chapter 6, Richard Valencia and Daniel Solórzano team to offer their analyses of Contemporary Deficit Thinking. Although their discussion of contemporary deficit thinking covers a period from the late 1950s to the present, the authors concentrate on the deficit thinking discourses of the 1980s and 90s. Valencia and Solórzano find that contemporary deficit thinking cannot be conveniently placed under a clear rubric as can be done for earlier deficit thinking eras, as current discourse on deficit thinking is a conglomeration of the previously discussed models — genetic pathology, culture of poverty, and cultural and accumulated environmental deficits. As such, Valencia and Solórzano divide their analyses into 1) description and critiques of neohereditarianism as seen in the cross-racial/ethnic studies of intellectual performance by Shuey (1966), Jensen (1969), Dunn (1987), and Herrnstein and Murray (1994); 2) an examination of current deficit thinking views of the poor, with a focus on the 'underclass' construct; 3) coverage of renewed assaults on 'inadequate parents, home, and child' as causes of school failure; here, Valencia and Solórzano highlight the recent, on-going deconstruction of the 'at-risk' discourse — a construct often implicitly classist and racist (Swadener and Lubeck, 1995).

Arthur Pearl presents Chapter 7, Democratic Education as an Alternative to Deficit Thinking. Pearl argues that deficit thinking is deeply embedded in American life and thought. It has too many offshoots to be effectively combated in a piecemeal fashion. Deficit thinking is part of larger frames of reference; it fits neatly into the 'natural law' foundation on which modern conservative thought rests; it is also part of the liberal commitment to help those unable to help themselves. Alternatives to deficit thinking will not be successful unless those alternatives are part of a general theory. Pearl proposes 'strong democracy' as the alternative to general theories that maintain deficit thinking. In schools, the alternative to deficit model policies and practices he offers is 'democratic education'. A democratic education has four requirements: 1) a curriculum organized so that all students are *equally* prepared to use knowledge to solve important social and personal problems; 2) a clearly enunciated student Bill of Rights that is made *equally* available to all students; 3) opportunity for all students to participate *equally* in decisions that affect their lives; 4) classroom practices that *equally* encourage all students to succeed in all of the school's sanctioned activities. What these requirements mean and how they can be used to provide an alternative to deficit thinking is briefly described by Pearl, and the evidence is presented to show that when democratic education principles are applied, so-called deficits tend to disappear. Lastly, a career ladder approach to teacher credentialing is outlined to provide evidence of the effectiveness of a democratic approach to teacher education, as a measure that would provide teachers who would be better able to encourage all students equally. The career ladder approach is contrasted with affirmative action as a non-deficit thinking alternative to an endangered practice.

Chapter 8, the final contribution, is entitled Epilogue: The Future of Deficit Thinking in Educational Thought and Practice and is written by Richard R. Valencia and Arthur Pearl. The authors assert that the momentum and currency contemporary deficit thinking hold in educational thought and practice are likely to increase into the twenty-first century, if this virulent social thought goes unchecked and unchallenged. Exacerbating this gloomy prognostication, Valencia and Pearl contend, is the dramatic increase in people of color (general and school-age populations) and the poor — two populations that are primary marks of deficit thinking. Further fueling the ascendant direction of deficit thinking discourse is the mounting and oppressive neoconservatism characterizing the national and state political levels. Valencia and Pearl's pessimistic vision of the future regarding the role of deficit thinking in educational thought and practice is based on the assumption that such discourse will go unabated. As the authors underscore, however, this is *not* the case. Current anti-deficit thinking discourse (e.g., Fine, 1990; Kozol, 1991; Pearl, 1991; Ronda and Valencia, 1994; Swadener and Lubeck, 1995; Valencia, 1991) is an extension of decades of dissent. Valencia and Pearl are cautiously optimistic that the contemporary deficit thinking movement can be slowed down significantly if the on-going anti-deficit thinking discourse launches a full-scale assault via a continuation of the deconstruction of deficit thinking notions, as well as the proffering of workable school reform based on principles of democratic education.

Note

1   In the present book, we use the term *American* in reference to the United States of America — a practice deeply embedded in historical and contemporary scholarship. We are well aware that America is a continent, not a country. We use the term American out

of convention, not as a geo-chauvinistic claim that the USA has exclusive ownership of the word.

References

BLACK, M.H. (1966) 'Characteristics of the culturally disadvantaged child', in FROST, J.L. and HAWKES, G.R. (Eds) *The Disadvantaged Child: Issues and Innovations*, Boston, MA: Houghton Mifflin, pp. 45–50.

BOYKIN, A.W. (1986) 'The triple quandary and the schooling of Afro-American children', in NEISSER, U. (Ed) *The School Achievement of Minority Children: New Perspectives*, Hillsdale, NJ: Erlbaum, pp. 57–92.

DUNN, L.M. (1987) *Bilingual Hispanic Children on the US Mainland: A Review of Research on their Cognitive, Linguistic, and Scholastic Development*, Circle Pines, MN: American Guidance Service.

EDWARDS, T.J. (1967) 'Pedagogical and psycho-social adjustment problems in cultural deprivation', in HELLMUTH, J. (Ed) *Disadvantaged Child*, New York: Brunner/Mazel, 1, pp. 161–71.

FINE, M. (1990) 'Making controversy: Who's "at-risk"?', *Journal of Cultural Studies*, 1, pp. 55–68.

GRASSIE, J. (Writer) (1995, December 1) *Dateline*, New York: National Broadcasting Corporation.

HERRNSTEIN, R.J. and MURRAY, C. (1994) *The Bell Curve: Intelligence and Class Structure in American Life*, New York: Free Press.

HESS, R.D. (1970) 'The transmission of cognitive strategies in poor families: The socialization of apathy and underachievement' in ALLEN, V.L. (Ed) *Psychological Factors in Poverty*, Chicago IL: Markham, pp. 73–92.

HESS, R.D. and SHIPMAN, V. (1965) 'Early experience and the socialization of cognitive modes in children', *Child Development*, 36, pp. 869–86.

JENSEN, A.R. (1969) 'How much can we boost IQ and scholastic achievement?', *Harvard Educational Review*, 39, pp. 1–123.

KOZOL, J. (1991) *Savage Inequalities: Children in America's Schools* New York: Crown.

NEISSER, U. (1986) 'New answers to an old question', in NEISSER, U. (Ed) *The School Achievement of Minority Students: New Perspectives*, Hillsdale, NJ: Erlbaum, pp. 1–17.

NIETO, S. (1996) *Affirming Diversity: The Sociopolitical Context of Multicultural Education* (2nd ed.) New York: Longman.

PEARL, A. (1991) 'Systemic and institutional factors in Chicano school failure', in VALENCIA, R.R. (Ed) *Chicano School Failure and Success: Research and Policy Agendas for the 1990s*, London: Falmer Press, pp. 273–320.

RONDA, M.A. and VALENCIA, R.R. (1994) '"At-risk" Chicano students: The institutional and communicative life of a category', *Hispanic Journal of Behavioral Sciences*, 16, pp. 363–95.

SHUEY, A.M. (1966) *The Testing of Negro Intelligence* (2nd ed.) New York: Social Science Press.

SWADENER, B.B. (1995) 'Children and families "at promise": Deconstructing the discourse of risk', in SWADENER, B.B. and LUBECK, S. (Eds) *Children and Families 'at Promise': Deconstructing the Discourse of Risk*, Albany: State University of New York Press, pp. 17–49.

SWADENER, B.B. and LUBECK, S. (Eds) (1995) *Children and Families 'at promise': Deconstructing the Discourse of Risk*, Albany, NY: State University of New York Press.

VALENCIA, R.R. (Ed) (1991) *Chicano School Failure and Success: Research and Policy Agendas for the 1990s*, London: Falmer Press.

Chapter 1

Conceptualizing the Notion of Deficit Thinking

Richard R. Valencia

As our nation approaches the new century, the improvement of schooling for economically disadvantaged racial/ethnic minority students presents one of the greatest challenges ever faced by educators and policymakers (Valencia, Menchaca and Valenzuela, 1993). Millions of low-socioeconomic status (SES) minority students (particularly, African Americans, Mexican Americans, and Puerto Ricans) attend schools that are segregated, inequitably financed, vapid in curricula delivery, teacher-centered and generally hostile in any sense of a learning environment. It is not surprising then that many students attending such schools perform very poorly on conventional measures of academic achievement, such as perform below grade level on standardized reading tests, drop out of secondary schools at extraordinarily high rates, and matriculate to four-year universities in small numbers (see Valencia, 1991).

What accounts for such school failure — which I have previously defined as persistently, pervasively and disproportionately low academic achievement (Valencia, 1991) — among a substantial proportion of low-SES minority students? To be sure, the educational literature has not been silent on this question. Explanations include 'communication process' models that emphasize differences, hence misunderstandings, between students and teacher in verbal and nonverbal communication styles (Erickson, 1987). Such misunderstandings from these marked boundaries often result in students being labeled unmotivated to learn. In sum, linguistic differences lead to trouble, conflict and school failure.

Another explanation of school failure lay in 'caste theory', a model advanced by Ogbu (see Ogbu, 1978, 1987; for a concise summary and critique of Ogbu's theory, see Foley, 1991). This model contends that castelike ethnic minority students (for example, African Americans; Mexican Americans) living in a racist society perceive their educational and life chances as quite limited, and thus adapt accordingly by collective action or hustling for example. Once overwhelmed, such minority students 'develop a dysfunctional oppositional culture that leads them to believe that they cannot be both academically successful and ethnically different. In short, caste theory makes a powerful case that involuntary minorities are not likely to succeed in school and life' (Foley, 1991: 67).

Still, another explanation of school failure is offered under the rubric of what

1

may best be called 'structural inequality' models (see Bowles and Gintis, 1976; Pearl, 1991). Pearl contends that the failure of many low-SES minority students 'can be fully understood only when analyzed in the broadest political, economic and cultural contexts' (1991: 273). Pearl's structural model posits that the 1) vicissitudes of the national economy, 2) political influence over school policy and practice (macropolitics), and 3) the top-down, authoritarian nature of schooling are all factors contributing to school failure.

The theory of school failure that is the subject of the present book is termed *deficit thinking*. Of the several theories that have been advanced to explicate school failure among economically disadvantaged minority students, the deficit model has held the longest currency — spanning well over a century, with roots going back even further as evidenced by the early racist discourses from the early 1600s to the late 1800s (see Menchaca, Chapter 2, this book). The deficit thinking model, at its core, is an endogenous theory — positing that the student who fails in school does so because of internal deficits or deficiencies. Such deficits manifest, it is alleged, in limited intellectual abilities, linguistic shortcomings, lack of motivation to learn and immoral behavior. The proposed transmitters of these deficits vary according to the intellectual and scholarly climate of the times. We shall see that genetics, culture and class, and familial socialization have all been postulated as the sources of alleged deficits expressed by the individual student who experiences school failure. Given the parsimonious nature of deficit thinking, it is not unexpected that advocates of the model have failed to look for external attributions of school failure. How schools are organized to prevent learning, inequalities in the political economy of education, and oppressive macropolicies and practices in education are all held exculpatory in understanding school failure.

Presently, many behavioral and social scientists hold the deficit thinking model in disrepute — arguing that it is unduly simplistic, lacks empirical verification, more ideological than scientific, grounded in classism and racism, and offers counterproductive educational prescriptions for school success. However, because deficit thinking is so protean, taking different forms to conform to what is politically acceptable at the moment, and while the popularity of different revisions may change, it never ceases to be important in determining school policy and practice. Given the strong conservative ascendancy it is not surprising that deficit thinking is currently experiencing a resurgence (see the neohereditarian works of Dunn, 1987; Herrnstein and Murray, 1994). Valencia and Solórzano (Chapter 6, this volume) examine this contemporary deficit thinking. Not only is deficit thinking penetrating current educational thought and practice (for example, the popular notion of the at-risk student; see Swadener and Lubeck, 1995, for a sustained critique), it is shaping national policies toward the economically disadvantaged such as welfare reform and immigration reform.

In light of the long-standing existence of deficit thinking and its powerful influence on educational practice, it is incongruous that very little has been written on the concept of deficit thinking. To wit, my goal in this introduction is to unpack the notion of deficit thinking. I will do so by establishing what the term means. In my treatise, I discuss six characteristics of deficit thinking in the following contexts: 1) blaming the victim; 2) oppression; 3) pseudoscience; 4) temporal changes; 5) educability; 6) heterodoxy.

Blaming the Victim and Deficit Thinking

In 1971, William Ryan offered the social sciences *Blaming the Victim* — a now classic book. With the striking force of a two by four, Ryan's blow to the backbone of deficit thinking was clearly felt.[1] In a penetrating and impassioned treatise, his social construction of the phrase, 'blaming the victim', masterfully got to the core of the nature of deficit thinking. Ryan's book was a reaction to deficit thinking and subsequent policies advanced in the 1960s, a time at which the deficit thinking model hit its apex with respect to volume of literature, policy interventions and popularity. His critique transcended deficit thinking in education and covered social programs in general. Commenting on the 'terrifying sameness in the programs' (p. 7) that arose from deficit thinking, Ryan observed:

> In education, we have programs of 'compensatory education' to build up the skills and attitudes of the ghetto child, rather than structural changes in the schools. In race relations, we have social engineers who think up ways of 'strengthening' the Negro family, rather than methods of eradicating racism. In health care, we develop new programs to provide health information (to correct the supposed ignorance of the poor) and to reach out and discover cases of untreated illness and disability (to compensate for their supposed unwillingness to seek treatment). Meanwhile, the gross inequalities of our medical care delivery systems are left completely unchanged. As we might expect, the logical outcome of analyzing social problems in terms of the deficiencies of the victims is the development of programs aided at correcting those deficiencies. *The formula for action becomes extraordinarily simple: change the victim.* [emphasis added] (1971: 8)

In sum, I believe Ryan's (1971) *Blaming the Victim* was especially valuable in exposing the ideological base of deficit thinking (i.e., the more powerful blame the innocent) and in showing us how deficit thinking translated to action. First, social problems were identified (by victim-blamers). Second, a study was done in order to find out how the disadvantaged and advantaged were different. Third, once the differences were identified, they were defined as the causes of the social problem. Fourth, governmental intervention was set in play to correct the differences (i.e., deficiencies). The great appeal of deficit thinking as a model of social reform in the 1960s and early 1970s lay in the framework's appearance of soundness. In reference to the above four steps, Ryan noted, 'All of this happens so smoothly that it seems downright rational' (p. 8).

Oppression and Deficit Thinking

It follows logically from Ryan's (1971) analysis of 'victim-blamers and victims' that deficit thinking is a form of oppression — that is, the cruel and unjust use of authority and power to keep a group of people in their place. As we shall see in some of the remaining chapters of the present book, the history of deficit thinking in education is filled with examples of how economically disadvantaged students of color were kept in their place by macro- and microlevel educational policies/ practices fueled by class and racial prejudice.

The historical and contemporary bases of such oppression are seen in a range of contexts: for example, state constitutional statutes, state educational agency policies, judicial outcomes, state legislation, local school board policies, and classroom teacher practices. Some actual examples are:

Compulsory Ignorance Laws

These laws were adopted in the US South in the middle of the eighteenth century. They called for heavy fines for any person who taught African slaves to write or used them as scribes (Weinberg, 1977). One explanation for the basis of compulsory ignorance laws lay in the belief that African slaves were mentally deficient and thus they had severe limitations on how much they could benefit from literary training. Another, and more plausible reason for such laws was that Southern whites used these statutes as means of keeping slaves in check. After all, becoming literate has the potential of raising consciousness and politicizing oppressed people. In short, knowledge takes on a liberating potential. As Weinberg notes, 'Whites seemed to fear not that Negroes could not learn but that they would' (p. 39).

School Segregation

The forced segregation of ethnic minority students has been a subject of great interest among scholars (for example, Donato, Menchaca and Valencia, 1991; Gonzalez, 1990; Menchaca and Valencia, 1990; San Miguel, 1987; Weinberg, 1977; Wollenberg, 1978). Clearly, segregationist laws and related practices constituted oppression. As Menchaca and Valencia have noted, there is considerable evidence that the ideological foundations of school segregation date back to the racial beliefs of the nineteenth century that white groups should not socially interact with peoples of colored races. Such white supremacy practices were predicated on the belief that colored races were biologically inferior and race mixing would contaminate whites (see Menchaca, Chapter 2 of this book, for full development of this idea).

The role of deficit thinking was very influential in the promotion of school segregation during the rooting of separate but equal education in the late 1890s and early 1900s, and in the subsequent decades of entrenchment (1920s, 1930s, 1940s). The forced segregation of African American and Mexican American students, for example, was based on deficit views that these children were intellectually inferior, linguistically limited in English, unmotivated, and immoral — all characteristics that would hold back the progress of white students if racial/ethnic mixing in schools was permitted. Suffice it to say, deficit thinking in its manifestation of schooling practices led to inferior schooling, hence such social thought and its subsequent policy recommendations contributed substantially to school failure for many low-SES minority students. Segregation, an oppressive act, resulted in 'colored' and 'Mexican' schools with run-down physical plants, insufficient supplies, dated textbooks and dead-end curricula.

High-stakes Testing

A modern form of educational oppression, driven by deficit thinking, is high-stakes testing, which is defined as:

> The exclusive, or near exclusive use of a test score to make a significant educational decision about students, teachers (prospective and incumbent), and schools. Such decisions can have desirable or undesirable consequences for students, teachers, and schools. That is, a great deal rides on the results of certain test scores. A significant gain or loss can result from test score outcomes (hence the notion of 'high-stakes'). (Valencia and Guadarrama, 1996: 561)

High-stakes testing programs, which have now swept the country, are state-mandated strategies founded on the premise (unvalidated) that schooling outcomes such as reading performance and graduation from high school can be improved through built-in sanctions. For example: Pass the test, graduate; do not pass, do not graduate. Valencia and Guadarrama contend that high-stakes testing constitutes test abuse. Using Mexican Americans in Texas as a case in point, the authors argue that for Mexican American students, who are forced to traverse an educational path filled with obstacles, the realization of school success becomes even more distant. High-stakes testing, a new hurdle, exacerbates the attainment of school success in a terrain where obstacles, inequities and adverse conditions abound. Furthermore, Valencia and Guadarrama make the point that the Texas Educational Agency's policy of threatening to close schools (meaning low-SES minority schools) that perform poorly on the state-mandated tests 'constitutes institutional bullyism' (1996: 584). The authors also note that such a rating policy is grounded in deficit thinking in that the practice ignores the schooling problems that teem in Texas, such as inequities in school financing; underserving of the limited-English-proficient student population; school segregation. Finally, the authors offer this criticism of the Texas Educational Agency (TEA): 'For the TEA to sidestep these issues and to place the burden of school reform solely on the local campus is an indefensible policy' (1996: 587).

In conclusion, I believe that the contention of characterizing deficit thinking as a form of oppression offers a fruitful area to develop intellectually. As our account of the evolution of deficit thinking unfolds, more will be discussed about the linkages among deficit thinking, educability perceptions, the politics of oppression, the practice of schooling, and school failure.

Pseudoscience and Deficit Thinking

Another central contention I assert here is that deficit thinking is a form of pseudoscience, which Blum (1978) defines as a 'process of false persuasion by scientific pretense' (p. 12). To some extent, the appeal of the deficit thinking paradigm among scholars, laypeople, and policymakers comes from the model's wrapping — the 'scientific method'. We are all familiar with the core of the scientific method: that is, empirical verification. Science rests on the process of beginning with sound assumptions and clear conjectures (or hypotheses), moves through the operation of collecting data with reliable and valid tools, and concludes with objective empirical verification (or disconfirmation) of the initial conjectures.

A close examination of research by deficit thinkers uniformly shows that the scientific method is frequently violated (see Garth, 1923). Typically, the study's assumptions are unsound, instruments used are psychometrically weak and/or data are collected in flawed manners and rival hypotheses for the observed findings are not considered. Of course, the preceding scenario can, and does, characterize just plain sloppy research. How does one draw the line between 1) legitimate scientific research that contains lethal flaws that prevent its publication from 2) pseudoscience? One can argue that the difference lays in the *degree of researcher bias* (which is ubiquitous), as well as the *degree of vigor* the researcher pursues hypothesis verification. On these distinctions between true and pseudoscience, Blum (1978) notes:

> All scientific work is guided by assumptions, and the defense of one's assumption becomes a likely source of bias. Particularly when controversial topics are being researched, some amount of bias is inherent in the position of any investigator. The label 'pseudoscience' becomes pertinent when the bias displayed by scientists reaches such extraordinary proportions that their relentless pursuit of verification leads them to commit major errors of reasoning. (pp. 12–13)

In addition to the above distinction between genuine science and pseudoscience, Blum (1978) also offers good advice to those who wish to discern whether pseudoscience exists. Blum contends that two different kinds of occurrences must join: 'First, there must be attempts at verification which are grossly inadequate. Second, the unwarranted conclusions drawn from such attempts must be successfully disseminated to and believed by a substantial audience' (p. 12). These two criteria will prove useful in our analysis of the development and maintenance of deficit thinking. As a case in point, I (in Chapter 3) draw on these standards when discussing hereditarianism, the intelligence testing movement, and deficit thinking from about 1900–1930.

Temporal Changes and Deficit Thinking

Given the pseudoscientific, hence ideological nature of deficit thinking, it makes sense to characterize it as a dynamic and chameleonic concept. That is, deficit thinking is greatly influenced by the temporal period and *Zeitgeist* in which it finds itself. Two points need to be made here. First, deficit thinking, though dynamic in nature, is shaped more by the ideological and research climates of the time — rather than shaping the climates.[2] For example, during the 1920s, deficit thinking *vis-à-vis* racial differences in intelligence was heavily affected by widespread hereditarian views — perspectives entrenched in cross-racial research endeavors, eugenics and psychometrics (Blum, 1978).

Second, the fluid aspect of deficit thinking is not seen in the basic framework of the model, but rather in the transmitter of the alleged deficits. The basic characteristics of the model (endogenous; imputational; oppressive) are fairly static. What is protean is the perceived *transmitter* of the alleged deficits. In the genetic pathology variant of deficit thinking, poor intellectual performance of people of color is believed to be transmitted through inferior genes. In the culture of poverty variant, autonomous and self-sustaining cultural systems of the poor are thought to be the carriers of deficits and subsequent problems, such as school failure. In the cultural and accumulated environmental deficits variant of deficit thinking, the familial and home environmental contexts are singled out as the transmitters of pathology.

In light of the changing nature of the scholarly and ideological spheres of society, it is possible to trace — with some sense of clarity — the evolving conformation of deficit thinking as well as its impact on shaping educational practices. To wit, this is the aim of the following chapters.

Educability and Deficit Thinking

The social and behavioral sciences have four goals with regard to understanding human behavior, to 1) describe, 2) explain, 3) predict and 4) modify behavior. As a scholarly pursuit, the deficit thinking model also strives to attain these objectives. As we have discussed, deficit thinking typically offers a *description* of behavior in pathological or dysfunctional ways — referring to deficits, deficiencies, limitations or shortcomings in individuals, families and cultures. With respect to an *explanation* of behavior, endogenous factors, such as limited intelligence or linguistic deficiencies, are claimed to be the etiological bases of the alleged behavioral deficits. It follows, then, that deficit thinking would posit a *prediction* of the maintenance and perpetuation of deficits, if intervention is not pursued. In sum, the three aspects of description, explanation and prediction of behavior are central to the way the deficit thinking model operates. It is also important to underscore that the fourth aim (modification or intervention) of the social and behavioral sciences regarding human behavior is integral to our understanding of the functioning of the deficit thinking framework. This means that deficit thinking sometimes offers a *prescription* in its approach to dealing with people who are targeted populations, for example, low-SES Puerto Ricans.

In the following chapters, the reader will be informed of numerous examples of how deficit thinkers have proposed and, directly or indirectly, helped shape the actual implementation of educational interventions for low-SES racial/ethnic minority students. Lewis Terman, a prominent figure (and deficit thinker) in the nascent period of the intelligence testing movement, advocated that 'Indians, Mexicans, and Negroes...' because of their alleged intellectual dullness and ineducability 'should be segregated in special classes and be given instruction which is concrete and practical' (Terman, 1916, pp. 91–2). In the 1920s, deficit thinkers argued successfully for the segregation of Mexican (i.e., Mexican American) students, for example, using the contention that these children had 'language handicaps' (i.e., were limited in English language skills) and thus should be segregated in special classes or Mexican schools. Such isolation of Mexican students, it was argued, was necessary as they would slow the learning process and academic development of white students. From an anti-deficit thinking perspective not only was this an unsound intervention (i.e., no bilingual education was provided), but some Mexican students who spoke no Spanish were *also* segregated — thus demonstrating racist overtones of this practice (Donato *et al.*, 1991). Deficit theorists in the 1960s were not content with a copious descriptive, explanatory and predictive framework of the 'culturally deprived' or 'culturally disadvantaged' child. These self-proclaimed experts also had specific policy recommendations for educating the so-called deprived child. Bereiter and Engelman (1966), for example, presented detailed language programs to improve the 'linguistic deprivation' of poor blacks. Such programs consisted of rote, unchallenging verbal stimulation in which the child had to adjust to the curriculum — not the other way around.

The notion of educability, particularly perceptions about the educability of economically disadvantaged minority students, will have a decidedly impressive presence in our analysis of the deficit thinking model. This salience of educability perceptions and curricula intervention stems from the basic nature of the student–teacher (and policymaker) relationships. Available research, observations, and anecdotes all inform us that most schools are teacher-centered, top-down, and elitist (Pearl, 1991). Many adults who develop educational policy or teach students frequently attribute school failure to students, and school success to themselves. Of course, such attributional distortions become magnified when deficit thinking is involved. As a colleague and I noted elsewhere (Valencia and Aburto, 1991: 233–4): 'Some scholars would have us believe that educability is largely dependent on individual intellectual ability and that social, political, and economic conditions within the schools and society are largely unrelated to "*why* some of our children are so much more educable than others" (Hawkins, 1984: 375).' In the proceeding analysis of deficit thinking in educational thought and practice, we will explicate the historical essence of the educability-intervention issue as advanced by Dabney (1980):

> The historical emphasis upon capacity for learning has been to perceive school learning as primarily dependent upon the presumed ability of the student, rather than upon the quality of the learning environment. However, there appears to be a growing recognition that school failure and student achievement are socially determined. Even so ... such recognition

has not prevented new interpretations of these failures which blame the victims and often co-exist with arguments about innate or class deficiencies. (p. 13)

Heterodoxy and Deficit Thinking

In Bourdieu's (1992) *Outline of a Theory of Practice* the concepts of 'doxa', 'orthodoxy' and 'heterodoxy' are key notions in his theories of capital and symbolic power — frameworks to understand class domination. To Bourdieu, doxa is that part of the class society in which the social world is 'beyond question' or there is a 'universe of the undiscussed (undisputed)'. When argument or crisis occurs in a class society, a 'universe of discourse (or argument)' is set in motion. According to Bourdieu, when the world of 'opinion' is opened, heterodoxy (i.e., unconventional opinions; dissent; nonconformity) comes into play as 'the dominated classes have an interest in pushing back the limits of *doxa* and exposing the arbitrariness of the taken for granted . . .' 1992: 169). On the other hand, 'the dominant classes have an interest in defending the integrity of doxa or, short of this, of establishing in its place the necessarily imperfect substitute, *orthodoxy*' (p. 169).

I find Bourdieu's (1992) discussion (as described above) useful in understanding the tension between the deficit-thinking and the anti-deficit thinking camps. In the evolution of deficit thinking, there have been eras, for example, 1920s, 1960s and early 1970s in which deficit thinking has clearly characterized the orthodoxy. Albeit having minimal impact at first in challenging the status quo during these periods, heterodoxic views did appear (see Bond, 1924; Ginsburg, 1972; Ryan, 1971; Sanchez, 1934). As I noted earlier, although the deficit thinking model is held in low esteem by many scholars today, its substantial historical influence in shaping educational thought and practice as well as its current resurgence deserves our attention. Furthermore, we need to be aware that heterodoxic opinions with respect to deficit thinking have been part of this evolution. The current book builds on this stream of academic discourse that critiques deficit thinking.

In conclusion, we can summarize the preceding discussion of six characteristics of deficit thinking in the context of schooling as follows:

1 Deficit thinking is a person-centered explanation of school failure among individuals as linked to group membership (typically, the combination of racial/ethnic minority status and economic disadvantagement). The deficit thinking framework holds that poor schooling performance is rooted in students' alleged cognitive and motivational deficits, while institutional structures and inequitable schooling arrangements that exclude students from learning are held exculpatory. Finally, the model is largely based on imputation and little documentation.
2 In light of the 'victim–blamers/victims' nature of deficit thinking and the lop-sided power arrangements between deficit thinkers and economically disadvantaged minority students, the model can be oppressive. As such,

the deficit thinking paradigm holds little hope for addressing the possibilities of school success for such students.

3   The deficit thinking model is a form of pseudoscience in which researchers approach their work with deeply embedded negative biases, pursue such work in methodologically flawed ways, and communicate their findings in proselytizing manners.

4   Depending on the historical period, the alleged deficits are transmitted via low-grade genes, inferior culture and class, or inadequate familial socialization. We shall see, however, that contemporary deficit thinking draws from all these bases.

5   Not only does the deficit thinking model contain descriptive, explanatory and predictive elements, it is also — at times — a prescriptive model based on educability perceptions of low-SES minority students.

6   Historically, the deficit thinking model has rested on orthodoxy — the dominant, conventional scholarly and ideological climates of the time. Through an evolving discourse, heterodoxy has come to play a major role in the scholarly and ideological spheres in which deficit thinking has been situated.

With this dissection of the deficit thinking construct now complete, we move to an analysis of the evolution of deficit thinking in educational thought and practice. Martha Menchaca begins by presenting her examination of the Early Racist Discourses: Roots of Deficit Thinking.

Notes

1   Ryan did not use the term *deficit thinking* in his book. He did, however, refer to 'defect' situated 'within the victim' (1971: 7). In any event, it is very clear that the theory he was critiquing was the deficit thinking model.

2   This is not to say that deficit thinking has been silent in shaping macrolevel social programs and schooling practices. A case in point was the structuring and implementing of Operation Head Start, a federal program of the mid-1960s built on a 'compensatory' approach (see Pearl, Chapter 5, this book).

References

BEREITER, C. and ENGELMAN, S. (1966) *Teaching Disadvantaged Children in the Preschool*, New York: Prentice-Hall.

BLUM, J. (1978) *Pseudoscience and Mental Ability: The Origins and Fallacies of the IQ Controversy*, New York: Monthly Review Press.

BOND, H.M. (1924) 'What the army "intelligence" tests measured', *Opportunity*, **2**, pp. 197–202.

BOURDIEU, P. (1992) *Outline of a Theory of Practice*, Cambridge, England: Cambridge University Press.

BOWLES, S. and GINTIS, H. (1976) *Schooling in Capitalist America: Educational Reform and the Contradictions of Economic Life*, New York: Basic Books.

DABNEY, M.G. (1980, April) *The Gifted Black Adolescent: Focus upon the Creative Positives*. Paper presented at the Annual International Convention of the Council for Exceptional Children, Philadelphia, PA (ERIC Document Reproduction Service No. ED 189 767).

DONATO, R., MENCHACA, M. and VALENCIA, R.R. (1991) 'Segregation, desegregation, and integration of Chicano students: Problems and prospects', in VALENCIA, R.R. (Ed) *Chicano School Failure and Success: Research and Policy Agendas for the 1990s*, London: Falmer Press, pp. 27–63.

DUNN, L.M. (1987) *Bilingual Hispanic Children on the US Mainland: A Review of Research on their Cognitive, Linguistic and Scholastic Development*, Circle Pines, MN: American Guidance Service.

ERICKSON, F. (1987) 'Transformation and school success: The politics and culture of educational achievement', *Anthropology and Education Quarterly*, **18**, pp. 335–56.

FOLEY, D.E. (1991) 'Reconsidering anthropological explanations of ethnic school failure', *Anthropology and Education Quarterly*, **22**, pp. 60–86.

GARTH, T.R. (1923) 'A comparison of the intelligence of Mexican and mixed and full blood Indian children', *Psychological Review*, **30**, pp. 388–401.

GINSBURG, H. (1972) *The Myth of the Deprived Child: Poor Children's Intellect and Education*, Englewood Cliffs, NJ: Prentice-Hall.

GONZALEZ, G.G. (1990) *Chicano Education in the Era of Segregation*, Philadelphia, PA: The Balch Institute Press.

HAWKINS, T. (1984) 'Vote of confidence', Commentary in 'Backtalk', *Phi Delta Kappan*, **65**, p. 375.

HERRNSTEIN, R.J. and MURRAY, C. (1994) *The Bell Curve: Intelligence and Class Structure in American Life*, New York: Free Press.

MENCHACA, M. and VALENCIA, R.R. (1990) 'Anglo-Saxon ideologies and their impact on the segregation of Mexican students in California, the 1920s–1930s', *Anthropology and Education Quarterly*, **21**, pp. 222–49.

OGBU, J.V. (1978) *Minority Education and Caste: The American System in Cross-cultural Perspective*, New York: Academic Press.

OGBU, J.V. (1987) 'Variability in minority school performance: A problem in search of an explanation', *Anthropology and Education Quarterly*, **18**, pp. 312–34.

PEARL, A. (1991) 'Systemic and institutional factors in Chicano school failure', in VALENCIA, R.R. (Ed) *Chicano School Failure and Success: Research and Policy Agendas for the 1990s*, London: Falmer Press, pp. 273–320.

RYAN, W. (1971) *Blaming the Victim*, New York: Random House.

SÁNCHEZ, G.I. (1934) 'Bilingualism and mental measures', *Journal of Applied Psychology*, **18**, pp. 765–72.

SAN MIGUEL, G., JR. (1987) *'Let Them All Take Heed': Mexican Americans and the Campaign for Educational Inequality in Texas, 1910–1981*, Austin, TX: University of Texas Press.

SWADENER, B.B. and LUBECK, S. (Eds) (1995) *Children and Families 'at promise': Deconstructing the Discourse of Risk*, Albany NY: State University of New York Press.

TERMAN, L.M. (1916) *The Measurement of Intelligence*, Boston, MA: Houghton Mifflin.

VALENCIA, R.R. (1991) 'The plight of Chicano students: An overview of schooling conditions and outcomes', in VALENCIA, R.R. (Ed) *Chicano School Failure and Success: Research and Policy Agendas for the 1990s*, London: Falmer Press, pp. 3–26.

VALENCIA, R.R. and ABURTO, S. (1991) 'The uses and abuses of educational testing: Chicanos as a case in point', in VALENCIA, R.R. (Ed) *Chicano School Failure and Success: Research and Policy Agendas for the 1990s*, London: Falmer Press, pp. 203–51.

VALENCIA, R.R. and GUADARRAMA, I.N. (1996) 'High-stakes testing and its impact on racial/ethnic minority students', in SUZUKI, L.A., MELLER, P.J. and PONTEROTTO, J.G. (Eds) *Multicultural Assessment: Clinical, Psychological and Educational Applications*, San Francisco CA: Jossey-Bass, pp. 561–610.

VALENCIA, R.R., MENCHACA, M. and VALENZUELA, A. (1993) 'The educational future of Chicanos: A call for affirmative diversity', *The Journal of the Association of Mexican American Educators*, pp. 5–13.

WEINBERG, M.A. (1977) *A Chance to Learn: The History of Race and Education in the United States*, New York: Cambridge University Press.

WOLLENBERG, C. (1978) *All Deliberate Speed: Segregation and Exclusion in California Schools, 1855–1975*, Berkeley CA: University of California Press.

Chapter 2

Early Racist Discourses:
The Roots of Deficit Thinking

Martha Menchaca

This chapter will examine the roots of deficit thinking in the United States and will delineate how racist discourses impacted the schooling practices towards racial minorities. This discussion will chronologically examine a series of long-standing debates over race beginning with the 1600s and ending in the late 1800s. Past racial beliefs about people of color were varied and arose from moral, political, pseudo-scientific and racist debates (Blum, 1978; Feagin, 1989). These discourses centered on the premise that people of color were either biologically or culturally inferior to Caucasians. In presenting this discussion I will support the theoretical position that in the past racial discourses were independent from, but were strongly interconnected to, colonial economic interests (Blauner, 1994; Lyons, 1975; Takaki, 1994). This interrelationship influenced many domains of American society, including schooling.

My intent in this chapter is to focus on the influence of this ideological and economic interrelationship upon the schooling practices of racial minorities. I will argue that between 1620 to 1870, whites enslaved or maintained racial minorities in a servitude position because it economically benefited them. Whites rationalized this economic interest by promoting various discourses alleging the inferiority of non-whites (Lyons, 1975; Weinberg, 1977).[1] By 1870, the reasons for subordinating racial minorities became more complicated, yet for many whites economics continued to be a motivating factor. As a consequence, when public education became available to whites in the United States, denying schooling to racial minorities continued to be strongly motivated by white economic interests. In most communities, whites refused to allow racial minorities to attend public schools. Because the main preoccupation of American racists was to prove blacks were inferior, my analysis will focus on the latter and then examine how this ideological dilemma impacted other racial minorities.

The Settlement of America and the Ideologies of
Racial Contact–1620 to 1732

My account of American deficit thinking begins with the arrival of the English Pilgrims in North America. My intent is not to charge that the Pilgrims were racist against 'tawny people' and that they subsequently cleared the land of the 'savage Indians', rather my purpose is to explain how the racial beliefs of the early seventeenth century arrived, via the Pilgrims, to America. In 1620, when the Pilgrims set foot in America and met the native inhabitants of the New World, biblical interpretations were the only accepted discourses used to explain the racial and cultural differences between the commuting parties (Feagin, 1989). The Pilgrims are believed to having been a pious people who sought religious freedom in the New World. Their goals were meritorious and provided an ethical foundation for the virtuous goals of the new republic which soon was to unfold upon our shores. There were problems, nonetheless, with the Pilgrims' presence in America. Although they were a 'good' people, they were colonizers. As they migrated away from English religious intolerance, they unwittingly became the servants and conduits of mercantile capitalism in America (Rose, 1989). Their financial backers used them and other early colonizers as agents of British economic interests. Under British law, the Crown and the mercantile capitalists, who sponsored the Pilgrims' voyage to the New World, had the right to set claim to America because the Pilgrims were among the first Europeans to set foot upon this land (see *United States v. Rogers*, 1846). British law did not recognize the Native Americans to be the legal owners of the New World. Only the first Europeans to inhabit America had such legal claim. The Pilgrims were rewarded for their role in the conquest and settlement of America by being granted moderate farming plots, adequately sufficient to sustain their families. For the financiers of the colonial encounter and the British Crown a much heftier reward awaited, as the Pilgrims had given them the legal basis to transform America into their real estate property (Rose, 1989).

Another problem was unwittingly introduced by the Pilgrims. This problem was not economic, but rather it dealt with the embroilment of religious beliefs and British economic interests. During the seventeenth century, Britain's economic interests in America centered on transferring land inhabited by Indians into British property (Takaki, 1990). Indian labor was not coveted or needed, for the colonizers and their financiers were obsessed with obtaining land. Thus, fraudulent legal practices were used by the British to usurp Indian lands while, concurrently, the British Crown used violent militaristic maneuvers to extricate the Indians from their homelands. If the Indians refused to be relocated, extermination was considered to be the only alternative practice. This oppressive land displacement was viewed by the colonizers as a sorrowful yet unavoidable practice God had destined them to enact, in order to salvage America from paganism.

The Pilgrims and the succeeding white generations rationalized their economic interests by proselytizing the religious tenet that they were 'God's Chosen People' (Feagin, 1989; Menchaca, 1995). To them it was clear that God had made the Anglo-Saxons a superior race destined to own and to govern America (Blum, 1978; Gossett, 1953, 1977). Allegedly, God had also bestowed upon them the obligation to encourage European immigration in order to populate America with Christians. It was therefore their religious right to take possession of America by any means necessary.

The religious views of America's early settlers were merely a reflection of the popular views held in Great Britain and by a large part by the scientific community of Europe. These views had been strongly influenced by the travel accounts of European explorers, government officials, adventurers and scientists. European travel accounts depicted people around the world as being either savages or barbarians, who lacked Christian faith and committed idolatrous acts by venerating demonic gods (Said, 1979; Weinberg, 1977). In essence, people of color were demonized. A common opinion was that the dark races were descendants of the devil. Such views were often manifested in British plays, novels and literary works and thus served to perpetuate stereotypes about people of color (Mintz, 1985; Said, 1979). Edward Said supports this position and comments that influential scholars adopted popular myths and subsequently published works where they demonized non-whites. He states that in the Orient and in other places where people of color resided, Europeans generated lies about them and transformed them into white truths. With respect to the Orient, Said observes:

> The European imagination was nourished extensively from this repertoire: between the Middle Ages and the eighteenth century such major authors as Ariosto, Milton, Marlowe, Tasso, Shakespeare, Cervantes, and the authors of the *Chanson de Roland* and the *Poem del Cid* drew on the Orient's riches for their productions, in ways that sharpened the outlines of imagery, ideas, and figures populating it. In addition, a great deal of what was considered learned Orientalist scholarship in Europe pressed ideological myths into service, even as knowledge seemed genuinely to be advancing. (1979: 63)

Said further comments that the reification of demonic stereotypes was astutely used by the British to justify colonialism around the world.

George Stocking concurs and comments that these popular racial views were opportune during the age of British exploration and colonial settlement as they became the bedrock foundation to rationalize British colonialism (Stocking, 1968). Colonization was often rationalized as being a Christian act that would lead to the moral upgrading of alleged savages and barbarians. Stocking further proposes that although these racial views did not generate the conditions to embark on the colonial enterprise, they served to condone it and justify its practice. For example, when the British Crown increased its massive real estate holdings in America, the West Indies and Africa, government officials rationalized their land acquisition policies by claiming that all 'vacant land' needed to be developed and transformed into profitable property. Moreover, this quest for profit was accompanied by a racist discourse that promoted the enslavement of non-whites — in particular blacks.

In America, this scenario began to unfold when the British military launched a campaign of destruction against the Indians by killing them or relocating them in areas not settled by whites (Wolf, 1982). With the near decimation of the indigenous population it became necessary to import slaves. For as Gramsci posits (in Forgacs, 1988), the economic needs of those in power are often rationalized as common sense practices, or in other words naturalized as inevitable acts that must be enacted for the common good of society. After most Indians were massacred, land became available to every British settler — wealthy and poor alike. Wealthy estate owners amassed thousands of acres formally owned by the Indians. These estates required massive amounts of slave labor if profit was to be made. However, the small-scale farmer also needed slaves, of course in less amounts, and in correspondence to the size of the farm and the economic means of the farmer. To the small-scale farmer, owning a slave meant the difference between having or not having luxuries and the opportunity to improve one's economic standing in the community.

Thus, the enslavement and exportation of Africans to the American-British colonies was an expedient response to the labor demands generated by Anglo-Saxon usurption of Indian lands and the increasing number of Anglo-Saxons and northern European immigrants establishing farms in America. By the late 1600s there were approximately 200,000 Anglo-Saxon colonists and by the mid-1700s there were close to 2 million Anglo-Saxons and 200,000 to 400,000 Scottish-Irish (Feagin, 1989).[2] Likewise, by the late 1600s Great Britain imported two-thirds of the slaves exported from Africa and sent 2 million slaves to its American and West Indies colonies (Barbados and Jamaica) (Wolf, 1982).

The enslavement of African people was perversely justified by the colonial government and its subjects. In America, the racial belief that Africans were not human beings and their enslavement was not against God's will was a popular argument used to condone slavery (Lyons, 1975; Weinberg, 1977). Although Francois Bernier in 1684 and Carlos Linnaeus in 1730 had published scientific studies challenging that belief, popular opinion in America continued to view Africans as animals (Blum, 1978; Gossett, 1953). Bernier's and Linnaeus' studies had found that Africans, Indians, Asians and Caucasians belonged to the same species and none of these races could be considered animals. Yet, deficit thinking about the nature of Africans remained the orthodoxy.

In the American-British colonies, the inferiority of Africans and other people of color was interpreted in various ways. To many individuals, inferiority was associated with biological differences, whereas to others it was a result of non-whites lacking European culture and/or Christian religion. As we shall see in later chapters of the present book, the themes of *biological inferiority* and *cultural deprivation* will play important roles in the evolution of deficit thinking. By 1730, these different views became apparent in popular, government and scientific discourses. Two dominant discourses took center stage, reflecting different moral attitudes toward non-whites. One discourse supported the common unity of mankind as presented by the biblical account of God's creation. Racial differences were explained by acclimation and migration accounts proceeding God's creation of Adam and Eve (see Lyons, 1975). It was alleged that after Adam and Eve's creation, their descendants migrated to different parts of the world, and after inhabiting new environmental niches, the climate produced distinguishing physical characteristics among groups of people. The opposing discourse also supported the creationist thesis, but disagreed with the explanation that the climate changed the physical appearance of people. This discourse proposed that only Caucasians were human and were created by God (see Nott and Gliddon, 1854, 1857).

With respect to the schooling of non-whites, the biblical interpretation proposing a common origin of mankind served to foster paternalistic attitudes. In the 1600s British missionaries and American Quakers set up a few schools to educate African slaves and American Indians (Feagin, 1989; Lyons, 1975). The missionaries were convinced that Africans and American Indians were human because they had the ability to undergo religious transformation. The organized efforts of these Christians were launched by the Society for the Propagation of the Gospel (SPG). The SPG was a Christian missionary organization with chapters in the United States, the Caribbean and Africa. Although these pioneers sought to educate Africans and American Indians because they were children of God, their Christian religious doctrine allowed them to retain the belief that people of color were inferior. Africans and American Indians were viewed to be savages whose cultural environment had prevented them from cognitively developing in the same manner as Caucasians (Nott and Gliddon, 1854). In the case of Africans, the SPG members believed the tropical climate in Africa had somehow stunned the natives' intellectual development and instead fostered indolence and dullness (Weinberg, 1977). A similar deficit thinking environmental explanation was offered about American Indians even though the climate of North America was vastly different from Africa. Nonetheless, members of the SPG advocated the education of Africans and American Indians because they believed that Christian doctrines would enlighten them and salvage their souls. The more progressive missionaries also sought to educate Africans as a means of teaching them competitive skills to enter the free labor market. Their intentions were motivated by anti-slavery sentiments for they considered slavery to be immoral and culturally damaging for both Africans and whites. Because they believed in the common unity of mankind, they disagreed with the position that God condoned slavery. Furthermore, they opposed slavery on the grounds that it made whites lazy and dependent on slaves. Likewise, for Africans, slavery was viewed to obstruct their cognitive development and made their learning of Christian doctrines nearly impossible. At that time, SPG missionaries were not met with open hostility by those who opposed the schooling of Africans and American Indians, in that very few mission schools had been opened and the participation of the African slaves was approved by their masters.

The Monogenist v. Polygenist Debate

By 1732, the biblical paradigm came under overwhelming attack for being unscientific. Many scholars claimed natural history provided scientific evidence that the human races previously classified by Bernier and Linnaeus actually belonged to different species (E. Agassiz, 1885; L. Agassiz, 1854; see Banton and Harwood, 1975; Brinton, 1890; Nott and Gliddon, 1854, 1857). These scholars claimed only Caucasians belonged to the human race. These scholars criticized biblical interpretations on the ground that they offered philosophical and not scientific perspectives about humankind. With the emergence of the natural sciences into a prominent position, the biblical paradigm began to lose its position as the elaborator of the basic principles of the origins of humankind (Nicholson, 1991). Many scholars sought to understand the basic ordering of society by searching for principles found in the essential features of natural and social reality.

Although the attack on the biblical paradigm obtained widespread support in the 1700s, it was not abandoned. In 1732, the opposing schools of thought on the genesis of mankind came to be known as the Monogenist v. Polygenist Debate (Stocking, 1968). The monogenist theorists claimed there was a common origin for mankind and supported their position by citing biblical parables. They, however, also began to support their claims with natural science research as many scholars were arguing that material evidence was necessary to support any origins argument. On the other hand, the polygenists claimed that the physical differences between the races were radical and thus could only be explained by divergent origins. At the forefront of the polygenist school of thought were the craniologists who were in the process of investigating the relations between the body and the environment. These individuals sought to support their claims by advancing pseudoscientific evidence that proved the races had different cranium sizes, hence there was a hierarchy of superiority. Craniologists were supported by other scholars who advanced less racist hypotheses, but who nonetheless considered non-whites not to be human.

Scholars such as Lord Kames, who was clearly a polygenist thinker, but was uncomfortable in denouncing all biblical interpretations in fear of being labeled a heretic, attempted to reinterpret various Old Testament passages in efforts to legitimize the polygenist discourse. Lord Kames' book, written in 1774 and entitled *Sketches of History of Man*, claimed that all the races had been created by God (see Stanton, 1966). He argued, however, that upon the dispersal of Adam and Eve's children from their parental homeland, they migrated to areas populated by non-humans, and subsequently propagated with them, resulting in the creation of species that were only *part* human. In this manner, Lord Kames illustrated why Christian theologians and many scholars mistakenly thought non-whites were human, given that interbreeding between Caucasians and animals had produced an animal that resembled humans. Citing the parable of The Tower of Babel, Lord Kames argued this event lent credence to the conclusion that some of the races were not human. To Lord Kames, the only acceptable explanation for the confusion of tongues was that some individuals were not speaking human languages. Lord Kames' convoluted perspectives played a significant role in the debate over the origins of mankind, for the polygenist position was given legitimacy and subtly allowed to remain within the confines of Christian theology.

Charles White was a polygenist scholar, as well as a craniologist (Nott and Gliddon, 1854, 1857; Stanton, 1966). He became one of the most influential scholars within the craniology movement. White and his colleagues claimed that the smaller brain cases of non-whites indicated they were of a different species from Caucasians. Physical similarities between non-whites and Caucasians were attributed to a common genus that had produced various species. To support his thesis, White compared animals with humans. According to White, foxes, wolves and dogs belonged to the same genus but were of a different species. Likewise, he claimed that whites and non-whites shared the same genus, but were of different species. He also advanced other subjective opinions and attempted to pass them as scientific data. White claimed that besides the cranial differences between the races, the anthropoid facial features of blacks and the dark skin of non-whites supported the divergent origins thesis.

Scholars such as Johannan F. Blumenbach offered a counter analysis to the views expressed by the craniologists (Banton and Harwood, 1975). Blumenbach was also a craniologist, but did not agree that the cranial differences between whites and non-whites supported the polygenist position. He claimed a common origin for mankind, arguing that all the races originated from a pair of Caucasian parents. Allegedly, climatic and environmental differences in the ecological niches inhabited by the various races had caused distinctions in physical appearance. Blumenbach claimed that the similarities between non-whites and the animals inhabiting the same ecological niche could be explained by how the environment had affected all of the inhabitants of the particular area. For example, physical similarities between monkeys, gorillas and blacks were explained in this way. As a means of explaining why cranial differences existed between whites and non-whites, Blumenbach argued the environment had caused the latter groups' brains to degenerate, and over time to become smaller. To him, however, this was insufficient evidence proving a distinct species argument. Blumenbach claimed that in the case of blacks, the hot environment had made them sluggish and their inactivity had stunned the development of their brains.

Peter Camper, also a monogenist, supported Blumenbach's research, yet became intensely involved in investigating the common facial similarities between blacks and monkeys (Lyons, 1975). He also concluded that the environment had caused blacks and monkeys to develop similar jaw structures. Unfortunately, Camper's research was used by the polygenists to further prove that Africans were animals. The jaw measurement data gathered by Camper were used to corroborate the claims advanced by the polygenists.

By the late 1770s, the craniology and facial feature data gathered by the polygenists appeared to be compelling evidence supporting their stance. However, the monogenists introduced a hybridity thesis that became difficult to refute (Stocking, 1968). Both the monogenists and polygenists recognized that non-whites were interbreeding with whites and successfully propagating mulattoes (a person of black and white ancestry) and mestizos (a person of white and Indian ancestry). Their explanations for this phenomenon, however, were analyzed differently by both camps. The monogenists argued that the proliferation of half-breeds proved whites and non-whites were of the same species, otherwise they would not have been able to reproduce. In turn, the polygenists offered two separate arguments. First, Charles White proposed that in the animal kingdom there were certain types of animals who were of different species and could interbreed. Interbreeding was possible because they belonged to the same genus. Once again referring to dogs, wolves and foxes, White claimed that these animals belonged to different species yet they could have offspring (Stanton, 1966). Their offspring, White claimed, would be born sterile. A second polygenist thesis was advanced by scholar Edward Long. His hybridity explanation, however, focused on ethnological observations rather then acclimation arguments. His thesis appears to have been appealing to the public for his book became the most widely circulated polygenist text of its time. In 1774, Long wrote *The History of Jamaica* where he examined miscegenation practices between English colonists and black slaves (see Stanton, 1966). Long concurred with White and other polygenists who claimed that because blacks had anthropoid facial features, this proved undoubtedly that blacks were not human. Using Charles White's hybridity thesis to corroborate his findings, Long posited that whites and blacks in Jamaica could interbreed and produce offspring. Mulatto offspring, however, allegedly were born infertile. To Long, the 'fact' that mulattoes were sterile supported the polygenist explanation that interbreeding was possible between different species and hybridity was not evidence of a common origin. Long, as a means of addressing ethnological observations contradicting his hybridity–sterility explanation, qualified his arguments by noting that only in rare cases did mulattoes have offspring. Allegedly, mulattoes could only be fertile if they interbred with pure blacks. Curiously, Long did not comment why in Latin America, whites, Indians, and blacks had been interbreeding for over two centuries and the hybrid populations continued to be fertile. Furthermore, Long failed to examine the interbreeding research that the monogenists had advanced against his thesis.

William Stanton argues in his book, entitled *The Leopard Spots* (1966), that even in Long's time his thesis was recognized to be severely flawed; yet it was embraced by polygenist thinkers because it served a political function. That is, by the late 1700s, the monogenist v. polygenist debate had become severely embroiled in the political debate over slavery. The origins of mankind became a very important political discourse used to justify or attack slavery (Gossett, 1953; Lyons, 1975). We must now turn to this topic and examine the interrelations between racist thinking and early American racial practices.

Racial Thinking and American Economic Practices–1776 to 1800

In 1776, the United States obtained its independence from England and in the new republic the founding fathers instituted a racial policy permitting slavery and denying non-whites the basic rights guaranteed to its white citizens (Menchaca, 1993). Whether the founding fathers of the new government supported the polygenist or monogenist discourse is difficult to determine. It is clear, however, that the policies they enacted and the documents they wrote indicate they considered non-whites to be inferior. Furthermore, as the new republic matured, racial laws were passed to maintain non-whites in a subordinate position and to promote the economic interests of whites. To delineate these historical issues, an analysis of the racial laws passed by the founding fathers in the late 1700s and a review of the racial philosophy of two great American statesmen will clarify how deficit thinking and economic interests were intertwined.

In the American Declaration of Independence, the founding fathers decreed that all men were created equal. Subsequent legislation passed by them and their successors, however, clearly illustrates that the Bill of Rights did not apply to non-whites. In the first draft of the Constitution of the United States, Native Americans were declared to be three-fifths of a person for purposes of taxation and census counts (Constitution of the United States, article 1, section 2, in United States Code Service Constitution, 1986: 18; see Menchaca, 1993; Takaki, 1990, 1994). And, when the 13 colonies ratified their first constitutional legislations, non-whites were not extended United States citizenship (Feagin, 1989; Heizer and Almquist, 1977; Menchaca, 1993). On the contrary, in the case of blacks and Indians it was legal to enslave them. In the passage of the first Naturalization Act of 1790 our founding fathers declared that only free 'white' immigrants had the right to apply for citizenship, when Indians and blacks were denied that right (Naturalization Act of 1790, chapter 3, section 1). In addition, beginning in 1797 the federal and state governments passed inheritance legislation to ensure that property in the United States could not be owned in perpetuity by racial minorities (in chronological order these cases are *United States v. Villato*, 1797; *McCreery v. Somerville*, 1824; *McKinney v. Saviego*, 1855; *Cross v. De Valle*, 1863). Native Americans and Spaniards (and later Mexicans and Asians) who owned land were prohibited from passing down their property to heirs.[3] The property was seized by the federal government after the death of the landowner. Indeed, these early laws and constitutional declarations clearly demarcate our founding fathers' racial views. Whether they thought non-whites were humans is unclear, but what is blatantly obvious is that they viewed them to be inferior and unworthy of receiving the political rights accorded to whites.

Furthermore, a few years after the American Revolution the writings left by two great statesmen reveal the rationale behind the passage of these racist laws. It also appears that the polygenist and monogenist arguments were fused together to condone the labor exploitation of people of color. The union of these pseudo-scientific tenets produced a discourse that appeared to be Christian and likewise, morally, to justify the exploitation of non-whites.

Thomas Jefferson, the main author of the American Declaration of Independence and of the first United States Constitution, believed in the monogenist origin of mankind (Sinkler, 1971). However, he staunchly defended the institution of slavery on the grounds that the success of the American farmer and the economy of the United States depended upon the maintenance of slavery and the absorption of the land inhabited by Indians (Takaki, 1990, 1994). Jefferson also proposed that slavery was not immoral nor did it violate the spirit of the Constitution in that non-whites were cognitively and morally inferior to whites. On blacks, Jefferson commented that they were a race of degenerate people who were dull and inclined to laziness. If they were not enslaved they would be unproductive, and if emancipated they would starve and soon find themselves destitute. Partly in response to abolitionist critics, Jefferson eventually revised his position on slavery. Jefferson was accused of professing compassion and humanity in the treatment of slaves, yet contradicting his words by his acts. Jefferson was a well known anti-abolitionist and throughout his life refused to free any of his slaves, including his own hybrid children. In particular, heightened criticisms were launched toward him when it became public knowledge that Jefferson had a black mistress and three illegitimate children (Sinkler, 1971; Takaki, 1990). To many of Jefferson's critics, his thoughts, actions and personal life were convoluted and morally reprehensible. Thomas Hamilton, for example, publicly reviled Jefferson. Hamilton wrote:

> The moral character of Jefferson was repulsive . . . Continually puling about liberty, equality, and the degrading curse of slavery, he brought his own children to the hammer, and made money of his debaucheries. Even at his death, he did not manumit his numerous offspring, but left them, soul and body, to degradation, and the cartwhip. (quoted in Stanton, 1966: 56)

Politically, however, Jefferson's actions indeed seem to be astute. By advocating a middle of the road position, Jefferson could receive support from both the monogenists and polygenists in that he advocated a racial inferiority thesis without demeaning the worth of the Bible. Likewise, his views justified a humane type of slavery.

By 1790, Jefferson's position toward slavery changed. He agreed with his critics that slavery should be abolished in the United States. However, his views on slavery were not morally motivated; rather, they were fueled by economic and racist interests. Jefferson proposed that slavery should eventually be abolished, for if not, it would lead to the moral degeneration of whites (Takaki, 1990). The profits wreaked from slavery gave white men excessive leisure time and prevented them from cultivating the American work ethic of hard work. Thus, Jefferson proposed if slavery was not abolished it would produce generations of white men interested solely in play and pleasures of the body. To the nation this could be disastrous. Jefferson, however, qualified his liberal stance. If slavery was abolished, Jefferson proposed it would be necessary to deport blacks to avoid the mulattoization of the United States. He speculated that once slaves were emancipated, white males would propagate with black females and in the succeeding generation the light-skinned mulatto offspring would intermarry with whites. Jefferson also proposed, for the benefit of the nation, that a deportation mandate would be necessary after emancipation. Allegedly, given that blacks were feeble-minded, they would become a burden upon the state. In the case of mulattoes, Jefferson did not consider them to be feeble-minded. However, he considered them to be an economic threat to whites. Because mulattoes would be cognitively enriched by their white fathers, they would pose a threat to the free labor market because they would have the ability to perform the same skills as whites.

With respect to Native Americans, Thomas Jefferson had a more compassionate attitude. He proposed that they too were humans, but they posed a threat to the moral consciousness of this nation. He acknowledged the fact that Indians had been fraudulently removed from their lands, and in the process, most of them had been exterminated. To Jefferson, this had been an inevitable dilemma. On the one hand the land had to be cleared for the farmers. Without land, Jefferson argued, America could not have been built. On the other hand, the extermination of the Indians was troubling the minds of Americans, producing a collective sense of national guilt. For Jefferson, the only form of abolishing this guilt would be either to assimilate the remaining Indians or to exterminate those who survived. Indians, unlike blacks, could be assimilated because they were an industrious people. Jefferson argued that before the white man set his foot upon this shore, many Indians led civilized lives as farmers. He believed that although in the future Indians could not reach the same level of intellectual development as white people, he was confident that they could live among civilized people. Jefferson warned, however, that if Indians refused to live among whites there would not be any place in society for them, because without the company of whites, Indians would become a savage people (Sinkler, 1971).

Similar views were shared by Benjamin Rush (MD), a second well known statesman and political philosopher of American republicanism, following the independence of the United States. Dr Rush's role within American politics is attributed to his well respected writings on the virtues of republicanism (Stanton, 1966; Takaki, 1990). He proposed that under republicanism Americans would develop an industrious work ethic and a religious ethic guided by the tenets of Christianity. His medical observations on race were also widely circulated and were used by abolitionist activists. Dr Rush was clearly a monogenist thinker — yet he was also a deficit thinker. Dr Rush proposed that the physical differences and intellectual inferiority of dark-skinned people were a result of the cultural degeneration they experienced proceeding their exodus from the Garden of Eden. He claimed that the original parental stock of all races descended from a pair of Caucasians. Therefore, Dr Rush believed that through education and Christian indoctrination, blacks could be civilized and taught to be industrious in that they descended from Caucasians. Dr Rush also disapproved of slavery, in spite of its economic advantages for the new republic. Slavery, he argued, led to the further cognitive degeneration of blacks as they were not allowed to think independently. Likewise, he considered slavery to be spiritually harmful to whites, for the same reasons that Jefferson proposed. Unlike Jefferson, Dr Rush disagreed that they should be deported. Instead, he proposed that they be segregated in all domains of social life for this would prevent the mulattoization of white Americans. Dr Rush did not favor racial miscegenation as he believed that blacks had cognitively degenerated to such a point that they were a threat to the intellectual superiority of whites.

Dr Rush supported his racial views by referring to his medical findings on leprosy. He observed that when blacks contracted leprosy their skin became white. Based on this discovery he concluded that the original color of all races was white. To support his findings he cited the case of one of his black patients, a former slave who had contracted leprosy. Upon his patient's recovery, Dr Rush clothed him and paid for his schooling. His patient became a prime example that blacks had the cognitive ability to learn and to be part of white society.

Dr Rush's views on American Indians were less sympathetic (Takaki, 1990). He felt that in America there was not any place for them. Dr Rush alleged that Indians, unlike blacks who had proven themselves to be an industrious people, refused to be civilized and put to work. To Rush, this indicated that Indians, although they also had descended from whites, had degenerated to such a point that they could no longer be regenerated. As such, it was necessary to exterminate them.

In sum, statesmen as Thomas Jefferson and Dr Benjamin Rush, personify the liberal views held by many of our founding fathers and provide insight as to why racist laws were passed after the American Revolution. These 'liberal' views also suggest that monogenist and polygenist perspectives were fused and significantly influenced the political practices of our founding fathers. It is unclear, however, if either the monogenist or polygenist school of thought was more popular. What is clear, though, is that people of color were viewed to be inferior. Inferiority was defined differently, but a common denominator was the perspective that people of color were intellectually dull, naturally lazy and unable to attain the level of civilization as whites.

Dr Rush's views on education and leprosy leads us to our next discussion on how the racial views of the late 1700s influenced the schooling practices toward racial minorities in the United States. By this time, most American colonies had passed laws prohibiting the schooling of blacks (Lyons, 1975). This, however, did not prevent the Society for the Propagation of the Gospel (SPG) from opening schools to educate blacks and Indians. By the turn of the nineteenth century, the target population of the mission schools were blacks, since by that time, most Indians had been either exterminated or driven out of the settlements where whites resided (see Indian Intercourse Act of 1802). To the missionaries, educating blacks continued to be extremely important for it was their quest to prove that God had created all the races of the earth, as cited in the Bible. SPG missionaries sought to teach blacks Christian doctrines for this would prove they were capable of abstract thinking like whites, and this evidence could be used to dispute the belief that they were animals. SPG missionaries also opposed slavery on the grounds that it was against God's will to enslave people (Lyons, 1975).

When the SPG schools were first set up in the late 1600s, whites did not oppose the mission schools and some liberal plantation owners allowed their slaves to attend school. At that time, the schools were few and located only in communities where compulsory ignorance laws had not been passed. By the late 1700s, however, when the missionaries became more involved in political organizations against slavery, slave owners became actively engaged in dismantling the mission schools. Slave masters did not necessarily propose that blacks were animals and therefore should not be schooled; their primary concern was economics. Slave masters opposed schooling blacks because they alleged it made slaves presumptuous and encouraged them to organize manumission movements (Nott and Gliddon, 1854, 1857). Slave owners were also against educating blacks because they felt it damaged their property, given that there was no place in society for an educated black person.

In response to the pro-slavery advocates, the number of townships adopting compulsory ignorance laws increased, and many mission schools were closed in the early 1800s (Weinberg, 1977). Interestingly, it also appears that compulsory ignorance laws were passed at this time because of the success of the mission schools. It was apparent that blacks who were educated by missionaries had the capability to learn and this threatened the main argument used to justify slavery. It became increasingly difficult for advocates to defend slavery on the grounds that blacks were animals in light of the fact that many blacks did have the capability to be schooled. The educability and education of blacks became a serious issue for polygenist thinkers to explain.

Slavery, Abolition, and Racial Thinking–1800 to 1859

In the United States, by the turn of the nineteenth century, the racial debates on the origin of mankind became further embroiled in the debate over slavery. On the one hand, the abolitionists, who took a monogenist stand, claimed that slavery was wrong on the basis that God had created the races from a common parental stock (Stanton, 1966). They continued to support their thesis by advancing research on the common origin of the races, focusing on acclimation and hybridity theories. On the other hand, the pro-slavery proponents, who advocated a polygenist position, argued that slavery was not immoral in that God had intended Caucasians to create a great nation and to enslave non-whites. They further proposed that God had created all the non-white races in the same manner that He had created the rest of the animal kingdom. Therefore, given that non-whites were animals it was not immoral to enslave inferior beings (Nott and Gliddon, 1854, 1857). This school of thought continued to support its positions with craniology and environmental data. However, they began to disassociate themselves from their hybridity–sterility claims as their projections failed to be supported by ethnological findings. Heated arguments ensued between the opposing philosophical and political camps. On the opposing sides were medical doctors Samuel Stanhope Smith and Samuel Morton. Their theoretical perspectives became the benchmark discourses used by their supporters.

Dr Stanhope Smith was an avowed abolitionist, who critically attacked the polygenist stand on the basis that it was pseudoscientific and a racist discourse used by those who favored the enslavement or labor exploitation of non-whites. Although Dr Stanhope Smith advocated a common origin thesis, he did not believe that the human races were equal. He proposed that unlike whites, non-whites descended from groups that lived in a state of savagery and this ancestry had produced cultures of intellectually inferior peoples. Dr Stanhope Smith, however, was not a cultural determinist and he held similar optimistic beliefs on education, as did Dr Rush. In 1810, Dr Stanhope Smith published a book entitled *Essays on the Causes of the Variety of Complexion and Figure in the Human Species* where he presented his thesis on how the cultures of non-whites could be regenerated (see Gossett, 1953, 1977; Stanton, 1966). He began his analysis by explaining why physical differences existed between whites and non-whites. On this issue, he concurred with the monogenist position on acclimation and added a political observation. Dr Stanhope Smith proposed climatic factors produced physical differences in mankind; and in the case of blacks, the hot climate of Africa had made them lethargic and prevented them from forming civilized cultures. In America, the cognitive problems blacks had been observed to have were exacerbated and perpetuated by slavery and not by any physical inferiority characteristic. Under slavery, blacks were not allowed to be schooled and were prevented from developing independent thinking. These were the real problems that perpetuated their dullness, and not the size of their brains, as alleged by the craniologists. Dr Stanhope Smith supported his findings by citing examples of educated blacks. He asserted that many blacks, once they were freed and educated in schools, showed a great advancement in cognitive skills.

On the opposing side was Dr Samuel Morton. He disagreed with the acclimation thesis advanced by the monogenists and argued that instead of speculating on prehistorical fictions, scholars should pay attention to the scientific findings advanced by the craniologists. In 1839 he wrote a widely circulated book entitled *Crania Americana* (see Nott and Gliddon, 1854). Dr Morton became an influential figure within the polygenist camp, as he influenced many of his colleagues to drop the origins debate and, instead, conduct research on the superiority of the white race. Dr Morton's recommendations were astute, for the hybridity evidence that had been advanced in Latin America overwhelmingly indicated that people of color were indeed human. With respect to his position on slavery, Dr Morton did not advocate the enslavement of people of color. However, he aligned himself with two leaders of the pro-slavery movement — Dr Josiah Clark Nott and George R. Gliddon (Banton and Harwood, 1975). Part of his research was funded by these well known American racists and after his death they inherited his skull collection.

Dr Morton proposed that the Caucasian race was superior and therefore should have the right to govern non-whites. He supported his claims by advancing biblical and craniometric research. He concurred with the biblical interpretation that God had created all the races. However, Dr Morton revised the monogenist thesis and added that God had created various pairs of parents. Each parent stock, in turn, begot the different races of man. Allegedly, Adam and Eve were the Caucasian parental set and God had made them a superior race. Because God had allegedly endowed them with superior intellect, Dr Morton concluded that the Creator planned for Caucasians to dominate the rest of the races. Dr Morton supported his biblical interpretation by ethnocentrically claiming that only whites had produced advanced civilizations, while the rest of the races had either produced savage or barbarian cultures. To him, this was clear evidence that only Caucasians had the capacity to excel and to govern others. To further support his racist views, Morton used his collection of cranioscopic measurement data based upon nearly 400 skulls. Morton found that whites had larger craniums, and this he concluded, proved whites were intellectually superior. He argued that the cubic inch measurements of the different skulls of men were: white 85, mulatto 80, and black 71 (cited in Stanton, 1966).[4]

Furthermore, after Dr Samuel Stanhope Smith advanced his acclimation thesis, Dr Morton contested it by using Dr Charles Caldwell's arguments. Dr Morton proposed that it was a ludicrous idea to account for physical differences among mankind via the acclimation thesis. To him, it was obvious that this was untrue because people of different races who lived in the same ecological niche did not change in appearance. Dr Morton concluded that changes in race and color were due to intermarriage and not climate. By the mid-1800s, Dr Morton was able to successfully discredit the acclimation thesis and provide the scientific evidence needed by those who defended slavery.

In the southern region of the United States, Dr Morton's research was well received. In Mississippi, Dr Josiah Clark Nott and George R. Gliddon, collaborated on two books to expand upon the findings of Dr Morton. In 1854 they published *Types of Mankind* and in 1857 *The Indigenous Races of the Earth*. Dr Nott was a physician and Gliddon a wealthy publicist and American Consul to Egypt. Dr Nott's research focused on biological issues whereas Gliddon was concerned with proving that non-whites were culturally inferior. Both research areas were inter-related in that a major aim of their investigations were to argue that biologically inferior people produced inferior cultures. Furthermore, unlike Dr Morton who preferred to disassociate his research from the 'divergent origins debate' because of its dubious validity, Nott and Gliddon were determined to prove this theoretical position. Paradoxically, they were unconcerned with the hybridity evidence that was overwhelmingly destroying the polygenist origins discourse. With respect to their views on slavery, both Nott and Gliddon proposed that slavery was justified because non-whites were of a different species from Caucasians. They proposed that enslaving blacks was the civilized way to uplift them for that was the only way they could live among civilized people and learn the ways of Christians (Banton and Harwood, 1975). To support their pseudoscientific and pro-slavery views, Nott and Gliddon advanced arguments covering linguistic, art history, cranioscopic, archeological and physical anthropology subjects.

On language, Nott and Gliddon conducted a survey and analysis of the languages spoken by over 50 non-white societies (Nott and Gliddon, 1857). They found that, unlike the 'complex languages' spoken by Caucasians, non-whites spoke primitive languages reflecting a simplistic mentality. Because they found these languages difficult to understand in grammar and tone, they concluded that it was quite clear that these were inferior languages spoken by primitive or savage peoples. On the subject of art, Nott and Gliddon concentrated on blacks and failed to say anything about other non-white races. Nott and Gliddon (1857) argued that in antiquity no black community had produced any art form. Nott and Gliddon stated, 'Long as history has made mention of Negroes, they have never had any art of their own. Their features are recorded by their ancient enemies and not by themselves' (p. 188). Both authors concurred that archeology supported their inferiority claim for there was no art artifact indicating that blacks had the mental ability to produce art. Nott and Gliddon, however, had to qualify their statements, in light of the fact that Egyptian monuments, statues and wall paintings demonstrated that the skin color of Egyptians was black. They argued, however, that Egyptians were not black, but rather a dark complected Caucasian race.

Nott and Gliddon's most racist arguments dealt with cranioscopic data. Focusing on blacks and Indians, Nott and Gliddon concluded that these two races descended from anthropoids. The scholars contended that blacks had evolved from gorillas and Indians from monkeys. Using Dr Morton's data, they concluded that the similar cranial structures of blacks, Indians, gorillas and monkeys supported their theory. Nott and Gliddon in reference to blacks stated:

> In the accompanying table will be found a series of figures representing the juvenile, or immature, and adult skulls of the anthropomorphous monkeys, the adult or permanent forms of the lower types both of men and monkeys, and, lastly a well-known representation of the highest form of the 'human divine', [referring to a Caucasian-Greek skull] . . . that for each of the lower human types of skull, there appears to exist among the monkeys a rude representative, which seems remotely and imperfectly to anticipate the typical idea of the former, and to bear to it a certain ill-defined relation; and, lastly that the best formed human skull stands immensely removed from the most perfectly elaborated monkey cranium. (1857: 205)

After having compared the skulls of two blacks, one Caucasian of Greek descent, two orangutans, one chimpanzee, one baboon and two extinct types of monkeys, Nott and Gliddon concluded that the skull of the Caucasian did not have any resemblance with the anthropoids, yet there were striking similarities between the skulls of the two blacks and the rest of the animal skulls under study. Furthermore, on Indians and monkeys Nott and Gliddon stated:

> what is extremely noteworthy, their 'species' is very nearly the same as that of each of their succedaneums skipping about Brazilian forests the present hour. There is a solidarity, a homogeneity here, of circumstances between monkeys and man, not to be contemptuously overlooked. (1857: 501)

Thus, to Nott and Gliddon not only did Indians resemble monkeys, they shared similar behavioral similarities.

Once again, to support their craniometric data and their subjective analysis on the behavior of blacks and Indians, Nott and Gliddon claimed archeologists had found that neither race had the intellect to establish advanced civilizations. Although they acknowledged that the Aztec of Mexico and the Inca of Peru had established advanced societies, they proposed these were archeological exceptions. They attempted to explain this phenomenon by using Louis Agassiz' 'independent evolution' thesis (Nott and Gliddon, 1857).

Agassiz, like Morton, at that time was a renowned researcher. Agassiz' 'independent evolution' thesis was based upon firsthand observations of animals and humans living in cold climates. Aggassiz also traveled extensively through Europe, Africa, and North America conducting similar research (see Agassiz, 1885; Nott and Gliddon, 1857). Agassiz' thesis proposed that because animals and humans who lived in the same ecological niche resembled each other, this constituted evidence of independent evolution. Each race of man had evolved separately from each other and only shared a similar evolutionary history with the fauna in its ecological niche. For example, in the cold regions of Europe the bears shared similar characteristics with the Caucasian inhabitants. Both were hairy and light colored. Likewise in Asia, many animals had elongated eyelids like the natives, while in Africa the faces and hands of Africans, Agassiz asserted, resembled the gorillas' facial characteristics and their manual dexterity. In the New World the Indians were small and anthropoid looking, like the monkeys. Thus, based on this observational data, Agassiz concluded that the races had evolved independently. Although Agassiz never actually claimed that blacks and Indians had evolved from anthropoids and whites from humans, Nott and Gliddon made this theoretical leap and argued that Agassiz' observations clearly proved that certain races were not human.

To support their racist thinking, Nott and Gliddon (1854) claimed that in England and France extinct species of animals had been excavated with remains resembling modern Whites, whereas in Africa Negroid skulls with ape features had been found aside extinct fauna. Likewise, in Latin America, an ancient Indian skeleton the size of a monkey was unearthed (Nott and Gliddon, 1854, 1857). This — to them — indicated that God had created whites in their present form, while blacks and Indians had evolved from early anthropoids. To explain how blacks and Indians eventually obtained human-like characteristics, Nott and Gliddon concluded that certain groups of Caucasians must have interbred with monkeys and gorillas and thus begot non-whites. In the case of blacks, they were begot by crossing Jews and gorillas (Nott and Gliddon, 1857). Allegedly, Jews were a primitive stock of Caucasians that had a different origin from the rest of the Caucasians of the New World. Jewish endogenous marriage practices had generated the conditions for making males lust after non-Jewish women. Given that Jews were prohibited from marrying non-Jews or having lovers outside their ethnic group, this norm became difficult to obey. Consequently, many Jewish men — in means of not disobeying their people — opted to copulate with gorillas. Apparently, this practice was also replicated in North America. Nott and Gliddon, however, admitted that they did not have any biblical evidence to verify how Indians acquired human characteristics. Unlike the case of Indians, Nott and Gliddon argued that the Bible supported their thesis as there were many passages stating that Jews often broke with tradition and did not follow their people's endogenous rules. In the case of Indians, they could only hypothesize that different types of Caucasian races intermingled with monkeys and begot Indians. Interestingly, they had a strange hypothesis about how the Aztec and the Inca were begot and why they differed from other Indian groups. Nott and Gliddon speculated that the architectural achievements of these two indigenous peoples could be attributed to their larger proportions of human descent in comparison to other Indians. They acknowledged, however, that their views on the Aztec and Inca were speculations because they did not have any data to support their claims. Finally, on the issue of hybridity, Nott and Gliddon disregarded all evidence dispelling their polygenist views. They held on to the belief that it was only a matter of time for mestizos and mulattoes to become infertile.

Suffice it to say, such racist and nonsensical theories did not go uncontested. Nott and Gliddon's racist views came under attack by John Bachman, an abolitionist and a natural scientist. He accused Nott and Gliddon of manipulating Morton's data to support Agassiz' absurd theory of independent evolution for the purpose of defending slavery (Stanton, 1966). He also accused them of inviting racist European scientists to speak to American audiences on the virtues of slavery. Their aim, he alleged, was political: to fuel pro-slavery sentiments. Bachman's critical assessments and public denunciations were accompanied by his study challenging the polygenist discourse. In his publication, entitled *Viviparous Quadrupeds of North America* (1854), Bachman presented his hybridity theory (cited in Stanton, 1966). He conducted the first crossbreeding study that used thousands of animal species. Bachman proved that it was rare for different species to crossbreed. In only two cases was crossbreeding possible and Bachman found that the offspring of these species were sterile. Bachman alleged that for generations polygenist scholars had falsely misled the public into believing that crossbreeding was common between species. They had done this, Bachman argued, because it had been their main ploy to explain why whites could interbreed with non-whites. Thus, Bachman proposed that because the polygenists were wrong, and the children of racially mixed parents were fertile, this proved that non-whites were human. Bachman's findings were supported by the interracial marriage practices of Latin America (Stocking, 1968). After 350 years of miscegenation, the mestizo and mulatto populations continued to reproduce and there was not any indication their fertility would cease. On the contrary, in most Latin American countries it had become an accepted social practice for people of different races to marry.

On the issue of acclimation, Bachman revised the monogenist analysis. He proposed that physical differences between humans were a result of adaptation and migration. Physical changes in humans occurred after they migrated out of their original homeland and began to adapt to their new environment. Changes in the body, however, took thousands of years to occur and did not radically alter the body. A case in point were the Indians of North America who migrated from Asia to the Americas thousands of years ago. Once in the New World, the migrants adapted to the new environment and cultural and physical changes ensued. To support his hypotheses, Bachman pointed to the fact that no prehuman skeleton had been unearthed in the New World, indicating that Indians must have migrated from the Old World and did not evolve independently.

Bachman's research became impossible to refute, and within a decade he disgraced the scholarly work of Nott and Gliddon. His research became popular among the abolitionists and it was successfully used to attack the scientific rationale for slavery. Unfortunately, throughout Bachman's life he was persecuted by pro-slavery advocates and in 1874 he was severely beaten in his home by a mob of angry citizens (Stanton, 1966). His house was also set on fire and his publications and manuscripts burned.

In 1859, the polygenist school of thought was struck its final blow after Charles Darwin wrote *The Origin of the Species* (Gossett, 1953; Lyons, 1975). Darwin advanced an evolutionary theory and supported it with skeletal evidence. He argued that all the races were of a modern human stock and had gradually, and in one line, evolved from a common origin. None of the races could be classified as pre-modern humans. In essence, he verified Bachman's hypothesis. Using advanced physical anthropology dating techniques and abundant skeletal data, Darwin proved that humans had evolved in one direct evolutionary line from earlier forms of humans. This evolutionary line began with a group of hominids that evolved into one homindae line. Later homo erectus evolved from this direct line and culminated in the evolution of modern man — Homo sapiens. Anthropoids were a distinct species and no race had directly evolved from them. When humans reached the stage of Homo sapiens, they dispersed throughout the world. The evolution of mankind was a result of successful adaptation to the environment. The future generations reflected the physical characteristics of those who had survived. The criterion of success was the number of viable offspring that members of a population left after their death.

Unfortunately, Darwin's discovery did not put an end to the racist discourses of the period. On the contrary, he provided the scientific rationale for new racist thinking (Blum, 1978). That is, according to Darwin a common origin did not necessarily mean the races were equal, in particular with respect to intelligence. Darwin's views on the inequality of mankind gave the craniologists a new scientific base to revise their racist theories. They and other racist thinkers proposed that although Darwin's evolutionary theory was sound, it did not prove that the races were equal, nor did it justify changing public policy towards non-whites. Racist craniologists introduced a 'cultural evolutionist' thesis based on a revision of old craniometric beliefs. They claimed that because Caucasians had larger brain cases they were cognitively superior to non-whites. To support their argument, they alleged only Caucasians had larger brain cases, and only they had founded advanced civilizations. People of color were alleged to have only produced savage or semi-civilized cultures because they were simpleminded (Stocking, 1968). In turn, these arguments were used by craniologists and other racists to defend slavery and to condone the labor exploitation of non-whites. In the United States a popular discourse emerged among whites, claiming their right to govern non-whites on the ground that they were superior (Brinton, 1890; Feagin, 1989; see Gossett, 1953, 1977). We now turn to this topic and examine the new racial discourses and their interrelationship with the economic interests of white Americans.

The Blurring of Boundaries Between Racial Discourses: Common Sense White Racial Ideologies

Following Darwin's scientific discoveries, new racial discourses were advanced to justify the economic, social and political subordination of non-whites, and to deny them educational opportunities. After Darwin introduced his research, it was clear that the monogenists had won the debate and the origins argument was laid to rest. Nonetheless, new racist discourses emerged proclaiming the cultural and cognitive inferiority of non-whites.

In 1865, the abolitionist movement triumphed in the United States and slavery was abolished under the Thirteenth Amendment. This, however, did not mean that blacks nor other non-whites were declared equal. Quite the contrary. Following emancipation, former abolitionists and pro-slavery advocates shared common racial views with respect to non-whites. It became difficult to discern the difference between racists and liberals, as both groups supported the segregation of non-whites, favored limited or no occupational mobility for them, and were unwilling to extend public education to non-whites (Barrera, 1979; Highman, 1994; Menchaca, 1993; Omi and Winant, 1994; Sinkler, 1971). It also appears that by the late 1800s these racial views became a commonly accepted dogma among white Americans and were not always motivated by economic interests (Highman, 1994; Takaki, 1990). By stating this, I do not intend to infer that whites had ceased to have economic motives for maintaining non-whites in a subordinate position — for indeed the opposite situation was the case. My point is that a blurring of the boundaries between the racial ideologies occurred and a common sense racial ideology emerged and became widespread among most whites. By 'common sense' I mean collective views that, for the most part, were unreflective and appeared sound and prudent by most whites (see Forgacs, 1988). For example, individuals who held economic interests for maintaining non-whites in a subordinate position, such as white union leaders who resided in high density racial minority areas and shared similar racial views with intellectual elites that did not. To illustrate the blurring of the boundaries between the racial ideologies I turn to an analysis of the racial views of Abraham Lincoln and those held by scholars during the late 1800s. I will then proceed to explain how these racial ideologies were manifested in educational policies and practices.

In 1865, the President of the United States, Abraham Lincoln, emancipated slaves after Congress declared slavery to be in violation of the Constitution of the United States. Indeed, this was a monumental event for it was the first step towards extending blacks and other racial minorities the basic rights guaranteed by the Constitution. The passage of the Thirteenth Amendment, however, did not mean that non-whites were equal to whites under the law. It only meant that no man, woman or child could be enslaved. During that period, only the newly conquered regions of Texas and New Mexico conferred upon part of the non-white populations the full political rights of United States citizenship (Menchaca, 1993).[5] These political rights had been granted to some non-white citizens under the Treaty of Guadalupe Hidalgo that had officially terminated the war between Mexico and the United States in 1848. New Mexico and Texas legislators gave Mexican mestizos the full political rights of United States citizens and extended to detribalized Indians partial political rights at the township level.[6] The rest of the states only conferred the full political rights of citizenship upon the 'free white male population' (Hull, 1985; Konvitz, 1946).

In the area of employment, racial minorities were subjected to a caste system as occupations became color coded (Barrera, 1979; Highman, 1994). Blacks and Mexicans were concentrated in agricultural and service occupations; Chinese were employed in the construction of the transatlantic railroad (Blauner, 1994; Takaki, 1990). (Beginning in 1850, thousands of Chinese had immigrated to the United States.)[7] Unless racial minorities were self-employed, it was uncommon for them to break out of these occupational fields. Within the educational domain, racial minorities were virtually ignored, even though public education had become available to most whites (Hendrick, 1977; Weinberg, 1977). In essence, racial minorities were denied basic political rights and the economic opportunities enjoyed by whites.

This was not surprising, for in the United States this was the closing of an era when non-whites were considered to be animals.

The emancipation proclamation, under the Thirteenth Amendment, thus marked the end of an era of slavery and the opening of a new political structure where racial minorities were considered human under the law. Unfortunately, what was professed was not truly practiced: Racial minority groups were still treated and viewed to be inferior. Clearly, Abraham Lincoln was a monogenist and liberal racial thinker. His attitudes toward race, however, indicate that the blurring of the social boundaries between racists and liberals were beginning to merge into a unified white American 'common sense' discourse. From 1858 to 1865, Lincoln gave many speeches where he revealed his racist beliefs, beginning with his senatorial campaign. In July 17, 1858, Lincoln gave a speech to an audience in Springfield, Illinois. He attempted to persuade the audience to support abolition, while concomitantly reassuring them he shared their views about black inferiority. Lincoln told his audience that after emancipation he would prohibit slaves from living among whites because they were inferior and should not mix with whites. Lincoln stated, 'There is a physical difference between the two which . . . will probably forever forbid their living together on the footing of perfect equality' (Abraham Lincoln, Speech at Springfield, Illinois, July 17, 1858, quoted in Sinkler, 1971: 29).

In another speech, Lincoln once again reassured his audience that if elected to state senator he would uphold the segregation of the races and be against any legislation promoting the social and political equality of blacks. Lincoln stated

> I am not or ever have been in favor of making voters, or jurors of Negroes nor of qualifying them to hold office, nor to marry with white people . . . I will say . . . in addition . . . that there is a physical difference between the white and black races which I believe will forever forbid the two races living together on terms of social and political equality. And inasmuch as they cannot so live, while they do remain together there must be the position of superior and inferior, and I as much as any other man am in favor of having the superior position assigned to the white races. (Abraham Lincoln, Speech at Charleston, Illinois, September 18, 1858, quoted in Sinkler, 1971: 40–1)

After becoming president of the United States, Lincoln's views towards blacks remained the same. His disdain for blacks was so great that he advocated they be deported from the United States after emancipation. This discourse was not dissimilar from the arguments espoused by racists. A case in point was his second annual presidential address to the nation, where Lincoln disclosed plans to establish a colony for American blacks in Latin America. They were to be deported after homes were built for them. Lincoln stated, 'If gradual emancipation and deportation be adopted . . . till new homes can be found for them [blacks] in congenial climes — and with people of their own blood and race' (quoted in Sinkler, 1971: 52). Following political pressures from black activists, Lincoln reconsidered his deportation plans. Instead, he proposed that if blacks preferred to remain in the

United States following emancipation they should be allowed to do so, however, they would not be permitted to live in the same neighborhoods with whites. After Lincoln's death, similar views were expressed by many contemporary historians and scholars.

Within the academic sphere, the blurring of the boundaries between the racial discourses became apparent in that the belief of non-white inferiority was widespread (Gossett, 1953). By the 1870s, racial discourses advanced by scholars shared a 'common sense' belief, beholding the superiority of whites and the need to practice racial segregation. On one side were the craniologists and social Darwinists who espoused a far-right white supremacy racist discourse, and on the other side were the historians who presented a moderate racist position. Today, the views advanced by both sides would be considered quite racist. In those days, however, the discourses advanced by the social Darwinists were more heinous as they advocated social engineering programs to maintain non-whites and poor whites in subordinate positions, whereas the historians merely wanted to prove the inferiority of non-whites.

Within the universities, the racial discourse advanced by the historians was called the Teutonic Origin Theory, and it became the historical explanation to account for racial differences (Gossett, 1953, 1977; Menchaca and Valencia, 1990). The theory originated in England and it was imported to the United States by Henry Main in 1870. The original version proposed that Anglo-Saxons were superior in intellect to all races, including other whites. Within a few years after it was introduced to the United States, it was revised to include all the descendants from northern European origin. This was done in order to be inclusive of the ethnic makeup of the elites, and other upwardly mobile whites, in that a large number of Germans were part of the upper classes and held political power in the United States (Feagin, 1989). Supporters of the Teutonic Origin Theory proposed that northern Europeans were a superior race because they shared a common genetic pool. Allegedly, they had never mixed with inferior racial groups, such as the southern and eastern Europeans who were considered to be intellectually dull. Since northern Europeans had practiced selective interbreeding, this had allowed them to remain racially pure and to develop distinct and superior cultures. Allegedly, the most important distinguishing characteristic of the northern Europeans was a superior intellect. To support their position, scholars claimed that only the northern Europeans had formed long-lasting governments and it was they who had founded the most advanced civilization in the history of the world — the United States. This historical discourse paralleled and complemented the racial discourse advanced by social Darwinists. Supporters of the Teutonic Origin Theory, however, unlike the social Darwinists, did not advance social engineering programs to maintain the purity of whites.

One of the most racist discourses was advanced by Herbert Spencer and Darwin's cousin, Sir Francis Galton (Blum, 1978). Together these two scholars spearheaded the era of social Darwinism. The central tenet of social Darwinism was that intelligence and all other social characteristics were genetically inherited (for more on the role of Galton, see Valencia, Chapter 3, this volume). Therefore, they argued that the social order was an outcome of intellectual differences between inferior and superior peoples. According to the social Darwinists, racial minorities and poor whites were economically disadvantaged because they were intellectually dull and did not have the cognitive capacity to improve their economic standing. On the other hand, northern Europeans were intellectually superior and this had allowed them to emerge as the political leaders and economic elites of the United States. As a means of explaining why many northern Europeans were part of the working-class, social Darwinists proposed that these individuals were racially or ethnically mixed and were not genetically pure. Thus, social Darwinists proposed that the purity of the northern Europeans must be maintained in order to preserve their intellectual superiority. To do so, social Darwinists became political activists and lobbied the government to pass legislation to support their pseudoscientific findings. Social Darwinists proposed that in the case of non-whites, they needed to be segregated in order to prevent miscegenation and thus avoid the cognitive degeneration of whites. And, in the case of poor whites, the social Darwinists proposed that the government should outlaw labor unions. Social Darwinists considered unions to be a threat to the welfare and racial purity of northern Europeans. Their rationale was that unions would assist southern and eastern Europeans to improve their economic standing by helping them obtain higher wages. This was a potentially dangerous practice for higher wages might make southern and eastern Europeans attractive marriage partners to the northern Europeans. Thus, the social Darwinists concluded that the class mobility of inferior whites could lead to the intellectual degeneration of the northern Europeans. To prevent the intermingling of northern Europeans with other groups, social Darwinists lobbied the government to pass legislation instituting racial segregation, prohibition of unionization and to begin a voluntary sterilization program to regulate the fertility growth of poor whites and racial minorities who were deemed undesirable, such as the feeble-minded. The latter program was called eugenics and its goal was to limit the number of poor whites and racial minorities (for more on the eugenics movement, see Valencia, Chapter 3). Social Darwinists proposed that the size of this population should be determined upon employers' needs for manual labor.

In sum, by the 1870s the alleged cultural and intellectual inferiority of non-whites became a popular discourse and was used to justify their inferior treatment. It also appears that within part of the scientific community a common argument was used to explain why poverty existed among whites. In the case of poor whites, although they too were considered to be intellectually inferior, they were not severely discriminated against in comparison to non-whites. Whites were not segregated, nor prohibited from entering most occupations, nor were they denied public education. Furthermore, in the case of poor whites, union leaders heatedly contested the arguments of the social Darwinists and accused them of advancing pseudoscientific theories in order to maintain a cheap labor force. Unfortunately, union leaders did not come to the defense of non-whites and did not attempt to include them in their union movements (Reisler, 1976). On the contrary, union organizers favored the preservation of industrial occupations and higher paid wage labor for whites. A similar practice occurred in the area of schooling. Political activists who disagreed with the social mobility argument of the social Darwinists saw education as a stepping stone for improving the social mobility of whites, however, this same attitude was not extended to non-whites.

In the United States public education was deemed by the federal government to be a state issue and was not considered to be the responsibility of the federal government nor to be a basic right guaranteed under the United States Constitution. Formal public education began to be offered by the states in 1825 (Katz, 1988). Prior to that date, public education had been uncommon and was available only to elites. Exceptions were made when philanthropic organizations gave cities grants to establish public schools or when a township decided to provide schooling for white children, irrespective of their social class. Between 1825 to 1870, all states and territories began funding public education that was professionally staffed and administered by a central bureaucracy. Schools became age graded, often compulsory, teachers were specially trained and school administrators were hired as full-time experts. Unfortunately, racial minorities were locked out of this system (Hendrick, 1977; Weinberg, 1977). In the southern region of the United States, most states passed compulsory ignorance laws prohibiting the schooling of blacks, and in the North a few cities allowed blacks to attend public schools as long as they were placed in segregated classrooms or schools. It was not until 1868 that compulsory ignorance laws were finally declared to be illegal. However, this practice continued on for many years afterwards as many local townships ignored the federal mandate.

In the case of other racial minorities there is no evidence indicating that they were included in the public education system during the nineteenth century. On the contrary, the states passed school funding laws to ensure that blacks and other racial minorities would not be schooled — even when a liberal school district chose to do so (Hendrick, 1977; Hertert, 1994; Katz, 1988; Menchaca, 1995; Weinberg, 1977). After 1868, state governments theoretically gave local school boards the right to decide if they wanted to provide public education for racial minorities; yet, government officials prevented the school boards from practicing this right. State governments prohibited school boards from using state funds to educate non-white students. If any public school district was found enrolling non-whites, the state could legally withhold the educational funds. State governments only allowed local school boards to educate racial minorities as long as their education was funded upon the property taxes of non-whites. Because very few racial minorities owned property in those days their property tax bases were insufficient to pay for the costs of building and sustaining schools (see Menchaca, 1995). In the South, matters were worse. The property taxes collected from non-whites were to be used to fund white schools, and only if money was left over could it be used to set up schools for non-whites (Weinberg, 1977).

The arguments used to deny racial minorities educational opportunities were varied, but quite obviously racist. Craniologists and many other scholars proposed that non-whites did not have the cognitive ability to learn, therefore it was a waste of time to educate them (Brinton, 1890; Lyons, 1975; Weinberg, 1977). Others believed that educated non-whites would become presumptuous and would try to move up socially by marrying whites, therefore this could cause serious social problems (Lyons, 1975; Sinkler, 1971). Yet others proposed that it was unwise to educate racial minorities for they would begin demanding better occupations in correspondence to their educational level, and this would create a strain in the skilled labor market (Takaki, 1990).

Although it was a common practice to deny education to racial minorities, there were some whites who opposed this educational practice. For example, a few years after the Fourteenth Amendment passed in 1868 and racial minorities born in the United States were declared citizens, President Grant authored legislation proposing that educational rights be extended to blacks. His intent was to educate blacks in order to make them better citizens and well informed voters. Unfortunately, his views were not shared by other government officials as the United States Congress did not support his legislation (Sinkler, 1971). Further efforts to offer education to blacks were launched by a few philanthropic women's societies (Katz, 1988). These social welfare societies set up schools for black students or donated money to black communities who had obtained approval from the states to establish segregated schools. These cases, however, were uncommon, for the standard practice was to deny racial minorities any semblance of equal education.

By the closure of the nineteenth century, it appears that at the federal level extending public education to non-whites was not an issue meriting consideration. On the contrary, the federal government passed educational policies endorsing the states' rights to do whatever they deemed appropriate. A case in point: In 1896 the federal Supreme Court passed *Plessy v. Ferguson* and officially gave the states the right to segregate racial minorities in separate schools. Although the states were already practicing segregated schooling, the significance of *Plessy* was that it made it clear to non-whites that they did not have any legal recourse to protest against the educational policies of the states. *Plessy* further supported the states' right to segregate racial minorities in all domains of social life and to deny them entrance into any public facilities where whites deemed it inappropriate to be in their company.

It was not until the twentieth century that most states finally extended formal public education to non-whites. Education, however, was provided in a segregated environment. By 1910, the majority of black children were attending school (Weinberg, 1977) and by 1920 the majority of Mexicans, Asians, and Native Americans were provided public education (Hendrick, 1977; Montejano, 1987).[8]

In sum, the roots of deficit thinking are inextricably tied to racist discourses that evolved from the early 1600s to the late 1800s. Out of these discourses came beliefs that racial minorities were physically, cognitively or culturally inferior to whites. Furthermore, such deficit thinking was used to justify the economic exploitation of people of color and to deny them the social and political rights enjoyed by whites. It appears that from the founding of the first American colony and until the late 1800s, white economic interests were strong motivations for upholding these practices. In the area of American education, most racial minorities were denied the privilege of being schooled until the early 1900s, and the rationales used to justify this practice ranged from ideological beliefs based upon racist assumptions to economic interests supported by whites.

Much of what transpired during the period of the early racist discourses helped to set the stage for the further articulation of hereditarian thought that characterized the first two decades following the beginning of the twentieth century. The impetus that made this new era of deficit thinking distinct from pre-twentieth century deficit thinking was the development of the first intelligence test in 1905 by Binet and Simon in France. With the importation of the new Binet–Simon scales to America and the appropriation of the measurement tool by United States scholars, the intelligence testing movement soon swept the country. Hereditarianism, the belief that all or most of human behavior was best explained by biological bases, had eventually found its calibrator of intelligence. It was not long before 'race psychology' studies 'scientifically confirmed' what pre-twentieth century deficit thinking scholars had asserted for decades: Racial differences in intelligence, it was contended, are most validly explained by racial differences in innate, genetically determined abilities. What emerged from these findings, regarding schooling, were curricular recommendations that the 'intellectually inferior' and the social order would best be served by providing these students concrete, low-level, segregated instruction commensurate with their alleged diminished intellectual abilities. Richard Valencia offers an analysis of this deficit thinking era, which he calls the *genetic pathology model* period, in the next chapter.

Notes

1   I am aware that the term *non-whites* is a condescending referent to people of color. In the present chapter, however, I use it deliberately to underscore the racist discourses that separate whites from those who are not.

2   See Feagin (1989) for a discussion of the ethnic heritage of the first colonists.

3   Spaniards were considered to be non-white in the United States during the eighteenth century; by the nineteenth century they were reclassified as Caucasians. For a discussion on the racial classification of Spaniards and Mexicans in the New World see Menchaca (1993).

4   Nott and Gliddon added Dr Morton's skulls to their own skull collection. They measured the brain cases of skulls from different races to determine which race had the largest brain case. These measurements were based on the sizes of the brains in cubic inches. Their results were: white 92, Asian 85, black 83 and Indian 79 (Nott and Gliddon, 1854: 450).

5   The United States government annexed Texas in 1845 and conquered most of northern Mexico in 1848. The present states of California, Arizona, New Mexico, Texas, Nevada, Utah, most of Colorado and parts of Oklahoma, Kansas and Wyoming were annexed to the United States after the termination of the Mexican–American War of 1846 to 1848 (see Weber, 1982).

6   Mexican women who were Caucasian were not extended the right of suffrage.

7   228, 201 Chinese immigrated to the United States between 1850 to 1880 (See Feagin, 1989: 338–40).

8   By 1910 nearly 60 per cent of black students (Weinberg, 1977: 57) and nearly 40 per cent of Mexican students (Hendrick, 1977: 60; see Menchaca, 1995) attended school.

References

AGASSIZ, E. (1885) *His Life and Correspondence*, New York: Houghton Mifflin.
AGASSIZ, L. (1854) 'Sketch of the natural provinces of the animal world and their relation to the different types of man', in NOTT, J.C. and GLIDDON, G.R. *Types of Mankind*, Philadelphia: Lippincott, Grambo, pp. viii–xxvi.
BANTON, M. and HARWOOD, J. (1975) *The Race Concept*, London: David & Charles.
BARRERA, M. (1979) *Race and Class in the Southwest: A Theory of Racial Inequality*, Notre Dame, IN: University of Notre Dame Press.
BLAUNER, R. (1994) 'Colonized and immigrant minorities', in TAKAKI, R. (Ed) *From Different Shores: Perspectives on Race and Ethnicity in America* (2nd ed.) New York: Oxford University Press. Article first published in 1972, pp. 149–60.
BLUM, J. (1978) *Pseudoscience and Mental Ability: The Origins of the Fallacies of the IQ Controversy*, New York: Monthly Review Press.
BRINTON, D.G. (1890) *Races and Peoples: Lectures on the Science of Ethnography*, New York: N.D.C. Hodges Publishers.
Constitution of the United States, art. 1, sec. 2, in United States Code Service Constitution, 1986, p. 18.
Cross v. De Valle (1863) 1 US (1 Wallace), pp. 5–16.
FEAGIN, J. (1989) *Racial and Ethnic Relations* (3rd ed.) Englewood Cliffs, NJ: Prentice-Hall.
FORGACS, D. (1988) *An Antonio Gramsci Reader: Selected Writings: 1916–1935*, New York: Shocken Books.
GOSSETT, T. (1953) *The Idea of Anglo-Saxon Superiority in American Thought 1865–1915*, Unpublished doctoral dissertation, Minneapolis: University of Minnesota.
GOSSETT, T. (1977) *Race: The History of an Idea in America*, New York: Shocken Books.
HEIZER, R.F. and ALMQUIST, A.F. (1977) *The Other Californians: Prejudice and Discrimination under Spain, Mexico and the United States*, Berkeley, CA: University of California Press.
HENDRICK, I. (1977) *The Education of Non-whites in California 1849–1970*, San Francisco, CA: R & E Associates.
HERTERT, L. (1994) A *History of the Changing Definition of Equity*, Madison, WI: The Finance Center Consortium for Policy Research in Education.
HIGHMAN, J. (1994) 'Strangers in the land: Nativism and nationalism', in TAKAKI, R. (Ed) *From Different Shores: Perspectives on Race and Ethnicity in America* (2nd ed.) New York: Oxford University Press, pp. 78–82.
HULL, E. (1985) *Without Justice for All: The Constitutional Rights of Aliens*, Westport, CT: Greenwood Press.
INDIAN INTERCOURSE ACT OF 1802 (1845) In 2 *United States Statutes at Large*, Chap. 13, pp. 139–46.
KATZ, M.B. (1988) 'Origins of public education: A reassessment', in MCCLELLAN, B.E. and REESE, W.J. (Eds) *The Social History of American Education*, Chicago, IL: University of Illinois Press, pp. 91–118.
KONVITZ, M.R. (1946) *The Alien and the Asiatic in American Law*, Ithaca, NY: Cornell University Press.
LYONS, C.H. (1975) *To Wash an Aethiop White: British Ideas about Black African Educability*, New York: Teachers College Press.
McCreery v. Somerville (1824) 9 US (9 Wheaton), pp. 354–61.

McKinney v. Saviego (1855) 18 US (18 Howard), pp. 235–40.

MENCHACA, M. (1993) 'Chicano Indianism: A history of racial repression', *American Ethnologist*, **20**, pp. 583–603.

MENCHACA, M. (1995) *The Mexican Outsiders: A Community History of Marginalization and Discrimination in California*, Austin, TX: University of Texas Press.

MENCHACA, M. and VALENCIA, R. (1990) 'Anglo-Saxon ideologies in the 1920s–1930s: Their impact on the segregation of Mexican students in California', *Anthropology and Education Quarterly*, **21**, pp. 222–49.

MINTZ, S. (1985) *Sweetness and Power*, New York: Penguin Books.

MONTEJANO, D. (1987) *Anglos and Mexicans in the Making of Texas, 1836–1986*, Austin, TX: University of Texas Press.

Naturalization Act of 1790, ch. 3, sec. 1.

NICHOLSON, L.J. (1991) *Feminism/postmodernism*, New York: Routledge.

NOTT, J.C. and GLIDDON, G.R. (1854) *Types of Mankind*, Philadelphia, PA: Lippincott, Grambo.

NOTT, J.C. and GLIDDON, G.R. (1857) *Indigenous Races of the Earth*, Philadelphia, PA: Lippincott & Company.

OMI, M. and WINANT, H. (1994) *Racial Formation in the United States from the 1960s to the 1990s* (2nd ed.), New York: Routledge and Kegan Paul.

Plessy v. Ferguson (1896) 163 US, pp. 537–64.

Reisler, M. (1976) *By the Sweat of Their Brow: Mexican Immigrant Labor in the United States, 1900–1940*, Westport, CT: Greenwood Press.

ROSE, D. (1989) *Patterns of American Culture*, Philadelphia, PA: University of Pennsylvania Press.

SAID, E. (1979) *Orientalism*, New York: Vintage Books.

SINKLER, G. (1971) *The Racial Attitudes of American Presidents: From Abraham Lincoln to Theodore Roosevelt*, Garden City, NY: Doubleday.

STANTON, W. (1966) *The Leopard's Spots: Scientific Attitudes Toward Race in America 1815–59*, Chicago, IL: The University of Chicago Press.

STOCKING, G.W., JR. (1968) *Race, Culture and Evolution*, New York: The Free Press.

TAKAKI, R. (1990) *Iron Cages: Race and Culture in 19th Century America*, New York: Alfred A. Knopf.

TAKAKI, R. (1994) 'Reflections on racial patterns in America', in TAKAKI, R. (Ed) *From Different Shores: Perspectives on Race and Ethnicity in America* (2nd ed.), New York: Oxford University Press, pp. 24–35.

United States v. Rogers (1846) 4 US (4 Howard), pp. 567–74.

United States v. Villato (1797) 2 US (2 Dallas), pp. 370–3.

WEBER, D. (1982) *The Mexican Frontier, 1821–1846: The American Southwest Under Mexico*, Albuquerque, NM: University of New Mexico Press.

WEINBERG, M. (1977) *A Chance to Learn: The History of Race and Education in the United States*, New York: Cambridge University Press.

WOLF, E. (1982) *Europe and the People without History*, Berkeley, CA: University of California Press.

Chapter 3

Genetic Pathology Model of Deficit Thinking

Richard R. Valencia

In this chapter, I focus on the genetic pathology model (a term I coin here). The genetic pathology model of deficit thinking — which contends that inferiority is transmitted by the genetic code — held currency from about 1890 to 1930. Although alleged personality defects and social deviance, such as criminal behavior, were also the subjects of hereditarian driven research efforts, our focus will be on that arm of the genetic pathology camp in which racial differences in measured intelligence were investigated. The hereditarian notion of genetically determined intelligence was firmly entrenched by the early 1920s, as was the deficit thinking position that intellectual differences favoring whites over certain ethnic minority groups, for example, blacks, Mexican Americans was largely due to an innate basis. Our analysis of the genetic pathology model, a variant of the parent deficit thinking paradigm, covers the following areas: 1) nature vs. nurture; 2) foundations; 3) ideology and intelligence testing, cross-racial research and actual use of tests in curriculum differentiation; 4) heterodoxy.

As an introductory note, I need to underscore that any analysis of the genetic pathology model and era has to be couched in the context of the key players. This is important in that a great deal of our discussion focuses on the collective social thought of these individuals who held hereditarian perspectives. These scholars and researchers, professors, designers of standardized, widely used tests, officers of scholarly organizations, consultants to government agencies, were frequently in positions of stature and authority. Initially, there were the likes of Herbert Spencer, Sir Francis Galton and Karl Pearson. Later, individuals such as Charles B. Davenport, Stanley Hall, Henry H. Goddard, Frederick Kuhlmann, Lewis Terman, Robert M. Yerkes, Edward L. Thorndike, Robert S. Woodworth and James McKeen Cattell became prime movers of hereditarianism and the eugenics movement during the genetic pathology era. The number of individuals was large, but in actuality these men formed small, tight-knit circles. For example, Galton — an avowed hereditarian and eugenicist — hand picked Pearson as his successor. Goddard, Kuhlmann, and Terman were students of Professor Hall, who believed strongly in inherited mental ability. Thorndike and Woodworth studied under Cattell, who in turn served as a research assistant for Galton (Blum, 1978). Many of these would go on to serve in eminent, influential positions. For example, Blum notes, 'An index of psychologists' respect for eugenics is the fact that Hall, Cattell, Yerkes, Terman, Thorndike and Woodworth all became presidents of the American Psychological Association' (1978: 57–8).

Perhaps of greater influence was the role of individuals, such as Terman and Thorndike, who were professors of education and psychology at major universities. Blum comments:

> Their work was extensively supported by the government and foundations. They trained many school psychologists and administrators. Future teachers read their textbooks in college. Moreover, their views were congenial to school authorities concerned with setting up a tracking system which would encourage acceptance of inequality and social class divisions. (1978: 64)

In this chapter we shall expand our discussion of how a powerful group of hereditarians helped to mold educational policies and practices through their deficit thinking.

Nature vs. Nurture

The debate concerning the relative contributions of nature (heredity) and nurture (environment) to intelligence remains prominent today. Historically, it is interesting to note that it was in Shakespeare's *The Tempest* that the nature–nurture distinction was first established (Samuda, 1975; see also Nunn, 1945). The character Prospero, in reference to Caliban said: 'A devil, a born devil, on whose nature/Nurture can never stick' (*The Tempest*, IV, 1). As Samuda describes (drawing on Nunn), Sir Francis Galton (1883) used the distinction in his *Inquiries into Human Faculty and its Development* and 'it was to be accepted this way thereafter' (p. 35).

Although the nature–nurture dissimilarity was first coined by Shakespeare, it appears that Aristotle is first credited with drawing a connection between the measurement of intelligence (and beauty) and the superiority of some groups of humans compared to others (Chorover, 1979). The unit of measurement was the facial angle — or more specifically, the slope of the forehead as seen in profile. It was contended that human facial lines ranged from a low of 70 degrees (Negroes) to a high of 100 degrees (ancient Greeks). Below 70 degrees were apes, and even lower, dogs.[1]

Most scholars would agree that the modern day nature–nurture controversy can be traced to Galton's 1870 work, *Hereditary Genius: An Inquiry into Its Laws and Consequences* (Chorover, 1979). The belief that heredity plays a monumental role in determining human behavior and outcomes was Galton's thesis. Note the opening sentence of *Hereditary Genius*: 'I propose to show in this book that a man's natural abilities are derived by inheritance, under exactly the same limitations as are the form and physical features of the *whole organic world*' [emphasis added] (p. 1). Using detailed genealogical data, for example, the judges of England who served the courts between 1660 and 1865, Galton presented a 'case . . . so overpoweringly strong . . .' (1870: 3) that few scholars of the times would challenge his thesis. According to Galton, men of eminence (such as statesmen, military commanders, scientists or poets) were in such positions due to their 'natural gifts' which were genetically inherited via their parents and ancestors who also held positions of eminence. Galton failed to consider, however, the rival explanation that in a highly socially stratified England, eminent people were in such fortunate positions because privilege, status and wealth were *socially* inherited.

In such an ambitious thesis (i.e., drawing from principles pertinent to the 'whole organic world'), Galton was not remiss at presenting his views of racial differences in *Hereditary Genius*. Galton's racist perspectives are forecast in the title of his chapter, The Comparative Worth of Different Races. According to his ranking system, the ancient Greeks were at the top, Anglo-Saxons held an intermediate position, and the African Negro and the 'Australian type' (I assume he was referring to the indigenous people of Australia) were at the bottom rungs. More specifically, Galton proffered, 'the average [intellectual] ability of the Athenian race is, on the lowest possible estimate, very nearly two grades higher than our own — that is, about as much as our race is above that of the African negro' (1870: 342). Commenting further on the intelligence of Negroes, Galton notes:

> the number among the negroes of those whom we should call half-witted men, is very large. Every book alluding to negro servants in America is full of instances. I was myself much impressed by this fact during my travels in Africa. The mistakes the negroes make in their own matters, were so childish, stupid, and simpleton-like, as frequently to make me ashamed of my own species. (1870: 339)

A number of events, developments and scholarly works during the period from 1890 to 1920 coalesced in which the 'discovery of nature' and the 'new biology' swept across American academia and 'skewed the scientific discussion of the nature–nurture problem toward the conclusion that heredity was all powerful and environment was of little consequence' (Cravens, 1978: 45).[2] The appearance of Galtonian biometrics, close ties between Galton and American psychologists, the development of the correlation coefficient (Galton and Karl Pearson), the eugenics movement, the development of the Binet–Simon intelligence scales in France, the appropriation of the Binet–Simon scales by American psychologists H.H. Goddard and Lewis Terman, individual intelligence testing, mass intelligence testing in World War II, Mendelian genetics, and instinct theory (William McDougall) all combined to help heredity become entrenched as a powerful explanatory base of human behavior in the nature–nurture controversy.

It must be noted, however, that the prevailing winds of hereditarianism and its novel scientific doctrines owed its development not only to the internal workings of science, but also to external forces and events of the times. As Cravens has observed, the new scientific doctrines of hereditarianism 'were seized upon by men in public life who possessed a direct stake in their application to American society' (1978: 86). As such, hereditarian ideas became the rationale for white racial superiority. Cravens notes that as racist ideas became linked with ideas of science, dissent emerged. Some scholars, who posited that environmental factors were the better explanations of human behavior and outcomes, viewed hereditarianism as anathema to the future of the social sciences and a democratic society.

Among historians of the nature–nurture controversy and race relations, there is agreement that the one individual most responsible for the development and advancement of the concept of culture was German-born Franz Boas (Cravens, 1978; Degler, 1991). Boas, born in Minden, Germany in 1858 was raised in a middle-class Jewish family. It is likely that his politically liberal upbringing and experience of anti-Semitism in Germany helped to shape his left-liberal world views as an adult (Cravens, 1978). Boas settled in New York City in 1887, hoping to launch a career as an anthropologist. In 1899 he was appointed professor of anthropology (Columbia University), and by the early 1910s Boas trained a number of students (Alfred Kroeber; Robert H. Lowie; Edward Sapir) who would eventually go on to distinction in their scholarly work in anthropology (Cravens, 1978). From about 1900 to 1920, Boasian environmentalism would indelibly make its mark on the landscape of the nature–nurture debate. Boas' 1911 book, *The Mind of Primitive Man*, his best-known commentary of his perspectives on culture and race 'declared war on the idea that differences in culture were derived from differences in innate capacity' (Degler, 1991: 62). To be sure, Boas' views on culture and race were indeed radical — considering the entrenchment of hereditarian thought during that era. His basic thesis was that the observed social differences among races (an undeniable fact) were products of 'different histories not different biological experiences' (Degler, 1991: 62). The influence of Boas in laying the foundation for cultural relativism and the eventual sovereignty of culture as an explanation of human behavior was so profound it led one historian, Degler, to comment:

> Indeed, his [Boas'] introduction of history of culture as the cause of differences among people might be said to have been the sword that cut asunder evolution's Gordian knot in which nurture was tightly tied to nature. It also constructed a single human nature in place of one divided by biology into superior and inferior peoples. (1991: 62–3)

Notwithstanding the far-reaching influence of Boas and his anthropology colleagues, the expunging of the belief that human behavior has a biological basis was no easy chore. As Degler has commented, the overturning of hereditarianism 'consumed most of the decades of the 1920s' (1991: 141). To better understand the tenacity of the hereditarian position, it is useful to examine the foundations of the genetic pathology era of deficit thinking, a subject we turn to next.

Foundations

Scholars who have studied the era in which the genetic pathology model prevailed have identified two major foundations that led to developments regarding deficit thinking. These were philosophical and measurement foundations (Blum, 1978; Gould, 1981; Guthrie, 1976). With respect to philosophical foundations, there were three epistemological developments germane to deficit thinking and social stratification: social Darwinism, Galtonian eugenics, and Mendelian genetics.

Social Darwinism

In a sense, social Darwinism was used to *explain* social stratification.[3] Those groups of people who were wealthier, brighter and moral — compared to the poor, intellectually dull and immoral — were in such privileged positions because of their alleged fitter genetic constitutions. Certainly, social Darwinism was a classic case of deficit thinking as it reified hereditarianism and said nothing about the inculpatory role societal structural forces had in creating a social hierarchy.

Given the new hereditarian doctrines that appeared at the turn of the twentieth century, it was not a huge leap for scholars to conclude that inherited intelligence *caused* one's social status. With respect to research endeavors, most psychologists and other social scientists in the 1910s who examined the subject of intelligence and social status concluded the association to be causal (Cravens, 1978). For example, English (1917) administered tests (such as measures of quickness, reasoning and memory) to students from two schools in contrasting environments. The lower-socioeconomic status (SES) students had parents who were college servants, small tradesmen, and the like. The higher-SES students came from homes in which their fathers held high posts, for example, in academic or civic occupations. Based on the demonstrative intellectual superiority of the higher-SES children over the lower-SES group, English interpreted such differences as being caused by heredity.[4] In some of these early research investigations, the correlation coefficient was calculated to quantify the relation between intelligence and SES. Hereditarian researchers violated the major dictum of what is often admonished about the concept of correlation: *Correlation does not imply causality.*

Galtonian Eugenics

A case can be made that Galtonian eugenics were utilized to *enforce* stratification. Galton was a staunch advocate of eugenics, the belief that improvement in the human race could and should be encouraged through selective breeding. The influence of Galtonian eugenics was eventually seen in 1) molding the political climate that led to the Johnson–Lodge Immigration Act of 1924 (which attempted to curtail southern and eastern European immigration so as to avoid the 'mongrelization' of Anglo-Saxon racial stock), 2) giving impetus to the forced sterilization practices *vis-à-vis* the 'mentally defective' and other undesirables. Let us examine each of these in turn.

The passage of the highly restrictive Johnson–Lodge Immigration Act of 1924 (commonly known as the Immigration Act of 1924), was actually a culmination of years of agitation to curtail immigration from southern and eastern Europe (for example, Italy, Russia, Poland and Greece). Although it goes uncontested that the provisions of the Immigration Act demonstrated racial and ethnic biases (Degler, 1991), the question remains, however, as to the roles of mental testing, hereditarian psychologists and the eugenics movement in influencing the passage of the statute. Several scholars have contended that hereditarianists and eugenicists — via intelligence test data — had profound influence in congressional debate and eventual passage of the Immigration Act of 1924 (see Chorover, 1979; Gould, 1981; Kamin, 1974; Karier, 1972).[5] These scholars, for the most part, point to Carl Brigham's 1923 book, *A Study of American Intelligence*, where he reanalyzed the Army intelligence data (WWI) by immigrant background and concluded the innate intellectual superiority of the Nordic-origin men over Army examinees whose ancestry could be traced to southern and eastern Europe (Chorover, 1979; Kamin, 1974). Brigham's conclusions were far-reaching: In the absence of restrictive and selective immigration policy, the possibility of racial admixture looms large — which in turn will 'allegedly' lead to the overall decline of American intelligence.

Other scholars have argued that contemporary and prominent hereditarian psychologists of the 1920s, such as Terman, Goddard, Thorndike, played very little, if any, role in influencing Congressional deliberations (Degler, 1991; Samelson, 1979; Snyderman and Herrnstein, 1983). For example, Snydermann and Herrnstein in an examination of congressional records pertinent to the Immigration Act of 1924 offer this observation regarding intelligence testing data:

[the data] are brought up only once in over 600 pages of congressional floor debate, where they are subjected to further criticism without rejoinder. None of the major contemporary figures in testing . . . were called to testify, nor were any of their writings inserted into the legislative record. (1983: 994)

The truth of the matter regarding the role of mental testing and hereditarian ideas in shaping the Immigration Act of 1924 probably lies somewhere between the two camps. Although archival research of congressional documents by Samelson (1979) and Snydermann and Herrnstein (1983) led to independent conclusions that the hereditarian roots of mental testing had little importance in molding the new immigration policy (Degler, 1991), there still remains suggestive evidence that the roles of intelligence testing and eugenics may have, at least, created a mind-set among some congressmen. First, the Honorable Albert Johnson, the congressman who served as chairman of the House Committee on Immigration and Naturalization and co-composer of the Immigration Act of 1924, was elected as chairman of the Eugenics Research Association in 1923. Second, Kamin admits that 'psychologists [Lewis Terman] failed to appear before the Congressional committees, but other patriotic thinkers carried their message for them' (1974: 24). For example, on January 5, 1924 the chairman of the Allied Patriotic Societies of New York — drawing from Brigham's 1923 book *A Study of American Intelligence* — testified in front of Congressman Johnson's committee. Francis Kinnicut of the Immigration

Restriction League — also liberally referring to Brigham's book — testified in front of the US Senate Committee on Immigration on February 20, 1923.

In my analysis, I do not think the roles of mental testing and eugenics and their alleged impact on restrictionist immigration policies can be placed in a context of all-or-nothing, as seen in the above debate. Although such roles were likely exaggerated by some scholars, having a eugenicist (Johnson) as the co-composer of the Immigration Act of 1924 coupled with some restrictionist and racist testimony to immigration committees of the Congress and Senate may have predisposed some policymakers to be influenced to vote for the act's passage. Just because mental testing data were not recorded in volumes of congressional floor debate does not exclude the possibility that some policymakers were indeed influenced by the contemporary ideological climate of hereditarianism and eugenics. Yet, the primary reason for restriction of immigration from southeastern Europe can most likely be attributed to the overall mood towards cultural diversity of the contemporary 1920s. Anti-immigration sentiment gained impetus in 1890, and grew substantially from 1905 to 1914 as millions and millions of 'new' immigrants arrived in the US.[6] As Degler (1991) has observed, the new immigrants were dramatically different compared with 'old-line Americans', as well as the earlier immigrants. The newcomers, Degler describes, were arriving in unprecedented numbers from relatively new sending areas (southern and eastern Europe), were generally poor, Jewish, Catholic, unskilled, illiterate and settling in large urban areas where criminal, immoral and violent behaviors were more likely to occur. Commenting on the forces that drove anti-immigration policies, Degler gives primary importance to the public's fears about threats to social cohesion and national unity and places in lower significance the roles of hereditarianism and mental testing. 'On balance, then, the more important motivation behind the successful effort to narrow the welcome to immigrants was the concern for social homogeneity, not mental fitness' (Degler, 1991: 53).

The second issue concerning Galtonian eugenics in which social stratification was enforced had to do with coerced sterilization of individuals who were deemed to be mentally insane or defective or socially deviant and engaged in criminal behavior. Contrary to what many people think, it was the United States, not Nazi Germany, that 'became the first nation in modern times to enact and enforce laws providing for eugenic sterilization in the name of 'purifying the race' (Chorover, 1979: 43). From 1907 to 1931, 31 states had passed (and many enforced) sterilization laws (Haller, 1963; also see Landman, 1932). By 1931, the sterilization of the mentally insane outnumbered the sterilization of the feebleminded at a ratio of 2 to 1. The numbers of criminals, epileptics and others that were sterilized was negligible (Haller). The number of sterilizations that were conducted during this period is believed to be 12,145, with 7548 of those forced operations in California.[7]

By far, California was the leader in legal sterilization. The Human Betterment Foundation, a eugenics organization established in 1928 in California, was founded by businessman E.S. Gosney. Included among the foundation's board members were Chancellor Emeritus of Stanford University, David Starr, Stanford University professor Lewis Terman, and biologist Paul Popenoe (Marks, 1981). The Human Betterment Foundation, in a far-reaching proselytizing fashion, sought 'to persuade intelligent people about the virtues of sterilizing the unfit' (Marks, 1981: 115). The primary means of accomplishing this goal was the publication and dissemination of sterilization literature. For example, 130,000 copies of a pamphlet (*Human Sterilization*) were printed and disseminated in 1932 (cited in Marks). The results of sterilization efforts in California were reported in a widely distributed book, *Sterilization for Human Betterment* (1929), co-authored by Popenoe and Gosney (Marks). Following the publication of the book, the Human Betterment Foundation reported a follow-up study in which the first 10,000 sterilizations in California were discussed. Marks describes:

> Predictably, a high percentage of those sterilized were either foreign-born or black. Although only 20 per cent of California's adult population were foreign-born and 1.5 per cent black, 39 per cent of the men and 31 per cent of the women sterilized were foreign-born, while 4 per cent of the total number were black. (pp. 115–16)[8]

The most massive sterilization plan ever articulated (but never implemented) came from the *Proceedings of the First National Conference on Race Betterment*. The conference was held in January, 1914, at Battle Creek, Michigan and was sponsored by the Race Betterment Foundation. The drafted plan (Race Betterment Foundation, 1914) sought to target undesirable groups, such as the feebleminded for large-scale sterilization. The proposed sterilization program assumed that in the US about 10 per cent of the general population constituted the undesirables that should not be allowed to reproduce. In order to reach an incidence proportion of about 6 per cent undesirables by the mid-1950s, approximately 5.8 million people would have needed to be sterilized from 1915 to 1955 (see Chorover, 1979; Karier, 1972). Certainly, the idea of sterilizing nearly 6 million people is abhorrent. Although the Race Betterment Foundation's plan was never put in action, forced sterilizations continued across the US. By 1958, 60,926 sterilizations had been done under state laws (Haller, 1963).

Some eugenicists were not just content with attempts to eliminate undesirables. A number of individuals actually offered concrete plans to promote eugenic measures among the economically and socially elite. For example, William McDougall, professor of psychology at Harvard University, provided readers with his views on eugenics, Negro intelligence, the relative worth of diverse social classes, and a plan of action in his 1921 book, *Is America Safe for Democracy?* McDougall's thesis about the descent of civilization is: '*the great condition of the decline of any civilization is the inadequacy of the qualities of the people who are the bearers of it*' (1921: 12). What are these inadequacies? Who are these people? An answer to the former query can be located in part by examining his views on the concept of *equality*. Note the following:

> The framers of the Declaration of Independence embodied in it the debated proposition that 'all men are created equal'. There are two senses in which this sentence may be interpreted. It may be taken to mean that all

men are equal in respect of their claims for justice, for humane treatment
and the kindly feeling of their fellows, for opportunities to make the best
of their powers of service and of happiness. On the other hand, it may be,
and sometimes has been, taken to mean that all men are born with equal
capacities for intellectual and moral development. There can be no doubt,
I think, that the former interpretation is the true one. (1921: 23–4)

Thus, McDougall — in classic deficit thinking form — posits that the ills of society
and the threats to the safety of a democratic society via the decline of American
civilization can be attributed to innate limitations of intelligence and morality among
some people. Who are these people?

Predictably, McDougall targets the 'Negro race' and the new immigrants.[9] The
key to understanding McDougall's racist and classist treatise, in light of a eugenics
plan, lay in his analyses of differential birthrates. In *Is America Safe for Democracy?* he presents his ideas about eugenics in an appendix entitled, The New Plan.
McDougall's basis for his plan rests on the contention that human physical, moral
and mental qualities are 1) hereditary, 2) unevenly distributed across some groups,
and 3) are fairly unmodifiable by 'good' environmental influences, such as education. Or, stated in another manner: 'The firm and sufficient basis of the demand
for eugenic measures is the long-recognized fact that you may not expect to gather
figs from thistles or grapes from thorns' (1921: 193). Continuing in his analysis,
McDougall cavalierly carves the world into two — the haves and the have-nots:

> Any population may in principle be regarded as consisting of two halves;
> the half made up of all individuals the sum of whose innate qualities or
> potentialities is above the average or mean value, and the other half made
> up of individuals the sum of whose qualities is below the mean value.
> (1921: 193–4)

McDougall continues by proposing a plan of eugenics in which the 'superior half'
of US society needs to dramatically increase its birthrate, which is substantially less
than the 'inferior half'. To counter the 'dysgenic' influence that was occurring in
McDougall's contemporary America, he proposed that the 'selected classes' should
receive monetary rewards for having more children. 'This increase of income should,
I suggest, be not less than one-tenth of the [yearly] earned income, and might well
be rated more' (1921: 199). Although McDougall's morally repugnant 'new plan'
was not implemented, it is of great historical interest that such a plan — in which
American citizens would be judged on biological worth — came from the country's
leading, and most well known, social scientist.

Mendelian Genetics

With respect to Mendelian genetics, one can argue that they were used, in a sense,
to *perpetuate* stratification. The Mendelian laws were 1) *segregation* (during gamete

formation hereditary units occur in pairs, thus every gamete receives but one member of a pair); 2) *independent unit characteristics* (height and skin color, for example, are inherited separately as units; 3) *dominance* (which states that in every individual there are a pair of determining genes for every factor — one from each parent, one gene being dominant and one recessive). Although Mendel's work was confined to inherited factors in plants, in due time Mendelian genetics (particularly Mendelian ratios) were posited in explaining the consequences of racial admixture.

In light of the growing general research activity of race differences during the first two decades of the twentieth century, it is not at all surprising that race mixture (miscegenation) also loomed significant as a research endeavor and social issue. To the anti-miscegenationist, the underlying problem of biological amalgamation was the notion of 'disharmony', or alleged poor fits due to disparate genetic contributions from disparate racial or extreme groups. As Davenport, an unequivocal opponent of race crossing, noted with his co-author (Steggerda) in *Race Crossing in Jamaica* (1929): 'A hybridized people are a badly put-together people' (quoted in Klineberg, 1935a: 212). Such malefic consequences of miscegenation were not restricted in instances of black–white crosses, but were also of concern in some cases of miscegenation between white ethnic groups. Otto Klineberg — an admirer of Franz Boas and a staunch opponent of the hypothesis of racial inferiority of some groups — wrote, in reference to Davenport's and Steggerda's (1929) claim and admonishment of white race crossing:

> The Scotch [sic] have a large frame and large viscera, whereas the Italians have a small frame and small viscera; in crossing, there is danger of the combination of large viscera in a small frame, which may cause crowding, or of small viscera in a large frame, resulting in inadequate support. (Klineberg, 1935a: 212–13)[10]

The debunking of the theory of anthropometric disharmony resultant of race mixture was systematically undertaken by researchers such as Castle (1923, 1926, 1930; cited in Klineberg, 1935a) who pointed out the misuse of Mendelian genetics. Specifically, the underlying assumption of alleged disharmony brought out by miscegenation was 'based on the fallacy of a unit character inheritance of specific organs' (Klineberg, 1935a: 213).

The study of the intelligence of mixed bloods (particularly the early Negro–white investigations) provides us with some insights to deficit thinking. The 'mulatto hypothesis' was a conjecture that in cases of Negro–white racial mixes, the intellectual abilities of the resultant hybrid were positively correlated with the amount of white genetic contribution (see Guthrie, 1976; Klineberg, 1935a). That is, as the proportion of white blood increases, the higher the measured intelligence in the racially mixed offspring. The deficit thinking aspect of the mulatto hypothesis rested, of course, on racist beliefs — the alleged intellectual superiority and inferiority of whites and Negroes, respectively. Under rigorous scientific scrutiny, however, the racial and racist foundation of the mulatto hypothesis collapsed. Researchers such as Herkovits (1926, 1934), Peterson and Lanier (1929), and

Klineberg (1928) concluded that the association among the amount of white ancestry, Negroid features, and intelligence was nonsignificant.

In research that did support the mulatto hypothesis, what rival explanations may have existed that could have explained the observed finding that 'mixed bloods' performed better than 'pure bloods'?[11] First, there is the measurement issue. Ferguson (1916; cited in Klineberg, 1935a) concluded that darker Negroes were inferior to lighter-skinned Negroes, based on the administration of simple psychological tests. Klineberg commented: 'This [study] was [done] before the days of the application of anthropometric measurements in the field, and the group was classified by inspection alone' (1935a: 120).

Second, there is the problem of not controlling for socioeconomic status. For example, Garth (1923) administered the National Intelligence Test (NIT) to 941 boys and girls, ages 12–18 years. The groups consisted of three full-blooded American Indian groups, one mixed-blooded Indian group, and a 'Mexican' (Mexican American) group. For analyses, NIT IQs were based on aggregate scores of all children by combining both sexes and all age levels for each group. The results showed that with respect to highest to lowest median scores the ranks were: 1) mixed-bloods; 2) Mexicans; 3) Plains and Southeastern full-bloods; 4) Pueblo full-bloods; and 5) Navajo/Apache full-bloods. Garth compared the median IQ score of each blood group with the median score of the Plains and Southeastern Indians, the group who scored intermediately. The author suggested a genetic hypothesis to explain the results: 'The mixed breeds excel the pure breeds in intelligence scores . . . If these groups may be taken as representative of their racial stocks, the results indicate differences between their racial stocks in intelligence as here measured' (1923: 401). Garth measured, but did not control for educational attainment of children in the five groups (an issue he admits). In fact, the school attainment by the five groups almost exactly corresponded to the rankings of their scores on the NIT.[12] The strong association between school attainment and IQ had been established by the time of Garth's study, yet he failed to control for the former. Thus, his suggestion of a racial admixture hypothesis denoting intellectual advantages of mixed bloods having white ancestry was unwarranted.

Third, another rival explanation for the mulatto hypothesis has to do with the social acceptability of hybrids. Klineberg (1935a), drawing from Woodson (1928) notes the following in a refutation of the mulatto hypothesis:

> This argument as it stands completely overlooks the important part played by social and educational factors. It is well known, for example, that even during slavery the light-colored Negroes were given special opportunities, engaged in domestic service instead of working in the fields and were encouraged to acquire an education. Since they were in many cases related to their master, the proscription against teaching slaves to read and write was not enforced so far as they were concerned and it is not strange that they should have far outstripped the Blacks. (1935a: 218)

In sum, the use (better yet, misuse) of Mendelian genetics constituted another attempt to perpetuate social stratification, arguing that miscegenation would create disharmonious, baleful unions between whites and racial/ethnic minorities (particularly, blacks). Likewise, the scientific racism that drove the mulatto hypothesis by glorifying alleged white intellectual superiority and pronouncing the alleged intellectual inferiority of blacks, Mexican Americans, and American Indians reeked of deficit thinking. Although the alleged disadvantages of racial mixture were uncloaked as inaccuracies by anti-deficit thinkers of the times, Mendelian genetics held currency as a prominent ideological foundation for deficit thinking during the era of the genetic pathology model.

The second major foundation of the genetic pathology model lay in measurement — that is, anthropometric classifications and assessment of intelligence. Before discussing these two aspects, it would be useful to comment on the notion of *measurement*. Technically speaking, 'measurement is the assignment of numerals to objects or events according to rules that give numerals quantitative meaning' (Wiersma and Jurs, 1985: 3). Several points are germane here. First, numerals — in themselves — are irrelevant to measurement *until* they are assigned quantitative meaning. Second, the rules or standards we use in measurement are crucial elements in comprehending and communicating what is being measured. Third, measurement — particularly of human attributes — frequently involves evaluation, the ideal of a value judgment being made. Taking these points together, measurement can be thought of as a powerful process leading to significant outcomes. With respect to human measurement, the process of conceptualizing a measurement tool, assigning numerals for meaning, using rules and making judgments can be a powerful undertaking because one has the authority to define. In our analysis of the evolution of deficit thinking, the notion of measurement becomes critical because of its influence over both the perceived arrangement and control of social relations. As Chorover has commented:

> After all, the power to measure is merely an extension of the power to define. The point is worth pondering because throughout its history the measurement of human diversity has been linked to claims of human superiority and inferiority and has thereby been used to justify prevailing patterns of behavior control. (1979: 33–4)

Regarding anthropometry, Guthrie (1976) has identified the following types of measurement: skin color, hair and eye color, hair type, lip thickness, and cranium shape and size (see Menchaca, Chapter 2 this volume, for a review and critique of craniometric research). Anthropometric investigations (Davenport, 1927) led researchers often to conclude that racial typologies could be described in which certain races were allegedly more superior to others. Suffice it to say, people of color were placed at the bottom of the continuum. It was not until 1928, at its annual meeting, that the American Anthropological Association adopted a resolution declaring that in anthropology there is 'no scientific basis for discrimination' against any group of people on the assumption of racial inferiority (Guthrie, 1976).

Although anthropometric research was significant in fueling the flames of racism, a more influential force during the era of the genetic pathology model was the measurement of intelligence, particularly the American invention of the intelligence quotient (IQ). Shortly after the development of the first intelligence test in 1905 by Binet and Simon in France, the intelligence scales were imported to the US. From about 1908 to 1911, H.H. Goddard — who had studied with Stanley Hall, a Galtonian hereditarianist — translated the Binet scale to English and contended it measured innate intelligence along a unilinear scale (Blum, 1978; Gould, 1981). Although Goddard was highly influential in launching the Binet scale in America, it was Lewis Terman[13] (also a student of Hall) who is considered the chief architect of its popularity (Gould, 1981). Terman's revisions (from about 1911 to 1915) of the Binet scale were substantial, including: 1) nearly doubling the number of items; 2) extending the upward part of the scale to 'superior adults'; 3) popularizing the ratio 'IQ' (calculated as one's mental age divided by one's chronological age and multiplying by 100[14]); 4) establishing a standard deviation of 15 to 16 points at each age level; 5) scaling the test to approximate a Gaussian (normal; bell-shaped) curve; 6) standardizing the scale near Stanford, California area (hence the 1916 Stanford–Binet Intelligence Test); it is important to note that Terman intentionally sought to obtain a standardization group that was middle class and white (Terman, 1916). Not only was the Stanford–Binet to become the standard of intellectual measurement for decades to come, but Terman — who believed measured intelligence was largely innate — also espoused views about the power of intelligence tests to define and control behavior:

> It is safe to predict that in the near future intelligence tests will bring tens of thousands of these high-grade defectives under the surveillance and protection of society. This will ultimately result in curtailing the reproduction of feeble-mindedness and in the elimination of an enormous amount of crime, pauperism, and industrial inefficiency. It is hardly necessary to emphasize that the high-grade cases, of the type now so frequently overlooked, are precisely the ones whose guardianship it is most important for the State to assume. (Terman, 1916: 6–7)

Very soon after the commencement of the Stanford–Binet test's commercialization, the seeds of the intelligence testing movement were planted. Immediately, scientists and lay people alike misconceived the construct of intelligence and its measuring tool, the IQ. Rather than accepting what the IQ was (a percentile rank on a test measuring a very small sliver of the construct of intelligence), people thought it to be a permanent part of one's psychological baggage. In short, the IQ took on a personal niche in an individual's identity. The dominant thinking by psychologists during the heyday of intelligence testing was almost sacred in nature. Intelligence, as measured by IQ, was believed to have three faces: It was *fixed* at the point of conception, *constant* over the life cycle, and *unalterable* by environmental influences (Kirk, 1973).

A major shortcoming of the Stanford–Binet, as well as other revised Binet scales (see Kuhlmann, 1912), was the lengthy administrative time. As any current school psychologist can testify, individually administered intelligence tests can take up to one-and-a-half hours or so. By 1917, group-administered *achievement tests* were widely available for use in schools. Citing a 1917 survey by Walter Monroe, Chapman (1988) noted that there were 218 group-administered achievement tests accessible for use with students (50 for high schools and 168 for elementary schools) covering 16 subject areas, such as algebra, history and spelling. Yet, at that time no group-administered intelligence test existed. To understand the emergence of group intelligence tests, we need to turn to what transpired shortly after the United States entry to WWI with respect to the mental testing of Army recruits.

The story of the Army mental tests in WWI has been told before, and told well (see Chapman, 1988; Gould, 1981). What I will focus on is the tenacity of deficit thinking of the test developers and how such thought strengthened the already strapping grip hereditarianism held regarding the explanation of racial and class differences in intellectual performance.

The prime mover of the development of the Army mental tests was Robert M. Yerkes, Harvard University professor and president of the American Psychological Association. As Gould (1981) has written, Yerkes proselytized within government sectors as well as within his profession for the Army to test all of its recruits on mental measures, arguing that such test data could provide valuable information for military placement that is, whether a recruit is best fit to be a private or an officer.[15] Yerkes' test development team consisted of the top hereditarians in mental measurement, including Goddard and Terman. Working fervently, Yerkes and his team developed two group administered intelligence tests — the Army Alpha (a written test for literate recruits) and the Army Beta (a pictorial test for illiterate recruits; men who failed the Alpha test also took Beta).[16] The content of the Army Alpha test, which included eight sections and took about an hour for administration, contained the all too familiar completion of numerical sequences, analogies, etc. The Alpha test, historically, is of great significance as this test 'was the granddaddy, literally as well as figuratively, of all written mental tests' (Gould, 1981: 199).[17]

The Army mental tests campaign under Professor (and Colonel) Yerkes was indeed an ambitious undertaking — the universal testing of recruits. By May, 1918 the Army had set up 24 camps for testing. By January, 1919 — about 8 months after testing had commenced — the testing program had fulfilled its mission: The mental ability of 1,726,966 enlisted men and officers had been assessed (Chapman, 1988). The reader can imagine: How does one go about analyzing such massive data, particularly at a time when computers were unavailable? Yerkes had a team member, E.G. Boring, select a subsample of 160,000 cases from the 1.7 million test files for analysis. After converting the scores of the Army Alpha, Beta, and individual test data to a common standard, the Yerkes team produced data and conclusions 'that reverberated throughout the 1920s with a hard hereditarian ring' (Gould, 1981: 196). As Gould has commented, three 'facts' from the data analysis of the army mental testing surfaced 'and continued to influence social policy in America long after their scores on the tests had been forgotten' (p. 196). In brief, these conclusions were:

1   The measured average mental age of white American adults (i.e., the Army recruits who were tested) was 13.08 years. In that the mental age of a

'moron' was from 8 to 12 years, and because the Army test data approximated a normal (but positively skewed) distribution, the shocking (and absurd) conclusion was that about 50 per cent of the white male adults in the American population were morons![18]

2   Based on disaggregated data analysis for the white sample, the mental ages of recruits were reported by national origin. The men from southern and eastern Europe were concluded to be less intelligent than those from Nordic ancestry. The average man, for example, of Russian origin (mental age, 11.34 years) and Italian origin (mental age, 11.01) were deemed to be morons.

3   The average mental age of the Negro recruit was measured at 10.41, solidly at the bottom of the mental measurement group comparisons.

So, we see, according to a group of well-known psychologists, the average white, new immigrant, and Negro male in 1920 is a moron — intellectually inferior via the genetic code. The Army Alpha and Beta tests, developed by the leading American hereditarians of the period, were so 'constructed to measure innate intelligence, and they did so by definition' (Gould, 1981: 198). Given the strength of the circular nature of this argument, the massive data base, and the prominent reputations of the Army test developers, the value of deficit thinking on the American stock market of social thought would rise dramatically. Already on the increase, the eugenics, anti-miscegenation, and restrictionist immigration movements looked to the Army data to bolster their political agendas. Perhaps this is seen most clearly in Princeton University professor Carl C. Brigham's book, *A Study of American Intelligence* (1923). Brigham's volume, directed to a popular audience as well as a scholarly one (published by Princeton University Press), provided a reanalysis of the Army mental test data. Hard-hitting themes of his treatise were the decline of American intelligence (imputed to racial admixture), the racial (intellectual) inferiority of the Negro, and the need to restrict immigration from southern and eastern Europe. Yerkes wrote a laudable foreword to his book, commenting that Brigham's treatment was fact-filled, not opinionated. Some scholars have noted, however, that Brigham's conclusions did not differ much from Madison Grant, the leading American theorist of racism of the period, who wrote *The Passing of the Great Race* (1916).

Suffice it to say, the conclusions drawn by hereditarian-bent scholars regarding the Army test data and racial/ethnic and class differences in intellectual performance demonstrate quite clearly how 'science' is adjusted to meet political priorities. Deficit thinking shuts debate. Deficit thinking has no room for heterodoxy. Deficit thinking allows no room for rival interpretations of the same data. Gould (1981), referring to Yerkes' (1921) mountainous monograph on *Psychological Examining in the United States Army* points out that 'scarcely a word do we read through eight hundred pages of any role for environmental influence' (1981: 198). More specifically:

As pure numbers, these data carried no inherent social message. They might have been used to promote equality of opportunity and to underscore the disadvantages imposed upon so many Americans. Yerkes might have argued that an average mental age of thirteen reflected the fact that relatively few recruits had the opportunity to finish or even to attend high school. He might have attributed the low average of some national groups to the fact that most recruits from these countries were recent immigrants who did not speak English and were unfamiliar with American culture. He might have recognized the link between low Negro scores and the history of slavery and racism. (Gould, 1981: 198)

In sum, out of the Army mass intelligence testing campaign (especially the Alpha tests), mass intelligence testing in the schools was born. On January 23, 1919 — the same day the Army ended its testing program — Yerkes and Terman requested a grant of $25,000 from the Rockefeller Foundation to fund their proposal for the purposes of 'developing and standardizing an intelligence scale for the group examination of school children — a scale for the measurement of native ability' (quoted in Chapman, 1988: 77). About a year later, the development of the National Intelligence Test (NIT) was complete and ready for distribution. Regarding the norming of the test, the NIT was just as inclusive as the Stanford–Binet; it appears that no African American, Mexican American, Asian American, and American Indian children were part of the standardization sample.[19] World Book Publisher printed 400,000 copies for public school use and had them for sale in the fall of 1920 (Chapman, 1988: 1). In an advertisement for the NIT, the publisher touted the role the Army mental tests had in the development of the new group intelligence test. As well, the advertisement was explicit about the classificatory use of the NIT. Note the following:

These tests are the direct result of the application of the army testing methods to school needs . . . The effectiveness of the army intelligence tests in problems of classification and diagnosis is a measure of the success that may be expected to attend the use of the National Intelligence Tests, which have been greatly improved in the light of army experiences . . . They [the NIT scales] are simple in application, reliable, and immediately useful for classifying children in Grades 3 to 8 with respect to intellectual ability. (cited in Gould, 1981: 178)

Soon after the publication of the NIT in early 1920, other group-administered intelligence tests were developed and ready for consumption by a very hungry and receptive public school system bent on promoting efficiency. The new corpus of group intelligence tests included the familiar 'general' instrument (i.e., similar to the NIT) as well as nonverbal and performance tests. Some of these tests (see, Valencia, 1985) with their respective publication dates, are: Terman Group Tests of Mental Ability (1920); Haggerty Delta I Test (1920); Detroit First Grade Intelligence Test (1921); Otis SA Test of Mental Ability (1922); Otis Classification Test (1923); Detroit Primary Intelligence Test (1924); Cole–Vincent Group Test (1924); and the Goodenough Draw-a-Man Test (1926).[20]

By the mid-1920s, group-administered intelligence tests were used with great frequency in our nation's public schools, and bureaucracies arose to handle the mass testing and use of test results.[21] In 1926, the US Bureau of Education published a survey that sought to report the use of homogeneous grouping and the use of group intelligence tests in classifying students to ability groups (Cities Reporting the Use of Homogeneous Grouping and of the Winnetka Technique and the Dalton Plan, 1926; cited in Chapman, 1988). Based on data from 292 cities with populations ranging from 10,000 to 100,000 plus, the percentage of cities reporting homogeneous ability grouping at the elementary, junior high and high school levels were 85 per cent, 70 per cent, and 49 per cent, respectively. In the same report, it was reported that 250 (86 per cent) of the 292 cities surveyed used intelligence tests in student classification. Thus, since the publication of the NIT in 1920 and by the mid-1920s, American public schools had become highly differentiated in curriculum, and the sorting mechanisms, by far, were group intelligence (and achievement) tests.[22]

In sum, the measurement foundation — presumed by its architects to be built with bricks of 'good science' — provided some legitimacy to the pseudoscientific nature of deficit thinking during the era of the genetic pathology model. From this boost given to deficit thinking, a raging controversy would emerge. With the development of the IQ — the new found 'calibrator' of human intellectual abilities — coupled with the contention that 'as late as 1925, most race psychology studies assumed innate racial differences' [in mental abilities] (Cravens, 1978: 239), it was not long before one of the most explosive psychological debates of the twentieth century would appear on the scene. Racial differences in intellectual performance, some argued, are best explained by racial differences in genetically determined abilities. Numerous studies of racial comparisons of intellectual performance from about 1915 to 1930 were conducted and concluded that whites were genetically superior to African Americans, Mexican Americans, and American Indians. As we shall see in the next section, these 'research' findings were not mere descriptions of racial differences. Many studies had clear policy implications for schooling practices.

Ideology and Intelligence Testing, Cross-racial Research and Actual Use of Tests in Curriculum Differentiation

Here, I will first discuss the function and role of ideology in early intelligence testing. This will be followed by a review and critique of a number of cross-racial research studies of intellectual performance. I close by examining some scholarly work that discusses the actual use of intelligence tests in schools with respect to schooling practices directed towards children of color and children of working-class backgrounds.

Ideology and Intelligence Testing

Although the intelligence testing movement did indeed have a measurement foundation, I assert that ideology played an equally influential function in its development. The contention that ideology had an important role in shaping the intelligence testing movement has been advanced by other scholars (e.g., Marks, 1981). In this section I explore Marks' thesis by focusing on two major themes. First, an attempt is made to identify, with some precision, the psychological construct of individual differences and how this notion fits into the early twentieth-century meritocratic worldview. Second, the relationship between ideology and intelligence testing in the context of minority schooling will be discussed by examining the views of Lewis Terman, as a case in point.

The purpose and direction of the intelligence testing movement were driven by a rapidly changing complex society and educational system in serious need of a socially 'powerful organizing principle' (Fass, 1980: 432). Urbanization, industrialization and massive immigration combined to force the schools to address a critical issue of democratic schooling, which was 'how to educate the mass without losing sight of the individual' (1980: 446). Stated in another manner: How could the United States educate an intellectually diverse student population while sorting, selecting and rewarding individual talent in a democratic and scientifically defensible manner? The answer, as Fass has noted, was the idea of IQ and intelligence testing, which coincidentally, were becoming available at a time when an organizing mechanism for selection and curriculum differentiation was so much desired.

To understand the conjecture that intelligence testing was, in part, driven by ideological or extrascientific factors, we first need to examine the notion of intelligence testing itself. Drawing from Fass (1980), I am using the term intelligence testing to denote collectively: 1) the procedure of measuring intelligence; 2) that which is perceived to be the measure of intelligence (the IQ); and 3) the organizational and social mechanism referred to as the intelligence testing movement. In that the prime movers of intelligence testing were, for the most part, hereditarians, eugenicists and even racists, it makes sense to conclude that intelligence testing — consisting of procedural, measurable and social movement aspects — was a value-laden idea with significant implications for the stratification of schooling practices and outcomes.

Let us now examine Marks' (1981) thesis about the social construction of IQ and its impact on a differentiated reward system. The development of the construct of 'individual differences', coined by J. McKeen Cattel in 1916, was a major accomplishment in the field of psychology. On this development Marks comments:

> The construct of individual differences . . . provided the basis for the claim that psychology was a science. It provided a common set of facts, methods, techniques, and theory for psychologists to build their discipline around and a common set of agreed-upon assumptions within which they could operate. (Marks, 1981: 5)

Individual differences was historically complex as a construct. Marks (1981) discusses the construct as being composed of five interrelated ideas. First, the concept of individual differences was constructed on the basis of evolutionary theory in which biological determinism was the explanatory foundation of human nature.

Environment was not ignored, but relegated to a status independent and secondary to heredity.

Second, regarding intelligence, the concept of individual differences was constructed on the notion that one's intellectual abilities were genetically inherited and unmalleable. Thus, at the moment of human conception — when sperm met ovum — a template for intelligence was laid down, setting limits on what one could accomplish.

Third, the 'new psychology' had no room in its perspective for ideas such as free will, the mind or consciousness — interests of the 'old psychology'. The construct of individual differences had as its focus, behavior. Drawing from the frameworks of the biological and physical sciences, psychologists viewed heredity as biological and behavioral. The logical extension was that the construct of individual differences, when used to understand social behavior, went well beyond scientific credibility. 'Psychologists viewed the behavior of people — including women, blacks, and immigrants — as inherently indicating their biological capacities rather than their socio-economic, cultural-biological conditions.' (Marks, 1981: 9).

Fourth, the concept of individual differences was constructed on the premise that human behavior could and should be measured and quantified. To be sure, the measurement of individual differences was a preoccupation among psychologists at the turn of the century. Such activity was inspired, to some degree, in hopes of advancing psychology as a science. Measurement advancements did indeed occur. Thorndike, commenting on the work of Cattell and other psychologists in promoting measurement, wrote in 1890 about three significant principles of method in measurement that had been produced:

> To describe a quantity by its position on a scale of measurement, not by a classificatory adjective; to keep in mind the variable error of every determination that one uses; to study things, qualities and events by studying their relations. (quoted in Marks, 1981: 12)

Some psychologists approached measurement with zeal. Thorndike and his student, McCall, once voiced: 'All that exists, exists in some amount and can be measured' (quoted in Marks, 1981: 12). Such a proclamation is, of course, not value free. As we have discussed earlier, the power to measure is an outgrowth of the power to define (Chorover, 1979).

Fifth, also central to the psychological construct of individual differences is the idea of variation, or in measurement terminology, the concept of variance. The new psychology sought to focus on differences among people, whereas traditional psychology was disposed to study similarities. The idea that human behavior could and should be examined from a perspective of individual differences is a powerful one for it has, as its basis, the ranking of individuals on some scale, for example, 'genius', 'moron'. In constructing intelligence tests, psychologists relied substantially on Galton's utilization of the normal distribution curve, a mathematical model of probability predicting — with some precision — dispersion of scores around the mean. Based on IQ rankings, such measurement data were used, in part, as gatekeepers to decide which students would have access to the higher levels of knowledge and instruction. Once again, I am struck by the potency of Chorover's statement — '. . . the power to measure is merely an extension of the power to define' (1979: 33–4). It is important to keep in mind that the normal distribution is not a feature inherent in the intelligence test. Test constructors develop standardized tests specifically so the scores of the standardization sample are distributed normally. In any event, the construct of intelligence has been given more research attention by twentieth-century psychologists than any other dimension of individual differences (Peterson, 1982). Furthermore, the belief that intelligence is normally distributed remains, even today, as one of the most entrenched assumptions in psychology.

The second idea Marks (1981) discusses in his thesis about the extrascientific underpinning of intelligence testing is 'meritocracy' — the ideology that rewards should be based on merit. The democratic and egalitarian version of meritocracy of the nineteenth-century was rooted in the idea that hard work and effort, independent of intellectual ability, would lead to equal education (the common school notion) and social mobility. The important shift, however, was in the early twentieth-century when the ideology of equal education was supplanted with the ideology of equal educational opportunity (Marks, 1981). The meritocratic worldview at that time was based on the idea that innate intellectual ability was the key factor accounting for variability in talent. Thus, the new meritocracy of the twentieth-century — a sophisticated and differentiated reward system — was driven by the construct of individual differences.

As Marks notes, the new meritocratic formulation — compared to the old view (hereditary aristocracy) — was distinguished by the embracement of the construct of individual differences. He contends that the basic ideas of the new meritocratic worldview consisted of: '(1) the existence of essentially innate, unmalleable intellectual differences, i.e., the construct of individual differences; (2) equality of opportunity; (3) differentiated rewards based on the formula Merit = Innate Ability + Effort; and (4) meritocratic leadership and expertise' (1981: 23). It is interesting to note, by the way, that the modern version of meritocratic ideology is still based on individual differences (but not necessarily is there the widespread belief that ability is innate). As Valencia, Menchaca, Valenzuela have observed in the workings of the current version of meritocracy: 'Those individuals who are deemed the most meritorious (as decided by cognitive tests) will reap the rewards of society (as defined by going to the good schools, obtaining the best jobs, and receiving higher salaries)' (1993: 10). This conception of meritocracy is clearly seen, for example, in *The Bell Curve* (Herrnstein and Murray, 1994).

Let us close this section on ideology and intelligence testing by commenting on the views of one genetic pathology era ideologue, Stanford University professor Lewis Terman — a hereditarian deficit thinker, eugenicist, the developer of the Stanford revision and extension of the Binet–Simon intelligence scale (which Terman named the Stanford–Binet), and the father of the intelligence testing movement in the US. In 1916, Terman published *The Measurement of Intelligence*, a book that was intended to provide a guide for the clinical use of the Stanford–Binet test. The series editor (Ellwood P. Cubberly), who provided the introduction, praised the book for its readability — so clearly written, he noted, that the layman could easily comprehend it. Cubberly also said, 'Besides being of special importance to school officers and to students of education in colleges and normal schools, this volume can confidently be recommended to physicians and social workers, and to teachers and parents interested in intelligence measurements . . .' (p. ix).

It is not known whether this intended wide audience actually read *The Measurement of Intelligence*. However, if these diverse groups had, Terman's views about the intellectual level and educability of racial/ethnic minority youth would have been undeniably registered. In his discussion of borderline cases of intelligence (typically between 70 and 80 IQ, according to the convention of the time), Terman described the cases of M.P. and C.P. — Portuguese brothers with measured IQs of 77 and 78, respectively.[23] Terman's prognosis for M.P. and C.P. was disheartening, predicting that each brother would 'doubtless become a fairly reliable laborer at unskilled work . . . [and] and will probably never develop beyond the 11- or 12-year level (of intelligence) or be able to do satisfactory school work beyond the fifth or sixth grade' (1916: 90). Regarding Terman's views toward 'Indians, Mexicans and Negroes', his sentiments about these children were unequivocally racist. Note the following:

> What shall we say of cases like the last two [M.P. and C.P.] which test at high-grade moronity or at borderline . . .? Hardly anyone would think of them as institutional cases. Among laboring men and servant girls there are thousands like them. They are the world's 'hewers of wood and drawers of water'. And yet, as far as intelligence is concerned, the tests have told the truth. These boys are uneducated beyond the merest rudiments of training. No amount of school instruction will ever make them intelligent voters or capable citizens in the true sense of the word. Judged psychologically they cannot be considered normal.
>
> It is interesting to note that M.P. and C.P. represent the level of intelligence which is very, very common among Spanish-Indian and Mexican families of the Southwest and also among Negroes. Their dullness seems to be racial, or at least inherent in the family stocks from which they came. The fact that one meets this type with such extraordinary frequency among Indians, Mexicans, and Negroes suggests quite forcibly that the whole question of racial differences in mental traits will have to be taken up anew and by experimental methods. The writer predicts that when this is done there will be discovered enormously significant racial differences in general intelligence, differences which cannot be wiped out by any scheme of mental culture.
>
> Children of this group should be segregated in special classes and be given instruction which is concrete and practical. They cannot master abstractions, but they can often be made efficient workers, able to look out for themselves. There is no possibility at present of convincing society that they should not be allowed to reproduce, although from a eugenic point of

view they constitute a grave problem because of their unusually prolific breeding. (Terman, 1916: 91–2)

The above quote is not only interesting in communicating Terman's racial views about intellectual differences and educability of minority youth, it also contains references to the four social and behavioral sciences goals with regard to understanding human behavior I discussed in Chapter 1 of this book. Let us examine these four aims in the context of Terman's quote. First, *description.* Terman describes the IQ of Indians, Mexicans, and Negroes as very commonly being at the border-line level (70–80 IQ). Second, *explanation.* He suggests that the cause of such low IQ is 'racial' or 'inherent in the family stocks', meaning that the substantially lower intellectual performances of children of color is genetically based. Third, *prediction.* Indian, Mexican, and Negro children are uneducable beyond the fifth- or sixth-grade level of instruction and cannot become intelligent voters or good citizens. Terman also implies that in the absence of a eugenic intervention, there will be a dysgenics effect — that is, the overproduction of the alleged genetically disadvantaged. Fourth, *modification.* Terman advocates the segregation of these children of color in 'special classes', where instruction is to be 'concrete and practical'. The goal of such intervention is to produce individuals who can become 'efficient [and unskilled] workers'. In sum, Terman's views of racial differences in intelligence and educability were clearly influenced by deficit thinking.

In conclusion, a case can be made that intelligence was substantially influenced by the extrascientific ideas we have discussed. It is important to inquire, however, to what degree intelligence testing research shaped the social engineering of schooling practices *vis-à-vis* out-groups, such as low-SES minority students. We consider this later, but first let us examine some examples of cross-racial research on intellectual performance.

Cross-racial Research

Among social scientists and their research activities, it appears that during the period from 1890 to 1915 the question of race as an explanation of behavior was not of central importance (Degler, 1991). Stocking (1960; cited in Degler) surveyed 23 social science journals published in this time frame and found a paucity of articles dealing with race and behavior. Between 1910 and 1915, however, research activity on race was prominent as a field of study, but the number of articles published was minuscule, accounting for about 5 per cent of the total. From 1916 to 1929, race related research grew substantially.

Regarding early mental testing research in the US in which children of color were compared to their white peers, investigations began shortly after Goddard imported and revised the Binet scales. According to Guthrie (1976), the first reported study of Negro–white differences in intelligence — as measured by the Binet scales — was by Strong (1913) who conducted his investigation in Columbia, South Carolina. The subjects included 225 white and 125 Negro children. Strong, a graduate student, concluded that the 'colored children are mentally younger than the white' (quoted in Guthrie, 1976: 54). Strong even evoked the familiar mulatto hypothesis, concluding that black children of lighter complexions outperformed their darker skin peers. Morse (1914), the mentor of Strong, in a study a year later commented on Strong's findings and wrote that while his student's investigation showed that 'the colored children did excel in rote memory . . . [they] are inferior in esthetic judgment, observation, reasoning, motor control, logical memory, use of words, resistance to suggestion and in orientation or adjustment to the institutions and complexities of civilized society' (quoted in Guthrie, 1976: 54). The tone of this sweeping, deficit thinking indictment of the alleged limited mental abilities of black children would reverberate for decades to come.

One of the first deficit thinking research studies in which schooling prescriptions were actually suggested was the investigation by Phillips (1914). After testing 137 white and 86 black children with the Binet scales, and finding the latter group inferior in intellectual performance, Phillips raises the question of providing separate education.

> If the Binet tests are at all a gauge of mentality it must follow that there is a difference in mentality between the colored and the white children, and this raises the question: Should the two groups be instructed under the same curriculum? (quoted in Guthrie, 1976: 55)

With the development of the Stanford–Binet intelligence test in 1916, followed by the proliferation of group-administered intelligence tests and the rise of the intelligence testing movement, the study of racial differences in mental ability took root. The parent field of the study of racial differences was termed 'race psychology' during this era. Thomas R. Garth — a psychology professor at The University of Texas and later at the University of Denver — was a leading scholar in race psychology. Garth, a hereditarian and believer in the mental superiority of the white race (something he later would recant), conducted two literature reviews on race psychology that are worthy to summarize. In his first review (Garth, 1925), the period of research publication spanned 1916 to 1924. Garth identified 45 studies in which 19 'racial' groups were studied.[24] In the 45 studies, 73 separate investigations were conducted. Of the 73 investigations, 55 (75 per cent) focused on intelligence. The remaining covered other 'mental processing' aspects such as learning, mental fatigue and memory. Regarding the 19 'racial groups' who served as subjects in the 73 investigations, in descending order the groups studied most frequently with their respective number of investigations were: American Negro (25), American Indian (8), Chinese (6), Italian (5), Portuguese (4), Mexican (4)[25], and Japanese (3). All other groups participated as subjects once or twice. With respect to a conclusion, Garth noted: 'These studies taken all together seem to indicate the mental superiority of the white race. There may be some question, however, about the indicated inferiority of the yellow races' (1925: 359).

In his second review of race psychology literature, Garth (1930) covered the period from 1924 to 1929. A major trend was the dramatic increase in the number of investigations and groups studied. He identified 73 studies in which 132 investigations were conducted; 29 'racial groups' served as subjects. Of the groups studied, once again the American Negro was the most tested (in 25 of the 132 investigations). Of the total 36,882 subjects studied, there were 7158 (19 per cent) Negroes. Next in frequency were American Indians (in 14 of the 132 investigations; 5795 [16 per cent] subjects), followed by Mexicans (in 7 of the 132 investigations; 4140 [11 per cent] subjects). Thus, we can see that Negroes, American Indians, and Mexican Americans — the three prime targets of deficit thinking — were studied the most frequently in race psychology studies from 1925–1929, accounting for nearly half (46 per cent) of all subjects tested.[26]

As was found in his first review (1925), Garth (1930) observed that the measure of racial differences in intelligence was the most frequent mental processing aspect studied from 1925 to 1929. This is indicated, in part, by examining the kinds of tests administered in the 73 studies. During this 5-year period, 12 different types of tests were administered 126 times. Of the 126, intelligence tests (group = 49; individual = 6) were administered on 55 (44 per cent) occasions. Regarding a major conclusion about racial differences in intelligence, Garth observes that a belief in the 'hypothesis of racial inequality' was losing ground to the 'hypothesis of racial equality'. Note the following:

> What then shall we say, after surveying the literature of the last five years, is the status of the racial difference hypothesis? It would appear that it is no nearer being established than it was five years ago. In fact, many psychologists seem practically ready for another, the hypothesis of racial equality. (p. 348)

Garth's (1930) conclusion about the race psychology literature regarding racial differences in intelligence is used as the basis for Cravens' point that although most race psychology studies by 1925 articulated a hereditarian explanation for differences, by 1930 no such studies did so. 'The change was that rapid and total' (Cravens, 1978: 239).

Notwithstanding the decline of the genetic pathology model by 1930, it is still informative to review some of the race psychology research of the 1920s that investigated group differences in intelligence. In brief, I will summarize representative studies that focused on Mexican Americans and African Americans.

Regarding Mexican American children, Garth's (1925, 1930) race psychology reviews showed that these children were frequent subjects in intelligence testing research. Based on my own analysis and drawing from Sánchez (1932a), I have identified eight such studies published between 1920–1929 in which Mexican American children were subjects (Garretson, 1928; Garth, 1923, 1928; Goodenough, 1926; Koch and Simmons, 1926; Paschal and Sullivan, 1925; Sheldon, 1924; Young, 1922). The point of most interest is that in all eight studies the author(s) concluded that the lower intelligence test performance of the Mexican American children — compared directly to their white peers or white normative data — was due to heredity. In some cases, the hereditarian conclusions of inferior genetic constitution of Mexican American children was made explicit (for example, Garretson, 1928; Young, 1922) or was suggestive (such as, Goodenough, 1926).

Although it appears that Terman (1916) is the first researcher to comment that Mexican American children are innately intellectually inferior (see our previous discussion), there is no research base or publication to which his conclusion can be attributed. The first publication I can identify in which Mexican American children were subjects of intelligence testing research is Kimball Young's *Mental Differences in Certain Immigrant Groups* published in 1922. Young's monograph — published in the University of Oregon Publication series — was based on his doctoral dissertation research, in which he worked under the influential Stanford University professors Terman and Cubberly. Young (1922) administered the Army Alpha and Beta tests to over 750 12-year-old students attending schools in the larger Bay Area (for example, San Francisco; San Jose) of California. The subjects included 'American' (i.e., white) and 'Latin' (Italian; Portuguese; Spanish-Mexican). The Spanish-Mexican students numbered 51 and consisted of children whose ancestry could be traced to Spain or Mexico. The Spanish-Mexican groups — whose socioeconomic status was consistently lower than their white peers — had a combined Alpha and Beta mean score of 77.95, compared to the white combined mean of 129.45. The mean scores of the Italian and Portuguese were approximately the same as the Spanish-Mexican groups.

Although Young did not assess the Latin children's competence in English language skills, he nevertheless readily dismisses this likely confounding variable. Whereas the Latin children performed considerably higher on the Beta test (a performance scale) compared to the Army Alpha test (a verbal scale), Young intractably held to the position:

> it is clear why the alpha may have proved too difficult for the Latins. It was not language, but ability, that brought out the lower scores . . . The upshot of the whole matter is that the alleged language handicap of the Latins simply *does not exist to the extent imagined.* (1922: 59)

Young, I contend, acted too swiftly in disregarding the language issue as a confound. He failed to consider whether any of the Italian, Portuguese or Spanish-Mexican children had 1) any difficulty in understanding the English instruction for both the Alpha and Beta tests; 2) the same cultural experiences as their white peers regarding the content of the highly verbal and culturally loaded Army Alpha test, for example, a multiple choice item, such as 'Christy Mathewson is famous as a: writer, artist, baseball player, comedian'; 3) similar learning opportunities with materials and tasks germane to the Army Beta test (cubes, geometric shapes; numerical seriation); and 4) similar academic learning opportunities in their respective schools, given that the white students were typically enrolled in higher grades (hence greater exposure to advanced curriculum) than the Latin students. The white students were principally located in the low seventh and low sixth grades; the Spanish-Mexican students were mainly located in the low sixth, low fifth, low fourth, and high fourth grades.

With respect to his conclusion regarding the observed findings of group differences in intelligence testing and school achievement, Young's thoughts resonate with deficit thinking:

> that the true difficulty is one of mental capacity, or general intelligence, which makes the Latins unable to compete with the children of North European ancestry in the mastery of the traditional American public school curriculum . . . If the facts of mental heredity be taken as valid, these findings throw great light on the problems of racial mental differences . . . The writer stands firmly on the ground that the cause of school difficulties must be found in the more innate intellectual differences. (1922: 60, 63–4)[27]

In addition to examining mental differences in certain immigrant groups, Young also sought to investigate 1) 'the possible implication of the findings for the larger problems of immigration and the future race mixture in this country' (p. 3), and 2) the application of the study's results for the modification of school policy. Regarding the former purpose, Young was not shy in drawing conclusions. He lamented the inevitable race mixture between the alleged superior 'older' Americans and the alleged inferior stocks from parts of Europe:

> If the racial stocks that are flooding this country from Southern and South-eastern Europe are of such inferiority, on the average, as to be contented with a lower standard of life, if they are incapable of taking on the best of modern culture, then the sociological significance of the entire matter is apparent. Add to this the fact that amalgamation between these stocks and the older American stocks is certain to take place, and between different levels of average intelligence, we have a more serious phase of the problem presented us. (1922: 81)

Young's anti-miscegenationist views went even further, attributing inferior native intelligence not only to inferior races, but the *interaction* of race *and* social class. 'It is not a problem of the mixture of the Latins in general with the Americans, but of those classes of South Europeans and Mexicans of less average ability than our own American stock of the lower middle classes' (1922: 81). As a basis for immigration policy, Young argued that such discussion 'should resolve around an appreciation of the significance of mental differences rather than economic' (p. 83). Implying that immigration policy was, in part, being led by economic interests (i.e., immigrants were serving as a cheap source of labor, thus it was in the best interests of capitalists not to curtail immigration), Young recommended the use of mass testing as a gatekeeper to entering the US:

> Restriction of immigration should go on in terms of capacity of the immigrants and not of their cheapness as laborers. A set of well-worked out physical and psychological tests with norms could be devised for a relatively slight cost which would be of untold benefit to the country's future

in the way of preventing any further flooding of our country with low-grade materials on which to build a coming nation. We have enough liability in poor stock without enhancing it. (1922: 83)

Let us now review one other race psychology study in which the intellectual performance of Mexican American children was assessed. In an attempt to explain the causes of 'retardation' (i.e., being overage for one's grade level) among Mexican American school children attending school in a small public school system in Arizona, Garretson (1928) compared the intellectual performance of 197 'American' and 117 'Mexican' pupils.[28] The children, who were enrolled in grades 1–8, were administered the National Intelligence test (NIT), the Pinter Cunningham Primary Mental Test (a verbal scale), and the Meyers Pantomine Group Intelligence Test (a nonverbal test).

The results of the study showed the median IQs for the three tests were higher (no significance testing reported) for the white children at almost all grade levels. After analyzing irregularity of school attendance and transientness as possible explanations for retardation of the Mexican American children, Garretson dismissed them as factors. Drawing from the previously discussed investigation by Young (1922), Garretson proffered a genetic interpretation for the group differences in intelligence: 'This [the finding] apparently agrees with the conclusion of Young, that the native capacity, if we assume that the intelligence quotients are indicative of native capacity, of the Mexican pupil is less than that of the American child' (1922: 38). As to why the Mexican American children were overage for their grade level and not making normal progress, Garretson suggested the underlying cause to be innate: 'Probably the principal factor governing retardation of the Mexican child is his mental ability as measured by the group test' (1928: 40).

Once again we see the triumph of deficit thinking. Once again we see a race psychology study — here published in one of the then and now flagship journals, *Journal of Educational Psychology* — with serious methodological flaws. To wit, Garretson (1928) 1) failed to control for SES, as the white children were over-whelmingly of higher SES;[29] 2) he did not fully consider the possibility of language confoundment, that is the depressed intellectual performance of the Mexican American children was due, in part, to limited English proficiency;[30] 3) Garretson failed to address the finding of overlap; that is, in grade 7 the Mexican American children outperformed their white peers on the NIT (97.0 IQ to 96.3 IQ, respectively). In grade 3, the Mexican American children also outperformed their white peers on the Pantomine (74.0 IQ to 72.0 IQ, respectively).[31] How did Garretson reconcile these findings in light of his genetic inferiority confusion? Well, he simply did not. So it goes with deficit thinking.

Regarding race psychology investigations focusing on the intelligence of African American children and youth, they were by far the prime subjects of study during the period from 1916 to 1930 (see Garth, 1925, 1930; Price, 1934). As was the general status of intelligence testing research, such studies with African American subjects proliferated after the commercialization of group intelligence tests pursuant to the development of the Army Alpha and Beta tests. Explanations for the observed, low intellectual performance of African Americans — compared to their white peers or white normative data — frequently were hereditarian based. Let us examine a couple of representative studies from the 1920s.

Florence Goodenough, the developer of the Goodenough Draw-a-Man Test, published a race psychology study in 1926 that deserves our attention. She begins by stating there are two theories that have been advanced to account for racial differences in intelligence:

> The first ascribes the inferior showing made by the South Europeans and the negroes to such post-natal factors as inferior environment, poor physical condition and linguistic handicaps. The second point of view, while it recognizes that the factors named may to some degree affect the tests results, nevertheless holds that it is impossible to account for all the facts which have been observed upon any other hypothesis than that of *innate differences* among the groups under consideration. (1926: 389–90) [emphasis added]

To shed light on the possible explanatory base of group differences in intelligence, Goodenough (1926) administered her drawing test to 2457 school children (grades 1 to 4) representing 22 'racial stocks'. Of the total, there were 682 Negroes (69 attending schools in California, 613 in Tennessee and Louisiana). The weighted mean IQ (computed by the present author) for the Negro group was 79.4, about 20 points lower than the mean IQ of 100.3 for the 500 'American' (i.e., white, primarily 'North European stock').

Goodenough's conclusion as how to best explain the observed Negro-white differences in IQ leaned in the direction of theory two — a genetic interpretation. She came to this conclusion, I gather, by the following reasoning. First, the issue of the Negro child having any form of a linguistic handicap was irrelevant because the Draw-a-Man test 'is entirely independent of language' (1926: 393). Second, the home environment and SES of the Negro is *both* a cause and effect of inferior mental ability. In an interesting and convoluted form of deficit thinking Goodenough commented:

> It seems probable, upon the whole, that inferior environment is an effect at least as much as it is a cause of inferior ability, as the latter is indicated by intelligence tests. The person of low intelligence tends to gravitate to those neighborhoods where the economic requirement is minimal; and, once there, he reacts toward his surroundings along the lines of least resistance. His children inherit his mental characteristics. (1926: 391)

It is my contention that Goodenough's (1926) conclusion, suggesting that Negro children were innately inferior in intelligence, was partially shaped by the hereditarian *Zeitgeist* of the times. The tone, language and data presented in the study point to this. I also speculate that her study and conclusions were influenced by self interests and research bias — that is, Goodenough's need to validate and legitimize her newly developed drawing test, an instrument she purported was completely free of language. Might it be that Goodenough viewed her test as a 'perfect' or 'culture free' test? If so, she was very likely wrong. For example, Klineberg — commenting about a decade later about the cultural boundness of verbal intelligence tests had this to say about performance tests:

> The non-linguistic, or performance, tests present similar difficulties. The Goodenough test of 'drawing a man' is based upon the concept of a fully clothed man as seen in our society. When Porteus gave this test to the Australians, he found that they would almost invariably draw the man naked and so lose points given for correct drawing of the clothes. This test also assumes that a man is the figure most frequently drawn by children; the writer found that among the Dakotas (Sioux) the horse was much more popular. (1935a: 158–9)[32]

More recently, Anastasi noted: 'Such [cross-cultural, cross-ethnic] investigations have indicated performance on this test [Goodenough Draw-a-Man] is more dependent on differences in cultural background than was originally assumed' (1988: 306). It also appears that Goodenough (writing with Harris in 1950) a quarter century after the original test was of the opinion that 'the search for a culture-free test, whether of intelligence, artistic ability, personal-social characteristics, or any other measurable trait is illusory' (quoted in Anastasi, 1988: 306). As such, the low mean IQ performance of the Negro children in Goodenough's 1926 study was likely associated with differential experiences with representational art and limited opportunities of drawing with pencil and paper. Later research strongly supports this conjecture. Dennis (1966; cited in Anastasi, 1988) analyzed comparative data from the Goodenough Draw-a-Man Test in 40 different cultural groups. The main finding was: 'Mean group scores appeared to be most closely related to the amount of experience with representational art within each culture' (quoted in Anastasi, 1988: 306). Furthermore, one study (Bakare, 1972; cited in Anastasi) with Nigerian children found Goodenough–Harris test performance to be positively correlated with the children's SES.[33] In any event, it was scientifically indefensible for Goodenough (1926) to claim that her test — whose directions are very simple ('make a picture of a man; make the very best picture that you can') and which can be completed in minutes by the child — was a measure of innate intelligence.

As previously discussed, the study of racial admixture and performance on intelligence tests was a prominent focus among race psychologists. Particularly popular were investigations of white–Negro group differences in the context of the 'mulatto hypothesis'. Let us examine one such study. Koch and Simmons' (1926) work is a 100-plus page publication that appeared in *Psychological Monographs*, a publication outlet of the American Psychological Association. The subjects were white, Mexican and Negro school children in Texas (our focus will be on Negro performance). Of the total sample of 3316 subjects (grades 1–7, ages 5 to 17 years), there were 613 Negro children. Four group intelligence tests were administered — three nonverbal (Meyers Pantomine Intelligence Test; Detroit First-Grade Intelligence

Test; Pintner–Cunningham Primary Mental Test) and one general (National Intelligence Test).

Early in their monograph, Koch and Simmons admonished that race psychology researchers investigating group differences in academic achievement or intelligence need to be very careful in drawing hereditarian conclusions:

> In a comparative study of the performances of different races and different nationalities, one needs, therefore, to be particularly cautious about attributing any differences in educational achievement or in intelligence-test reactions primarily to an innate or hereditary cause. (1926: 6)

Notwithstanding the importance of this warning, it appears that Koch and Simmons felt themselves to be above their own advice, as they concluded the results of their study to be suggestive of genetic inferiority of the Negro sample. Let us see how this conclusion came to be.

Though Koch and Simmons (1926) reported that in virtually every possible comparison (age level × intelligence test) the white sample had higher mean performance than did the Negro sample, no hereditary explanation was presented. Such a cause was suggested, however, in the authors' analysis of the 'Negro color groups', that is, the presumption of racial admixture.[34] Arguing that it was impossible to undertake a pedigree study of the extent of hybridization among the children in the Negro group, the authors settled for the 'objective' color scale (color card) approach. In this method — which the authors admitted was a rough index — Koch and Simmons held up the color cards to the face of the children to ascertain 'the depth of skin-pigmentation' (1926: 83). Ignoring the wide spectrum of skin hue among African Americans, the authors conveniently collapsed the color card findings into three color groups — 'light', 'intermediate' and 'dark'.

Koch and Simmons were not reticent about what the findings might be using the color scale methodology. 'The theory underlying this procedure is . . . the light [skin] pupils . . . are intellectually most capable' (1926: 83). According to the authors, the mulatto hypothesis was confirmed: 'the mean and median scores of the various total color groups discloses the fact that in all the tests, except the Pintner–Cunningham, on which the intermediate groups excel, the lightest children outstrip the others . . .' (1926: 92). This, in turn, led Koch and Simmons to suggest innate intelligence was the primary (though not conclusive) cause of within-group intellectual performance of the Negro children; 'we may conclude that success in test performance tends to vary inversely with the depth of the pigmentation in the Negro subjects. This is an argument in favor of the intellectual superiority of the whites . . .' (1926: 96).[35] Once again we see a 1920s race psychology investigation that permeates with deficit thinking. Koch and Simmons' hereditarian conclusion is unwarranted on several grounds. First, the authors failed to control for SES between and within the white and Negro groups. Second, no discussion is considered about the possibility that the lighter skin Negroes were preferred (over darker skin Negroes) by whites in various social contexts. Thus, the lighter skin Negroes may have had, in their previous encounters with whites, better learning opportunities.

Third, the authors did not consider the invidious impact of school segregation on the academic development of the Negro children. For example, in the mid-1920s (the time of the investigation), Negro school children in Austin, Texas (one of the sites in this study) attended segregated schools.[36] Fourth, the authors, although acknowledging it, failed to discuss why the mean IQ differences between the 'intermediate' and 'dark' skin Negroes were, for the most part, inconsequential (and, in some cases, flip-flopped in rankings).

To be sure, 1920s race psychology research of racial/ethnic differences in intelligence was a prominent activity. As we have seen, the conclusions drawn about intellectual differences between white and some children of color (i.e., African American; Mexican American) were, in frequency, predominantly hereditarian based. Children of color, it was alleged, performed lower than their white peers largely because of inferiority in native intelligence. This research claim, in and of itself, is indeed a significant social statement of the nature of race relations during the height of the genetic pathology era. The allegation of the intellectual inferiority of these racial/ethnic minority groups speaks to the descriptive and explanatory aspects of deficit thinking during this period. The question remains, however, about the prescriptive role of intelligence testing research and the use of tests in shaping school curriculum.

Actual Use of Tests in Curriculum Differentiation

As we have earlier noted, the US was a dramatically transforming society in the decades sandwiching the turn of the twentieth century. Urbanization and massive immigration, as factors of change, were putting great pressure on public schools to become more efficient in the management and delivery of curricula. This was particularly the case at the secondary level. As Oakes (1985) has observed, from 1880 to 1918, the 14- to 17-year-old school age population grew from 200,000 to over 1.5 million students (a 700 per cent increase). The need for high schools was so pronounced during this time period (1890–1918) that 10,000 such schools were built (an average, mathematically, of one school built each day for 28 years). The need for public schools to become more skillful in sorting and selecting students for instruction was driven by a movement in search of some tool that could be utilized as a grand organizer. Part happenstance, part purposeful, historical analysis of this period informs us that the development of the first school-based group intelligence test (National Intelligence Test) in 1920, set in motion the use of the construct of IQ and the practice of intelligence testing as the desperately needed organizer of curriculum differentiation. Given the imbeddedness of the notion of IQ in American social thought and measurement theory, it was inescapable that IQ testing would be embraced as the management tool of choice (Fass, 1980).

As we turn to a discussion of some scholarly writing that is pertinent to the prescriptive role of testing in curriculum differentiation — which I conceptualize here as *the sorting of students into instructional groups based on perceived and/ or measured educability* — it would be useful to comment on the views of two men who had much to say about the sorting role of tests in the school context. These individuals are Lewis Terman and Virgil Dickson.

As the leader of the intelligence testing movement, and the chief proponent for the use of intelligence tests in school reform, Lewis Terman's influence was unrivaled in the 1920s. Paul Chapman (1988), in *Schools as Sorters: Lewis M. Terman, Applied Psychology, and the Intelligence Testing Movement, 1890–1930*, cogently supports this assertion. Terman's contributions to the development of tests and their application to curriculum differentiation were astounding, given the short period of time in which such school reform was implemented.

As Chapman has noted, Terman was an active leader on many fronts — a man with a mission, whose declaration in 1920 was 'A mental test for every child' (quoted in Chapman, 1988: 84). Terman published two major books on the use of intelligence tests in schools (*The Intelligence of School Children*, 1919; *Intelligence Tests and School Reorganization*, 1922) and numerous articles. In addition to the development of the Stanford–Binet intelligence test, Terman was the author or co-author of other prominent tests, for example, the National Intelligence Test; Terman Group Test of Mental Ability; The Stanford Achievement Test. He was the editor of six scholarly journals (including the *Journal of Educational Psychology and Journal of Applied Psychology*), as well as the series editor for World Book's Measurement and Adjustment Series (which eventually published nearly 20 textbooks). Terman was no loafer when it came to supervising graduate student research, sponsoring over 35 MA and PhD degrees in education and psychology at Stanford University from 1910 to 1925. A number of his students went on and made their own names in the field of intelligence testing and applied psychology, researchers such as Arthur Otis and Virgil Young. In 1921, Terman with 18 well known psychologists founded the Psychological Corporation in an effort to promote test usage and psychological research. Today, the Psychological Corporation stands as one of the leading developers and marketers of tests. Terman's crowning achievement came in 1922 with his election as president of the prestigious American Psychological Association, a solid indication of the high esteem his colleagues held for him. In sum, Terman was indeed the 'networker'. Chapman has commented on Terman's leadership as such:

> In the early twenties his prescriptions for the use of tests, his research on the technology of testing, and his conscious attempt to forge a network of applied psychologists all helped to galvanize the intelligence testing movement. Those efforts led directly to the adoption of tests in schools. (1988: 106)

What were Terman's prescriptions for the use of tests in schools? In order to understand Terman's recommendations for school reform via testing, one must first examine his views regarding individual differences in intelligence in the classroom. In most of Terman's writings, as well of those of other applied psychologists in Terman's camp, the fundamental problem of schools lay in heterogeneity of student abilities in American class rooms. Certainly, Terman was a strong believer in the existence of individual differences in intelligence. After all, individual and group intelligence tests were designed around the notion that intellectual variability among individuals could be assessed. However, *too many differences* in ability levels among students — the argument went — create inefficient teaching and learning climates for teachers and students, respectively. By having slow learners and fast learners learn together, the former face frustration, the latter boredom. Therefore, having classes with an undue amount of variability in mental ability makes for a pedagogical disadvantage. The solution? Curriculum differentiation. The sorting tool? Intelligence tests. The result? Efficiency. Terman's proposed system of using intelligence tests for classification, and the explicit need to eliminate heterogeneity in ability, led him to lay down this major principle in *Intelligence Tests and School Reorganization*; 'A reasonable homogeneity in the mental ability of pupils who are instructed together . . . is a *sine qua non* of school efficiency' (quoted in Chapman, 1988: 86–7).

Terman's views on the prescriptive role of tests in school reform are most clearly articulated in his 1922 book, *Intelligence Tests and School Reorganization*. His plan, a universal proposal, contained the following features (Chapman, 1988). First, all children in the first grade should be administered an individual intelligence test. Second, beginning at the third grade, children should be tested at least every other year with the use of group intelligence tests. Third, based on the test results, Terman advocated the adoption of 'homogeneous class groups'.[37] Although in practice most school districts that used tests for curriculum differentiation employed a three-track tier, Terman believed the ideal plan should use a 'multiple track plan' with five groups. The five homogeneous groups with their respective percentages of students of the total student body are: 'gifted' (2.5 per cent), 'bright' (15 per cent), 'average' (65 per cent), 'slow' (15 per cent), and 'special' (2.5 per cent).[38]

Thus, Terman's universal plan, he contended, could make it possible for intelligence tests to be used in some fashion that both teachers and students would have a more clearly 'differentiated course of study, as regards both content and method' (quoted in Chapman, 1988: 89). To be sure, Terman had great confidence in the power of intelligence tests to assess and predict a child's educability and course of study:

> the grade of school work which a child is able to do depends chiefly upon the level of mental development he has attained . . . *The limits of a child's educability can be fairly accurately predicted in the first school year* [emphasis added]. By repeated tests these limits can be determined accurately enough for all practical purposes by the end of the child's fifth or sixth school year. (Terman, 1920: 21)

Terman was not only a staunch advocate of the use of intelligence tests for educational tracking via homogeneous grouping, he also argued for such tests to be used in an applied manner for work force concerns and interests — that is, vocational guidance. In 1916, the year of the development of the Stanford–Binet intelligence test, Terman predicted, 'The time is probably not far distant when intelligence tests will become a recognized and widely used instrument for determining vocational fitness' (Terman, 1916: 17). Admitting that current intelligence tests were not infallible in revealing the occupation an individual is best fitted to follow, he still lauded the robustness of such present and future tests in determining the best match:

> when thousands of children who have been tested by the Binet scale have been followed out into the industrial world, and their success in various occupations noted, *we shall know fairly definitely the vocational significance of any given degree of mental inferiority or superiority* [emphasis added]. Researchers of this kind will ultimately determine the minimum 'intelligence quotient' necessary for success in each leading occupation. (1916: 17)

What were these 'minimum IQs' for various occupational classes, and how did Terman derive them? Regarding the latter part of the query, it appears that Terman (several years later in 1920) simply reviewed data from studies in which *adults* in different vocational groups were administered intelligence tests. Based on correlational analysis between occupational status of adults and their measured IQs, Terman reasoned — in a cause and effect manner — the following:

> Preliminary investigation indicates that an IQ below 70 rarely permits anything better than unskilled labor, that the range from 70 to 80 is preeminently that of semi-skilled labor, from 80 to 100 that of the skilled or ordinary clerical worker, from 100 to 110 or 115 that of the semi-professional pursuits, and that above all these are the grades of intelligence which permits one to enter the profession or the larger fields of business. Intelligence tests can tell us whether a child's native ability corresponds approximately to the median for: 1) the professional classes; 2) those in the semi-professional classes; 3) ordinary skilled workers; 4) the semi-skilled laborers; or 5) unskilled laborers; and *this information is of great value in planning a child's education.* [emphasis added] (Terman, 1920; 31)

Notwithstanding the reputation Terman had as a scholar and researcher, the above reasoning indicating a rather tight fit between measured intelligence of a school child and his or her subsequent attained occupational status during adulthood is faulty on several grounds. First, Terman concluded causality from correlational analysis. Second, the data he relied on were ex post facto in nature — that is, formulating conclusions from current data in the absence of not having or using base (past) data. Terman violated his own 1916 advice of testing many children on intelligence tests and then following them longitudinally, eventually into the world of work. Third, Terman in his conclusion about IQ and vocational fitness failed to control for key variables, such as SES or schooling attainment and did not consider obstacles in occupational mobility, such as employment discrimination faced by people of color and women.

In conclusion, Terman, the patriarch of the intelligence testing movement, was undoubtedly one of the most influential individuals in the history of using testing for school reform. His work as a scholar, researcher and test developer is well known. We must not forget, however, Dr Lewis M. Terman, as the applied psychologist and social reformer. As Marks (1972, 1981) has written, Terman approached his work with 'a burning faith in human improvability . . . he maintained unshakable commitment to equality of opportunity and social amelioration . . . Terman was involved in much more than creating and selling tests; he was involved in the construction of a meritocratic social reality' (1981: 167–8). At the surface level, Terman's conception of 'equality of opportunity' appears democratic and inclusive. At a deeper layer, however, his idea about this important notion is antithetical to basic principles of democracy such as fair play, equality and freedom. To Terman, to have equality in opportunity was for the individual to have education and training — commensurate to his or her *innate* ability — in order to attain his or her occupational status. Guided by deficit thinking, this perversion of equality of opportunity meant that people of color and the poor would be virtually locked out of the upward flow of educational and social mobility. Chapman — commenting on Terman, ideology and intelligence testing — compresses matters as such:

> The ideology of the emerging test movement, as expressed by Terman's views, can be reduced to its most essential components. Intelligence could be measured by tests and expressed in a single, numerical ratio. This ability was largely constant and determined by heredity. Class and racial inequality could be explained in large part by differences in intelligence. Used in schools, intelligence tests could be used to identify ability, prescribe curricula and determine students' futures. (1988: 92)

One of the reasons Terman became so influential in persuading administrators of the use of intelligence tests for curriculum differentiation in public schools was through his professorial duties in teaching, supervising and producing students with graduate degrees who carried on his mission. One such student was Virgil E. Dickson who, under Terman's supervision at Stanford University, earned his MA (1917) and PhD (1919). The subject of both degrees was in the realm of applied psychology, 'the relation of mental testing to administration'.

Dickson's star in the intelligence testing soared quickly. His master's and doctoral work focused on the experimental use of intelligence tests for student classification and instruction in the public school system in Oakland California — a city located in the Bay Area north of Stanford University. Based on his testing research with first graders, he gained the support of the superintendent of Oakland schools to establish a testing program. In 1917, Dickson (who was appointed as the Director of the Oakland Department of Research) had supervised the testing of 6500 students,[39] and by 1919–1920 he reported that 20,000 or so had been tested — about half the Oakland school district student enrollment (Chapman, 1988). As these 'experiments' culminated and gained further administrator and teacher support in 1919 and 1920, by 1923 Oakland had adapted a systemwide program of mass intelligence testing for homogeneous groupings. Students at all grade levels were administered group intelligence tests for general classification into ability groups and for counseling and guidance when students were promoted, for example, from sixth grade to junior high school.[40] Dickson's reorganization of the Oakland schools resulted in a 'three-track plan', consisting of classes for 'accelerated', 'normal' and 'slow' students.[41] The accomplishments of Dickson are very noteworthy in the history of test use in schools, as Oakland, it appears, was the first city in the nation to implement a district-wide program of mass mental testing and curriculum differentiation. Chapman has observed, 'By the middle of the decades, the use of intelligence tests for sorting students had been institutionalized in Oakland' (1988: 108), and subsequently, 'school districts around the country would be following Oakland's lead' (1988: 64).

By 1923, Dickson had become a leader in testing and ability grouping in the Bay Area, serving as the Director of Bureaus of Research and Guidance in both Oakland and nearby Berkeley, California. Also in 1923, Dickson published his *Mental Tests and the Classroom Teacher* under the auspices of the Measurement and Adjustment Series edited by Terman. In the preface of the book, Terman praised the book's applied implications for actual classroom practice and school organization. He also lauded the author: 'Dr. Dickson's experience in the educational use of test results has probably been more extensive than that of any other living educator' (1923: xiii).[42] *In Mental Tests and the Classroom Teacher* — which was written in a non-technical prose and geared for teachers, principals and administrators — Dickson's views on the nature of intelligence, individual differences, equality of opportunity, educability of children, curriculum differentiation and social engineering are clone-like in Termanian thought:

> Let us repeat that democracy does not mean equality of achievement, but equality of opportunity for achievement. Snedden [1921] defines the term 'democracy' as 'not the equality of all individuals in general, but equality in the exercise and enjoyment of those obligations, rights, and privileges which the state, through collective political action, creates and controls.' Not equality, then, in that which is *within*, through native endowment, but equality in the enjoyment of those things which are *without*, as the state's contribution to the welfare of the individual; not equality in innate ability but equality of opportunity to develop ability; this is the essence of true democracy, and this is the standard by which we must measure our educational and social program. (Dickson, 1923: 223)

In addition to the work of Dickson, there is also Kimball Young (1922) — a former student of Terman. As we reviewed earlier, Young's (1922) race psychology study concluded that 'Latin' students (i.e., Italian; Portuguese; Spanish-Mexican) compared to their white peers in San Jose, California schools (and nearby communities) were innately inferior in intelligence. Young did not stop there. He also had much to say about the need to modify the school curriculum using intelligence test scores. Young, contending that Italians, Portuguese and Spanish from Europe, 'and the Mexican immigration from our neighboring republic bring us *retarded material which the public schools have to handle'* [emphasis added] (1922: 65), offered these points of reform. First, ' The notion that we must have a common school organization for all pupils must be given up' (p. 66). The idea that all pupils can proceed uniformly in educational progress through the curriculum, he argued, needs to be abandoned. Particular emphasis (reclassification) should be on those schools that are overwhelmingly Latin, 'because it is there the largest number of the backward are found' (p. 67). Second, after mass intelligence testing, teaching should be reorganized around a structure of three kinds of classes: for 'superior', 'normal' and 'mentally retarded' students. Third, there needs to be a close cooperation between the schools and business regarding students' futures, especially those 'backward' pupils who are best suited for 'hand and eye education . . .' (p. 70):

> If much more vocational and manual arts work be introduced, if contacts with outside industry and business be established to care for the older pupils wishing to go over into occupations at once, the flexibility of the school system must be greater than it is at present. (Young, 1922: 71)[43]

I close this section by bringing our lens closer to the actual use of intelligence testing for curriculum differentiation regarding children of color, focusing on Mexican American students in Los Angeles public schools in the 1920s, as a case in point. Educational historian Gilbert Gonzalez' (1974a, 1974b, 1990) research has found that institutionalization of mass intelligence testing, homogeneous groupings, curriculum differentiation and counseling programs in Los Angeles schools were used in ways that effectively stratified students along racial/ethnic and SES lines. During the 1920s, mass intelligence testing in Los Angeles was indeed a big enterprise. By decade's end (1928–1929) a total of 328,000 tests were administered, for example, at the elementary level alone (Gonzalez, 1974a). Based on IQ test results, in large part, students were placed in one of four types of elementary classes: normal classes, *opportunity* rooms, *adjustment* rooms or *development* rooms. *Opportunity* rooms were designed for both the mentally superior (opportunity A) and slow learner (opportunity B — children whose IQs were above 70 but below the normal range). *Adjustment* rooms, on the other hand, were structured for normal children (i.e., average range IQ) who had specific skill problems, such as remediation in reading, limited English proficiency, or were 'educationally maladjusted' (most likely this was what we currently refer to as emotional and behavior disorders). *Development* rooms (sometimes referred to as centers) were designed for children whose IQ was below 70; these children were typically referred to as 'mentally retarded' or 'mentally deficient'. Gonzalez (1974a) has noted that the median IQ for Mexican American elementary school-age children in Los Angeles in the late 1920s was about 91.2.[44] He has suggested, given the observed median IQ of 91.2, that 'there was a very high probability that nearly one-half of the Mexican children would find themselves placed in slow-learner rooms and development centers' (p. 150). Gonzalez' suggestion that about 50 per cent of Mexican American elementary students were placed in classes for the mentally subaverage (opportunity B classes) and for the mentally retarded (development centers) translates into an astounding overrepresentational disparity, in that it has been estimated that Mexican American students comprised only 13 per cent of the student population in 1927 in Los Angeles City and County (Taylor, 1929; cited in Gonzalez, 1974a).[45]

It appears that the impact of curriculum differentiation with respect to a Mexican American student's job future was felt as early as the higher elementary grades. Gonzalez (1974a) has stated that some development rooms and centers (for the alleged mentally retarded) served as training grounds for manual training, and subsequently as sources for producing cheap labor. These development centers were run by full-time manual education, crafts and home economics teachers. The larger centers had the services of a full-time agricultural teacher. Gonzalez (1974b) reports that by 1929, there were 2500 children in eleven development centers in Los Angeles schools. Ten of the centers were in 'laboring class communities', and of the total enrollment, Mexican American children were 'highly represented in five of them, constituting the entire population of one, one-third in two, and one-fourth in two others' (1974b: 298). The development centers were geared to training unskilled and semi-skilled workers for industry, such as menial occupations in restaurants, laundries and agriculture. Gonzalez (1974a) reports that 325 students graduated from the development centers in 1928–1929. Of those '65 were working in agriculture as fruit pickers, 60 sold newspapers, and the remainder scattered over a wide range of unskilled manual occupations' (p. 167). Gonzalez offers an interesting insight to the development center–business connection by quoting a school administrator who viewed the center as bonanzas to local industry:

> several employers have told us that a dull girl makes a very much better operator on a mangle than a normal girl. The job is purely routine and is irksome to persons of average intelligence, while the sub-normal seems to get actual satisfaction out of such a task. Fitting the person to the job reduces the 'turn over' in an industry and is, of course, desirable from an economic point of view. (1974b: 298)

In addition to what occurred at the elementary school level, Gonzalez (1974a, 1990) has also researched the role of intelligence testing and its partial role in secondary school curriculum differentiation in Los Angeles schools. Gonzalez has commented that 'By the mid-twenties a four-tiered tracking system, each with its specific teaching methods, curriculum, and educational objectives and consequences was in full swing' (1990: 83). The Division of Psychology and Educational Research, using mass IQ testing to identify the type of course work that allegedly would be commensurate with students' mental capacity, designed four curricular tracks — very superior, normal, dull-normal, and mentally retarded. Given the widespread belief that Mexican American children were not cut out for 'book study' and thus should be trained for hand work (see Stanley, 1920), it is not at all surprising that Los Angeles schools undertook a systematic curricula plan of 'training for occupational efficiency for Mexican Americans', a term used by Gonzalez (1990). The success of the Los Angeles vocational educational program was due, in part, to the marriage between the educational system and local business. Gonzalez (1990) has noted that vocational education was partially shaped by modifying its curriculum based on local labor needs. It was not uncommon for the Los Angeles Chamber of Commerce and the public school system to be bedfellows. These connections were such that:

> the purpose of schooling became interwoven with, and in a number of ways, shaped by industry. The preparation of students to enter 'the business and industrial world' was more than just a preparation for life. It was an education molded by business and industry. (Gonzalez, 1974a: 168–9)

Vocational education in Los Angeles public junior and senior high schools — which was designed to prepare students for manually oriented occupations (skilled, semiskilled, or unskilled) — hit its pace in the 1920s. By 1929, the school district offered 70 regular vocational educational courses at about half of the city's high schools (Gonzalez, 1974a). Yet, these courses were not distributed evenly across the city — overwhelmingly being located in poor, working-class and 'foreign-born' (e.g., Mexican, Jewish) and black neighborhoods. Referring to the eastside sector of Los Angeles (predominantly racial/ethnic minority), Gonzalez found 'Lincoln, Roosevelt and Jefferson [high schools] combined made available for their students forty-six of the seventy regular vocational courses taught in the entire city. Roosevelt and Lincoln alone offered 35 vocational courses' (1974a: 180). In 1932, the schools were offering 'class A' all-day vocational courses for the male students (about 5 hours for trade instruction and 1½ for academic instruction). Gonzalez (1974a) notes that three high schools (Lincoln, Roosevelt, and Fremont) — all located in working-class areas of the city — provided 26 of the total 31 class A vocational courses in the school district. None of the class A courses were offered in the westside of Los Angeles, a predominantly white, higher-SES area.

Many Mexican American female students were not immune to having their economic and social mobility thwarted by the limitation imposed on them by vocational education. Furthermore, a case can be made that Mexican American females, compared to their male counterparts, faced more oppressive occupational outcomes as vocational training in the schools often channeled the girls into the most menial jobs (such as, domestic servants; laundry workers; seamstresses). It appears that the schools' emphasis on very low-level vocational education for Mexican American females was partially influenced by inaccurate and disparaging images educators had of these girls. For example, Pearl Ellis in her 1929 *Americanization Through Homemaking* commented: 'Mexican Americans have inherited this remarkable aptness with the needle. We should strive to foster it in them . . .' (quoted in Gonzalez, 1990: 49). Regarding homemaking as vocational education, it was a major course of study for many Mexican American girls. A rationale for homemaking courses appears to have been driven by observations among educators that these girls married early and had large families, and thus the role of the schools should be to prepare them for homemaking. For example, Hazel Bishop in her 1937 master's thesis (*A Case Study of the Improvement of Mexican Homes Through*

Instruction in Homemaking) egregiously commented: 'The Mexican woman seems to exist just to bear children' (p. 79). Bishop, quoting a fourth-grade teacher in Santa Ana, California from her survey noted:

> The fact that the Mexican girl marries young and becomes the mother in the home at the age the American [white] girl is in high school means that the junior high school is trusted with her education for homemaker. For this reason, it seems to me that *all* or *most all* [emphasis added] of her junior high training should be directed toward making her a better wife, mother and homemaker. (1937: 91)

The geographic distribution of vocational educational courses for girls broke along similar patterns as seen in the location of vocational courses for boys — such offerings were in schools located in predominantly working-class, racial/ethnic minority neighborhoods:

> For instance homemaking was offered at only four schools: Lafayette Junior High (with an enrollment of 36 per cent Black, 14 per cent Mexican, and 30 per cent Jewish), Belvedere Junior High (51 per cent Mexican), Hollenbeck (Mexican and Jewish) and Jefferson (mixed working class). Lincoln offered dressmaking, millinery and power-sewing. Roosevelt offered dressmaking, sewing, power-sewing and personal hygiene. Fremont offered dressmaking and personal hygiene. What this in fact meant, was that of six vocational subjects for females Lincoln offered three, Roosevelt four, Fremont two. Only seven schools taught vocational courses for women. All of them were located in working class neighborhoods. (Gonzalez, 1974a: 180–1)

In sum, historical analysis of intelligence testing and curriculum differentiation in 1920s and early 1930s Los Angeles public schools informs us that deficit thinking in relation to the schooling of Mexican American boys and girls was influential in shaping very limited educational and occupational opportunities for these students. It appears that Mexican American students in Los Angeles public schools during the era of the genetic pathology model routinely faced one of two unequally attractive educational pathways — 1) dead-end special education for alleged slow learners or 2) non-academic vocational education that emphasized low-level skills. For the most part, either trail led to manual occupations, typically requiring minimal or no skills. Offering a macrolevel analysis of the linkages between intelligence testing and consequences for Mexican Americans, Gonzalez ties up matters this way:

> On the basis of IQ tests administered by guidance counselors, inordinate numbers of Mexican-American children were placed in coursework which prepared them for a variety of manual operations . . . This movement was a reaction of the privileged classes to the rising numbers of the working

classes. Schools were redefined in the era of monopoly capitalism to be instruments through which social order could be preserved and industrialization expanded. Thus American schools were not and still are not agents of change, but rather bolster the social stratifications and values of our society. In such an educational system, Mexican-Americans were not provided with opportunities to improve their lot but instead were subjected to a socialization process that reinforced the status quo and was opposed to social change. (1974b: 301)

In this chapter, I have attempted to present a thesis that the deficit thinking framework of the genetic pathology era was fortified by both 'extrascientific' and 'scientific' foundations — the former being ideological and epistemological in nature (social Darwinism; Galtonian eugenics; Mendelian genetics), and the latter dealing with measurement, particularly intelligence testing.

Historical analysis and interpretation informs us that indeed intelligence testing led to inferior schooling via curriculum differentiation for a substantial number of low-SES students of color, particularly African American and Mexican American pupils. It would be inaccurate, however, to argue that the misclassifications and inappropriate channeling of these students into unchallenging, low-status curriculum depended *exclusively* on IQ tests. To be sure, the perspective that intelligence testing during the era of the genetic pathology model served as oppressive sorting tools has some value in theory building about educational inequality. Educational historians must be cautious, however, in giving credit to intelligence tests as *sole* forgers of inequality. To do so would be a failure to understand that educational oppression during the era of the genetic pathology theory was fueled by the collective mind of a fundamentally unequal society that viewed, through a deficit thinking lens, the educability of low-SES children of color as being very limited.

It is also important to keep in mind that the low educability perceptions of racial/ethnic minority students held during the genetic pathology era had their own historical context, predating the intelligence testing movement. The ideological foundations of racial segregation of African American and Mexican American children can be traced to the nineteenth-century racial belief that white groups should not socially interact with races that were believed to be biologically inferior (see Menchaca, Chapter 2, this volume; Menchaca and Valencia, 1990). About a decade prior to the 1905 development of the Binet–Simon scales in France, the *Plessy v. Ferguson* Supreme Court decision of 1896 ruled favorably on the 'separate but equal' decision, creating a system of social apartheid in the South, including a legally sanctioned dual school system. By 1920 — two years before the first race psychology dealing with the intelligence testing of Mexican American children appeared (Young's 1922 investigation), and several years before the mass IQ testing of these students — the segregation of Mexican American pupils in inferior schools was in motion (Gonzalez, 1990). By 1930/1931, 85 per cent of California schools surveyed by the state government reported segregating Mexican American students either in separate classrooms or in separate schools (Hendrick, 1977). At the same time, 90 per cent of schools in Texas were practicing a tripartite structure of racially segregated schools — separate schools for white, Mexican American, and African American students (Rangel and Alcala, 1972).

In the final analysis, it appears that the inferior and unequal education received by many poor and working-class Mexican American and African Americans during the height of the genetic pathology era would have occurred even had the intelligence testing movement not existed. So pervasive and powerful was racial animus toward Mexican American and African American people, and so embedded was hereditarianism and deficit thinking in American social thought, that it was predictable that few educators and school administrators expected, or even desired, these children of color to succeed academically.

But, the historical reality is that intelligence testing did exist and was clearly implicated in classifying many racial/ethnic minority students for instruction and curricula content 'commensurate with their abilities'. Intelligence testing, I contend, served as a powerful role of legitimization. That is, through the softness of symbolic validation — and not rigorous psychometric inspection — intelligence tests became measurement tools of the new 'scientific applied psychology', a field that claimed it could accurately measure innate intelligence and could prescribe appropriate curriculum that was in the best interests of the student and the social order. As such, preconceived perceptions about the alleged limited educability of African American and Mexican American students easily became verified, 'scientifically', based on IQ test scores. Thus, intelligence testing in the 1920s with respect to these students of color came to be a tool of domination and intrusiveness. The alliance of intelligence testing, deficit thinking and curriculum differentiation helped to legitimize the meritocratic ideology of 'equality of opportunity' (one gets in curriculum what one deserves, based on innate ability) and economic inequality as expressed in a stratified workforce (one gets in occupation status where one best fits, based on innate ability). Finally, we should not forget that the success of the IQ test in serving as a powerful organizing principle of the schooling process was due, in part, to the ideologues who had unbridled faith in the value of intelligence testing in reforming the schools and pressed ever so diligently for its mass use. Henry Herbert Goddard (1920) in his book, *Human Efficiency and Levels of Intelligence*, spoke clearly to this mission:

> Testing intelligence is no longer an experiment or of doubted value. It is fast becoming an exact science.
>
> The facts revealed by the army tests cannot be ignored. Greater efficiency, we are always working for. Can these new facts be used to increase our efficiency? No question! We only await the Human Engineer who will undertake the work. (p. vii)

Heterodoxy

During the epoch of the genetic pathology model, the reign of deficit thinking in educational thought and practice did not prevail without contestation. Though the remonstrations to the orthodoxy were slow in developing, fairly unorganized in the beginning, and met at times with fierce resistance from deficit thinkers, dissenters through their heterodoxic perspectives were eventually able to mount an effective challenge. Our account of the evolution of deficit thinking in the genetic pathology era would be incomplete without examining this discord. Given that we have previously discussed the heterodoxic views in anthropology (by focusing on Franz Boas) contra deficit thinking, here I will confine our discussion to dissent within psychology, applied psychology and educational psychology.[46] I have divided this discussion into two parts — research efforts and perspectives by white, as well as racial/ethnic minority scholars (i.e., African American and Mexican Americans). This division is intentional on my part because the anti-deficit thinking views held by scholars of color (compared to their white peers) were, for the most part, more strongly voiced and incisive — probably due to their insider perspective. Furthermore, many scholars of color were likely more sensitive to the nature of deficit thinking, having faced it first hand. Robert Guthrie (1976), in *Even the Rat was White: A Historical View of Psychology*, has written that racism and discrimination made it very difficult for African Americans during the 1910s to be awarded college scholarships, to attain graduate-level training in psychology, and once in professional positions (i.e., at black colleges) to publish frequently due to poor wages and excessive teaching responsibilities. Guthrie also notes:

> Traditional psychologists rarely considered any form of scholarship, let alone criticism from black scholars. This academic racism led black scholars to publish their own journals and to establish other media of communication. A leading periodical of this era was *The Crisis*, edited by W.E.B. DuBois. (Guthrie, 1976: 74)

White Scholars

As we have discussed earlier, the hereditarian perspectives during the genetic pathology era were not restricted to explaining racial differences in intelligence. There was also an assumption that a high social and occupational standing was a result of inherited superior intelligence, and in contrast, low standing was likewise predominantly influenced by innate inferior intellectual capacity. Many behavioral and social scientists who took up the question of intelligence and SES during the late teens and 1920s posited the hereditarian explanation.

One of the first empirical studies in psychology — as opposed to anthropology and sociology — to challenge the hereditarian position linking genetics with SES was published by S.L. Pressey, a former graduate student of Robert Yerkes. It appears that Pressey's motivation to pursue this line of research was shaped in part by his skepticism 'of the hereditarians' apparent problems with methodological rigor' (Cravens, 1978: 255). Pressey and co-author Thomas (1919) administered a 'group scale of intelligence' developed at Indiana University to 321 country children in Southern Indiana. This intelligence test included the standard type of items (for example, analogies; opposites; word completion). The participating children, ages 10 to 13 years, consisted of two subsamples: children from a 'poor rural farming district' and from a 'fairly good agricultural district'. The children were, with a few exceptions, of 'American stock' (meaning white). The authors sought to compare the intelligence test scores of 1) poor farming district children vs. good farming district children, and 2) the country sample, as a whole, with a sample of 2800 city children who had previously been tested on the same instrument (see Pressey and Teter, 1919).

The results revealed that the children from the poor farming districts, as a group, performed lower on the intelligence test than did their counterparts from the good farming district. The authors discussed, however, that these findings were not as reliable as one would want because of methodological problems, for example, children in the two districts were tested by different examiners, one which was not as skilled as the other. The major finding was the country children, as an aggregate, performed uniformly more poorly (about 1½ years below in mental age) than their city peers. Pressey and Thomas (1919) suggest that the country children's lower test scores were related to having less experiences in testing (i.e., they showed less 'testability'), were shyer, were less dexterous with pencils and had fewer opportunities in developing test-related verbal skills compared to city children. The authors concluded that the typical forms of intelligence tests are inadequate for the study of SES comparisons (as well as racial differences; see Pressey and Teter, 1919). Pressey and Thomas' suggestion was, 'It is urged that the usual type of intelligence tests does not give adequate measures of the ability of country children; performance tests and materials more relevant to their environment are needed' (1919: 286).

Another challenge to the biological basis of social and occupational attainment was by Ada Arlitt, a psychologist. Arlitt's (1921) investigation — fittingly titled, 'On the Need for Caution in Establishing Race Norms' — was particularly important in that it appears to be one of the first psychological studies to compare directly white with racial/ethnic minority children and to control, modicumly, social class. Arlitt administered the 1916 Stanford–Binet intelligence test to 'native born white' ($n = 191$), Italian ($n = 87$), and Negro ($n = 71$) primary grade children living in the same community and attending the same grades in the same schools.[47] The children's social status was ascertained by father's occupation using a conventional SES scale. The five groupings were in descending order: 1) Professional; 2) Semiprofessional (and higher business); 3) Skilled; 4) Semiskilled; and 5) Unskilled. For reasons not too clear, Arlitt relabeled the occupational groupings, using value-laden categories.[48] Group 1 became 'Very Superior', group 2 'Superior', group 3 'Average' and because of small sample size, groups 4 and 5 were combined and labeled 'Inferior'.

Based on aggregated IQ data analysis by race/ethnicity (i.e., SES was free to vary within each of the three racial/ethnic groups), the median IQs for the native white, Italian, and Negro samples were 106.5, 85, and 83.4, respectively. Thus, the native white group's median IQ was 21.5 points higher than the Italian group and 23.1 points above that of the Negro sample. In that about 92 per cent of the Italian and Negro children were of Inferior social status, Arlitt (1921) was unable to compare IQ scores by SES within these two groups. However, because of adequate sample sizes and SES variability, she was able to do so with the native white group. The observed median IQ scores for the four occupational groups were: Very Superior (125.9), Superior (118.7), Average (107), and Inferior (92). As can be seen, the median IQ difference between the Very Superior and Inferior native white children was 33.9 points — a substantial gap. Arlitt then compared the median IQ (92) of the native white Inferior groups with the median IQs of the Italian (85) and Negro (83.4) children of the same social class (Inferior). The median IQ of the native white groups was 7 points above the Italians and 8.6 higher than the Negroes — strikingly less than was seen between the Very Superior and Superior native white groups. This led Arlitt to conclude:

> the difference in median I.Q. which is due to race alone is in this case at most only 8.6 points whereas the difference between children of the same race but of Inferior and Very Superior social status may amount to 33.9 points. It is apparent that such differences as we have between the negro and Italian children and between these and children of native born white parents are not nearly so striking as the difference between children of the same race but of different social status. Of the two factors social status seems to play the more important part. To such an extent is this true that it would seem to indicate that *there is more likeness between children of the same social status but different race than between children of the same race but of different social status* [emphasis added]. (1921: 182–3)

In the context of the history of cross-racial/ethnic research on intellectual performance in the US, Arlitt's (1921) study of three-fourths of a century ago indeed is a significant investigation. First, *direct* comparisons of diverse racial/ethnic groups' intelligence test performance were made. Second, all the children in the study were enrolled in the same schools and classes. Third, there was the major finding that social class was a considerably stronger predictor, compared to race/ethnicity, of intellectual performance. The finding that SES transcended race/ethnicity as a predictor of performance on intelligence tests — a result that would be consistently observed in later research (see Christian and Livermore, 1970; Oakland, 1978) — was a blow to hereditarianism, but its impact was slow in coming.[49]

Any analysis of heterodoxy during the period of the genetic pathology model would be remiss without mentioning the work of the indefatigable Columbia University professor, Otto Klineberg. As Degler has commented, 'Many psychologists expressed reservations about the reality of race differences during the 1920s debate, but none was more tireless or ingenious in creating those doubts than Otto Klineberg . . . ' (1991: 179). Arriving at Columbia University in 1925, young professor Klineberg (26-years-old) — a native Canadian — was part of the orthodoxy (i.e., he held conventional beliefs that mental and character differences among racial/ethnic groups were racially based.) As Degler notes, due to his professional connections with linguist Edward Sapir and Franz Boas, Klineberg would shed such views forever. From 1925 to about 1930, Klineberg worked with vigor through his ambitious research and publication agenda to answer, or at least to offer responses, to practically all existing research that proffered the position that certain groups were racially inferior. So far-reaching were Klineberg's heterodoxic goals and efforts that they led Degler to note categorically that Klineberg was to psychology as Boas was to anthropology. 'He [Klineberg] made it his business to do for psychology what his friend and colleague at Columbia had done for anthropology: to rid his discipline of racial explanations for human social differences' (Degler, 1991: 179).

Klineberg's industrious research program was also quite varied in scope. For example, he traveled to villages in Europe in order to test the Nordic superiority hypothesis advanced by Carl Brigham's (1923) analysis of the Army mental testing. Klineberg also examined the school records of 500 Negro children who attended schools in Tennessee and subsequently migrated to Northern cities (see Klineberg, 1932). His intention here was to examine the 'selective migration' hypothesis, the conjecture that the higher IQ scores seen among Northern Negroes was due to the more intelligent Negroes who migrated from the South to the North (see Klineberg, 1935b). Klineberg's research pursuits and scholarly interests also involved such topics as biochemistry, anthropology, physiology, race mixture, deviance (i.e., criminal behavior), 'fundamental drives' (i.e., instincts) and language.

Much of Klineberg's original research publications and his criticisms of deficit thinking and hereditarian orthodoxy can be seen in his now classic book, *Race Differences* (1935a). In all, he was quite successful in debunking biologically based research regarding racial/ethnic group comparisons. In his book — which is written mainly for students and the 'intelligent layman' — it is clear that Klineberg was greatly influenced by Boas (to whom the book is dedicated). Methodically, Klineberg, in the introductory section of the book, outlines and critiques racial superiority theories, rejects polygenetic theory, speaks to the unjustification of assuming that 'race' and 'nationality' are synonymous, and argues for the importance of culture in understanding group differences. Also, as was Boas, Klineberg was ideologically committed in his scholarly work to notions of equality, inclusivity and the application of research to social problems. In the conclusions to *Race Differences*, Klineberg wrote:

> There is no reason . . . to treat two people differently because they differ in their physical type. There is no justification for denying a Negro a job or an education because he is a Negro. No one has been able to demonstrate that ability is correlated with skin color or head shape or any of the anatomical characteristics used to classify races. A man must be judged as an individual, not as a member of a group whose limits are arbitrary and artificial. Our racial and national stereotypes — the 'pictures in our minds' of the Oriental, the Italian, the Jew, the Mexican — will be wrong much more often than right; they are based on current opinions which have never been verified, and they cannot be trusted in the treatment of human beings. (1935a: 345–6)

Although Klineberg's *Race Differences* was published in 1935, it is still very germane to our discussion of the genetic pathology era. For example, in his coverage of methodological confoundment in intelligence testing research (for example, SES; language), Klineberg primarily relied on race psychology studies published in the 1920s. As a case in point, let us examine his criticisms of possible language confoundment in such research. Klineberg notes that beginning very early in the development of intelligence tests it was known that an examinee's familiarity with the English language was important to consider (today, we refer to this concern as one of 'cultural loading'). This issue was so critical, as we have seen, that Yerkes, *et al.*, in the development of the Army group intelligence tests developed the Army Beta test, a nonverbal measure (pictorial) for illiterate recruits in which language does not appreciably play a role. Notwithstanding the caution about administering verbal tests to those who are limited or non-proficient in English, a substantial proportion of race psychology studies of group differences used verbal tests in the absence of first assessing the language status of examinees.[50] Children who were most likely to be penalized under these testing circumstances were those who were raised in environments in which English was not the mother tongue and had limited second language skills or were developing bilingually, for example, American Indians, Italian Americans, Chinese and Japanese Americans, and Mexican Americans.

In order to examine his conjecture that such children would be penalized on verbal intelligence tests, Klineberg (1935a) — in a demonstration of his methodological adroitness — reviewed a number of studies in which IQ data were available for linguistically diverse groups, such as Italians, on both 'linguistic' tests (i.e., verbally loaded tests such as the Stanford–Binet and National Intelligence Test) and 'performance' tests (i.e., nonverbal tests, such as the Army Beta; actual performance tests, such as the Goodenough Draw-a-Person Test or the Porteus Maze test). Klineberg then compared the grand mean IQ of the linguistic tests with the grand mean IQ of the performance tests. For all racial/ethnic groups studied, the mean IQ on the performance tests was higher than the mean IQ on the linguistic tests, thus supporting Klineberg's hypothesis that language was indeed a penalizing factor in the intellectual assessment of culturally/linguistically diverse groups.[51] The groups examined and the linguistic test-performance test gap in IQ was as follows: Italians (8 points), Chinese/Japanese (12.4 points), American Indians (16.4 points), and Mexicans (10 points). Klineberg concluded, 'If we compare the studies of various racial groups by these two types of tests, it becomes clear that the linguistic tests place many of them at a disadvantage' (p. 169). Implicit in Klineberg's conclusion about the language factor (as well as his discussion of other control problems) is that any research-based statements about white superiority in innate intelligence are unwarranted in light of methodological flaws — particularly the failure to control variables.

Klineberg's views on racial equality and his anti-deficit thinking research publications were certainly significant in creating doubt about the dogma of hereditarianism. In my view, his major contribution as a scholar was his dedication to methodological rigor in his own research efforts, as well as an advocate of such practice in general. Specifically, Klineberg argued, there was a need to control for variables, that if left free to vary, would confound the results. On the issue of control and Negro–white comparisons in intelligence, a high priority research topic for him, Klineberg (1935a) noted:

> It is this writer's opinion that this is where the problem of Negro intelligence now stands. The direct comparison between Negroes and Whites will always remain a doubtful procedure because of the impossibility of controlling the various factors which may influence the results . . . The real test of Negro–White equality as far as intelligence tests are concerned can be met only by a study in a region in which Negroes suffer no discrimination whatsoever and enjoy exactly the same educational and economic opportunities. (1935a: 188–9)

Although the above opinion has a utopian ring regarding race relations, the methodological import of his message is not lost. Continuing, Klineberg commented on a more realistic level, 'It is safe to say that as the environment of the Negro approximates more and more closely that of the White, his inferiority tends to disappear' (1935a: 189).

On a final note, one of Klineberg's conclusions in *Race Differences* (1935a) appears a bit peculiar at first glance. Notwithstanding his strong beliefs in the equality of Negroes and whites and his research findings debunking the substantive and methodological shortcomings of racial explanations for social and psychological behavior, Klineberg commented at book's end:

> The general conclusion of this book is that there is no scientific proof of racial differences in mentality. *This does not necessarily mean that there are no such differences* [emphasis added]. It may be that at some future time, and with the aid of techniques as yet undiscovered, differences may be demonstrated. *In the present stage of our knowledge, however, we have no right to assume that they exist* [emphasis added]. (1935a: 345)

One interpretation of Klineberg's closing words is that he has backpedaled on his views about intellectual equality, perhaps retreating into being noncommittal on the issue. Another rendering and understanding of his statement — which I find more credible — lay in the italicized sentences above. It appears that his general conclusion, and his caveats, are framed in the context of Klineberg the scientist and researcher. That is, in light of all the available research findings and methodological problems germane to Negro–white investigations of intellectual performance, the null hypothesis cannot be rejected. Put in a clearer but still scientifically worded manner, the conjecture that there are no innately based differences in Negro–white intelligence must be accepted, and thus cannot be rejected.

In 1921, the *Journal of Educational Psychology* sponsored a symposium on 'Intelligence and its measurement' (see Terman *et al.*, 1921). Seventeen psychologists were invited to share their views on how they conceived intelligence and what research was needed in the general area.[52] The symposium sparked controversy on several topics, for example, the constancy of IQ, the specific nature of intelligence, and methodology in research investigations. Regarding the psychologists' conceptions of intelligence, clear differences arose. For example, note the following views: Thorndike, 'intellect in general [is defined as] the *power of good responses from the point of view of truth or fact . . .* ' (p. 124); Terman, '*An individual is intelligent in proportion as he is able to carry on abstract thinking*' (p. 128); Colvin, '*An individual possesses intelligence insofar as he has learned, or can learn to adjust himself to his environment*' (p. 136). One contributor, Ruml, did not even offer a conception of intelligence as he believed its nature was undebatable at the time. This was the case, he argued, for two reasons: 'first, the lack of precision in the terms and concepts that must form the basis for such a discussion and second, the absence of factual material on so many of the essential points' (p. 143). On the latter point, he asserted that inadequate samplings of populations, control problems, and contradictory reports from investigators made any debate difficult to ensue. Thus, the 1921 symposium attended by top psychologists would set the climate for further controversy and dissent during the 1920s.

The debate among psychologists was greatly intensified in 1922 when William C. Bagley, psychologist at Teachers College (Columbia University), presented a scathing attack on IQ testing in an address before the Society of College Teachers of Education. Bagley's talk, which was later published in the year in *School and Society* and reprinted in his 1925 book on *Determinism in Education*, was a *tour de force* assault on a number of aspects of intelligence testing. Criticisms included, for example: 1) mental measures do not directly measure innate intelligence; they measure 'acquired' intelligence; 2) scientific validity of group differences is specious, given the faulty assumption that members of diverse groups have had identical environments, education, and experiences; 3) the belief that one's limits of educability can be accurately ascertained is false, given the inherent problems with the measuring tool — IQ tests; 4) the practice of curriculum differentiation through IQ testing is undemocratic in that such sorting intensifies societal stratification.

Bagley (1922), in his essay, refers throughout to some fellow psychologists (who are his targets of criticism) as 'the determinist'. Only once does he attach a name to 'the determinist', and this referent is Terman (1919) mentioned in a footnote. But, what is 'educational determinism'? Bagley writes:

> As used in this discussion, educational determinism means the attitude of mind consequent upon the conviction or the assumption that the influence of education is very narrowly circumscribed by traits or capacities which, for each individual, *are both innate and in themselves practically unmodified by experience or training* [emphasis added]. (1922: 373)

Suffice it to say, the barbs slung by Bagley did hit his main target — Terman. As Chapman (1988) has observed, rebukes and rejoinders between Bagley and Terman lasted a good year. After a short lull of this intellectual war, Terman rekindled the debate with his 1924 article on 'The possibilities and limitations of training'.

Although he did not renew his fight with Bagley, he did resume his campaign for curriculum differentiation (Chapman, 1988: 133).

In sum, the intraprofessional disagreements — some fierce — among white psychologists, applied psychologists and educational psychologists created a mounting heterodoxy to hereditarian thought and, to some degree, curriculum differentiation. Not only does this internal dissent inform us about the tension between scholars of diverse views during the genetic pathology era, it also reveals that many of the issues raised by critics then still have currency today. Note the following comment by Chapman (1988) on the criticisms of early mental testing. Although Chapman's referent is the Stanford–Binet intelligence test of 1916, his points are pertinent to group intelligence testing of the 1920s:

> Early work on the Stanford–Binet by Terman and others was criticized on several grounds. Some questioned the validity of this test, its reliability, and the degree to which it was influenced by heredity. They argued, too, that the sample for the Stanford–Binet norms produced standards that were biased against the lower classes, immigrants and blacks. Others objected to the great expectations for the use of the tests, suggesting that the tests were fallible and should not be used to determine the fate of individuals. (1988: 29)

The criticisms of intelligence tests then and now share much in common. Current issues and concerns about test reliability and validity, class and ethnic bias, inadequate norming and unfairness in test use clearly have historical roots.

Scholars of Color

As Thomas (1982) has appropriately noted, 'The role of black scholars in the mental testing controversy of the 1920s has been largely overlooked' (p. 258). My review of pertinent literature certainly supports Thomas' assertion. For example, Fass' (1980) historical analysis of the intelligence testing movement in the late teens and 1920s, and Cronbach's (1975) and Haney's (1981) broader historical coverages of mental testing and standardized testing — both studies published in the *American Psychologist* — are all silent on the contributions of black scholars. Books that deal, in part, on the topic of early mental testing (see Blum, 1978; Chapman, 1988; Cravens, 1978; Kamin, 1974; Marks, 1981; Samuda, 1975) also fail to discuss the role of black scholars during the contentious nature–nurture debate over intelligence in the 1920s. There are, however, a few exceptions. For example, Guthrie (1976, 1981) and Thomas (1982) present keen insights to a number of black scholars who 'launched a concerted intellectual assault upon racist conclusions which white psychologists extrapolated from mental test data' (Thomas, 1982: 259). Why many contemporary scholars have disregarded the historical contributions of black scholars in helping shape the early mental testing debate is not clear. In any event, our discussion of heterodoxy contra the genetic pathology era would be negligent without commenting on the participation of black psychologists and educators.

One of the first publications by a black scholar that appeared in a mainstream journal was by a black woman educational psychologist, Martha MacLear of Howard University.[53] MacLear's (1922) investigation was inspired, it appears, by Yerke's conclusion from the Army testing program that the northern Negroes were mentally superior to southern Negroes. To address this issue, MacLear first obtained the record cards (i.e., academic marks in which 70 was a passing mark) for 116 Negro graduates of the Howard University Academy, a first-class high school; 58 students were from the north, 58 from the south. The results showed that the marks for English and Mathematics classes, compared by geographic region, were very similar, (for example, English IV: south median = 77, average = 78; north median = 76, average = 77). (An eye-balling of all the marks indicates the differences are not statistically different.) MacLear also did a similar analysis of marks, by region, of the record cards of 200 Howard University graduates (College of Arts and Sciences and the Teachers College); 100 of the graduates were from the north, 100 from the south. The marks of the college graduates were compared in the same way as the academy graduates; the results were the same — no significant differences.

Offering, at that juncture, a self criticism that the schools in question may have selected students of 'the same grades of mentality from the north and south' (p. 677), MacLear (1922) examined the Army mental test records of 220 Howard University Negro students who had taken the test (Army Alpha, I presume). Based on her analysis of the test scores (110 students from the north, 110 from the south), MacLear found the medians to be 116 and 99 for the northern and southern students, respectively. Apparently surprised by the results, which she referred to as 'a wide and striking divergence in intelligence, if such is measured by the Army tests' (p. 677), she conjectured that the two sets of data (marks and mental test scores) were probably measuring different things. MacLear contended that because the Army tests were used to sort young men 'to fit into positions requiring varying degrees of executive ability' (p. 677) — for example, officers, privates, infantry men — the tests 'really measure executive ability, which is not general intelligence although closely related to it' (p. 677). In sum, it appears that MacLear was questioning the construct validity of the Army tests, a subject some later scholars would do (see Gould, 1981). As an explanation for the observed differences on the Army tests, she offered this interesting, and quite plausible, environmental hypothesis:

> the . . . suggestion might be made that the Army tests measure opportunity
> for observation and practice in forming judgments. It is perfectly appar-
> ent to anyone who knows the two sections studied that no comparison
> between them can be made in this respect. In the south, the negro is a
> subject race, segregated with his own race and limited to the very meager
> offerings which they can give him. In the north, although still handi-
> capped, he has freedom of motion and, and as he lives chiefly in the city,
> he has the constant stimulus of city life and contact, although superficial,
> with a race to which the world of opportunity is open. This would stimulate

observation and the habit of forming judgments, although these are of minor importance in scholarship as seen in our undergraduates in the American college. (MacLear, 1922: 678)

Perhaps the most comprehensive coverage of the role of black scholars in the mental testing debate of the 1920s is William Thomas' (1982) article on 'Black intellectuals' critique of early mental testing: A little-known saga of the 1920s'. Thomas' review discusses the contributions of 9 black intellectuals (all men) who published articles critical of intelligence testing, with particular focus on allegations by white scholars that blacks were innately inferior in intelligence. These nine scholars were Horace Mann Bond, Francis C. Sumner, E. Franklin Frazier, Charles H. Thompson, Charles S. Johnson, Howard H. Long, Ira DeA. Reid, Joseph St. Clair Price and Herman G. Canady. The majority of these 1920s scholars published their research in *Crisis* and *Opportunity*, periodicals of the National Association for the Advancement of Colored People and the Urban League, respectively. In that mainstream journals were frequently controlled by editors and editorial boards who were hereditarians, for example, Terman's editorial control over the *Journal of Educational Psychology* and the *Journal of Applied Psychology*, the new black academic outlets, as the *Crisis*, were welcome forums for the black intellectual. This is not to say, however, that all black scholars critical of differential race psychology research on intelligence testing in the 1920s were locked out in publishing their work in the standard journals. For example, Sumner (1925) and Price (1929) published in *School and Society*.

Nevertheless, a case can be made that black intellectuals encountered enormous difficulty in getting their data and conclusions presented in the wider context of academic debate in the 1920s. A prime example is the appointment of Terman to chair a committee commissioned by the National Society for the Study of Education (NSSE). The charge of the NSSE committee, which consisted of all white male scholars, was to investigate the nature–nurture issue with respect to influence on intelligence and school achievement.[54] In 1924, Terman announced in an article (published in the *Journal of Educational Research*) his appointment to the committee and the goal: to publish, based on empirical work, a yearbook on the topic under the auspices of the NSSE. His call for assistance was national. 'The cooperation of qualified investigators *everywhere* [emphasis added] is solicited' (1924: 343). After several years of research activity, totaling 38 separate investigations (funded by money from foundation, private and university sources), the effort resulted in the 1928 NSSE *Yearbook* (see Terman, 1928).[55] It is not clear whether any black scholars applied for the NSSE research funding, but it is clear that *no* blacks served on the NSSE committee and '*no* [emphasis added] contributions from the black intellectual community appeared in the 1928 *Yearbook*' (Thomas, 1982: 263).

In his review of black intellectuals' assault on 1920s mental testing, Thomas (1982) systematically cataloged the responses into three areas.[56] First, there were publications that focused on an environmental critique, for example, differences in educational opportunity between whites and blacks best accounted for racial differences in intellectual performance. A case in point was the investigation by Bond

(1924). Bond, who earned his PhD from the University of Chicago, sought to refute the assertion that blacks were inherently inferior in intelligence by examining schooling effects on mental test performance (i.e., Army Alpha test). Using an ingenious research design, Bond turned the table on hereditarians. Thomas notes this of Bond's study:

> By limiting his comparison to interracial differences among whites, he removed completely from his analysis the issue of differences due to race. This allowed him to question whether, as a result of differences in test performance, the exponents of intelligence testing as a discriminator of racial differences would assert that southern white draftees were inherently and racially inferior to whites in other regions of the country. (1982: 272)

In an analysis of existing data, Bond (1924) compared the rank order of white draftees' intelligence test scores with the rank order of the 'educational efficiency' (i.e., schooling achievement) of the respective states of the recruits. Thomas (1982), in a discussion of Bond's study, reports that the observed rank order correlation between test scores and state educational efficiency was a robust magnitude of .74. Regarding education in the south, Bond reported that nine southern states occupied the nine bottom ranks in educational efficiency. Likewise, the Army mental scores of the white draftees from these states were also among the lowest ranks. In contrast, states outside the south, for example, California and Connecticut, were among the highest in educational efficiency, and recruits from these states were among the highest in intelligence test scores. Thomas' conclusions of Bond's study is well taken:

> Bond's astute observations put hereditarian proponents on the defensive. They had to admit either that the racial stock of these so-called racially pure [southern] states was distinctly inferior to whites in states having a higher percentage of southern and eastern European stock or that test performance was dependent on environmental conditions and cultural advancement reflected in schools. (1924: 272–3)

Second, some of the research scholars and scholarly treatises, Thomas (1982) notes, zeroed in on methodological flaws (such as not controlling for gain score effects in the Army testing program; that is, Johnson [1923] found that white recruits that failed the Army tests were retested much more frequently than black recruits who failed). Also included in this second category were studies highly critical of instrumentation, that is, the IQ test itself. For example, Long (1925) — who earned his doctorate in experimental psychology from Clark University — presented a technical criticism of IQ tests, contending that they contained numerous measurement problems, such as 'mental age scores are inadequate for comparing the mentality of races unless account is taken of the correlation of the raw scores with chronological age' (Thomas: 280).

Finally, the third category of responses included research in which black scholars conducted their *own* original research and generated their *own* data, thus providing alternative explanations to hereditarian-based conclusions drawn by white scholars. For example, Canady (1928) in his master's thesis was one of the first scholars to investigate examiner effects on intelligence testing with white and black children.[57] In his study, 48 black and 25 white elementary school children were administered (in a counter-balanced design) the Stanford–Binet intelligence test by black and white examiners; 23 black and 18 white children were first tested by the black examiner then by a white examiner; the other 25 black and 7 white children were tested by the black examiner and then the white examiner. Canady sought to study the assumption that 'if it is true that a white examiner cannot gain the full cooperation of Negro children because of racial barriers, it might also be true that a Negro examiner would encounter the same difficulty in testing white children' (quoted in Guthrie, 1976: 68). Canady reported that the average IQ increase for the black children (when tested by both black and white examiners) was nearly the same as the average IQ loss of white children (when tested by both examiners). In that the fluctuations appeared random, Canady concluded that the race of the examiner was not a factor in test performance. That is, 'the group-for-group comparison of the performances of black and white subjects failed to reveal any differences that might be legitimately interpreted as due to the personal equation of the examiners' (Thomas, 1982: 285). As such, Canady spoke to the influence of rapport establishment between examinee and examiner during testing situations.

In conclusion, black scholars of the 1920s were not silent on the allegations of deficit thinkers who asserted that blacks were innately inferior in intelligence.[58] As we have seen, using Thomas' (1982) account as a basis of discussion, black intellectuals did not take lightly these frequent racial pronouncements of hereditarianism. Examining pointed hypotheses and using clever research designs and methodological rigor, a cadre of black scholars of this period joined the rising heterodoxy. Although their research, rejoinders to the orthodoxy of hereditarian thought, and dissent have gone unrecognized by many scholars, the black intellectual critique of early mental testing is a vital part of the history of challenges to deficit thinking in educational thought and practice.[59]

Regarding Mexican American intellectuals of the 1920s, who criticized mental testing research in which Mexican American students served as subjects, there were no such scholars. This is ironic given that Mexican American students in the Southwest were subject to frequent intelligence testing and resultant curriculum differentiation. For these children not to have someone of their own ethnic group to speak against contentions that they were innately inferior to white children in intelligence and to expose the inferior schooling they received via curriculum differentiation was, indeed, a sad state of affairs. This lamentable situation would change, however, in 1931 with the arrival of the indomitable George Isidore Sánchez on the academic scene.

Sánchez, born in 1906 in Albuquerque, New Mexico in a working-class neighborhood, apparently had early interests in becoming an educator. After graduation from high school at 16 years of age, Sánchez became a teacher in a rural New Mexican town. There, he saw first hand the schooling inequities, such as disproportionate monetary funding, that Mexican American children experienced. At age 24, Sánchez graduated, with honors, from the University of New Mexico (Romo, 1986).

In 1930, Sánchez enrolled as a master's student at the University of Texas at Austin. His academic interests were educational testing and evaluation. In 1931, he completed a master's degree, writing his thesis on 'A study of the scores of Spanish-speaking children on repeated tests' (this was published later in Sánchez, 1932b). Sánchez' master's thesis dealt with the implications of drawing conclusions about a child's academic achievement or mental ability based on just one administration. To study this, he administered the Stanford Achievement Test and Haggerty Intelligence Test to 45 Spanish-speaking New Mexican pupils (grades 3 to 8).[60] Both tests were administered four times over a period of two years (intervals between testing was 4 to 5 months). Sánchez found that beyond the second test administration significant gain scores occurred, with improvement varying by grades, ages and relative brightness of students. He surmised that the 'language factor' (which I assume is variation in English competence) was key, and a failure to consider it may impair, even invalidate, the value of achievement and mental tests.[61] Sánchez' study was important in that his results 1) challenged the notion that IQ is constant, one of the main assertions in hereditarian thought about the nature of intelligence, and 2) as competence in English (of Spanish-speaking children) increases over time, so does academic and mental ability.

One of Sánchez' most judicious assaults on mental testing and conclusions drawn by white scholars about the intellectual performance of Mexican Americans is seen in 'Group differences and Spanish-speaking children — a critical review', an article that appeared in a 1932 issue of the *Journal of Applied Psychology* (a noted journal of the American Psychological Association). Based on his review of the existing literature of Mexican American children's performance on intelligence tests (and in some studies, academic achievement tests), Sánchez observed that three major types of explanations for performance prevailed among white scholars. Note the degrees of deficit thinking implicitly or explicitly expressed:

a   Innate capacity is differentiated racially, and intelligence tests measure such differentiation.
b   Environment (in its broader sense) is largely responsible for 'intelligence' as measured by tests. It at least conditions innate ability, and intelligence tests are in part measures of environmental effects.
c   Bilingualism, over and above its environmental attributes, is a handicap acting not only upon language expression and language understanding but upon more intricate psychological processes. At the very least it presents an extra obstacle in the learning process of foreign language children. (Sanchez, 1932a: 550)

In refutation of these three categories of explanations, Sánchez (1932a) presented several counterpoints, some substantive and some methodological in character. In my analysis of his review, I believe his critique can be compressed into two major assertions: 1) Mexican American children, compared to their white peers, have vastly different environmental backgrounds — especially living in poorer SES conditions. Most researchers have virtually ignored controlling for environmental factors. As such, there is little scientific data and analysis of the influence of environment on mental test performance. One exception, however, is Sánchez (1931) where he demonstrated the role of school training. 2) For the most part, Mexican American children in existing research studies are non- or limited-English proficient, or are in varying stages of developing bilingually. For researchers (see Goodenough, 1926) to assume that language is totally eliminated from nonverbal and performance tests is questionable. On this point, Sánchez was right on target as later research (see Mitchell, 1937) would aptly confirm his position. Furthermore, limited-English-speaking Mexican Americans do better on nonverbal, compared to verbal IQ tests. Klineberg's (1935a) review of this point (as we have previously discussed) would later support Sánchez' contention.

Another article of significance by Sánchez (1934a) is his critical essay of mental measures and testing as they relate to Mexican American students, especially those who are limited in English competency. In this insightful analysis, he castigates myopic scholars and unsophisticated applied personnel who, without question, accept intelligence tests as valid tools. The seven issues he raised were, in a sense, prognosticatory as their relevance for Mexican Americans would hold for decades to come and would serve as beacons for reform in test development, individual assessment, and social concerns involving test use. Padilla and Aranda (1974), in their synopsis of Sánchez' essay, summarized these issues as follows:

1 Tests are not standardized on the Spanish-speaking population of this country.
2 Test items are not representative of the Spanish-speaking culture.
3 The entire nature of intelligence is still a controversial issue.
4 Test results from the Spanish-speaking continue to be accepted uncritically.
5 Revised or translated tests are not necessarily an improvement on test measures.
6 Attitudes and prejudices often determine the use of test results.
7 The influence of testing on the educational system is phenomenal (p. 222).

After completing his MA degree in 1931, Sánchez enrolled at the University of California at Berkeley and earned his PhD in 1934 ('The education of bilinguals in a state school system' Sánchez, 1934b). In 1940, Sánchez joined the faculty of the University of Texas at Austin in the Department of History and Philosophy of Education (which he served as the department chair from 1950 to 1959). In a short time he became a champion of Mexican American civil rights, challenging school segregation and discrimination in housing and employment (Romo, 1986). Sánchez taught at UT Austin until his death in 1972. So illustrious was his career that UT Austin in 1994 named the College of Education building the George I. Sánchez Building.

In conclusion, the genetic pathology model of deficit thinking certainly made its mark in influencing American educational thought and practice. Predictably so, with a paradigm based on pseudoscience and proselytized by influential researchers and scholars, low-SES children of color were losers from the beginning. However, with such an oppressive model serving as the orthodoxy, it was just a matter of time before the genetic pathology model would collapse. Douglas Foley, the author of the next chapter, begins his discussion with an overview of a number of factors that led to the passing of the genetic pathology model. Although the genetic pathology paradigm was no longer tenable as a basis to explain human behavior, deficit thinking in intellectual thought and in the worlds of research and education persisted. Let us turn to this subject.

Notes

1   Chorover (1979) draws upon the writings of eighteenth-century Dutch anatomist and art historian, Peter Compli, who introduced the facial angle concept and discussed the role of Aristotle in first recognizing an association between physical beauty, mental perfections and facial angles.

2   Any detailed discussion of this period is well beyond the scope of this chapter. Pertinent and excellent analyses can be seen, for example, in Blum (1978), Cravens (1978) and Degler (1991).

3   The term *social Darwinism*, stemming from Darwin's account and principles of evolution, was derived 'as a part of the general effort to apply concepts of biological evolution to problems of human societies' (Blum, 1978: 25). English philosopher Herbert Spencer is given credit for coining the key phrase in social Darwinism — 'survival of the fittest' (Degler, 1991). In the late twentieth century, social Darwinism became an important evolutionary rationale to explain the alleged inevitability of poverty, attainment of wealth and social stratification in general.

4   Of course, not all scientists who investigated the relation between intellectual performance and SES concluded the link was genetic in nature. In the late 1910s and early 1920s, some researchers concluded that the association between intelligence and social standing was greatly influenced by environmental factors (see Cravens, 1978). However, notwithstanding this growing body of environmental interpretations, Rudolph Pintner, a mental testing specialist, concluded this as late as 1930 in his book, *Intelligence Testing:*

> We may sum up these studies of the relationship of the intelligence of the child to the occupational or social status of the parent by saying that they fit in very well with the theory that intellectual potentiality is largely inherited. (1930: 518)

5   For example, note the following: ' "scientific" data derived from the testing and Eugenics Movement . . . entered into the dialogue which led to the restrictive immigration quota of 1924, that clearly discriminated against southern Europeans' (Karier, 1972: 163). Also note: 'the findings of the IQ tests emerged as a crucial source of support for the selective exclusion of aliens from certain countries' (Chorover, 1979: 71). And finally, 'Congressional debates leading to passage of the Immigration Restriction Act of 1924 continually invoke the army data' (Gould, 1981: 232).

6 From 1830 to 1930, America experienced its greatest period of immigration. For this century-long era, historians typically divide the period in two: the 'old' immigration (1830–1882), and the 'new' immigration (1882–1930) (Chorover, 1979).

7 Such figures are conservative. As Haller has commented: 'The figures are minimum, since such states kept poor records and since a few institutions preferred not to reveal the extent of sterilization being done' (1963: 231).

8 Mark's (1981) figures come from the follow-up study by the Human Betterment Foundation (*Human Sterilization Today*, pamphlet, 1938: 9–10).

9 McDougall (1921) also briefly refers to Mexicans and Indians of the US Southwest as being genetically inferior in intelligence. He cites Terman (1916) as his reference.

10 Regarding the study by Davenport and Steggerda (1929), the focus is on Negro-white crosses and alleged disharmonious anthropometric outcomes. For example, the authors note that the legs and arms of the Negro are disproportionately long in comparison to the trunk, whereas the limbs of the white are disproportionately short. Miscegenation, according to Davenport and Steggerda, might result in an individual with long legs (via Negro constitution) and short arms (via white constitution) — leading the authors to conclude, '[the resultant individual would have] to stoop more to pick up a thing on the ground than one with the opposite combination' (1929: 471). In a response, Klineberg quipped, 'This does not seem to be a very serious inconvenience; but in any case it is just as probable that he [the Negro] would have the "opposite advantage", which would put him at an advantage in picking things up from the ground!' (1935a: 213).

11 Technically speaking, a mulatto is the first-generation offspring of a black and a white individual. The three issues to follow, however, can generalize beyond the mulatto hypothesis to other racial studies that examined white/other admixture (such as hybridity among American Indians; see, Garth, 1923 below).

12 I calculated a Spearman rank order coefficient in which the five groups' ranks in IQ and schooling attainment were compared. The observed p (rho = .99) was significant at the .01 level of confidence.

13 Although Terman is often given credit for developing the first widely used American version of the Binet scale, Henry Goddard and Frederick Kuhlmann (1912) were the first to produce highly useful versions (see Freeman, 1926). It is believed that Terman's success in having his Binet scale version more widely used and known was due to the assertiveness of the test's publisher (Houghton Mifflin book company) and Terman's reputation as a scholar and author of many books, articles and tests (French and Hale, 1990).

14 William Stern (1914) was the developer of the construct of 'mental quotient' (a child's mental age divided by his or her chronological age). For example, a 12-year-old child whose mental age was estimated to be 14 years would have a mental quotient of 1.17. Terman, in his development of the Stanford–Binet, extended the construct of mental quotient by multiplying it by 100. In the above example, the IQ would be 117.

15 Gould (1981) believes that the Army probably did not make wide military placement use of the tests. He does contend, however, that they had considerable influence in screening men for officer training.

16 Recruits who failed both Alpha and Beta tests were administered an individual intelligence test, typically a Binet scale version (Gould, 1981).

17 C.C. Brigham, a follower of Yerkes as well as the author of the racist, xenophobic *A Study of American Intelligence* (1923), became the secretary of the College Entrance Examination Board and in the development of the Scholastic Aptitude Test he used the Army tests as models (Gould, 1981).

18   Goddard is credited with devising the name 'moron' (a Greek word meaning foolish) to those he deemed to be 'high-grade' defectives (Gould, 1981). Citing a classification scheme from the American Association for the Study of the Feeble-Minded, Goddard noted:

>   Feeble-mindedness [a moron designation] has been defined as a 'state of mental defect existing from birth or from an early age and due to incomplete or abnormal development in consequence of which, the person affected is incapable of performing his duties as a member of society in the position of life to which he was born'. (1923: 4)

19   In addition to Terman and Yerkes, there were three other co-developers of the NIT — M.E. Haggerty, E.L. Thorndike and G.M. Whipple. It is interesting to note that the NIT team did not always see eye-to-eye on the test's development. For example, regarding the development of standard norms, Thorndike wanted 'foreign' populations and rural districts represented in the standardization sample. Haggerty desired separate age norms for 'colored' children. On the latter, 'Yerkes replied, "No, we don't want to use them. The political situation here will prevent us from going into colored schools"' (quoted in Chapman, 1988: 81). As Chapman notes, due to the pressure of time, the schools finally selected for the norming of the NIT were in the cities of Cincinnati, Pittsburgh, Kansas and New York City. For a test that used 'National' in its name, the final locations chosen for norming were certainly not representative of American culture. On this issue, Chapman's point is well taken:

>   The point to be drawn from this discussion is that the examination board, like Terman in his work on the Stanford–Binet, made rather broad assumptions about the nature of American culture and what constituted the 'normal' American experience. These standards were then used to judge the intelligence of many Americans whose cultural background was not adequately reflected in either the tests or the norms. These decisions would have important consequences, too, for in little more than a year, the National Intelligence Tests would be in wide use around the country. (1988: 81)

20   Hildreth, in *A Bibliography of Mental Tests and Rating Scales* (1933; cited in Chapman, 1988), reported that from 1920 to 1929, 70 'mental tests' were developed. From 1900–1932, 133 were available. Unfortunately, Hildreth used the term 'mental test' in an omnibus fashion, including achievement and aptitude tests and tests measuring various types of ability. Thus, her analysis does not inform us of the number of intelligence tests. In any event, the mental tests she did identify were used, according to her, for large-scale classification of school children's abilities.

21   As Chapman (1988) has noted, group achievement tests were about as widely used as their sister test, group intelligence instruments. Achievement tests were used in an accountability role to evaluate the performance of local schools, as well as for homogeneous grouping. Achievement tests were produced in greater numbers than intelligence tests by far. Hildreth (1933; cited in Chapman (1988) reported that between 1920 and 1929, 741 achievement tests were developed. From 1900–1932, 1298 such tests were produced.

22   It should be noted that the administrative practice of ability grouping in public schools did not follow one uniform organizational plan. Chapman (1988), commenting on a

1929 survey by Otto (1931) of 395 superintendents in cities ranging in size from 2500 to 25,000, wrote 'he [Otto] discovered 20 different plans to classify students within classrooms, and 122 different promotion schemes' (1988: 159).

23 Terman defined border-line cases as 'those which fall near the boundary between that grade of mental deficiency [70 to 80 IQ] which will be generally recognized as such and the higher group usually classified as normal but dull. They are doubtful cases, the ones we are always (rarely with success) to restore to normality' (1916: 87).

24 Garth, as well as a number of other race psychologists of this period, used 'race' in a biological sense. We know now that race is best viewed as a social concept. Also, Garth and others confused race with national origin and ethnicity.

25 The term 'Mexican' was typically used during the first four decades of the twentieth century to refer to Mexican-origin children living in the United States. A substantial proportion of these children were citizens of the US.

26 It needs to be noted that not all race psychology studies of this period were deficit thinking in nature. For example, Gesche (1927) tested 1152 Mexican children for their color preference — a study apparently neutral regarding social implications.

27 Young's conclusions of the innate intellectual inferiority of the Italian, Portuguese and Spanish-Mexican children in his study, I daresay, were influenced by his wider racist beliefs. For example, in his discussion of the racial backgrounds of the Spanish-Mexican group, he wrote:

> Biologists and anthropologists both look with little favor on a violent mixture of races so divergent as some of these elements are. It is not impossible that part of the socio-economic difficulties of Latin America, especially Mexico, are due to the 'character of an unfortunate hybrid race'. (1922: 78)

It appears that Young's reference to the peoples of Latin America, particularly Mexicans, as being a product of a 'violent mixture of races' resulting in 'an unfortunate hybrid race', is drawn from Keller's (1908) book, *Colonization*. Young, quoting Keller, wrote:

> It is certainly important to try to appraise the Spanish-American stock, for there has never existed in historic times any such experiment in the mixture of really alien races . . . In its net results race-mixture plus other factors seem scarcely to have produced a favorable human type in Spanish-America; taken at its very best it has not represented a striking success. (quoted in Young, 1922: 78)

28 The term *retardation* was commonly used in the 1920s. It was used in three ways. *Pedagogical* retardation referred to children who were overage for their grade level. Simply put, 'A retarded child is a child who is too old for the grade he is in' (quoted in Taylor, 1927: 13). *Psychological* retardation was used to convey 'mental retardation'. The indexes used were mental and chronological ages. For example, 'if the pupil is in the first grade and his mental age is from six to seven, he is normal in respect to mentality. In case this same pupil should score less than six years of age in the first grade, he is retarded mentally' (Taylor, 1927: 15). *Physiological* retardation, which we today would view as dealing with physical growth of children, had to do with developmental phases, for example, puberty. 'Physiological age refers to the stage of development in contra-distinction to age, in years and months, which is the usual method of designating age' (quoted in Taylor, 1927: 152).

29 Garretson (1928) reported that the monthly mean incomes for the parents of the white and Mexican children were $250 and $110, respectively.

30 Garretson commented:

> With few exceptions, Spanish is the language spoken in the homes and on the streets of the Mexican part of town. It is unusual for a Mexican child to be able to speak English when he enters the kindergarten or first grade. (1928: 32–3)

Even after admitting the above and presenting data to show that the IQ differences in grade 1 — favoring the White sample — on the verbal Pintner-Cunningham and the NIT were substantial, and after commenting that the Mexican children's language difficulty operated to their disadvantage, Garretson still suggested a genetic explanation for group differences.

31 Furthermore, on several other grade levels the IQ differences — though favoring whites — were negligible and, I daresay, statistically nonsignificant; for example, on the Pantomime test, grade 5, the mean IQs were 92.0 and 91.5 for the whites and Mexican Americans, respectively.

32 In Goodenough (1926), there were 79 American Indian subjects (Hoopla Valley); their mean IQ was 85.6.

33 The Goodenough–Harris Drawing Test is an extension and revision of the 1926 Goodenough Draw-a-Man Test.

34 It is of interest to note that Koch and Simmons (1926) found racial admixture analysis *vis-à-vis* intelligence testing to be a truly bona fide scientific approach. Commenting that it was almost impossible to establish the role that innate ability had in intellectual performance because of differences in social opportunities between racial/ethnic stocks, the authors, with great confidence, commented:

> We may, however, control with considerable success the factor of environment by limiting our investigation to the racial or nationality group itself and examining the behavior of those who have a mixed ancestry, a white–Mexican or white–Negro, for instance, in contrast to those who come from almost a pure native stock. (1926: 83)

35 Koch and Simmons (1926) also conducted an analysis of intellectual performance of the Mexican 'color groups'. The results showed that the mean IQs on all tests (except one) were higher for the 'light' groups compared to the 'intermediate' and 'dark' Mexican groups. Although the mean IQ differences across the three groups were typically statistically nonsignificant, the authors still hinted at an hereditarian conclusion: 'The rather consistent tendency of the mean scores of the light group to exceed those of the other color population is, perhaps, worthy of slight consideration' (1926: 84).

36 From the time of establishment of the Austin Independent School District (AISD) in 1881 up to the *Brown v. Board of Education* in 1954, the AISD operated — pursuant to Texas law — a dual school system for African American and White students (from 'Plaintiffs' Proposed Findings of Facts and Conclusions of Law', *Samantha Price et al. v. Austin Independent School District et al.* (1987).

37 Chapman (1988) has commented that Terman's use of 'homogeneous class groups' is one of the first uses of the notion, which subsequently became a common term in education.

38   It is interesting to note that Terman's five percentage breakdowns coincide nearly identically to the way in which measured intelligence on later intelligence tests was distributed (by design). The breakdowns are strikingly similar to the areas (i.e., cases) under the normal curve. For example, about 2.5 per cent of the area is contained in two standard deviations above the mean (IQ of 130 and above — Terman's 'gifted' group). About 15 per cent of the area is contained between the first and second standard deviations above the mean (IQs between 115 and 130 — Terman's 'bright' group). And so on. The point I make here is that Terman's a priori groupings were manufactured given his knowledge of the normal distribution. Such groupings are reflections of probability theory through a human-made construction, which subsequently became a social construction of reality.

39   Dickson used the individually administered Stanford–Binet intelligence test as well as the Otis Group Intelligence Test, developed by Arthur Otis, a former graduate student of Terman (Chapman, 1988).

40   The Stanford–Binet was also administered in special circumstances, for example, for kindergarten pupils, see Chapman, 1988.

41   Two points are noteworthy here. First, as Chapman (1988) has commented, there were actually five different types of classes: accelerated (10 per cent of students), normal (82 per cent), and slow (8 per cent). The latter category was divided into three subgroupings: 'limited' (6 per cent), 'opportunity' (1 per cent; entry-level students that needed help to catch up), and 'atypical' (1 per cent; students 3 or more years behind grade level).

Second, as one would predict, immigrant and poor children were overrepresented in the slow classes due to their typically low IQ scores. Chapman (1988) has written that Young shared the common beliefs of ethnic and class mental inferiority, thus reinforcing prejudices frequently voiced during the genetic pathology era.

42   Terman noted in the preface that by 1923, 50,000 students in Oakland and Berkeley school systems had been tested and classified on ability.

43   For further discussion of Young's (1922) ideas about curriculum differentiation see Chapman (1988) and Gonzalez (1990).

44   Gonzalez (1974a) drew this median IQ data from McAnulty (1929), whose study in turn drew on a compilation of IQ test data survey in Los Angeles from 1926, 1927 and 1928.

The observed median IQ of 91.2 of Mexican American children in 1920s Los Angeles was about two-thirds of a standard deviation below the typical white median (and mean) of 100. This difference of two-thirds of a standard deviation was frequently found in other race psychology studies of the time. Furthermore, Valencia (1985) in a comprehensive review of research on intelligence testing and Chicano school-age children, has estimated an aggregated mean IQ of 87.3. His analysis is based on 10,739 Mexican American children in 78 studies spanning six decades. Valencia has noted, however, that this aggregated mean IQ of 87.3 is entirely misleading and greatly confounded by the failure of researchers to control critical variables.

45   There is at least one educational historian that challenges the thesis that IQ testing played a demonstrative role in curriculum differentiation in Los Angeles schools in the 1920s and early 1930s. Rafferty (1988, 1992) contends that educational historians have greatly exaggerated the role intelligence testing played in ability grouping placements of Mexican American and other minority students in Los Angeles. Rafferty's case study does shed some light on the role of IQ testing — particularly how classroom teachers may or may have not used test results for grouping purposes. I think, however, that her thesis and final analysis are misleading. Rafferty criticizes other educational historians for stating that IQ tests were used *exclusively* for educational placement. My reading

of the same material (see Gonzalez, 1974a) leads me to believe that such historians *did* speak to *other* factors than just IQ testing. Gonzalez notes 'placements into the various curricular levels considered more than just IQs; counselors also considered nationality, parents' occupation, teacher evaluations, grades, school progress and behavior. However, IQs provided the key to placement' (1990: 80).

46 Although my focus here is on dissent within the academic/research community, challenges to deficit thinking (particularly dealing with intelligence testing) were also brought forth by journalists, school administrators, teachers and labor figures. For a brief, but cogent, coverage of these exchanges see Chapman (1988).

47 Arlitt, a psychology professor at Bryn Mawr College, collected the data with the assistance of four graduate students. Thus, I assume that the location of the study was in the Bryn Mawr, Pennsylvania area.

48 It appears that Arlitt relabeled the occupational groupings because of her perceptions of the home environments of the children. Note, 'The home conditions followed closely the division by occupation' (1921: 180).

49 Degler (1991), in his own analysis of Arlitt's (1921) study, contends that she captured a central issue in the field of race psychology, but the implications of controlling for SES in cross racial/ethnic investigations were not recognized quickly by researchers:

> An indication of how slowly social scientists recognized the implications of findings such as those published by Arlitt is provided by some research Arlitt [1922] herself reported the following year. In this study Arlitt found that black children of ages five and six scored above white children of the same age and social class, but that, as the students grew older, the whites surpassed the blacks. That shift, Arlitt attributed 'to a genuine race difference'. On the basis of her article the previous year, one would have thought she would have asked how it came about that black children fell below whites as they grew older. Instead, she proceeded to explain why the superior scores of the black children at an earlier age may have been influenced by factors other than intelligence. In short, she fell back to the traditionalist position of assuming that race was controlling even when scores clearly called it into question. (p. 173)

50 The failure of race psychologists to assess (prior to intelligence testing) the language status of children and youth who were most likely to be limited-English proficient was a frequent occurrence during the genetic pathology period. For example, in my analysis of intelligence testing research of Mexican American children during the 1920s (Valencia, 1985), I found that of the total eight such studies, none of the investigators attempted to assess the children's language for dominance and fluency. Furthermore, in the same review of the literature, I found that in the 124 intelligence testing instances I identified in 106 studies (spanning six decades), the language status of the Mexican American children *was not even reported* in 63 (50.8 per cent) instances. Furthermore, in those studies that did report language status of the subjects, about two-thirds assessed language (predominantly through indirect means and not through the more precise, direct procedures), but still one-third of the studies *failed* to assess language. Thus, one can conclude that taking all pertinent studies of Mexican American intellectual performance (from 1922 through 1984), the strong majority of investigators failed to assess language status.

51 The results of Klineberg's analysis must be examined with caution (for reasons he acknowledges). First, the comparison of IQ scores across different intelligence tests

may be misleading in that the assumption of the various tests being equivalent in validity and reliability is certainly shaky. Second, Klineberg's method of averaging IQ scores across tests was done using simple averaging. The preferred, and most accurate, procedure is to use the weighted mean method. In any event, Klineberg's finding that the various groups studied scored higher on performance than linguistic IQ tests was certainly the case. Support for this is seen in Valencia (1985) where I employed the same procedure as Klineberg (1935a), except that I used the weighted means analysis. In 22 investigations (spanning decades) involving 2380 Mexican American children, their mean IQ on verbal tests was 85.6 and 94.7 on performance tests, a difference of 9.1 points (very close to Klineberg's observed differences of 10 points in a much smaller number of studies involving Mexican American children).

52 Participating in the symposium were Drs Bell, Buckingham, Colvin, Dearborn, Freeman, Haggerty, Henmon, Peterson, Pintner, Pressey, Ruml, Terman, Thorndike, Thurstone, Whipple, Woodrow, and Yerkes.

53 I give credit to Degler (1991) who pointed out the existence of this study. It is important to note that MacLear's investigation, an important empirical investigation and critique of the Army mental tests, has been virtually unrecognized by scholars who have written on this early period of testing. Even Thomas (1982), in his comprehensive discussion of the contributions of nine black males of the 1920s who criticized mental testing, failed to include this black woman's work.

54 Members of the committee included Bagley, Baldwin, Brigham, Freeman, Pintner, Whipple and Terman (chairman) (see Terman, 1924). As can be seen, the committee was represented by a cross section of opinion (Chapman, 1988). For example, Bagley was a staunch critic of intelligence testing, and Brigham was a racist and a firm believer in hereditarianism.

55 See Chapman (1988) for a discussion of a 1928 conference sponsored by the NSSE to discuss the results of *Yearbook's* findings.

56 Thomas' three categories are not mutually exclusive. For example, in McLear's (1922) study she focused on all three areas: (1) the environmental hypothesis; (2) a critique of instrumentation; (3) the generation of her own data.

57 His master's thesis was eventually published in Canady (1936).

58 Research and interest on mental testing by black scholars was not isolated to the 1920s, as such activities spilled over into the 1930s. One such study was by Beckham (1933) who examined the relation between intelligence and SES of 1100 'colored' adolescents (ages 12 to 16 years) attending schools in New York City, Washington, DC and Baltimore. The children in the sample — which is believed to be the largest number of black children participating in one study (Guthrie, 1976) — were administered the Stanford–Binet. Among many findings, Beckham observed: 1) the mean IQ of the total sample was 95.2, which was only one-third of a standard deviation below the white normative mean of 100; most previous research had reported a difference of one standard deviation (15 points) between the whites and blacks; 2) 60.2 per cent of the total sample fell in the normal IQ range (90–109); previous studies typically showed a considerably smaller proportion of blacks falling in the normal range; 3) Stanford–Binet IQ scores were positively correlated with SES.

Shuey (1966) has criticized Beckham's (1933) study, contending that the Washington, DC sample was not selected randomly. She argues that all of the Washington, DC subjects were brought to Howard University for testing by Howard psychology students as part of a course requirement. Thus, I gather, Shuey is contending that the grand IQ mean may be spurious (inflated) because 'the subjects were heavily biased in favor of siblings, neighbors and friends of the *Howard* students' (p. 35). However, Shuey fails to mention that Beckham, in his sample of 1100 colored adolescents, included 100 'delinquents' (inmates in a school for delinquents). Their mean IQ was 86, the lowest mean of the subsamples. I deleted the mean of the delinquents, recalculated the grand mean for the three metropolitan groups, and observed a new grand mean of 97.7 (2.5 points higher than Beckham's grand mean of 95.2 for the four subsamples). One could assume that the grand mean of 95.2 was spurious (pulled down) by the delinquent group's mean due to an unrepresentative sample of colored adolescents. In short, given Shuey's criticism plus my recalculation, there could be a cancelling out effect, and thus Beckham's initial grand mean is valid.

Another example of 1930s testing research by black scholars is Jenkins' (1936) study of Negro children of superior intelligence, a topic of virtual neglect by white scholars. Jenkins' sample included children, grades 3 to 8, attending seven public schools in Chicago. After rigorous screening, the author identified 103 Negro children who scored IQs of 120 and above on an abbreviated form of the Stanford–Binet. Jenkins' major findings included: 1) the incidence of Negro children of superior intelligence was found to be similar to the incidence percentage in research with superior white children; 2) contrary to research studies of superior white children in which such exceptional boys and girls were found only in middle-class, upper-middle class and professional groups, Jenkins' found that in addition to this pattern, one-third of the superior Negro children were of low SES and working-class backgrounds; 3) based on geneological data given by parents, the racial composition of 63 of the 103 children was estimated; Jenkins found that 14 (22.2 per cent) of the children had no white ancestry and 29 (46.1 per cent) had more Negro ancestry than white, thus providing a refutation of the mulatto hypothesis. Jenkins noted, 'The discovery of a [pure blood] Negro child who scores in the very highest range of the Stanford–Binet scale constitutes one of the most significant findings of the study' (1936: 189).

59   It is noteworthy to mention, however, that in his essay of the black intellectual assault on early mental testing, Thomas (1982) discusses an irony. He describes that some black colleges and secondary schools in the 1930s used intelligence tests for purposes of educational/vocational guidance and curriculum differentiation. Thomas speculates that mental testing was used as such for two reasons: 1) black students from lower-class backgrounds were finding greater access to black colleges via their matriculation to middle-class secondary schools (which were the conduits to black colleges); as a result, curriculum differentiation was needed to meet the needs of individual students (examine the views espoused by some black scholars who were active in the 1920s — Bond, 1937; Canady, 1937); 2) black intellectuals deemed it very important to identify black students with superior abilities and talent in order to create leaders, role models and to demonstrate to white America that blacks of uncommon talent existed.

Thomas suggests these developments raised the question:

> whether the early black critics of mental testing were as devoutly opposed to the underlying assumptions of individual intellectual differences as their critiques suggest they might have been . . . In an academic climate validating the notion that it is as important that one discovers what one cannot do as it is to discover what one can do, black educators had not come too far afield from the postulations of Lewis Terman . . . By employing the tool which had been used to build a body of racist data, blacks were co-opted into an ironic and paradoxical legitimation of the instrument. (1982: 287–8)

Thomas' (1982) contention that black intellectuals' shift from a critique to an embracement of mental testing has some merit as being referred to as an irony. I think, however, Thomas makes more of this than there is. First, to argue that black intellectuals were closely aligned with Terman's postulations of mental tests is a tenuous position. Terman was a hereditarian. I daresay that none of the black intellectuals believed IQ tests measured innate intelligence. Second, black scholars were highly critical of mental testing *abuse* — specifically, using IQ testing for classifying students for instructional groupings that led to dead-end, inferior schooling. Black colleges that used mental testing for curriculum differentiation were, I suggest, utilizing them for individual guidance and career development. If some black students, because of social class differences, had doors either opened or closed due to curriculum differentiation, then this would need to be documented. Thomas does not.

60 I am assuming that Sánchez' (1931) 'Spanish-speaking' sample was comprised of children who had no, to some, good command of English. Sánchez, unfortunately, made the common mistake of failing to assess the children's language status. Also, it appears that both the achievement and intelligence tests were administered in English. Had Sánchez assessed the children's English skills and then analyzed test data by such divisions, his study would have been more revealing about the influence of the 'language factor'.

61 Two points are noteworthy here. First, Sánchez (1931) commented that the observed gain scores due to practice effect were likely negligible because of the rather long intervals between testing. Second, he surmised that the gain in scores was most likely due to 'school training', which he viewed as 'the influence of an increasing facility in the use of English' (p. 69). Strong evidence for this conjecture was present in that Sánchez reported the correlations between reading achievement and all other measured abilities (especially mental ability) were high.

References

ANASTASI, A. (1988) *Psychological Testing* (6th ed.), New York: Macmillan.

ARLITT, A.H. (1921) 'On the need for caution in establishing race norms', *Journal of Applied Psychology*, **5**, pp. 179–83.

ARLITT, A.H. (1922) 'The relation of intelligence to age in Negro children', *Journal of Applied Psychology*, **22**, pp. 278–381.

BAGLEY, W.C. (1922) 'Educational determinism; or democracy and the I.Q.', *School and Society*, **15**, 373–84.

BAGLEY, W.C. (1925) *Determinism in Education*, Baltimore, MD: Warwick & York.

BAKARE, C.G.M. (1972) 'Social-class differences in the performance of Nigerian children on the Draw-a-Man test', in CRONBACH, L.J. and DRENTH, P.J.D. (Eds) *Mental Tests and Cultural Adaptation*, The Hague: Mouton, pp. 355–63.

BECKHAM, A.S. (1933) 'A study of the intelligence of colored adolescents of different social-economic status in typical metropolitan areas', *Journal of Social Psychology*, **4**, pp. 70–90.

BISHOP, H.P. (1937) 'A case study of the improvement of Mexican homes through instruction in homemaking', Unpublished master's thesis, University of Southern California, Los Angeles.

BLUM, J.M. (1978) *Pseudoscience and Mental Ability: The Origins and Fallacies of the IQ Controversy*, New York: Monthly Review Press.

BOAS, F. (1911) *The Mind of Primitive Man*, New York: Macmillan.

BOND, H.M. (1924) 'What the army "intelligence" tests measured', *Opportunity*, **2**, pp. 197–202.

BOND, H.M. (1937) 'The liberal arts college for Negroes: A social force', in (Ed) University of Louisville, *A Century of Municipal Higher Education*, Chicago, IL: Lincoln Printing Co.

BRIGHAM, C.C. (1923) *A Study of American Intelligence*, Princeton, NJ: Princeton University Press.

Brown v. Board of Education of Topeka (1954) 347 US 483, at 494.

CANADY, H.G. (1928) 'The effects of "rapport" on the IQ: A study in race psychology', Unpublished master's thesis, Northwestern University, Evanston, IL.

CANADY, H.G. (1936) 'The effect of "rapport" on the IQ: A new approach to the problem of racial psychology', *Journal of Negro Education*, **5**, pp. 209–19.

CANADY, H.G. (1937) 'Individual differences and their educational significance in the guidance of the gifted and talented child', *Quarterly Review of Higher Education Among Negroes*, **5**, pp. 202–5.

CASTLE, W.E. (1923) *Genetics and Eugenics*, Cambridge, MA: Harvard University Press.

CASTLE, W.E. (1926) 'Biological and social consequences of race crossing', *American Journal of Physical Anthropology*, **9**, pp. 145–56.

CASTLE, W.E. (1930) 'Race mixture and physical disharmonies', *Science*, **71**, pp. 603–6.

CHAPMAN, P.D. (1988) *Schools as Sorters: Lewis M. Terman, Applied Psychology, and the Intelligence Testing Movement, 1890–1930*, New York: New York University Press.

CHOROVER, S.L. (1979) *From Genius to Genocide: The Meaning of Human Nature and the Power of Behavior Control*, Cambridge, MA: The Massachusetts Institute of Technology Press.

CHRISTIANSEN, T. and LIVERMORE, G. (1970) A comparison of Anglo-American and Spanish-American children on the WISC. *Journal of Social Psychology*, **81**, pp. 9–14.

Cities Reporting the Use of Homogeneous Grouping and of the Winnetka Technique and the Dalton Plan (1926) Department of the Interior, Bureau of Education, City School Leaflet no. 22. Washington, DC: Government Printing Office.

CRAVENS, H. (1978) *The Triumph of Evolution: American Scientists and the Heredity-Environment Controversy, 1900–1941*, Philadelphia, PA: University of Pennsylvania Press.

CRONBACH, L.J. (1975) 'Five decades of public controversy over mental testing', *American Psychologist*, **30**, pp. 1–14.

CUBBERLY, E.P. (1916) 'Editor's Introduction', in TERMAN, L.M., *The Measurement of Intelligence: An Explanation of and a Complete Guide for the Stanford Revision and Extension of the Binet–Simon Scales*, Boston, MA: Houghton Mifflin, pp. vii–ix.

DAVENPORT, C.B. (1927) *Guide to Physical Anthropology and Anthroposcopy*, Cold Spring Harbor, NY: Eugenics Research Association.

DAVENPORT, C.B. and STEGGERDA, M. (1929) *Race Crossing in Jamaica*, Westport, CT: Negro Universities Press.

DEGLER, C.N. (1991) *In Search of Human Nature: The Decline and Revival of Darwinism in American Social Thought*, New York: Oxford University Press.

DENNIS, W. (1966) Goodenough scores, art experience, and modernization', *Journal of Social Psychology*, **68**, pp. 211–28.

DICKSON, V.E. (1923) *Mental Tests and the Classroom Teacher*, Yonkers-on-Hudson, NY: World Book.

ELLIS, P. (1929) *Americanization Through Homemaking*, Los Angeles, CA: Wetzel Publishing Co.

ENGLISH, H.B. (1917) 'An experimental study of mental capacities of school children correlated with social status', *Psychological Monographs*, **23**, pp. 266–331.

FASS, P.S. (1980) 'The IQ: A cultural and historical framework', *American Journal of Education*, **88**, pp. 431–58.

FERGUSON, G.O. (1916) 'The psychology of the Negro', *Archives of Psychology*, **36**.

FREEMAN, F.N. (1926) *Mental Tests: Their History, Principles and Applications*, Boston, MA: Houghton Mifflin.

FRENCH, J.L. and HALE, R.L. (1990) 'A history of the development of psychological and educational testing', in REYNOLDS, C.R. and KAMPHANS, R.W. (Eds) *Handbook of Psychological and Educational Assessment of Children: Intelligence and Achievement*, New York: Guilford Press, pp. 3–28.

GALTON, F. (1870) *Hereditary Genius: An Inquiry into its Laws and Consequences*, New York: D. Appleton & Co.

GALTON, F. (1883) *Inquiries into Human Faculty and its Development*, London: Macmillan.

GARRETSON, O.K. (1928) 'Study of the causes of retardation among Mexican children', *Journal of Educational Psychology*, **19**, pp. 31–40.

GARTH, T.R. (1923) 'A comparison of the intelligence of Mexican and full blood Indian children', *Psychological Review*, **30**, pp. 388–401.

GARTH, T.R. (1925) 'A review of race psychology', *Psychological Bulletin*, **22**, pp. 343–64.

GARTH, T.R. (1928) 'The intelligence of Mexican school children', *School and Society*, **27**, pp. 791–4.

GARTH, T.R. (1930) 'A review of race psychology, *Psychological Bulletin*, **27**, pp. 329–56.

GESCHE, I. (1927) 'The color preferences of 1152 Mexican children', *Journal of Comparative Psychology*, **7**, pp. 297–311.

GODDARD, H.H. (1920) *Human Efficiency and Levels of Intelligence*, Princeton, NJ: Princeton University Press.

GODDARD, H.H. (1923) *Feeblemindedness: Its Causes and Consequences*, New York: Macmillan.

GONZALEZ, G.G. (1974a) 'The system of public education and its function within the Chicano communities, 1910–1930', Unpublished doctoral dissertation, University of California, Los Angeles.

GONZALEZ, G.G. (1974b) 'Racism, education and the Mexican community in Los Angeles, 1920–1930', *Societas*, **4**, pp. 287–301.

GONZALEZ, G.G. (1990) *Chicano Education in the Era of Segregation*, Philadelphia, PA: The Balch Institute Press.

GOODENOUGH, F.L. (1926) 'Racial differences in the intelligence of school children', *Journal of Experimental Psychology*, **9**, pp. 388–97.

GOULD, S.J. (1981) *The Mismeasure of Man*, New York: W.W. Norton.

GRANT, M. (1916) *The Passing of the Great Race*, New York: Scribner's.

GUTHRIE, R.V. (1976) *Even the Rat was White: A Historical View of Psychology*, New York: Harper & Row.

GUTHRIE, R.V. (1981) 'IQ testing: Some historical perspectives', *Generator*, **14**, pp. 1–12.

HALLER, M.H. (1963) *Eugenics: Hereditarian Attitudes in American Thought*, New Brunswick, NJ: Rutgers University Press.

HANEY, W. (1981) 'Validity, vaudeville, and values: A short history of social concerns over standardized testing', *American Psychologist*, **36**, pp. 1021–34.

HENDRICK, I. (1977) *The Education of Non-whites in California, 1848–1970*, San Francisco, CA: R & E Associates.

HERKOVITZ, M.J. (1926) 'On the relation between Negro-white mixture and standing in intelligence tests', *Pedagogical Seminary*, **33**, pp. 30–42.

HERKOVITZ, M.J. (1934) 'A critical discussion of the mulatto hypothesis', *Journal of Negro Education*, Yearbook III.

HERRNSTEIN, R.J. and MURRAY, C. (1994) *The Bell Curve: Intelligence and Class Structure in American Life*, New York: The Free Press.

HILDRETH, G.A. (1933) A *Bibliography of Mental Tests and Rating Scales*, New York: Psychological Corporation.

HUMAN BETTERMENT FOUNDATION (1938) *Human Sterilization Today* (pamphlet), (location of publisher not known): Author.

JENKINS, M.D. (1936) 'A socio-psychological study of Negro children of superior intelligence', *Journal of Negro Education*, **5**, pp. 175–90.

JOHNSON, C.S. (1923) 'Mental measurement of Negro groups', *Opportunity*, **1**, pp. 21–5.

KAMIN, L.J. (1974) *The Science and Politics of IQ*, Potomac, MD: Lawrence Erlbaum Associates.

KARIER, C.J. (1972) 'Testing for order and control in the corporate liberal state', *Educational Theory*, **22**, pp. 154–80.

KELLER, A.G. (1908) *Colonization*, Boston, MA: Ginn.

KIRK, S.A. (1973) 'The education of intelligence', *Slow Learning Child*, **20**, pp. 67–83.

KLINEBERG, O. (1928) 'An experimental study of speed and other factors in "racial differences"', *Archives of Psychology*, **93**.

KLINEBERG, O. (1932) 'A study of psychological differences between "racial" and national groups in Europe', *Archives of Psychology*, **132**.

KLINEBERG, O. (1935a) *Race Differences*, New York: Harper & Brothers.

KLINEBERG, O. (1935b) *Negro Intelligence and Selective Migration*, New York: Columbia University Press.

KOCH, H.L. and SIMMONS, R. (1926) 'A study of the test performance of American, Mexican, and Negro children', *Psychological Monographs*, **35**, pp. 1–116.

KUHLMANN, F. (1912) 'Binet-Simon's system for measuring the intelligence of children' [monograph supplement], *Journal of Psycho-Asthenics*, **1**, pp. 76–92.

LANDMAN, J.H. (1932) *Human Sterilization: The History of the Sexual Sterilizaion Movement*, New York: Macmillan.

LONG, H.H. (1925) 'On mental tests and race psychology — a critique', *Opportunity*, **3**, pp. 134–8.

MCANULTY, E.A. (1929) 'Distribution of intelligence in the Los Angeles elementary schools', *Los Angeles Educational Research Bulletin*, **8**, pp. 6–8.

MACLEAR, M. (1922) 'Sectional differences as shown by academic ratings and Army tests', *School and Society*, **15**, pp. 676–8.

MARKS, R. (1972) 'Testers, trackers, and trustees: The ideology of the intelligence testing movement in America 1900–1954', Unpublished doctoral dissertation, Urbana-Champaign, IL: University of Illinois.

MARKS, R. (1981) *The Idea of IQ*, Washington, DC: University Press of America.

MCDOUGALL, W. (1921) *Is America Safe for Democracy?*, New York: Charles Scribner's Sons.

MENCHACA, M. and VALENCIA, R.R. (1990) 'Anglo-Saxon ideologies and their impact on the segregation of Mexican students in California, the 1920s–1930s', *Anthropology and Education Quarterly*, **21**, pp. 222–49.

MITCHELL, A.J. (1937) 'The effect of bilingualism in the measurement of intelligence', *Elementary School Journal*, **38**, pp. 29–37.

MONROE, W.S. (1917) *Educational Tests and Measurements*, Boston, MA: Houghton Mifflin.

MORSE, J. (1914) 'A comparison of white and colored children measured by the Binet scale of intelligence', *The Popular Science Monthly*, **84**, pp. 75–9.

NUNN, SIR P. (1945) *Education: Its Data and First Principles* (3rd ed.) London: Edward Arnold.

OAKES, J. (1985) *Keeping Track: How Schools Structure Inequality*, New Haven, CT: Yale University Press.

OAKLAND, T. (1978) 'Predictive validity of readiness tests for middle and lower socioeconomic status Anglo, black, and Mexican American children', *Journal of Educational Psychology*, **70**, pp. 574–82.

OTTO, H.J. (1931) 'Administrative practices followed in the organization of elementary schools', *American School Board Journal*, **83**.

PADILLA, A.M. and ARANDA, P. (1974) *Latino Mental Health: Bibliography and Abstracts*, Rockville, MD: Alcohol, Drug Abuse, and Mental Health Administration.

PASCHAL, F.C. and SULLIVAN, L.R. (1925) 'Racial differences in the mental and physical development of Mexican children', *Comparative Psychology Monographs*, **3**, pp. 1–76.

PETERSON, J. and LANIER, L.H. (1929) 'Studies in the comparative abilities of whites and Negroes', *Mental Measurement Monographs*, **5**.

PETERSON, P.L. (1982) 'Individual differences', in MITZEL, H.E. (Ed) *Encyclopedia of Educational Research* (5th ed.), New York: Macmillan, pp. 844–51.

PHILLIPS, B.A. (1914) 'The Binet test applied to colored children', *Psychological Clinic*, **8**, pp. 190–6.

PINTNER, R. (1930) *Intelligence Testing*, New York: Henry Holt & Co.

Plessy v. Ferguson (1896) 163 US, pp. 537–64.

POPENOE, P. and GOSNEY, E.S. (1929) *Sterilization for Human Betterment*, New York: Macmillan.

PRESSEY, S.L. and TETER, G.F. (1919) 'A comparison of colored and white children by means of a group scale of intelligence', *Journal of Applied Psychology*, **3**, pp. 277–82.

PRESSEY, S.L. and THOMAS, J.B. (1919) 'A study of country children in 1) a good and 2) poor farming district by means of a group scale of intelligence', *Journal of Applied Psychology*, **3**, pp. 283–6.

PRICE, J. ST. CLAIR (1929) 'The intelligence of Negro college freshmen', *School and Society*, **30**, 749–54.

RACE BETTERMENT FOUNDATION (1914) *Proceedings of the First National Conference on Race Betterment*, Battle Creek, MI: Author.

RAFFERTY, J.R. (1988) 'Missing the mark: Intelligence testing in Los Angeles public schools', *History of Education Quarterly*, **28**, pp. 73–93.

RAFFERTY, J.R. (1992) *Land of Fair Promise: Politics and Reform in Los Angeles Schools, 1885–1941*, Stanford, CA: Stanford University Press.

RANGEL, S.C. and ALCALA, C.M. (1972) 'Project report: De jure segregation of Chicanos in Texas schools', *Harvard Civil Rights-Civil Liberties Law Review*, **7**, pp. 307–91.

ROMO, R. (1986) 'George I. Sánchez and the civil rights movement: 1940 to 1960', *La Raza Law Journal*, **1**, pp. 342–62.

Samantha Price et al. v. Austin Independent School District (1987) Nos. 87–1576, 87–1635 (5th Cir.).

SAMELSON, F. (1979) 'Putting psychology on the map: Ideology and intelligence testing', in BUSS, A.R. (Ed) *Psychology in Social Context*, New York: Irvington.

SAMUDA, R.J. (1975) *Psychological Testing of American Minorities: Issues and Consequences*, New York: Harper & Row.

SÁNCHEZ, G.I. (1931) 'A study of the scores of Spanish-speaking children on repeated tests', Unpublished master's thesis, Austin, TX: The University of Texas.

SÁNCHEZ, G.I. (1932a) 'Group differences in Spanish-speaking children: A critical review', *Journal of Applied Psychology*, **16**, pp. 549–58.

SÁNCHEZ, G.I. (1932b) 'Scores of Spanish-speaking children on repeated tests', *Journal of Genetic Psychology*, **40**, pp. 223–31.

SÁNCHEZ, G.I. (1934a) 'Bilingualism and mental measures', *Journal of Applied Psychology*, **18**, pp. 765–72.

SÁNCHEZ, G.I. (1934b) 'The education of bilinguals in a state school system', Unpublished doctoral dissertation, Berkeley, CA: University of California.

SHELDON, W.H. (1924) 'The intelligence of Mexican children', *School and Society*, **19**, pp. 139–42.

SHUEY, A.M. (1966) *The Testing of Negro Children* (2nd ed.), New York: Social Science Press.

SNEDDEN, D. (1921) *Sociological Determination of Objectives in Education*, Philadelphia, PA: J.B. Lippincott.

SNYDERMAN, M. and HERRNSTEIN, R.J. (1983) 'Intelligence tests and the immigration act of 1924', *American Psychologist*, **38**, pp. 986–95.

STERN, W. (1914) *The Psychological Methods of Testing Intelligence*, Baltimore, MD: Warwick & York.

STANLEY, G. (1920) 'Special schools for Mexicans', *The Survey*, **44** (September, 15), pp. 714–15.

STOCKING, JR., G.W. (1960) 'American social scientists and race theory — 1890–1915', Unpublished doctoral dissertation, Philadelphia, PA: University of Pennsylvania.

STRONG, A.C. (1913) 'Three hundred fifty white and colored children measured by the Binet–Simon measuring scale of intelligence', *Pedagogical Seminary*, **20**, pp. 485–515.

SUMNER, F.C. (1925) 'Environic factors which prohibit creative scholarship among Negroes', *School and Society*, **22**, pp. 294–6.

TAYLOR, M.C. (1927) 'Retardation of Mexican children in the Albuquerque schools', Unpublished master's thesis, Stanford, CA: Stanford University.

TAYLOR, P.S. (1929) *Mexican Labor in the United States: Racial School Statistics*, Los Angeles, CA: University of California Publications in Economics, V.

TERMAN, L.M. (1916) *The Measurement of Intelligence: An Explanation of and a Complete Guide for the Use of the Stanford Revision and Extension of the Binet–Simon Scales*, Boston, MA: Houghton Mifflin.

TERMAN, L.M. (1919) *The Intelligence of School Children: How Children Differ in Ability, the Use of Mental Tests in School Grading and the Proper Education of Exceptional Children*, Boston, MA: Houghton Mifflin.

TERMAN, L.M. (1920) 'The use of intelligence tests in the grading of school children', *Journal of Educational Research*, **1**, pp. 20–32.

TERMAN, L.M. (1922) *Intelligence Tests and School Reorganization*, Yonkers-on-Hudson, NY: World Book.

TERMAN, L.M. (1924) 'The possibilities and limitations of training', *Journal of Educational Research*, **10**, pp. 335–43.

TERMAN, L.M (Ed) (1928) *Twenty Seventh Yearbook*, Bloomington, IL: Public School Publishing Co.

TERMAN, L.M., THORNDIKE, E.L., FREEMAN, F.N., COLVIN, S.S., PINTNER, R. and RUML, B. (1921) 'Intelligence and its measurement: A symposium', *Journal of Educational Psychology*, **12**, pp. 123–47, 195–216, 271–5.

THOMAS, W.B. (1982) 'Black intellectuals' critique of early mental testing: A little known saga of the 1920s', *American Journal of Education*, **90**, pp. 258–92.

VALENCIA, R.R. (1985) '*Chicanos and intelligence testing research: A descriptive state of the art*', Unpublished manuscript.

VALENCIA, R.R., MENCHACA, M. and VALENZUELA, A. (1993) 'The educational future of Chicanos: A call for affirmative diversity', *Journal of the Association of Mexican American Educators*, pp. 5–13.

WIERSMA, W. and JURS, S.G. (1985) *Educational Measurement and Testing*, Boston, MA: Allyn & Bacon.

WOODSON, C.G. (1928) *The Negro in our History* (5th ed.), Washington, DC: The Associated Publishers, Inc.

YERKES, R.M. (Ed) (1921) 'Psychological examining in the United States Army', *Memoirs of the National Academy of Sciences*, **15**, pp. 1–890.

YOUNG, K. (1922) *Mental Differences in Certain Immigration Groups: Psychological Tests of South Europeans in Typical California Schools with Bearing on the Educational Policy and on the Problems of Racial Contacts in this Country*, **1** (no. 11), Eugene, OR: University of Oregon Press.

Chapter 4

Deficit Thinking Models Based on Culture: The Anthropological Protest

Douglas E. Foley

This chapter will trace the shift in deficit thinking from a model based on genetics to one based on cultural attributes and behaviors. This transformation in deficit thinking was largely based on the appropriation of one particular anthropological theory of culture. Oscar Lewis' (1965) *'culture of poverty'* theory provided deficit thinkers with the type of culture concept that served well their ideological agenda. This selective, pernicious appropriation of anthropological theory did not go un-challenged, however. The response of anthropologists was resoundingly critical and can be broken into two general phases.

The first phase was marked by a strenuous effort to refute empirically the culture of poverty view of poor people. Many anthropologists produced a wide array of empirical studies on the politics, life-styles, families and value-orientations of low-income ethnic minority communities that cast them in an entirely different light than Lewis did. The second phase of the anthropological protest against culture-base deficit thinking produced a major reformulation of the culture concept and dismantled the ontological premises of Lewis' theory. Before recounting the anthro-pological response to deficit thinking, it is important to sketch why deficit thinkers had to replace a genetic model of deficit with a cultural model.

Changing Deficit Models: From Genetics to Culture

Through the 1940s and 1950s, many US scholars were left searching for models that eschewed the implicit racism of the earlier genetic pathology theory. As Valen-cia (Chapter 3, this volume) has discussed, beginning around 1930, the genetic pathology model of deficit thinking began a rapid decline in popularity and accept-ance. It is not surprising that a framework built on a foundation of hereditarianism and legitimized through pseudoscience would eventually collapse. A number of factors and events helped contribute to the demise of the genetic pathology model.

First, as Blum (1978) has noted, the eugenics movement of the 1920s was severely weakened by the impact of the Great Depression when some middle-class citizens became economically devastated. Such an experience was not supposed to happen, as the eugenicist position held that inherited limited intelligence caused poverty.

Second, the eugenics movement had its reputation further defiled by the atrocities occurring in Nazi Germany (Chase, 1977; cited in Blum, 1978). It appears that Hitler's racial purification program was inspired by the eugenics movement in the US and its success in getting sterilization laws passed. Thus, due to the rise of Hitler and Nazism many US eugenicists did not want to align themselves with any model and program that smacked of racism — as did the genetic pathology model. Blum observes:

> As England and America moved toward war with Germany, and Hitler's actions came to be viewed as less defensible, the number of persons who wanted to be considered eugenicists declined. The Carnegie Institution stopped funding the Eugenics Record Office in 1939; after that the movement was never more than a shadow of its former self. (1978: 65)

A third force, as described by Valencia (Chapter 3, this book), that contributed to the downfall of the genetic pathology model was the research and writings of some anthropologists, particularly Franz Boas (1911). Boas, an early critic of hereditarian pseudoscience through his debunking of craniometric arguments (Boas, 1899), repeatedly attacked white racial superiority theories in his forceful and influential writings from 1911 to the mid-1940s (Blum, 1978). As such, 'by 1945 racial theories were no longer considered scientifically respectable. Most psychologists decided that the hypothesis of black genetic inferiority should be abandoned' (Blum, 1978: 65).

Fourth, there was a sharp decline in research activity dealing with intelligence testing during the 1940s. In a review of intelligence testing publications in the general periodical literature (from 1910 to 1980), Haney (1981) observed that such research activity hit a peak in the 1920s, fell substantially in the 1930s and plummeted even further in the decade of the 1940s. Regarding intelligence testing research in which ethnic minority children/youth served as subjects, a similar trend has been observed. In a literature review of Mexican Americans and intelligence testing research, Valencia (1985) identified 18 journal articles published from 1920 to 1939 — but only one article was located that was published from 1940–49. His review suggests that the abrupt decline in intelligence testing research (in general and on ethnic minority groups in particular) was related to many scholars being absent from the world of research as they participated in World War II.

A fifth and final factor that contributed to a shift away from the genetic pathology model was a growing body of theory and research that challenged the beliefs about the immutability of intelligence. The foremost scholar was Jean Piaget, the noted Swiss child psychologist and professor of child psychology and history at the University of Geneva. Piaget (1926/1929) incorporated both genetic and environmental influences in his theorizing as to how children cognitively develop. Central to his theory was 'that the epigenesis of behavioral and thought structures derive from the invariant functions of accommodation and assimilation that operate in the child's continuous interaction with his environment...' (Hunt, 1961: 258). Piaget's theory of cognitive development, which contends that knowledge is derived from action, 'revolutionized and still dominates the study of human development' (Slavin, 1986: 34).

Another influential scholar was J. McV. Hunt, who in 1961, published *Intelligence and Experience*. Hunt developed new conceptions of intelligence and emphasized that environmental factors were critical in shaping intelligence. It should be noted, however, that Hunt was a deficit theorist, as he argued that the homes of the poor and minority — compared to white middle-class homes — were less likely to provide the necessary forms of cognitive stimulation.

In short, the five preceding factors were highly instrumental in the dissension of the genetic pathology model of deficit thinking. Although the hereditarian model itself was held in disrepute by the 1930s, deficit thinking in educational thought and practice would persist for decades to come.

Deficit Thinkers Appropriate the Culture of Poverty Theory

As deficit theorists began searching for a more cultural explanation of failure in school and life, many turned to the work of anthropologist Oscar Lewis and his *culture of poverty* theory. Lewis wrote a series of studies on the urban poor in Mexico, New York, Puerto Rico and Cuba (1959, 1961, 1965, 1966). He emphasized that people living in poverty tend to create a unique, self-sustaining life-style or way of life marked by a host of negative values, norms and social practices. The culture of poverty that is allegedly passed on to successive generations consisted of 70 traits which can be compressed into four clusters: 1) basic attitudes, values and character structure of poor people; 2) the nature of the poor's family system; 3) the nature of the slum community; and 4) the poor's social and civic relationship with the larger society.

Lewis' list of 'cultural traits' of the poor evokes a powerful negative image of poor people as a lazy, fatalistic, hedonistic, violent distrustful people living in common law unions, as well as in dysfunctional, female-centered authoritarian families who are chronically unemployed and rarely participate in local civic activities, vote or trust the police and political leaders. Lewis argues that the poor create an autonomous, distinct subculture or way of life that becomes encapsulated and self-perpetuating over generations. Ultimately, the poor's way of life, which is allegedly inferior to the mainstream way of life, keeps them impoverished. For anyone wanting to indict the poor, the culture of poverty theory is a powerful metaphor that spawns a sweeping, holistic image. It provides public policymakers and the general public with a relatively nontechnical, yet 'scientific' way to categorize and characterize all poor people.

One of the great ironies of Lewis' work is how critics of the poor misread and misused his theory for political ends. Lewis' ethnographic accounts of culture of poverty families are far more nuanced than the secondary accounts of his studies. A careful reading of his major books will reveal positive attributes and practices not listed among his 70 traits. Moreover, the texts contain little moralizing about the poor's immorality and lack of character. Lewis (1965) also qualified his theory with the bold assertion that the culture of poverty was found in capitalist countries only.

Unfortunately, his formal culture of poverty model was stated in such a categorical, objectivist manner that it was easy to appropriate as a literal, absolute truth claim. In the end, the subtleties of the actual accounts and Lewis' qualifying statements (Valentine *et al.*, 1969) vanished in the rhetorical bombast of his most ardent admirers. His work was generally used to provide a broader context in which to situate a variety of narrower linguistic, developmental psychology and parenting studies. Early critics of deficit thinking (see Ginsburg, 1972) concentrated more on debunking the myth of the deprived child, however, than on explicating how these thinkers created an interdisciplinary discourse based on a flawed theory of culture.

Ginsburg (1972) concentrated on how deficit thinkers of the 1960s emphasized linguistic and developmental deficiencies among the lower classes. Early deficit thinkers based their notion of language deficits on the work of British sociolinguist Basil Bernstein (1975). Bernstein portrayed middle-class children as using an 'elaborated code' characterized by the values of order, rationality, stability and the control of emotion. Their speech allegedly contained many relational and abstract terms suitable for complex intellectual activity.

In sharp contrast, lower-class children use a 'restricted code' with short simple, syntactically incomplete sentences, few subordinate if–then type clauses, limited adjectives and adverbs, and many idiomatic, concrete descriptive phrases. Such an impoverished language, it was argued, is much less suited for communicating complex ideas or relationships or doing the abstract reasoning tasks of academic work (Ginsburg, 1972). Lurking beneath this formulation is the general view of working-class families and parents as highly nonverbal, impulsive, authoritarian and dysfunctional. These parents fit neatly into Lewis' list of cultural traits that people living in a culture of poverty allegedly share.

Deficit thinkers also expanded their notion of a culturally deficient poor or lower-class family with studies of 'parenting styles' that purportedly retard intellectual development (Hess and Shipman, 1965, 1967). These studies often interviewed Aid to Families of Dependent Children (AFDC) welfare mothers and observed mother–child interactions in a sterile experimental setting. Such investigations concluded that middle-class parents prepare their children for tasks with better verbal feedback and less negative reinforcements. In contrast, lower-class parents are generally portrayed as more authoritarian, less verbal and less skilled parents. Moreover, the home environment is allegedly far less stimulus rich and orderly, hence deficient (see Pearl, Chapter 5, for an extended discussion of this deficit model). Once again, the image of the poor in Lewis' work is strikingly similar.

The 'way of life' that Lewis describes has all the deficient linguistic and familial practices, and much, much more. The more holistic culture of poverty concept allowed deficit thinkers to situate their more focused studies of negative linguistic and cognitive development in a much broader conceptual framework. Lewis describes a wide range of everyday cultural and community practices that are allegedly deficient in work ethic, morality and civic responsibility as well. His theory provided public policymakers with a much more accessible, dramatic popular image that the technical deficit studies of language, parenting and cognitive development lack. Public policymakers, seeking to indict the poor, fused culture of poverty and cultural deficit theories into a general, interdisciplinary discourse on poverty and the poor.

Michael Katz's book, entitled *The Undeserving Poor* (1989), brilliantly demonstrates how several generations of these policymakers have wielded what he calls a 'poverty discourse'. His study demonstrates a clear continuity from the 1960s War on Poverty liberals through the 1980s Reagan conservatives. Conservative policymakers turned liberal's paternalistic War on Poverty of the 1960s into a powerful rhetoric against big government and the welfare state. In the conservative view, the social benefits of the welfare state have destroyed poor people's work ethic and basic morality. Worse still, New Deal liberalism and its social welfare and affirmative action policies have helped perpetuate a pernicious, dependent culture of poverty among welfare recipients.

In sharp contrast, liberals, who embraced the culture of poverty/deficit perspective, were much more sanguine about the welfare state and its War on Poverty. The usual liberal package of education, job training, child care programs, food stamps and grants to single-parent mothers was supposed to help people lift themselves up by their bootstraps, not create dependent, morally bankrupt 'welfare slaves'. On the other hand, liberals like Daniel Moynihan (1965) shared the classist and racist bias of conservatives who viewed the black family as 'pathological' (i.e., matriarchal and lacking in male role models and networks of support). Moreover, such liberals also shared the conservative view of ghetto communities as dysfunctional and lacking in civic virtues. Ultimately, white liberals developed privileged middle-class institutions and life-styles in ways not unlike conservatives. Both ideological persuasions imagined the way of life of poor people as inferior to the white middle-class, mainstream way of life.

Katz (1989) documents how a host of the key academic writers, both liberal and conservative, debated fiercely the culture of poverty perspective, but he limits his discussion of the critics of culture of poverty/deficit thinking to Marxists. These leftist scholars generally shifted the blame for poverty from a deficient culture of the poor to an exploitive economic system that turns urban ghettos into internal colonies. What Katz leaves out of his account, however, is the way various anthropologists sought to counter deficit thinkers' misuse of the anthropological concept of culture.

Generating A Positive Empirical Portrait of Poor Peoples' Culture

Two seminal books (Leacock, 1971; Valentine, 1968) pointed out a variety of empirical, methodological and conceptual problems with Lewis' work. Leacock notes that non-anthropologists were drawn to his psychological notion of culture which was stripped of any historical and socioeconomic dimensions. She adds that Lewis' culture construct greatly exaggerates the continuity and power of intergenerational socialization. His model overstates the extent that any culture, especially a so-called culture of dysfunctional families and disorganized communities, can produce uniformly negative character, motivational, attitudinal and values traits in its residents.

Leacock (1971) goes on to say that a culture concept based on socialization and the transmission of cultural values invariably underestimates the autonomy of individuals to resist socialization, thus often understates in-group variation. She and others advocated replacing Lewis' highly abstract, universalistic set of largely negative traits with more situational studies of how cultural groups use their particular cultural traditions to adapt to historical circumstances. At this point, anthropologists and sociologists had not worked out an alternative model of the culture of the poor. The primary thrust of this early critique was to develop a host of empirical studies that refuted the culture of poverty theory.

The response of anthropology and various social scientists is far too widespread to document fully, but a new generation of post-sixties scholars arose, quickly challenging the images of a dysfunctional, negative culture of the poor. Robert Coles (1967), the Harvard psychiatrist turned social critic, generated what may be the most exhaustive, accessible set of empirical studies on children from all races who live in poverty. Armed with a tape recorder, Coles produced heart-rending portraits that leave little doubt about the resiliency and character of poor people. Oral historian Studs Turkle (1972) added an equally impressive, highly accessible volume on the dignity of the American working class.

More formal anthropological and sociological studies of poor whites (Howells, 1973; Rubin, 1976), African Americans (Hannerz, 1969; Williams, 1981), and Chicanos (Anchor, 1978; Foley et al., 1977) also generate in-depth portraits of functioning low-income communities with positive values and social practices. Hannerz' (1969) portrait of a ghetto in Washington DC suggests a dynamic African American culture with a diverse range of adaptive strategies. Foley's et al. (1977) study of the civil rights movement in a South Texas town highlights high levels of civic pride and political activism among low-income Chicanos. The previously cited community studies are a selective sample of scholarly works that refute the culture of poverty view of poor communities as socially disorganized and uninvolved in civic affairs.

In addition, various scholars of the African American family (Ashenbrenner, 1975; Stack, 1974; Willie, 1976) and of Chicano family and gender roles (Baca Zinn, 1980; Montiel, 1970; Paredes, 1993) attacked the notions of pathological, broken authoritarian families with poor parenting models. Stack's (1974) now classic study of the black extended family confounds the image of female-dominated, male-absent, socially disorganized single-parent families. The women in Stack's study bond together and practice collective childrearing while various males — brothers, uncles, boyfriends and street-corner men — provide role models for the children. Stack and others (Ashenbrenner, 1975; Willie, 1976) suggested that a new more flexible single-parent family, based on traditional African norms of reciprocity and extended kinship, was common in low-income communities.

As the years have passed, various ethnic minority scholars produced additional studies of African Americans (Dickerson, 1995; McAdoo, 1988; Sudakarsa, 1988). African American scholars have rejected earlier studies that labeled the African American family pathological, that emphasized matriarchy, high rates of illegitimacy, and the lack of male parenting models. They have called for more studies of functioning, stable working-class families (Dodson, 1988; Willie, 1976) and of single-parent, female-centered families (Dickerson, 1995). Their efforts are directed at showing that the middle-class ideal of a two-parent nuclear family has been replaced by a variety of less conventional, yet functional families (Littlejohn and Darling, 1993). Many of these studies also attempt to refute earlier assimilationist studies that overemphasize the impact of slavery at the expense of African cultural practices. Unlike Lewis' culture of poverty theory that obliterates historical cultural differences, these scholars take ethnic cultural traditions seriously.

A second wave of Latino family studies (Alvarez, 1987; Baca Zinn, 1989; Griswold del Castillo, 1984; Williams, 1990; Zavella, 1987) continues to attack the mythological mainstream model of family (Taylor, 1989) that underpins many deficit studies of ethnic minority families (Montiel, 1970). These studies have begun to challenge the stereotypic gender roles of domineering, emotionally distant 'macho' males and of dependent, passive females (Baca Zinn, 1980, 1989; Mirande, 1986). In addition, Williams (1990) highlights social class differences in the Mexican American family and the continuing importance of traditional religious rituals and values in low-income families. The new wave of family studies suggests that the culture of poverty view of poor families conflates the families of 'underclass' or 'lumpen proletariat' with stable, productive working-class families. Such a sweeping, negative view of 'non-white minority' families overstates greatly the utility of the culture of poverty theory.

On the linguistic front, various sociolinguists (Baratz and Shuey, 1969; Cazden, John and Hymes, 1972; Kochman, 1972; Labov, Cohen, Robins and Lewis, 1968) have attacked the notion of the poor as having a restricted, less abstract, simpler language code and cognitive reasoning style. As in the community studies, they emphasize a host of positive linguistic differences, not language deficiencies. Labov, *et al.* thoroughly demolishes the mainstream notion of a 'non-standard' form of English. He shows convincingly that African Americans speak a unique dialect of English that incorporates various non-standard English linguistic resources.

Both Labov *et al.* (1986) and Kochman (1972) also show the poetic richness of the African American dialect. A second wave of sociolinguistic studies demonstrate that African American oral (Baugh, 1983) and literacy practices (Heath, 1983) were equally rich and complex. Studies of Chicano dialect (Hernandez-Chavez, Cohen, and Beltramo, 1975; Sanchez, 1983) and folkloric and expressive culture performances (Limón, 1994; Paredes, 1993) head in a similar direction. In sum, the notion of poor people having an impoverished speech style or 'restricted' cognitive code is untenable in the face of numerous linguistic and folkloric studies.

Educational anthropologists working out of a sociolinguistic paradigm of culture generated an even more direct refutation of the linguistic deficit thesis. Several excellent studies of minority children — African American (Heath, 1983), American Indian (Erickson and Mohatt, 1982; Philips, 1983), and indigenous Hawaiian

The Evolution of Deficit Thinking

(Au and Jordan, 1981; Boggs, 1985) — highlight how linguistic differences, not linguistic deficits, help explain poor school performance. These studies of mis-communication (Foley, 1991) shift the blame for school failure to pedagogies organized around mainstream speech styles and highly standardized lessons (Mehan, 1979). The sociolinguists emphasize important cultural differences in oral speech styles and home literacy practices that put minority youth at a disadvantage.

Reconceptualizing the Culture of Poverty as a 'Class Culture'

Meanwhile, some sociologists began transforming Lewis' conceptually vague notion of 'the poor' with extended debates on the cultural attributes of social classes. Historically, sociologists have conceptualized social classes from either a Marxian or a Weberian perspective (Foley, 1990). Classical Marxists emphasize that the great mass of wage laborers are a relatively powerless, economically exploited group with common interest to overthrow the capitalist class who controls the society. This view of classes as antagonistic political groups says a great deal about the psychology or political 'consciousness' of the working class but relatively little about a distinct working-class culture or way of life. Marx never conceptualized the working-class as a culture in the anthropological sense.

In sharp contrast, the German sociologist Max Weber, a major critic of Marxism, reconceptualized social classes as 'status groups'. Weber was much more interested than Marx in viewing social classes as cultural groups with different life-styles, thus different value orientations, occupations, and patterns of consumption. The Weberian concept of class as a subjective, shared group orientation has a strong family resemblance to the anthropological concept of culture as socialization.

Although Oscar Lewis never explicitly grounded his culture of poverty concept in class theory, he talks about subcultures the way Weber talks about status groups, that is, as life-styles with specific value orientations. Had Lewis been familiar with the sociological debates over class cultures, he probably would have adopted a Weberian perspective of class. Unfortunately, for Lewis and those who have uncritically adopted his view, he never differentiated among various poor people; or as class theorists would put it, Lewis never differentiated among various sectors of the working class. As we shall see, the indiscriminate classification of all working-class people as 'the poor' is the Achilles heel of Lewis' theory. This theoretical lacuna becomes clear when one contrasts his theory to the more nuanced perspective of class cultures in modern sociology. The sociological debate over class cultures generates a more sophisticated perspective of the working class than a culture of poverty view.

Initially, mainstream sociologists used a Weberian perspective of classes to produce a model of the American class structure which had six levels, ranging from lower-lower to upper-upper class (Warner, 1949). Along with the studies of occupational rankings (Duncan, 1967), many American sociologists searched for a common value system that united all social classes in a national occupational/life-style status hierarchy. Not until the turbulent 1960s do questions of change, conflict and inequality come to the fore in studies of stratification.

As sociologists began reacting to the culture of poverty thesis in the 1960s, they developed a more complex view of the culture of working-class people (Gans, 1968; Liebow, 1967; Rainwater, 1970; Rodman, 1963). Initially, they viewed the lower class as having relatively minor value differences from the mainstream society that were temporary rationalizations of oppressive circumstances. For these 1960s sociologists, a distinct subculture does develop among the poor, but it is portrayed as far less intractable and different than Lewis portrayed it. Liebow (1967) affords us a particularly poignant view of black street corner men struggling unsuccessfully to be more 'mainstream' in value orientations.

A second major theme in sociological studies of class revolved around what came to be called the 'embourgeoisment thesis' (Goldthorpe, Lockwood, Bechhofer and Platt, 1969). Writers in this vein (Berger, 1960) emphasized that the working class was becoming a consumer class that shared basic mainstream value orientations. This type of Weberian class analysis also emphasized that the working class had a semi-autonomous 'class culture.' Frank Parkin (1971) summarizes both Weberian themes with his portrayal of the shrinking gap between working-class and mainstream culture in a consumer society.

Other sociologists in France gave the Weberian view of social classes as lifestyles an original Marxian twist. Pierre Bourdieu's (1984) opus on 'taste cultures' laid out empirically the vast differences between working- and middle-class culture in aesthetics, consumption patterns and everyday linguistic and expressive cultural practices. He conceptualized these class cultural differences as a form of 'symbolic capital' that the public schools and other high cultural institutions, such as museums, theater, opera, symphony, distribute unequally to the privileged classes, thus 'reproduce culturally' social class inequalities (Bourdieu and Passeron, 1977).

In Bourdieu's formulation, class cultural differences are not rational adaptations to the harshness of poverty. Unlike many American sociologists and Oscar Lewis, Bourdieu's 'taste culture' paradigm contains no psychologizing or moralizing about the working-class' immorality, civic inactivity or pathological family systems (however, for a perspective that Bourdieu does contribute to deficit thinking, see Pearl, Chapter 5, this book). He concentrates on showing how cultural institutions ideologically reproduce invidious class culture differences through the 'symbolic violence' of imposing middle-class taste culture and language upon the working-class (Bourdieu and Passeron, 1977). This perspective on class cultures, which is aptly labeled 'cultural Marxism', has become very popular in anthropological circles (Brightman, 1995).

Writing from a somewhat more traditional Marxist perspective, British historian E.P. Thompson (1963) created a very positive portrait of the culture of British working-class communities. Inspired by Italian Marxist Antonio Gramsci (1971), other British sociologists emphasized the vibrant local institutions, large extended families, unique folklore, sports, music, pubs and political organizations of working-class communities (Clarke, Critcher and Johnson, 1979). In anthropological terms, the working class' distinct 'expressive culture' was created from both traditional folk art and from their appropriation of mass popular cultural forms. From this perspective, working-class culture was not a failed copy of mainstream culture that American sociologists found in black street culture.

According to British sociologists, what was being passed from generation to generation was pride in one's working-class origins. In his now classic study of working-class lads, Paul Willis (1982) portrayed how working-class school youth drew upon the vibrant, shop floor culture of their fathers to create a rebellious anti-school subculture. In effect, the studies of class cultures conducted at the Center for Contemporary Cultural Studies at Birmingham University replaced the pessimistic culture of poverty view with an optimistic view of working-class people's strong, semi-autonomous culture. These studies of working-class culture are part of a much larger reformulation of the culture concept taking place in American cultural anthropology (Marcus and Fischer, 1986).

Reconceptualizing the Anthropological Concept of Culture with Theories of Class Culture and Ethnicity

The influence of British and French contemporary cultural studies scholars (Brantlinger, 1990) has been enormous in American anthropology. As the 1970s shaded into the 1980s, a new, more philosophical debate swept anthropology and has shaken the foundations of cultural theory (Clifford, 1989; Marcus and Fischer, 1986). Intense debates between postmodernists, cultural Marxists, critical theorists, feminists and ethnic minority scholars has produced a thorough critique of earlier models of culture. The debate over models of culture is, of course, a manifestation of a much broader philosophical revolt against positivistic, functionalist social science theories and methods (Bernstein, 1983; Polkinghorn, 1983).

Contemporary critical cultural theorists emphasize practice, agency, constructivism, contradiction, contestation, change and intercultural variation (Brightman, 1995). As Brightman points out, a new paradigm may be emerging that has injected sociological constructs of class and power into the anthropological concept of culture. Many contemporary anthropologists (Appadurai, 1990; Clifford, 1994; Fox, 1991; Harrison, 1991; Rosaldo, 1989) have completely dismantled the static model of culture as socialization passing a coherent, shared value systems from generation to generation. Such a view of American society and the cultures of ethnic Americans cannot explain the complex fusions of cultural practice found in many ethnic or 'hybrid' and 'borderland' cultures (Gilroy, 1993; Foley, 1995; Rosaldo, 1989). Nor do static socialization models of culture challenge the persistence of class, race and gender inequalities in American society.

This general shift in anthropological thinking has informed various ethnic minority scholars writing about working-class Chicano and African American culture. Their reconceptualizations of ethnicity and ethnic cultures contain some of the best critiques of poverty/deficit thinking. Americo Paredes (1993), a leading Chicano folklorist, and several of his students (Limón, 1994; Peña, 1985, 1996) have produced a provocative body of work on the 'expressive culture' of Mexican Americans. Texas Mexican Americans have resisted racial stereotypes and ideological domination through their verbal art, music and dance, which is a complex blend of traditional Mexican and modern American popular cultural practices. Coupled with recent studies of the family (Alvarez, 1987; Williams, 1990; Zavella, 1987) language (Sanchez, 1983) and cultural politics (Foley *et al.*, 1988, 1990), the culture of working-class Mexican Americans is clearly a robust variant of working-class culture found in Britain.

African American scholars have also developed an interesting response to the recent revival of culture of poverty and deficit thinking. Anthropologist Ted Gordon (1995) has produced a major review of studies on African American culture and males. Gordon finds a new generation of African American scholars working out of a critical cultural studies paradigm (Anderson, 1990; hooks, 1992; Naison, 1992; West, 1994). They are challenging essentializing notions of a pathological black family system and an immoral, destructive street culture in several important new ways.

These African American scholars highlight the respectability or virtues and solidarity in African American community and family traditions as opposed to an 'outlaw culture' of 'cool' and 'reputation' that a segment of African American males living on the mean streets of urban America have embraced (Majors and Billson, 1992; Naison, 1992). African American scholars emphasize that a segment of their community has appropriated an extreme version of mainstream individualism and hedonistic consumption characteristic of a capitalist culture. They characterize this cool, hip street culture as an extreme, nihilistic form of predatory entrepreneurship. Such deviant cultural practices have little to do with the communal, deeply spiritual values passed from generation to generation in most African American communities.

These new race-based theories of ethnic culture make two crucial distinctions that Oscar Lewis failed to make. First, Lewis acknowledged that the culture of poverty only existed in capitalist countries, but he failed to distinguish between the vast productive working-class and the chronically unemployed lumpen proletariat or 'underclass' (Massey and Denton, 1993). Second, he never acknowledged the positive pre-capitalist cultural traditions of various ethnic immigrant communities trapped in decaying urban economies. Instead, Lewis essentializes all poor as a 'cultural other' with the cultural traits and practices of the most downtrodden class sector.

In retrospect, Lewis' lack of familiarity with sociological theories of class and his downplaying of positive, distinct ethnic working-class cultural traditions are serious deficiencies. Such blind spots in his theory have made it susceptible to appropriation for ideological purposes. Too often, hard-working, stable working-class people from all races and cultures have been portrayed as a morally reprehensible category that Katz (1989) so aptly labels 'the undeserving poor'.

Recent Trends in Anthropological Studies of Minority Education

The aforementioned theoretical debates over the constructs of class and class cultures have gradually filtered into educational anthropology and the studies of ethnic minorities. Earlier sociolinguistic and community–school studies of minority youth tended to focus on why these youth failed in mainstream schools (Foley, 1991). One of the most important general explanations in the literature is John Ogbu's thesis that colonized, conquered 'involuntary minorities' (African Americans, Mexican Americans and Native Americans) developed oppositional cultures to school that were self-defeating (Ogbu, 1991). Those African American youth who did exhibit the optimism and effort necessary to succeed in white mainstream schools often had to 'act white' and assimilate culturally (Fordham and Ogbu, 1986). Although Ogbu and the sociolinguists explain why some minorities have failed, they tend to underemphasize the factors leading to success and empowerment.

More recently, a number of anthropologists, many influenced by the paradigmatic shift in cultural anthropology, have focused on why some minority youth succeed in school. In a recent special edition of the *Anthropology and Education Quarterly*, a number of anthropologists document the empowering practices and moments of minority youth and community (Ernst, Statzner and Trueba, 1994). Of special note is the work of Delgado-Gaitan on parental involvement (1990) and family narratives (1994), and of Velez-Ibañez and Greenberg (1992) on community 'funds of knowledge'. Far from being passive and fatalistic, low-income Mexican American parents are active in civic and school affairs and draw upon a rich fund of community knowledge (also, see Valencia and Solórzano, Chapter 6, this book).

Other developments in Afrocentric philosophies of education (Asante, 1987; Collins, 1990), and pedagogy (Delpit, 1988; Foster, 1993; Henry, 1992) suggest a new emphasis among ethnic minority educators on cultural politics. Others have focused on the assertiveness of ethnic minority students. Solomon (1992) and MacLeod (1987) document the cultural resistance among Afro Caribbean and African American high school students, yet these same students accept an achievement ideology. In related studies, Foley (1990) describes how middle-class Mexican American adolescents manage their images to achieve school success, and Harklau (1994) shows how Asian Americans negotiate their way out of lower tracks and remedial language programs. There is also the ethnographic (communication process perspective) study of Ronda and Valencia (1994) of middle-school, 'at-risk' Chicano students who were found to both reproduce *and* resist the at-risk label given to them.

Other anthropologists are searching for ways to empower minority youth through cultural therapy and ethnic consciousness-raising (Trueba and Zou, 1995) or critical pedagogical approaches. Others, working out of a cultural production perspective, are documenting how subordinate groups are actively constructing positive individual and cultural identities (Levinson, Foley, and Holland, 1996). What all these studies, and many others not cited, emphasize are ethnic cultural pride and community practices which empower individuals and groups. The shift towards a much more dynamic model of culture that takes into account power and cultural politics is obvious in the 'new anthropology of education'. All of these studies have left the culture of poverty concept of culture and deficit thinking in the dust bin of intellectual history.

Summing Up

This chapter used a critical cultural studies perspective to reinterpret the culture of poverty/cultural deficit debate of the 1960s and 70s. To this end, I have abandoned Lewis' conceit that culture is a 'neutral', apolitical transmission or socialization process between generations. Such a perspective assumes that the study of any group's culture is never this innocent, apolitical, neutral, objective enterprise. Consequently, many cultural anthropologists have redefined the traditional descriptive study of a cultural group as the study of how competing cultural groups — divided along class, racial and gender lines — socially construct images of each other (Foley, 1995).

Following recent trends in cultural studies (Brightman, 1995), I have utilized constructs of culture from Michel Foucault (1980) and Antonio Gramsci (1971) to rethink the culture of poverty/cultural deficit debate. From a Foucaldian perspective, the leaders of postindustrial societies typically maintain political order through a complex mix of popular (political) and professional (social science and public policymakers) opinion-makers. These opinion-makers use cultural institutions such as the media and schools to create powerful public discourses or discursive regimes that construct images of threatening, marginalized groups or cultural others.

Other critical theorists have pointed out (Habermas, 1971), that class interests lurk behind such discursive regimes and their images of marginalized groups. Antonio Gramsci's (1971) notion of a 'historical bloc' or class alliance between various political elite, public policymakers and cultural workers (scholars, journalists) makes Foucault's notion of a discursive regime more concrete and sociological. From Gramsci's perspective, a historical bloc invariably tries to preserve the ruling class by making its ideas the ruling ideas or conventional wisdoms of the times. In this particular case, the poverty policymakers and their intellectual allies become a historical bloc in post-World War II America that sought to regulate a growing, threatening urban underclass.

Unfortunately, few contemporary historians have chronicled how America's poverty intellectuals and policymakers rule, but Michael Katz's (1989) study is highly suggestive. He details how these policymakers and intellectuals developed a poverty discourse, based on culture of poverty/deficit thinking, to advance their political interests over poor people of color (also, see Valencia and Solórzano, Chapter 6, this volume). What Katz (1989) did not show, however, was the oppositional discourse that developed among the marginalized and their intellectual allies (for such discourse, see the recent book by Swadener and Lubeck, 1995).

Following Gramsci (1971), a counter-hegemonic bloc of scholars, many products of the turbulent 1960s era with ethnic and working-class backgrounds, emerged to speak out against deficit and culture of poverty thinking. As we saw earlier, many anthropologists and sociologists rebelled against the poverty/deficit paradigm. They produced a host of empirical studies and eventually a new paradigm for the study of culture that is informed by theories of class and class cultures (also, see Valencia, Chapter 3, this volume, who also finds considerable heterodoxy by anthropologists and psychologists during the genetic pathology era).

Hopefully, this account of some anthropologists' counter-hegemonic struggle against poverty/deficit thinking will help educational researchers and policymakers understand that selecting a conceptual model is never easy. The culture of poverty/ cultural deficit debate leaves a vivid legacy of how images of cultural others were created in highly politicized contexts. In this case, Lewis' pseudoscientific theory of the poor never served their interest, but it *did* serve the interest of reactionary politicians and policymakers. At this point, few cultural anthropologists familiar with this debate imagine that the cultural descriptions they produce will be read in the manner intended. Moreover, most would eschew a construct of culture devoid of cultural politics and power considerations. Constructs of culture that emphasize socialization and cultural continuity are too easily appropriated for reactionary political ends.

Despite these conceptual advances, various hegemonic discourses of the American ruling bloc are alive and well. American society seems to be experiencing a depressing revival of racist, classist and sexist thinking, epitomized by the publication of *The Bell Curve* (see Valencia and Solorzano, Chapter 6, this volume). Anthropologists like myself are astonished by the resiliency of deficit and culture of poverty thinking. Various economists, psychologists and educators continue to ply these racist and classist theories against working-class people of color. Apparently, they simply ignore the new empirical studies and paradigms of culture.

To better understand why this discourse is so resilient, we must explore what various psychologists were writing during the 1960s and 1970s. The psychological discourse on deficit thinking and poverty is crucial for at least two reasons. First, psychologists were the primary group of social scientists during this era who produced a deficit discourse for (and embraced by) educators and public policymakers. Thus, it is imperative to examine what these scholars contributed to the general discourse on deficit thinking. Second, deficit thinking — with respect to targeted populations of the poor, Latinos and African Americans — hit an apex in theorizing, production of publications, and recommendations for educational practice during this period. In the next chapter, Art Pearl provides an analysis of this era and these developments by focusing on the Cultural and Accumulated Environmental Deficit Models.

References

ALVAREZ, R. (1987) *Familia: Migration and Adaptation in Baja and Alta California*, Berkeley, CA: University of California Press.

ANCHOR, S. (1978) *Mexican Americans in a Dallas Barrio*, Tucson, AZ: University of Arizona Press.

ANDERSON, E. (1990) *Streetwise: Race, Class and Change in the Urban Community*, Chicago, IL: University of Chicago Press.

APPADURAI, A. (1990) 'Disjuncture and difference in the global cultural economy', *Public Culture*, 1, pp. 1–24.

ASANTE, M. (1987) *The Afrocentric Idea*, Philadelphia, PA: Temple University Press.

ASCHENBRENNER, J. (1975) *Lifelines: Black Families in Chicago*, New York: Holt, Rinehart and Winston.

AU, K.H. and JORDAN, C. (1981) 'Teaching reading to Hawaiian children: Finding a culturally appropriate solution', in TRUEBA, H., GUTHRIE, G. and AU, K.H. (Eds) *Culture and the Bilingual Classroom*, Rawley, MA: Newbury House, pp. 139–52.

BACA ZINN, M. (1980) 'Chicano men and masculinity' *Journal of Ethnic Studies*, **10**, pp. 19–44.

BACA ZINN, M. (1989) 'Family, race and poverty in the eighties', *Signs: Journal of Women in Culture and Society*, **14**, pp. 856–73.

BARATZ, J. and SHUEY, R. (Eds) (1969) *Teaching Black Children to Read*, Washington, DC: Center for Applied Linguistics.

BAUGH, J. (1983) *Black Street Speech: Its History, Structure and Survival*, Austin, TX: University of Texas Press.

BERGER, B. (1960) *Working Class Suburb*, Berkeley, CA: University of California Press.

BERNSTEIN, B. (1975) *Class, Codes and Control*, London: Routledge.

BERNSTEIN, R. (1983) *Beyond Objectivism and Relativism*, Oxford, England: Basil Blackwell.

BLUM, J. (1978) *Pseudoscience and Mental Ability: The Origins and Fallacies of the IQ Controversy*, New York: Monthly Review Press.

BOAS, F. (1899) 'The cephallic index', *American Anthropology*, **1**, pp. 448–61.

BOAS, F. (1911) *The Mind of Primitive Man*, New York: Macmillan.

BOGGS, S. with WATSON-GEGEO, K. and MCMILLEN, G. (1985) *Speaking, Relating and Learning: A Study of Hawaiian Children at Home and at School*, Norwood, NJ: Ablex.

BOURDIEU, P. (1984) *Distinctions: A Social Critique of the Judgment of Taste*, Cambridge, MA: Harvard University Press.

BOURDIEU, P. and PASSERON, C. (1977) *Reproduction in Education, Society and Culture*, Newbury, CA: Sage.

BRANTLINGER, P. (1990) *Crusoe's Footprints: Cultural Studies in Britain and America*, New York: Routledge.

BRIGHTMAN, R. (1995) 'Forget culture: Replacement, transcendence, relexification', *Cultural Anthropology*, **10**, pp. 509–46.

CAZDEN, C., JOHN, V. and HYMES, D. (Eds) (1972) *Functions of Language in the Classroom*, New York: Teachers College Press.

CHASE, A. (1977) *The Legacy of Malthus*, New York: Knopf.

CLARKE, J., CRITCHER, C. and JOHNSON, R. (1979) *Working Class Culture: Studies in History and Theory*, London: Hutchinson.

CLIFFORD, J. (1989) *The Predicament of Culture*, Cambridge, MA: Harvard University Press.

CLIFFORD, J. (1994) 'Diasporas', *Cultural Anthropology*, **9**, pp. 302–38.

COLES, R. (1967) *Children of Crises: A Study of Courage and Fear* (**1–3**), Boston, MA: Little, Brown.

COLLINS, P.H. (1990) *Black Feminist Thought: Knowledge, Consciousness and Pedagogy*, Boston, MA: Unwin Hyman.

DELGADO-GAITAN, C. (1990) *Literacy for Empowerment: The Role of Parents in Children's Education*, London: Falmer Press.

DELGADO-GAITAN, C. (1994) 'Consejos: The power of cultural narratives', *Anthropology and Education Quarterly*, **25**, pp. 298–316.

DELPIT, L. (1988) 'The silenced dialogue: Power and pedagogy in educating other people's children', *Harvard Educational Review*, **58**, pp. 280–98.

DICKERSON, B. (Ed) (1995) *African American Single Mothers: Understanding their Lives and Families*, Newbury, CA: Sage.

DODSON, J. (1988) 'Conceptualizations of black families', in MCADOO, H.P. (Ed) *Black Families*, Newbury, CA: Sage, pp. 77–89.

DUNCAN, O.D. (1967) *The American Occupational Structure*, New York: Free Press.

ERICKSON, F. and MOHATT, G. (1982) 'Cultural participation structures in two classrooms of Indian students', in SPINDLER, G. (Ed) *Doing the Ethnography of Schooling*, New York: Holt, Rinehart & Winston, pp. 132–75.

ERNST, G., STATZNER, E. and TRUEBA, H.T. (Eds) (1994) 'Alternate visions of schooling: Success stories in minority settings' [Special issue], *Anthropology and Education Quarterly*, **25**, (3).

FOLEY, D. (1995) *The Heartland Chronicles*, Philadelphia, PA: University of Pennsylvania Press.

FOLEY, D. (1990) *Learning Capitalist Culture: Deep in the Heart of Tejas*, Philadelphia: University of Pennsylvania Press.

FOLEY, D. (1991) 'Anthropological explanations of minority school failure', *Anthropology and Education Quarterly*, **4**, pp. 60–86.

FOLEY, D. with MOTA, C., POST, D. and LOZANO, I. (1977) *From Peones to Politicos: Class and Ethnicity in a South Texas Town, 1900–1977*, Austin: University of Texas Press.

FOLEY, D. with MOTA, C., POST, D. and LOZANO, I. (1988) *From Peones to Politicos: Class and Ethnicity in a South Texas Town, 1900–1987*, Austin: University of Texas Press.

FORDHAM, S. and OGBU, J. (1986) 'Black students' school success: Coping with the "burden of acting White"', *Urban Review*, **18**, pp. 176–206.

FOSTER, M. (1993) 'Educating for competence in community and culture: Exploring the views of exemplary African-American teachers', *Urban Education*, **27**, pp. 370–94.

FOUCAULT, M. (1980) *Power and Knowledge: Selected Interviews and Other Writings*, New York: Pantheon Books.

FOX, R. (Ed) (1991) *Recapturing Anthropology: Working in the Present*, Santa Fe, NM: School of American Research Press.

GANS, H. (1968) 'Culture and class in the study of poverty: An approach to anti-poverty research', in MOYNIHAN, P. (Ed) *On Understanding Poverty: Perspectives from the Social Sciences*, New York: Basic Books, pp. 201–28.

GILROY, P. (1993) *Black Atlantis: Modernity and Double Consciousness*, Cambridge, MA: Harvard University Press.

GINSBURG, H. (1972) *The Myth of the Deprived Child: Poor Children's Intellect and Education*, Englewood Cliffs, NJ: Prentice-Hall.

GOLDTHORPE, H., LOCKWOOD, D., BECHHOFER, F. and PLATT, J. (1969) *The Affluent Worker in the Class Structure*, London: Cambridge University Press.

GORDON, T. (1995) 'Cultural politics of the African-American male experience', Unpublished manuscript, Austin, TX: Department of Anthropology, The University of Texas.

GRAMSCI, A. (1971) *Prison Notebooks*, New York: International Publishers.

GRISWOLD DEL CASTILLO, R. (1984) *Chicano Families in the Urban Southwest: 1848 to Present*, South Bend, IN: Notre Dame University Press.

HABERMAS, J. (1971) *Knowledge and Human Interest*, Boston, MA: Beacon Press.

HANEY, W. (1981) 'Validity, vaudeville and values: A short history of social concerns about standardized testing', *American Psychologist*, **36**, pp. 1021–34.

HANNEZ, U. (1969) *Soulside: Inquiries into Ghetto Culture and Community*, New York: Columbia University Press.

HARRISON, F. (1991) *Decolonizing Anthropology: Moving Further Toward an Anthropology for Liberation*, Washington, DC: Association of Black Anthropologists. American Anthropological Association.

HARKLAU, L. (1994) 'Jumping tracks: How language minorities negotiate evaluations of ability', *Anthropology and Education Quarterly*, **25**, pp. 347–62.

HEATH, S.B. (1983) *Ways with Words: Language, Life and Work in Communities and Classrooms*, New York: Cambridge University Press.

HENRY, A. (1992) 'African Canadian women teachers' activism: Recreating communities of caring and resistance', *Journal of Negro Education*, **61**, pp. 392–404.

HERNANDEZ-CHAVEZ, E., COHEN, A.D. and BELTRAMO, A.F. (Eds) (1975) *El Lenguaje de los Chicanos: Regional and Social Characteristics used by Mexican-Americans*, Arlington, VA: Center for Applied Linguistics.

HESS, R.D. and SHIPMAN, V. (1965) 'Early experience and socialization of cognitive modes in children', *Child Development*, **36**, pp. 869–86.

HESS, R.D. and SHIPMAN, V. (1967) 'Cognitive elements in maternal behavior', in HILL, J.P. (Ed) *Minnesota Symposia on Child Psychology* (**1**), Minneapolis, MN: University of Minnesota Press, pp. 57–81.

hooks, b. (1992) *Black Looks: Race and Representation*, Boston, MA: South End Press.

HOWELLS, J.T. (1973) *Hard Living on Clay Street: Portraits of Blue Collar Families*, New York: Anchor.

HUNT, J. McV. (1961) *Intelligence and Experience*, New York: Ronald Press.

KATZ, M.B. (1989) *The Undeserving Poor: From the War on Poverty to the War on Welfare*, New York: Pantheon.

KOCHMAN, T. (Ed) (1972) *Rappin' and Stylin' Out: Communication in Urban Black America*, Urbana IL: University of Illinois Press.

LABOV, W., COHEN, P., ROBINS, C. and LEWIS, J. (1968) *A Study of the Non-standard English of Negro and Puerto Rican Speakers in New York City* (**1–2**), Washington, DC: Office of Education.

LEACOCK, E. (Ed) (1971) *The Culture of Poverty: A Critique*, New York: Simon and Schuster.

LEVINSON, B., FOLEY, D.E. and HOLLAND, D. (Eds) (1996) *The Cultural Production of the Educated Person: Critical Ethnographies of Local Practice*, Buffalo, NY: State University of New York Press.

LEWIS, O. (1959) *Five Families: Mexican Case Studies in the Culture of Poverty*, New York: Basic Books.

LEWIS, O. (1961) *The Children of Sanchez*, New York: Random House.

LEWIS, O. (1965) The Culture of Poverty, *Scientific American*, **215**, 19–25.

LEWIS, O. (1966) *La Vida: A Puerto Rican Family in the Culture of Poverty*, New York: Random House.

LIEBOW, E. (1967) *Talley's Corner: A Study of Negro Street Corner Men*, Boston, MA: Little Brown Co.

LIMÓN, J. (1994) *Dancing with the Devil: Society and Cultural Poetics in Mexican-American South Texas*, Madison WI: University of Wisconsin Press.

LITTLEJOHN, S.M. and DARLING, C.A. (1993) 'Understanding the strengths of African American families', *Journal of Black Studies*, **23**, pp. 160–71.

MAJORS, R. and BILLSON, J.M. (1992) *Cool Pose: The Dilemmas of Black Manhood in America*, New York: Lexington Books.

MARCUS, G. and FISCHER, M. (1986) *Anthropology as Cultural Critique*, Chicago, IL: University of Chicago Press.

MASSEY, D.S. and DENTON, N.A. (1993) *American Apartheid: Segregation and the Making of the Underclass*, Cambridge, MA: Harvard University Press.

MACLEOD, J. (1987) *Ain't no Makin' it: Leveled Aspirations in a Low-income Neighborhood*, Boulder, CO: Westview Press.

McAdoo, H.P. (Ed) (1988) *Black Families*, Newbury, CA: Sage.

Mehan, H. (1979) *Learning Lessons: Social Organization in the Classroom*, Cambridge, MA: Harvard University Press.

Mirande, A. (1986) *Chicano Fathers: Response and Adaptation to Emergent Roles*, Stanford, CA: Stanford University Press.

Montiel, M. (1970) 'The social science myth of the Mexican American family', *El Grito: A Journal of Contemporary Mexican American Thought*, **3**, pp. 56–63.

Moynihan, D. (1965) *The Negro Family: The Case for National Action*, Washington, DC: Office of Planning and Research, US Department of Labor.

Naison, M. (1992) 'Outlaw culture and black neighborhoods', *Reconstruction*, **1**, pp. 128–131.

Ogbu, J. (1991) 'Immigrants and minorities in comparative perspective', in Gibson, M. and Ogbu, J. (Eds) *Minority Status and Schooling: Comparative Study of Immigrant and Involuntary Minorities*, New York: Garland, pp. 3–33.

Paredes, A. (1993) *Folklore and Culture on the Texas–Mexican border*. Austin, TX: University of Texas Press, Center For Mexican American Studies.

Parkin, F. (1971) *Class Inequality and Political Order*, New York: Praeger.

Peña, M. (1985) *The Texas–Mexican Conjunto: History of a Working-class Music*, Austin, TX: University of Texas Press.

Peña, M. (1996) *Mexican American Orchestra: Music, Culture and the Dialectic of Conflict*, Austin, TX: University of Texas Press.

Philips, S.U. (1983) *The Invisible Culture: Communication in Classroom and Community on the Warm Springs Indian Reservation*, New York: Longman.

Piaget, J. (1929) *The Child's Conception of the World* (Tomlinson, J. and A., Trans.) New York: Harcourt, Brace, & World. (Original work published 1926).

Polkinghorn, D. (1983) *Methodology for the Human Sciences: Systems of Inquiry*, Albany, NY: State University of New York Press.

Rainwater, L. (1970) 'The problem of lower-class culture', *Journal of Social Issues*, **26**, pp. 133–48.

Rodman, H. (1963) 'The lower class values stretch', *Social Forces*, **42**, pp. 205–15.

Ronda, M.A. and Valencia, R.R. (1994) '"At-risk" Chicano students: The institutional and communicative life of a category', *Hispanic Journal of Behavioral Sciences*, **16**, pp. 363–95.

Rosaldo, R. (1989) *Culture and Truth: The Remaking of Social Analysis*, Boston, MA: Beacon Press.

Rubin, L.B. (1976) *Worlds of Pain: Life in Working-class Families*, New York: Basic Books.

Sánchez, R. (1983) *Chicano Discourse: Socio-historical Perspective*, Rawley, MA: Bergin and Garvey.

Slavin, R.E. (1986) *Educational Psychology: Theory into Practice*, Englewood Cliffs, NJ: Prentice Hall.

Solomon, P. (1992) *Black Resistance in High School: Forging a Separatist Culture*, Albany, NY: State University of New York Press.

Stack, C. (1974) *All our Kin*, New York: Harper & Row.

Sudarkasa, N. (1988) 'Interpreting the African heritage in Afro-American family organization', in McAdoo, H.P. (Ed) *Black Families*, Newbury: Sage, pp. 27–43.

Swadener, B.B. and Lubeck, S. (Eds) (1995) *Children and Families 'at promise': Deconstructing the Discourse of Risk*, Albany, NY: State University of New York Press.

Taylor, E. (1989) *Prime Time Families*, Berkeley, CA: University of California Press.

THOMPSON, E.P. (1963) *The Making of the English Working Class*, New York: Vintage.

TRUEBA, H.T. and ZOU, Y. (1995) *Education and Power: A Case Study of Miao University Students and its Significance for American Society*, London: Falmer Press.

TURKLE, S. (1972) *Working*, New York: Avon.

VALENCIA, R.R. (1985) 'Chicanos and intelligence testing research: A descriptive state of the art', Unpublished manuscript.

VALENTINE, C. (1968) *Culture and Poverty: Critique and Counterproposals*, Chicago, IL: University of Chicago Press.

VALENTINE, C., BERNDT, C., BOISSERIAN, E., BUSHNELL, J., GLADWIN, T., HANNERZ, V., KOCHAR, V.K., LEACOCK, E., LEWIS, O., MANGIN, W., MATZA, D., MEAD, M., MILLER, W. and MOYNIHAN, D. (1969) 'Culture and poverty: Critique and counterproposals', *Current Anthropology*, **10**, pp. 181–201.

VELEZ-IBAÑEZ, C. and GREENBERG, J.B. (1992) 'Formation and transformation of funds of knowledge among US–Mexican households', *Anthropology and Education Quarterly*, **23**, pp. 313–33.

WARNER, L. (1949) *Democracy in Jonesville: A Study in Equality and Inequality*, New York: Harper & Row.

WEST, C. (1994) *Race Matters*, New York: Vintage.

WILLIAMS, M. (1981) *On the Street Where I Live*, New York: Holt, Rinehart and Winston.

WILLIAMS, N. (1990) *The Mexican American Family: Tradition and Change*, New York: General Hall.

WILLIE, C.V. (1976) *A New Look at Black Families*, New York: General Hall.

WILLIS, P. (1982) *Learning to Labor: How Working-Class Kids Get Working-Class Jobs*, New York: Columbia University Press.

ZAVELLA, P. (1987) *Women's Work and Chicano Families*, Ithaca, NY: Cornell University Press.

Chapter 5

Cultural and Accumulated Environmental Deficit Models

Arthur Pearl

In this chapter we examine *nurture* deficit theories — ones that retain the notion of deficits but look to something other than genetics to explain them. We trace their rise, importance and their proliferation. The 1954 Supreme Court decision that struck down segregated schools also marked the low point in genetic deficit thinking. Deficit thinking returned, however, with both anthropological and psychological emphases, and we describe and explain the proliferation of these forms of thinking.

The genetic pathology model has not been the only wall deficit thinkers have leaned on. As genetic explanations became increasingly unpopular, or, in today's jargon 'politically incorrect', alternative explanations for persistent school failure and social reproduction were developed.[1] Genetic theories were espoused by conservatives. With the ascendancy to power of liberals in the 1960s came liberal deficit theories.

Explanations of an existing social hierarchy rose to public consciousness and political importance after World War II. It is with the emergence of fair employment practices legislation, reawakened interest in civil rights, and a GI Bill that opened the doors of higher education to heretofore excluded populations, that attention was turned not only to existing arrangements but also to policies and practices that would make for a more fair system.

The 1954 Supreme Court decision to end racial segregation with 'deliberate speed' reversed the 19th century 'separate but equal' doctrine, and by doing so, mandated rethinking of equity and access to education. That decision marked a high watermark for social scientists and gave impetus to their importance in social policy decisions.[2]

The 1954 Supreme Court decision marked the low point of genetic interpretations of racial differences.[3] Thomas F. Pettigrew (1964), whose analysis of race relations at that time was generally held to be definitive, was able to find only three American psychologists who were willing to publish that the persistent black–white difference in measured intelligence (IQ scores) was genetically determined. One of the three was Henry Garrett (1961), whose heated debates with Columbia University colleague Otto Klineberg (1935, 1940), had largely shaped the understanding of racial differences in measured intelligence in the 1930s. Henry Garrett was not easily dismissed; he was sufficiently respected among his colleagues to be elected president of the American Psychological Association in 1946 (for more discussion on Klineberg and Garrett, see Chapter 3 by Valencia, and Chapter 6 by Valencia and Solórzano, respectively, in the present volume).

If the differences in school achievement were not genetic then they had to be either the result of some other deficit, *or*, caused by persistent unequal treatment, that is, individual and institutional bias. Preponderance of social policy and social science thinking chose the former, which opened the door for the rise to prominence of *cultural deficit* arguments.

Cultural deprivation — largely a psychological model — characterized deficit thinking during the 1960s. This model was not a new departure of deficit thinking; it is best understood as an outgrowth of the anthropological *culture of poverty* model that was previously described by Foley (Chapter 4). The *cultural deprivation model*, also known as the *cultural disadvantagement* or *social pathology* model, singled out the family unit (rather than genes) as the transmitter of deficiencies. Although culture (or the alleged lack of it, as indicated by the notion of deprivation) was central to the cultural deprivation model, the family was key to this deficit framework. The family unit — mother, father, home environment — was pegged as the carrier of the pathology.

An enormous corpus of literature on cultural deprivation theory emerged during the 1960s (e.g., Deutsch, 1967; Frost and Hawkes, 1966; Gladwin, 1961; Hellmuth, 1967; Lewis 1961, 1966b; Miller, 1958). Taking this literature as a whole, the families of the poor were frequently depicted in very negative ways. The inadequate father was often described as an abusive or neglectful parent who frequently engaged in physical punishment of his children, was a substance abuser, a poor provider and sexually promiscuous. The mother was characterized as equally inadequate, being described as a poor teacher of her children, as she does not read to her children, unable to communicate the value of education and importance of high academic achievement to her children, sporadic with her affection and love, and so on. The home environment of the poor was also deemed inadequate. One major description that appeared with frequency in the deficit thinking literature of the 60s was that the home environment of the poor did not provide adequate (i.e., quality and quantity) sensory stimulation for optimal development of children. Also, according to the theory of cultural deprivation, the home environment was managed in such a manner that the child had difficulty in developing a proper sense of time and space. Furthermore, multiple mothering, as seen in extended Mexican American and African American families, usually resulted in inconsistencies in caretaker–child relationships, creating situations in which the dependency needs of children were not met.

The logical consequence of such a hypothesized family was a child saddled with deficits. These children were described in the literature as irreparably intellectually impaired (for example, cognitively underdeveloped) as well as linguistically impaired (such as, restricted vocabulary; impoverished linguistic system). The culturally deprived child was also described as having pathogenic personality characteristics, was fatalistic; mistrustful; had low self-esteem; poor impulse control;

inability to distinguish right from wrong; was anti-intellectual; ad nauseum). Thus, with the invention of the culturally disadvantaged/culturally deprived child we see one of the most significant social constructions of the 1960s.

Deficit theorists in the decade of the 60s were not content with a copious descriptive and explanatory conceptual framework of cultural deprivation; they also had specific policy recommendations for educating the deprived child. Bereiter and Engelman (1966) for example, presented detailed language programs to improve the 'linguistic deprivation' of poor blacks. Such programs consisted of rote, unchallenging verbal stimulation in which the child had to adjust to the curriculum. The most significant of the schooling programs was the 'compensatory' approach, such as Operation Head Start and the Elementary and Secondary School Act, both federal programs. As I have noted elsewhere (Pearl, 1991), these programs were almost exclusively early intervention strategies with clear deficit thinking messages:

> The dominant theoretical explanation for disproportionate school failure of the poor and the minority was 'accumulated environmental deficit' — that is, students entered school with a build-up of handicaps incurred in early formative years that would be irreversible unless significant action was taken when children were very young . . . If, however, intervention begins early enough the child can recover from the lack of intellectual stimulation at home and the dearth of language . . . (1991: 285)

It is possible to distinguish at least three different cultural theses that have been used to explain differential school achievement by race, class, gender or ethnicity. All have had powerful influence on public opinion and social policy. One, *cultural deprivation* (which became, inaccurately, a rubric for the cultural thesis), is drawn from sociology and anthropology and postulates the existence of alienated cultures that are so antagonistic to schooling to effectively prevent members from succeeding in school. A second cultural thesis, *inadequate socialization*, derives from psychoanalysis and postulates a chaotic home situation resulting in the character disorder of arrested development, for example, an inability to delay gratification, thus negatively affecting school performance. A third thesis, *accumulated environmental deficits*, based on cognitive development theory, contends that accumulated environmental deficits in critical early years lead to irreversible cognitive deficits. All three meet our criteria of deficit because they are used to explain behaviors and attitudes that are inimical with school success. Technically, all three models are more cultural, as opposed to environmental, because effects are enduring and are attributed to ways of life that serve to bind together identified groups (common values; parenting patterns; ways at looking at the world; distinctive use of language). A purely environmental explanation would not have long-term residual effects and once the environment was altered, it would be expected that the deficits would soon disappear. In a sense, the major thrust of our argument is that what are called deficits are really organizations of the environment that biases the opportunity structure to increase the likelihood of certain groups to succeed at the expense of others; that is, the environment does not provide the 'disadvantaged' and the 'at risk' with the same encouragements and opportunities provided the 'advantaged'.

As Riessman noted:

> Culture would include the traditions, values, and mores of a specific group, many of which have a long history. Values and attitudes of the under-privileged that are relevant for the educator would include beliefs about punishment, authority, games, cooperation, competition, introspection, intellectuals, etc. (1962: 6)

Riessman's contribution to the debate was particularly interesting in that he speaks to both sides of the controversy. He attributes some deficits to the disadvantaged, but he also identifies strengths that schools and other social agencies refuse to recognize and build on. Riessman identifies school practices that place obstacles in the path of the disadvantaged that discourage, if not deny, school success. He later became involved in creative experiments to demonstrate the potential of the disadvantaged (Riessman and Hollowitz, 1965) when opportunities are created for them; furthermore, he was a leader in the development of an experiment in democratic education (Pearl and Riessman, 1965) that I discuss in Chapter 7 (Democratic Education as an Alternative to Deficit Thinking).

In this chapter we explain the logic and evidence that supported these theories and how they have evolved over the past three decades. In actual practice, the justification for school decisions blurs the distinction between the theories. The different cultural deficit theses tend to merge and separate and are often combined with genetic theories depending on the specifics of the situation. The variety of theories to explain deficits, their elusiveness, and their protean nature undermines attempts to hold schools accountable for decisions that negatively affect individuals and groups. Whether the decision is assignment to a low-level ability group or track, explanation for a failing grade, establishing the nature of teacher–student relationships, defense of the curriculum, or the treatment of persons accused of violating school rules, the justification of the decision ultimately rests on one or more deficit theories. The range of theories gives the latitude to school authorities to respond with, 'If you don't like that theory, how about this one?'

The Cultural Deficit Theses

Cultural deficit models have been around for a long time. They can be traced to Aristotle, and during the heady days of The Enlightenment, to Rousseau and Pestalozzi (who effectively combated them). These models reemerged in the liberal spirit of the social movements and general optimism of the 1960s. They largely informed the War on Poverty and had long-term subtle, but corruptive, influences on the Civil Rights Movement. In the past 30 years they have been altered as the changing political climate brought more conservative orientations to social policies.

In the late 1950s and 1960s, the sociological/anthropological deficit theories gained considerable credibility via a series of influential publications (Chilman, 1966; Gladwin, 1961; Lewis, 1961, 1966a, 1966b; Miller, 1958). Oscar Lewis, in a series of popular vivid descriptions, depicted a self-perpetuating culture that repudiated not only schooling but any meaningful participation in the dominant culture's social, economic and political life (see Foley, Chapter 4, for a sustained analysis and critique of Lewis' concept of the 'culture of poverty'). The culture of poverty and the culture of the school were incompatible. The anti-intellectual nature of the culture of poverty and its basic lack of future orientation prohibited academic or economic success.

> Once the culture of poverty has come into existence it tends to perpetuate itself. By the time slum children are six or seven [years old] they have usually absorbed the basic attitudes and values of their subculture. Thereafter they are psychologically unready to take full advantage of changing conditions or improving opportunities that may develop in their lifetimes. (Lewis, 1966b: 7)

Walter Miller (1958) insisted that between 40–60 per cent of America is affected by 'lower-class culture' and that 15 per cent are immersed in it. From his studies he is widely acknowledged for having detected the 'focal concerns' of the lower class that includes '*excitement, autonomy, smartness* and *toughness*' (Ryan, 1971: 124). Those focal concerns stimulated William Ryan to comment that such a culture would be distinguished from one that values, '*boredom, stupidity, subjugation* and *weakness*' (Ryan, 1971: 124). Miller titillates with his presentation of a female-dominated African American lower-class culture that propelled black youth into gangs, and thus not only was it incompatible with dominant culture but was, in addition, a physical threat to it. For supportive data he used vernacular that he insisted revealed an obsession with incest. He argued that only when the gang member matured to a point where he was willing to submit to female domination would gang activity cease. As gangs became an ever more menacing activity, Miller's dire predictions either inspired or were harmonious with an increasingly draconian approach to gang suppression.

Oscar Lewis, although deeply committed to a deficit thesis, is also sympathetic to the poor and a supporter of equalization of resources. Walter Miller is not totally unsympathetic. The most devastating portrayal of poverty culture was presented in a United States governmental publication, *Growing Up Poor* (Chilman, 1966). In 108 pages the author, Catherine Chilman, lists 51 debilitating cultural characteristics that would prohibit the poor from enjoying the good life if somehow it would be made available to them. Ryan (1971) has characterized *Growing Up Poor* as a 'revolting', 'nefarious' and 'emetic' publication. For those who have genuine concerns about the poor, he recommends they read Chilman's pamphlet 'in order to understand what social workers and social scientists are whispering to each other behind their cupped hands' (1971: 115–16).

The cultural deficit theses did not readily lend themselves to ameliorative social policy initiatives. It is difficult to invite cultures with allegedly little or no positive attributes into a school and make them a part of a multicultural approach. There is little incentive for the dominant culture to learn from a 'deficient' or 'deprived' culture. Moreover, if one accepts the Chilman (1966) argument, it would be a waste of money to try to ameliorate the condition of poverty.

The cultural deficit arguments were not informed by well articulated theory; there is very little effort to explain exceptions — for example, the substantial number of disciplined musicians, artists, authors, scholars and business executives who were or had been 'culturally deprived' or 'disadvantaged'. Weakness in theory, however, is not a major impediment for those who accept deficits. Theoretical justification is not deemed necessary in situations where deficits are believed to be self evident. Those who oppose the attribution of deficits to the 'underclass' — and more specifically to certain ethnic and racial minorities — are required to build a much stronger case. Culture which is treated in broad and general terms by deficit theorists cannot be treated so cavalierly by those that find deficit theorizing inadequate.

Culture reemerges as a major focus in recent years as part of interest in diversity and an emphasis on multicultural/bilingual education with 'deficit' transmogrified into 'difference'. One observer credits Riessman for initiating the change from deficit to difference by his emphasis on the strengths of impoverished minority populations and the importance of recognizing their culture (Pai, 1990).

Culture as a concept grows in importance and changes in emphasis in the years between its reemergence as a deficit argument to its current use as multicultural education which has been instituted as an educational reform designed to promote equity and access. The initial efforts at reform emphasized assimilation with little efforts to alter the system to accommodate the diversity of school populations. However, schools were moved, in many instances with great reluctance and with much foot-dragging, to accommodate diversity by modifying curriculum and instruction. Culture — and in particular a vital component of culture, language — became salient issues in the 1970s.

Multiculturalism produced an altered curriculum. It tinkered with the Western Canon, which was the culmination of 'The Enlightenment'. It was 'truth and beauty' and 'all ye need to know'; the established single standard whose magnificence could inspire all; whose understanding defined intellectuality and against which all else could be judged (and found wanting).

Multicultural education included that which had been ignored in history and thus amended the heretofore unchallengeable Western Canon. The East and South were added to the West to produce a broader doctrine, but that new canon had neither the force of history nor the power of persuasive argument. It did not lead to the reemergence of a new centripetal center. To the contrary, multiculturalism coincided with the evacuation of the center in what has come to be known as postmodernism or deconstructionism.

Multicultural education was not the only challenge to the Western Canon and the wonders of The Enlightenment. Feminists denounced the patriarchy they discovered in it (e.g., Pateman, 1985). The Enlightenment was being battered from many directions. The demise of the Soviet Union and its impact on Marxist thought and the lack of credibility of established authority in the West, as well as influences in, for example, literature, music and architecture led to the demise of the 'great narratives' (Lyotard, 1984), salient among which was the Western Canon. A detailed examination of postmodernism goes far beyond our immediate concerns. For our purposes it is merely sufficient to know that postmodernism precluded a new grand narrative, a generally recognized multicultural canon.

It is one thing to speak down from Olympus and quite another to try to shout up to it. The multicultural canon celebrated difference and thus unwittingly helped tear away the fabric of cherished tradition. It gained acceptance not by elevation, but through reduction. Additions to the Western Canon did not enhance it, they subtracted from its status. The destruction of intellectual icons did not create new ones. There was nothing organic in the process. Rather than reintegrating into a dynamic whole — with established new standards — the canon splintered. An anarchy of culture replaced the old elitist hierarchical culture. The limited and essentially peripheral changes in curriculum had more far-reaching effects in stimulating a backlash (D'Souza, 1991) than it had in changing the life conditions of the poor.

Although I find the multicultural/bilingual approach inadequate and riddled with deficit thinking, those efforts cannot be blamed for the general intellectual malaise of the academy. The following quotes summarize my interests in postmodernist thinking.

> There is, perhaps, a degree of consensus that the typical postmodernist artifact is playful, self-ironizing and even schizoid; and that it reacts to the austere autonomy of high modernism by impudently embracing the language of commerce and the commodity. Its stance towards cultural tradition is one of irreverent pastiche and its contrived depthlessness undermines all metaphysical solemnities, sometimes by a brutal aesthetics of squalor and shock. (Terry Eagleton (1987), quoted by David Harvey (1989: 7–8))

> ... [t]he overall impact of postmodernism is that many other groups now share with black folks a sense of deep alienation, despair, uncertainty, loss of a sense of grounding even if it is not informed by shared circumstance. (bell hooks (1990), quoted by Harper (1994: 27))

> Post-modern culture is more and more a market culture dominated by gangster mentalities and self-destructive wantonness. The culture engulfs all of us — yet its impact on the disadvantaged is devastating, resulting in extreme violence ... (Cornel West, 1993: 10)

> The first business of educational reformers in schools and universities — multiculturalists, feminists, progressives — ought to be to sever their alliance with esoteric postmodernism; with literary metatheory (theory about theory); with fun-loving, self-annihilating hyperskepticism. As pedagogy these intellectual practices court catastrophe. They proffer to desperate travelers trying to find their way between Scylla and Charybdis a clever

little volume on Zeno's paradoxes. They give to people whose very lives depend on the right choices a lesson in the impossibility of judgment. They tell emerging citizens looking to legitimize their preferences for democracy that there is no intellectually respectable way to ground political legitimacy. (Benjamin Barber, 1992: 125)

With the loss of a center the concept of culture changes. With no accepted standards, words lose meaning, but life conditions do not necessarily change. Multicultural education became a part of the school vocabulary, and some changes were made in curriculum; bilingual education sputtered into a contentious existence without a politically grounded legitimacy. What did not change to any significant degree was the academic and economic success of African Americans and Mexican Americans. These populations continued to be underrepresented in the academy and overrepresented in prisons.

One person who brings a different slant to culture is Pierre Bourdieu. We are fascinated by Bourdieu because he provides powerful arguments against deficit thinking while also providing strong arguments for it (for a different perspective on Bourdieu and deficit thinking, see Foley, Chapter 4). French sociologist Pierre Bourdieu provides a theoretical framework that can be used as a road map into understanding various features of the rapidly changing intellectual terrain; he brings to the table a reference to frame the cultural deficit argument. Bourdieu brought a unique stamp to the enormous increase in access to higher education that in many ways has inspired the backlash against multiculturalism. While many observers found this phenomenon to be a big step in the direction of equity, Bourdieu insisted that increased educational access merely created new forms of social stratification. In a sense, Bourdieu reconstructed social reproduction. He was hardly alone, or the first, to recognize the school's role in systematic reproduction of social and economic status. That thesis has been presented and revisited in many forms (see Bowles and Gintis, 1976). According to Bourdieu, opening higher education to the lower classes did not change power relationships, and privileged status is maintained without the general public being aware of it. Bourdieu elevates the importance of education in social reproduction, claiming that education has more influence on maintaining inequality than family, church or business. He maintains that there is a need in modern economically developed democracies to replace the more openly brutal and physical oppression that characterized the past, with subtle symbolic control. Thus, Bourdieu and his colleagues have discovered that higher education has maintained inequality without violating democratic ideology by 'transmuting (social inequalities) into academic hierarchies' (Bourdieu and Passeron, 1977: 153).

Bourdieu recognizes the link between education and occupation and that credentials earned in school provide access to desirable work. He also makes clear that there is little to be gained by increasing the number of persons with credentials. When qualifications exceed occupational openings the dominant classes redefine the criteria for admission and thus maintain a privileged status for their children (and others with whom they share class membership). Thus, Bourdieu is able to show that merely increasing educational achievement in the dominated classes will not necessarily lead to economic success. It is not a particularly novel discovery.

> If we maintain a nation in which there are insufficient jobs to go around, and if some jobs are so menial, so dead-end, and so low-paying that persons employed in them are locked into perpetual poverty, then even the perfect education is going to leave some people out. A good education and an imperfect employment system can only lead to many well-educated people being unable to find work. (Pearl, 1972: 82)

Bourdieu recognizes that education has helped maintain inequality by permitting existing cultural advantage to be passed down from generation to generation in both educational and occupational achievement.

Bourdieu refines the social reproduction analysis; to him it does not reduce to simple class determinism. Working-class youth can be academically successful, *but* they succeed by developing a stiff, formal academic style that is qualitatively inferior to the deeper and richer style of successful upper-class students. Furthermore, higher education is hierarchically ordered and thus occupational attainment depends as much if not more on the type of institution attended as it does on the level of education attained. The upper classes go to elite schools that impart a different culture than the higher education working-class students receive. And lastly, educational institutions are not mere adjuncts to the dominant institutions of society, but they develop their own cultures that may deviate significantly from the dominant class interests and values.

In *La Distinction* 1979 (translated *Distinction: A Social Critique of the Judgment of Taste*, 1984) he concludes on the basis of his 'scientific' observations that cultural needs are the product of education (1984: i). Bourdieu emphasizes the importance of capital which he divides into two types: economic and cultural. Cultural capital is knowledge and style that serve to maintain social inequality. Credentials are capital assets that can be inherited or bought through the investment of time, energy and money and be exchanged for valued occupations. Cultural capital includes, in addition to different levels of credentials, many other attributes, for example, verbal facility, general cultural awareness and a working knowledge of the educational as well as connected systems. Cultural capital is unequally distributed. Few children of farmers or workers have higher degrees; few children of professionals do not. (Although this relationship is changing in subtle and complicated ways; more children of professionals are alienated from education, and slightly more from the lower classes are succeeding in higher education. Education may not be the 'great equalizer' that Horace Mann hoped it would be, but narcotics and other control substances are.) The maldistribution of credentials is not a profound observation; far more interesting is Bourdieu's contribution of how the higher education system reproduces, rather than redistributes, cultural capital. Children from dominated classes, even after years in higher education, never quite make up for their initial 'handicap'. One reason for dominant class superior educational performance is the school emphasis on the knowledge and cultural ideals of the privileged class. The emphasis on humanities (classical education; perennialism; foundationalism) is not compatible with the technical skills required in the fastest growing sectors of the job market. The dominant-class definition of cultural capital can only be appreciated by those who are economically secure. That definition also acts as a selection device. Success, Bourdieu (1984) insists, depends on broad cultural awareness and an elaborate language style (here his argument resembles the accumulated environmental deficit thesis that we discuss later in this chapter).

Many other factors conspire to maintain an imbalanced distribution of cultural capital-mastery of language and culture: Books in the home, music listened to, private art collections, even the dinner menu, are part of inherited culture and can only be acquired in a dominant-class family. The reliance on classic oral and written essays emphasize the 'inherited' style as much as they feature content (Bourdieu and de Saint Martin, 1974). Bourdieu, in this latter instance, reveals the nature of class bias in supposedly neutral and objective systems. In an analysis of university student responses to language tests, Bourdieu and Passeron (1977) demonstrate that dominant-class origin students do much better than dominated-class origin students on vocabulary questions, whereas the dominated students are equal to the dominant on academic questions. Middle-class students tend to have the lowest scores because they have neither inherited the cultural capital of the dominant nor are they as highly selected as the dominated (Bourdieu and Passeron, 1977).

Where Bourdieu bridges the modern and the postmodern is in the relative autonomy that he assigns to the educational system. The educational system, according to Bourdieu, has a self-reproductive capacity.[4] Drawing upon Durkheim (1893/1933) he points to the educational system's recruitment of leadership from its own ranks and as a result resembles more the church than business or government. The educational system controls the training, recruitment and promotion of teachers; thus, he explains, there is the widespread anti-capitalist attitudes of academics and the successful resistance to efforts to fashion curriculum to meet business interests.

The intellectual elite invests heavily in education and thereby accumulates cultural capital. They take on the responsibility to maintain humanist traditions and strongly oppose efforts to bend the most prestigious higher education institutions to the pressures emanating from the most powerful business sectors. They point their youth to the *Grandes Écoles* (the Stanfords, the Yales, the Harvards) and they in turn become the distinguished professors of the next generation of students. The motivation for continued study of the dominant class differs greatly from middle-class aspirations. The middle class looks to education to provide financial security for their children and thus, they lobby for utilitarian education and are impatient or even hostile to the luxury of a course of studies in humanities.

Class differences in understanding of the purposes of education has produced turmoil in the academy. A heterogeneous student population and a somewhat disharmonious relationship between junior and senior faculty has led to frustrations, anger and, according to Bourdieu, the May 1968 student revolt in France. Uprisings in universities in the United States and elsewhere could be explained by the

Bourdieuian analysis. Bourdieu's analysis of the university seems to us somewhat dated. He tends to ignore the raging postmodernist debates. The university's mission is certainly much more obscure since the postmodernists have gained eminence than it was before. Bourdieu seems stuck halfway between the critical theorists and the postmodernists, which he reveals by minimizing the importance of the postmodern equating of high and low culture expressions. Bourdieu is criticized for downplaying the more direct economic efforts to control education and maintain reproduction. Others fault him for underestimating the influences of government, teacher unions and other interest groups. For us, he helps explain how the quest for equity has given way to the struggle for place in a rudderless system. The ugly battles for power and privilege by those within the academy leave little room or attention for those who have never had access.

To Bourdieu, all cultural habits within the dominant class are part of a cultural game to establish legitimacy. Legitimacy requires both acceptance and distinction. Acceptance of a cultural habit or a standard or a work of art involves both approval by those on top of the social hierarchy and the exclusion of the dominated class from a voice in the matter. The struggle for legitimization involves all other intellectual endeavors — the arts, etc. This raises for us the question of the kind of education a student should receive to further the development of an undominated, that is, a democratic, cultural taste. It also raises another important question about whether a system designed to be closed can be opened. One of the consequences of *assuming* that systems are closed is that questions never get asked, let alone answered. In these postmodern days when solid foundations for decisions have been destroyed, one would expect there would be unlimited inquiry, and yet there appears to be less openness and invitation for creativity in educational innovation now than there was in the good old days when grand narratives were inspirations.

Bourdieu may be best known for his concept of '*habitus*' — a hypothesized approach to cognitive functioning and possibilities. Habitus sets the boundaries on thought processes and allows the individual to locate his or her sense of place. It thus establishes the limits to educability. Which means, unless there is careful examination of the foundations of that thought, there will be a readiness to accept deficits as a determinant of the boundaries of educability. Bourdieu defines a system of schemata that is both unlimited in its capacity for 'products-thoughts, perceptions, expressions, actions' (1977: 95), but at the same time bounded 'by the historically and socially situated conditions of its production' (1977: 95). 'Habitus . . . represents a cultural matrix, varying by people's background, that generates self-fulfilling prophecies' (Swartz, 1990: 72). Habitus thus tells us less about what humans can do or think and more about the limits on creativity. Bourdieu establishes for himself a middle ground between humans-have-an-infinite-capacity-for-creativity position and the behaviorist notion that creativity is a fiction, and all credit should be given to the contingencies of rewards and punishments that are provided by social and physical environments. The 'cultural freedom it secures is as remote from a creation of unpredictable novelty as it is from simple mechanical reproduction of the initial conditionings' (1977: 95). Habitus is the dialectical resolution of conflicting pressures toward coerced conformity and efforts to be free of oppression. Bourdieu has been taken to task for defining a habitus that does not take into account the wide shifts in expectations and aspirations among different groups. Bourdieu has made our job more difficult. *He has developed a highly sophisticated defense of deficit theory while he ostensibly positions himself on the side of equity.*

Bourdieu's dialectical approach to cognition differs significantly from the pancultural Jean Piaget, who sees cognition as the resolution of universal efforts to resist change, assimilation and a requirement to change or grow, via accommodation. There are differences between Bourdieu's formulation and Vygotsky's *zone of proximal development*, with whom he shares a similar foundation of thought. The process of cognition, its potentialities and limitations, is something every general theory and every educator must address. Bourdieu focuses on the hold that a culture has on its members and thus warns against being overly optimistic or making naive errors. Such a warning may be necessary in ebullient times, but now, when the mood is already overly pessimistic, Bourdieu becomes an advocate for the status quo.

Inadequate Socialization

> At the heart of the deterioration of the fabric of Negro society is the deterioration of the Negro family. It is *the* fundamental source of weakness of the Negro community at the present time . . . Unless this damage is repaired, all the effort to end discrimination and poverty and injustice will come to little. (Moynihan, 1965: 5) . . .

> At the center of the tangle of pathology is the weakness of the family structure. Once or twice removed, it will be found to be the principal source of most of the aberrant, inadequate or anti-social behavior that did not establish, but now serves to perpetuate the cycle of poverty and deprivation. (Moynihan, 1965: 30)

Inadequate socialization replaced genetic theories as the principle explanation of deficits. No one made its case more forcefully than Daniel Patrick Moynihan, the Harvard academic President Kennedy appointed as Special Assistant to the Secretary of Labor, and who had been a key player in the development of the War on Poverty. His reaffirmation of a deficit thesis was in effect a renunciation of much of what he shortly before advocated. It put a chill on the optimistic pronouncements of a date when poverty and its residual effects would be eliminated.

The inadequate socialization argument was deeply embedded in psychodynamic theory and was a key element in psychoanalysis. As a deficit thinking model, the inadequate socialization thesis was generally accepted at that time.[5] It fit neatly into the Freudian theory of ego and character development. A stable and supportive family provided the basis for healthy growth. The desired pattern of growth was movement from the infant's demand for immediate gratification (that is, operating according to *the pleasure principle*) to a well established ego and the ability to delay gratification and meet the requirements of the *reality principle*. Children who grew up in chaotic families, without a father figure and inconsistent parenting, the absence of love and support would not be able to develop a healthy ego and would exhibit various forms of psychopathology.

An inability to delay gratification was used to explain student failure in school. The student who operated on the pleasure principle could not study for future examinations, but rather he or she engaged instead in activities that provided instant gratifications. That such students were often truant could be explained by the future orientation of classroom, an orientation that required delayed gratification, an orientation that a student operating under the pleasure principle was unprepared to accept.

Inadequate socialization not only explained academic failure it also was used to explain disruptive behavior. The lack of a strong father figure in the home precluded the development of a superego and the capacity to distinguish right from wrong. A flawed superego led to sociopathology and a likely career in crime and other antisocial activities. A flawed ego led to psychopathology and an inability to take care of oneself. Furthermore, a defective ego precluded an ability to adjust to reality and opened the way for a likely life of repeated failure.

The inadequate socialization thesis not only deflected attention away from schools and other agencies, it also cautioned against expecting positive responses to increasing equity and access. That was perhaps the most important element in the Moynihan message, which is worth reiterating: 'Unless this damage [to the Negro family] is repaired, all the effort to end discrimination and poverty and injustice will come to little' (Moynihan, 1965: 5). How does one repair a family? How does one repair the African American family when one in three African American males between the ages of 15 and 30 years is in prison or otherwise caught up in the justice system? It is but a short step from the Moynihan Report to the current mantra of 'family values' that has become one of the current deficit models that we address later.

Repairing a 'tangle of pathology' would logically be a call for significant investment in rehabilitation and therapy. Today, such recommendations tend to be dismissed as soft liberalism. This means that inadequate socialization becomes a problem without a solution, except for yet another Moynihan recommendation, 'benign neglect'. To a very large extent, such neglect has become social policy, as investment in social programs continue to shrink and the differences in public expenditures for education by race and class increase dramatically (Kozol, 1991).

The inadequate socialization thesis, while less important today than it was 25–30 years ago in explaining school failure, continues to be the most powerful thesis in the treatment of crime and delinquency. August Aichhorn's 1925 classic, *Wayward Youth* (Aichhorn, 1925/1983), provides a solid practitioner's support to the Freudian explanation of social pathology. There is an important difference, however, in how inadequate socialization was considered then and how it is considered now. Aichhorn is oriented to ameliorating the problem. He believes he has discovered a cure for a persistent and troubling social problem. Today the thesis is promoted in the absence of a cure, which translates into longer and longer periods of incarceration.

August Aichhorn's book deals with one part of the great problem of the application of psychoanalysis to education, namely, that of influencing the dissocial adolescent by means of education. The author had worked for many years in an official position as director of state institutions for the care of delinquents before he became acquainted with psychoanalysis. His treatment of his charges had its source in a warm sympathy for the fate of these unfortunates and was rightly guided by his intuitive understanding of their psychic needs. Psychoanalysis could teach him little that was new to him in a practical way, but it offered him a clear theoretical insight into the justification of his treatment and enabled him to explain his method to others in this field.

We cannot assume that every educator has this intuitive gift. Aichhorn's experience and achievement lead us to [conclude] . . . that the educator should be psychoanalytically trained; otherwise the child, the object of his effort, remains an inaccessible enigma to him. Such training is best achieved when the educator subjects himself to an analysis in order to experience it within himself. Theoretical teaching of analysis does not penetrate deeply enough and brings no conviction. (Sigmund Freud, 1925/1983: vi)

Psychiatric thinking was at the core of the notion of rehabilitation of criminals, delinquents and students with serious behavioral problems. Support for rehabilitation declined precipitously, however, with the testimony of Robert Martinson before a Senate committee in 1974 and his publication in the influential journal, *In The Public Interest* (Martinson, 1974). Many other prominent social scientists joined the chorus against rehabilitation and lent their voices in support of the idea that 'nothing (or very little) works' (Greenberg, 1977; Sechrest, White, and Brown, 1979; Wilson, 1975). The 'nothing works' argument was not a renunciation of deficit thinking. To the contrary, the attack on rehabilitation was support for more hardened deficit thinking (genetic deficits or cultures so perverted and deficient that integration to mainstream society was not a feasible consideration), and only long-term imprisonment could provide effective protection to a beleaguered public whose safety had been imperiled by soft-hearted, do-gooder liberals. A slightly less strident form of this argument can be found in efforts to remove unworthy students from the classroom, as they threatened the academic growth of the more able. Although the attack on inadequate socialization took place in the field of corrections, it has impacted schools also. With the decline in rehabilitation, the inadequate socialization thesis (combined with new genetic arguments that identify genetic predisposition for crime; for a critique, see Chorover, 1979, who asserts that 'criminal defectology' is a 'bogus field' (p. 182)) has been used to justify increased police presence on school grounds and a willingness to expel more students from school. The increase in emphasis on security has served to exclude and isolate more disadvantaged youth and the predisposition to use draconian methods on vulnerable populations effectively militates against movement toward equity and access. The heavy emphasis on exclusion discourages analysis of early indication of incipient problems for those students who encounter discouragements and rejection in school, and are not provided with opportunities to establish positive relationships with others. Persistent rejection impacts culture. When students find themselves excluded from the dominant culture they, in effect, are encouraged to create new cultures.

Psychoanalysis was not the only foundation for the inadequate socialization thesis. Maslow's 'third force' also made a case for inadequate socialization. Abraham Maslow developed a hierarchy of needs, the lowest of which are the basic physiological needs, for example, food. For a person to achieve the highest order of human functioning — self-actualization, knowing and understanding, and finally, aesthetic appreciation — he or she must be able to satisfy, in order: safety needs, belonging and love needs and esteem needs. The lower four needs are *deficiency needs* the top three are *growth needs*. According to Maslow, one cannot gratify a higher need until the lower need is met, which means that the disadvantaged are mired in deficiency needs and therefore cannot enjoy growth (Maslow, 1970; 1971).

Maslow (1971) makes his deficit argument very clear when he attempts (with R. Diaz-Guerrero) to describe the differences between Mexican and 'American' delinquents. After dismissing superficial socioeconomic theories, such as Mexicans are poorer, more neglected, etc., he arrives at his sophisticated deficit theory. American parents of delinquents are weaker and less rooted in tradition than Mexican parents. American parents have failed in their socialization mission.

> We postulate that [American] juvenile violence, vandalism, cruelty, defiance of authority, and war against adults is not only a matter of growth dynamics of the standard Freudian variety (trying to be grown-up, fighting one's dependency needs, counterphobic mechanisms against weakness, childishness, cowardice, etc.), but also implies a hostile and contemptuous lashing-out in understandable retaliation against the *weak adults who have failed them* [emphasis added]. We feel this to be more directed toward the father than the mother, and more vehemently by boys than by girls, and would expect that the most common interpersonal attack would be attacks upon males (and everything that they represent), by boys. (Maslow with R. Diaz-Guerrero, 1971: 377)

The lack of social concern and a preoccupation with self, which is the heart of Maslowian psychology, lends itself to deficit thinking. Once removed from social responsibility it is but a short step to find reasons to blame those who are unable to help themselves. Self-growth, which is the primary goal, if not the sole goal of persons with such psychological orientation, is incompatible with social responsibility. Selfishness replaces citizenship as the primary human attribute. Deficit thinking rose as it became more and more acceptable to mainstream people so concerned with self aggrandizement they lost interest in others. The vacuum created with a loss in social consciousness was filled with calls for tax cuts and reduction in social programs. Distancing oneself from a problem made it much easier for the descendants of Cain to proclaim, 'I am not my brother's keeper'.

> By now millions of Americans have garnered extensive — and painful — experience in personal struggles with the new, Maslow inspired duty-to-self ethic. It has, to be sure, some benefits to offer the individual, but the core idea is amoral and social absurdity. It gives moral sanction to desires that do not contribute to society's well-being. It contains no principle for synchronizing the requirements of the society with the goals of the individual. It fails to discriminate between socially valuable desires and socially destructive ones, and often works perversely against the real goals of both individuals and society. It provides no principle other than hedonism for interpreting the meaning of the changes and sacrifices we must make to adapt to new economic-political conditions. (Yankelovich, 1981: 47)

Inadequate socialization can take many forms, and in each, the consequence is an alleged deficit. Lawrence Kohlberg generated a theory of moral development that he derived from Piaget (whose approach to cognitive development can be readily modified to conform to an inadequate socialization argument). Kohlberg hypothesized a six-step moral hierarchy beginning with preconventional childhood concerns of avoiding punishment and maturing to decisions based on pleasing those in power. In preadolescence, morality is initially based on maintaining good relationships with others, advancing to observing rules because this is the good thing to do, and developing a law-and-order orientation. These steps are to be followed by the highest levels of morality–legality apart from authority, and finally recognition of universal principles of justice, human rights, etc. This approach becomes an inadequate socialization theory because Kohlberg provided data to show that the poor and the individual racial/ethnic minority were much more likely to be fixated at the lower end of the morality scale than advantaged populations (Kohlberg, 1963, 1973, 1975; Kohlberg and Gilligan, 1971). Only those who have social and economic advantage are able to graduate to Kohlberg's higher levels of morality. Kohlberg, using similar logic, found women to be morally underdeveloped. Carol Gilligan, who began as a Kohlberg colleague, broke from him and devised an alternative theory that women with their feminine voice were not only different, but morally superior to men (Gilligan, 1982).

> The moral imperative that emerges repeatedly in interviews with women is an injunction to care, a responsibility to discern and alleviate the 'real and recognizable trouble' of this world. For men, the moral imperative appears rather as an injunction to respect the rights of others and thus to protect from interference the rights to life and self-fulfillment. Women's insistence on care is at first self-critical rather than self-protective, while men initially conceive obligation to others negatively in terms of non-interference. Development for both sexes would therefore seem to entail

an integration of rights and responsibilities through the discovery of the complementarity of these disparate views. (Gilligan, 1982: 44)

Gilligan (1982) can be seen as a significant figure in the rising number of different feminist strategists. During this period of rapidly expanding deficit theorists, feminist voices were heard and given a measure of credibility. While Gilligan brought into question judgments against women deficiencies, she did nothing to challenge deficit theorizing when applied to class, race and ethnicity.

Erik Erikson, another highly regarded psychologist whose 'Eight Stages of Man' has been much acclaimed, concocts yet another theory that lends itself to an inadequate socialization deficit interpretation. According to this theory, a child will have a healthy development only if provided the resources at earlier stages that lay the foundation for healthy development at later stages. Therefore, if in infancy a child is deprived of love, nurturing contacts, or is subjected to chaotic care, he or she will develop chronic mistrust and not be ready to develop autonomy at the next stage. According to Eriksonian theory, this means that the child is ravaged with shame and doubt and is thus organized to accept defeat, which in turn means predisposition, on entering school, the acceptance of inferiority as distinct from industriousness. That in turn, leads to an inability to form a well defined identity in adolescence. The cycle of deficit continues into the next generation because the maldeveloped person becomes a non-responsive and irresponsible parent, which culminates in an old age of despair and self disgust (Erikson, 1959, 1963, 1964, 1968). A theory, such as Erikson's, that puts responsibility on a previous stage, for example, a student enters school predisposed to fail, removes the school from examining obstacles to success that the educational system may have put in the path of students who fail. When school failure persistently correlates with class, race and ethnicity, an exhaustive examination of the school practices is vitally needed before conclusions about student deficiencies can be advanced. The powerful hold that deficit theories have on school decisionmakers deters the serious examination of inequitable schooling practices.

The Accumulated Environmental Deficit Thesis

Although inadequate socialization theories have grown substantially in recent years, it was 'accumulated environmental deficits' that dominated policy and practice in the 1960s (e.g., Bernstein, 1958, 1959, 1960, 1961, 1970, 1971; Bernstein and Henderson, 1969; Bloom, Davis and Hess, 1965; Deutsch, 1967; Hess and Shipman, 1965; Hunt, 1961). The accumulated environmental deficit thesis was the heart of the Great Society programs. It was the liberal answer to the ultraconservative and defeatist genetic explanation of lower-class failure. Accumulated environmental deficit theorizing was cultural to the extent that it was the culture of the lower class that allegedly organized a life without the necessary intellectual stimulation — that is, the absence of books and other printed material, the limited exposure to adequate language, and so on. It was also the most limited of the deficit theories. It was fairly restricted to language development, and that made it most amenable to social intervention. A major assumption was that through language interventions, the deprived student's cognitive development could be enhanced. It spawned compensatory education and the belief that deprivation of language could be repaired by an enriched preschool and through focused school interventions.

Many scholars embraced the accumulated environmental deficit argument. It was an extension of laboratory experiments that had convincingly demonstrated severe sensory deprivation inevitably led to equally severe permanent negative effects. Many psychologists and some sociolinguists found the life conditions of the poor, particularly African American poor, to be analogous to sensory deprivation. There were, however, difficulties in such an argument. For example, Martin Deutsch added 'sensory overload' as an equivalent to sensory deprivation, arguing that the noise and tumult of the ghetto home inhibited cognitive growth (Deutsch, 1967). This theoretical twist, of course, raised an apparent contradiction: Deprived children were receiving *too little* and *too much* sensory stimulation. But even more problematic was the *lack* of significant deficit observed at the time poor children entered school. It was not noted that until the fourth grade significant differences in academic or measured intellectual achievement appeared, and it is the tardiness of deficiency that the concept of *accumulation* was added to the deficit (Deutsch and Brown, 1964). In short, it took time for the early established deficits to be become perceptible. That early home experiences should be responsible for inadequate school performance was hardly the most parsimonious explanation; a far more logical explanation for emerging differences in school performance would be differences in treatment at school, but in this instance the less parsimonious was the more convincing.

The stamp of the accumulated environmental deficit thesis derived from quite diverse forms of cognitive development theory: a mechanistic behaviorist environmental thesis and more complex psycholinguistic and sociolinguistic theses. The differences between these models stimulated heated academic debates, but they had little impact on social policy. However complicated the arguments, the remedial programs were conceptually quite simple and programmatically muddled. Head Start, Follow Through, and most notably in compensatory education — the center piece of which was The Elementary and Secondary Education Act of 1965 — provided a range of enrichments with preferences given to the most simplistic (Bereiter and Engelmann, 1966). These interventions initiated during the rise of liberalism in American politics have survived fundamental political change and have remained firmly entrenched throughout the ascendancy of conservatism. What remains is a form of inertia without either historical reference or careful analysis.

The survival of the deficit-based programs is not a vindication of their effectiveness. To the contrary, the results of these programs — where performance across race, ethnicity and class are sometimes unequal — have served to reinforce deficit arguments.

An example is Arthur Jensen (1969) who overstated the case in renewing his thrust for acceptance of genetic differences when he opened his *Harvard Educational Review* article with 'compensatory education has been tried and failed' (1969: 1).

The available evidence neither supports nor refutes such a conclusion. Head Start programs appear to have long-term salutary effects; disadvantaged children exposed to such interventions do significantly better on a wide range of variables than do comparable children not offered Head Start, and the differences in Head Start student performance and the normal school population is narrowed considerably (see Berrueta-Clement, Schweinhart, Barnett, Epstein and Weikert, 1984; Hubbell, 1983). The Head Start students when contrasted with controls have better grades, are more regular in attendance, have fewer special education placements, do better on standardized tests, are more likely to graduate and continue on to higher education (Berrueta–Clement *et al.*, 1984). However, Head Start did not succeed either. The Head Start students did not catch up with the normal school population. Do the continued differences demonstrate the existence of an irremediable deficit? Not necessarily. It may reveal the limitations of operating within a deficit frame of reference. Programs that worked with similar populations, but challenged deficit thinking, have had much more powerful results. These results appear to hold up even though the theory underlying the interventions were widely disparate.

The Effective School Movement showed dramatic results using traditional instruction in a traditional school setting (Edmonds 1979, 1984; Haycock and Navarro, 1988). Deborah Meier's disadvantaged students' performances (in Central Park Secondary School) mirrored that of elite schools in an alternative high school whose emphasis was on habits of the mind and where intimate relationships between teachers and students were markedly different than the standard public high school and resembled more elite private schools (Meier, 1995). In another instance, students with nearly two decades of 'accumulated environmental deficits' were able to keep pace with students who met the entrance requirements at the University of Oregon in a program where the emphasis was on enhancing student participation in decisions that affected their lives and on consciously providing them with the gratifications of belonging, usefulness and competence (Hollins, 1991). Perhaps the largest and most significant indication of how far 'deprived populations' can go was revealed in the New Career programs of the 1960s (Pearl and Riessman, 1965) in which persons with alleged deficits and long mired in cultures of poverty were admitted to career ladder programs. The entry position in the ladder required no prior training, skill or experience. Students were able to move up the ladder by learning on the job and in the institutions of higher education through intermediate steps until attaining the terminal professional credential. Here again, persons reputedly suffering from a variety of deficits were able to match and even exceed the performance of the non-deficit professional (Amram, Flax, Hamermesh and Marty, 1988; Carter, 1977).

The accumulated environmental thesis met with serious criticism in the early 1970s. A number of psycholinguists and sociolinguists insisted that what were called *deficits* were *differences* and these differences were not inferior to the standard recognized code (Baratz and Baratz, 1970; Labov, 1970). For a period of time, this argument had some credibility. Although through this approach there was a well reasoned criticism of deficit thinking, the approaches to amelioration were inadequate and to some extent failed to sufficiently appreciate the capacity of disadvantaged students to adapt to new situations if given the same kind of encouragement that advantaged students receive. Thus, from my perspective, the *difference* argument while critical of the deficit thesis was in reality a variation of deficit thinking.

Basil Bernstein was one of the most influential of the language deficit theses. (I include him here because of his emphasis on language, although his framework is more an anthropological/sociological cultural thesis). Bernstein differentiated between a restricted code that he attributed to the lower-working class and the elaborated code of the upper classes (Bernstein, 1958, 1959, 1960, 1961). In a later article, he recognizes that his work had been used to defend compensatory education interventions and he tries to distance himself from deficit thinkers who abused his analysis by 'directly [equating it] with linguistic deprivation, linguistic deficiency or being nonverbal' (Bernstein, 1970: 26).

> Thus the relative backwardness of many working-class children who live in areas of high population density or in rural areas, may well be a culturally induced backwardness transmitted by the linguistic process. Such children's low performance on verbal IQ tests, their difficulty with abstract concepts, their failures within the language area, their general inability to profit from the school, all may result from the limitations of a restricted code. For these children the school induces a change of code and with this a change in the way the children relate to their kin and community. At the same time we often offer these children grossly inadequate schools with less than able teachers. No wonder they often fail — for those who have 'more', tend to receive more and become more, while those who have 'less', receive less and become less. (Bernstein, 1970: 37)

Thus Bernstein puts himself in the *difference* versus the *deficit* camp. He further speaks to the inequity of schools and how compensatory education deflects attention away from inequities in school finance and in the nature of teacher–student relationships. He further rails against the attacks made against families on whom deficit arguments are based. To this extent, his argument parallels ours. However, except for a request that teachers become broadly accepting and become familiar with and appreciative of the backgrounds, linguistic styles and strengths that the low-income child brings to the school, he has nothing to offer in making school better places not only for the poor but for all children.

In summary, we can conclude that cultural and accumulated environmental deficit models, with their person-centered frameworks, were attractive to scholars and policymakers in that they were more parsimonious theories than ones that examined the complexity of institutionalized inequity. They were also safer. These deficit theories could ignore external forces — that is, the complex makeup of macrolevel and microlevel mechanisms that helped structure schools as inequitable and exclusionary institutions. By accepting the simplicity of the cultural and accumulated environmental deficit models, scholars and policymakers were excused from addressing the real issues of inequality. In short, these deficit models were powerful, entrenched and inadequately critiqued paradigms in the 1960s. Given impetus by the Civil Rights Movement and revisionist scholarship, critiques of such deficit thinking began to appear by the end of the decade (see Baratz and Baratz, 1970; Ryan, 1971). Criticism was not a sufficient response. What was needed were powerful models of equity. Some of these deficit theories have survived, however. By the mid-1990s, a weakened impetus towards civil rights and the general conservative ascendancy has triggered a return of deficit thinking, some more powerful and more deeply entrenched than ever before (see Valencia and Solorzano, Chapter 6, for an analysis of Contemporary Deficit Thinking). Cultural deficit theses continue to influence educational thought and practice. Although the original models no longer have a powerful sway over policy or social thought, their current conservative manifestation has even more negative implications for equity.

In the 1950s and throughout the 1960s, the nation's attention was directed to the existence of inequality and overt racism. As the attention was focused, so too were efforts made to understand and explain the phenomena. Culture became one of the pegs on which analysis was tethered. A nation was prepared to accept past injustices, but was not ready to seriously examine current injustices. Thus, the concoctions of deficient cultures as the residual effects of historical wrongs found a hungry audience ready to uncritically accept cultural deprivation in that such acceptance required no important systemic change, nor did it require any change in behavior in those who continued to be beneficiaries of existing injustice.

Over the course of three decades, as a result of both court cases and legislation, *pluralism* and *multiculturalism* have been reluctantly included in school policy and practice. Unfortunately the acceptance of pluralism did not bring with it a critical analysis of deficit thinking. Rather than *difference* replacing *deficit*, both concepts co-exist.

'Difference' — the key concept of postmodernists, and certainly powerful albeit divisive in feminism — is a target for conservative efforts to sustain an existing system. Typical of the thought processes that inform the process that shape current educational initiatives is Thomas Sowell, a black economist who as senior fellow speaks from the ghetto that is the elite, isolated, conservative Hoover Institution at Stanford University. Here is his take on multiculturalism and its expression as 'Black English':

> Ghetto youths who think that talking jive, getting girls pregnant and being belligerent are all part of black identity do not realize how much they are just a throwback to ignorant whites. . . . Young people in the ghettos do not have any kingdoms to lose. They only have a future to lose. That future is going to belong to whoever can function in the high-tech, internationally competitive world. Those who cling to the obsolete past are going to be left behind. . . . most blacks and most whites no longer behave as they did before a changing world led them to adjust to new circumstances and new opportunities. But those blacks who have not yet made it beyond the cultural handicaps of the past are being encouraged to cling to this millstone around their necks.

Why? Because such blacks have been readopted as mascots by the white counterculture. (Sowell, 1995: 8)

First it should be abundantly clear to anyone, even remotely conversant with what is happening in schools, that there is no connection between ghetto youth and white counterculturalists (whoever and whatever they may have been, their influence was never more than minimal among blacks and is insignificant today anywhere). Secondly, it is not the language of the ghetto that precludes ghetto youth from a high-tech future, but the lack of encouragement to succeed in the school which of course discourages them to become fluent in the language of the school. But perhaps of greatest importance is the extent to which a cultural deficit argument has been mangled to deflect attention away from actual school practices and the dearth of options available to those locked into poverty.

The programs that derived from liberal cultural deficit theses in the 1960s — compensatory education and affirmative action — were predicated on the residual effects of previous injustice in a society where inequity and lack of access to opportunity structures no longer exist. The cultural deficit arguments promulgated by current conservatives are directed against the hangover effect that liberal devotion to programs that foster dependency and slothfulness and thus prevent African Americans and other minorities from securing the virtues of a high-tech society where they claim inequity and lack of access to opportunity structures that no longer exist. Both types of cultural deficit thinking serve to deflect attention away from the inequity and lack of access to opportunity structures that not only exist, but are growing at an alarming rate.

As fear of crime and violence molded an increasingly powerful grip on public opinion, more potent forms of cultural deficit theory were developed to inform legislation and policy with respect to poverty, gangs, immigration and the war on drugs. An example of the new wave of deficit thinking can be found in *On Alert! Gang Prevention* (California Department of Education, 1994). Very little in this pamphlet deals with prevention, as its primary message is for schools to unite with police to successfully complete a search and destroy mission. Because gangs are a threat to schools, schools must extirpate them. In this narrow focus, First Amendment rights must be sacrificed and gang attire and symbols banned on campus (California Department of Education, 1994: 28). I believe that gangs are a threat to schools, but I also believe that gangs have largely been created by schools. It is the unwillingness of schools to welcome, equally, all students and to encourage them, equally, to succeed in school that eventually encourages students to look elsewhere for vital gratifications. Gangs fill the vacuum that school creates. There is a glimmer of such understanding in the *On Alert!* pamphlet. But that glimmer is overshadowed by the prevailing deficit arguments that set the tone for the document.

Every young person needs feelings of self-worth, identity, acceptance, recognition, companionship, belonging, purpose, and security. When families, schools, churches, and communities cannot meet those needs, gangs may. Gangs often can supply what traditional systems have failed to provide. (California Department of Education, 1994: 15)

Gangs satisfy other important needs not mentioned in the pamphlet: usefulness, competence, meaning and creativity; these, like the above cited gratifications, are carefully rationed in school — some students get them, some do not. Race, class, ethnicity and gender are very important determinants of whose needs get gratified and whose do not.

In *On Alert! Gang Prevention*, the proposed changes in curriculum and instruction reveals how pervasively deficit thinking saturates the school. Schools are urged to develop gang resistant curriculum. There are no specific suggestions for curriculum change. Not mentioned is the degree to which gangs flourish in minority communities and the extent to which gangs grow as access to legitimate success is reduced. Schools are urged to 'help [gang members and those who aspire to become gang members] . . . see the value of obtaining skills that provide a place for them in productive society' (1994: 30). Not mentioned is how to demystify the route these students must take, the degree of encouragement they should receive, and how to make more credible the message. Cooperative education is strongly recommended with gang members working 'toward common goals shared by other students outside the gang' (p. 30). Teachers are advised to become more aware of gang infiltration (p. 35). Not mentioned is the altering of the nature of teacher relationships with vulnerable students, or recruiting persons into teaching from the communities where gangs fester and grow. Apart from some peripheral changes in school functioning, mostly in the direction of greater security, the school remains as fixed and the accommodations to it must be made by the students. With gangs, the emphasis is on compelling students to conform, and when that fails the next step is expulsion.

What about the recent growth of curricular changes in the area of multicultural education? Advantaged youth are delivered lessons on Cinco De Mayo and Martin Luther King Jr.'s birthday without understanding the significance of either. Multicultural education acquaints advantaged youth with Caesar Chavez, Diego Rivera (actually more with Frida Kahlo), Sandra Cisneros, Bob Marley, Alice Walker and Toni Morrison. Poor children of color, in contrast, remained mired in disadvantage and often are not given the opportunity to become acquainted with the above racial/ethnic minority individuals (characters those in authority attributed to be culturally disadvantaged).

What the advantaged learn from multicultural education is superficial, disjointed and fragmentary. Such learning does not inspire social action. Moreover, simultaneously with their newly acquired multiculturalism, advantaged students encounter virulent deficit cultural arguments in the analysis of *gang culture* and the practices that emanate from that analysis: such as, the legislative arguments used to reduce benefits for *welfare mothers*, the discussion about drug cultures, and the mounting campaign against *illegal immigrants*. In each of the above, the deficits of culture are clearly enunciated and each have equally clear implications for policy and practice. Multiculturalism, as currently conceived, does not lead to greater access or equity; the newly derived cultural deficit arguments based on fear have had powerful effects in reinforcing exclusion.

To be sure, the cultural and accumulated environmental deficit models we have discussed in this chapter have had substantial influence in shaping the evolution of deficit thinking in educational thought and practice. Although these theses hit their zenith in the golden age of deficit thinking, the 1960s, their tenacious and protean nature allowed them to surface and resurface — as does an obstinate virus — over the last few decades. In the 1980s, and particularly the 1990s, the deficit models we have covered have reappeared with some vigor as explanatory bases of school failure experienced by poor and working-class children/youth of color, as well as economically disadvantaged white youngsters. To a large extent, the current deficit thinking models are recycled theories with retooled constructs, such as 'at-risk' students. In the next chapter, Contemporary Deficit Thinking, Richard Valencia and Daniel Solórzano provide a comprehensive analysis of these current developments.

Notes

1   Social reproduction is a term used to describe, if not explain, social stability — the maintenance of economic and social hierarchical arrangements from generation to generation.
2   The most important contributor to that decision was the African American psychologist, Kenneth Clark, who — with his wife, Mamie — found that African American children (between the ages of 3 and 7 years), when presented with identical dolls (except for skin and hair color), preferred the white doll over the black doll. The older the children got, the more pronounced was the preference (Clark and Clark, 1947). The Clarks' findings were provided as evidence that African American children held themselves in very low esteem because of attending segregated schools. However, for a critique of this then popular 'Black self-hatred thesis', see White and Parham (1990).
3   The decline in support for genetic explanations of race and class differences in intellectual achievement was only temporary; genetic explanations for differential life success did not wither and die. To the contrary, such theses have amazing recuperative powers and reemerged with new vigor in the late 1960s, late 1980s, and mid-1990s (see Valencia and Solórzano, Chapter 6, current book).
4   Here, Bourdieu reverses the observation that brought so much recognition to C. Wright Mills who had insisted that church, family and school had paled in importance to the military, business and government. It was this Millsian argument that President Eisenhower appropriated in his farewell address, warning of the growing power of the 'military–industrial complex'.
5   In 1961, Art Pearl and Frank Riessman organized a Ford Foundation sponsored conference. The purpose was to invite social scientists who had written about the causes and consequences of poverty. Of the more than 50 scholars who attended, only a few questioned deficit thinking, and the vast majority supported the inadequate socialization thesis.

References

AICHHORN, A. (1983) *Wayward Youth*, Evanston, IL: Northwestern University Press. (Original work published 1925).

AMRAM, F., FLAX, S., HAMERMESH, M. and MARTY, G. (1988) *New Careers: The Dream that Worked*, Minneapolis, MN: University of Minnesota Press.

BARATZ, S.S. and BARATZ, J.C. (1970) 'Early childhood intervention: The social science base of institutional racism', *Harvard Educational Review*, **40**, pp. 29–50.

BARBER, B. (1992) *An Aristocracy of Everyone*, New York: Oxford University Press.

BEREITER, G. and ENGELMANN, S. (1966) *Teaching Disadvantaged Children in the Pre-school*, Englewood Cliffs, NJ: Prentice-Hall.

BERNSTEIN, B. (1958) 'Some sociological implications of a linguistic form', *British Journal of Sociology*, **9**, pp. 159–74.

BERNSTEIN, B. (1959) 'A public language: Some sociological implications of a linguistic form', *British Journal of Sociology*, **10**, pp. 311–26.

BERNSTEIN, B. (1960) 'Language and social class', *British Journal of Sociology*, **11**, pp. 271–76.

BERNSTEIN, B. (1961) 'Social class and linguistic development: A theory of social learning', in HALSEY, A.H., FLOUD, J. and ANDERSON, A. (Eds) *Education, Economy and Society*, New York: Free Press, pp. 288–314.

BERNSTEIN, B. (1970) 'A sociolinguistic approach to socialization with some reference to educability', in WILLIAMS, F. (Ed) *Language and Poverty*, Chicago IL: Markham Press, pp. 25–61.

BERNSTEIN, B. (1971) *Class, Codes and Control*, New York: Schocken Books.

BERNSTEIN, B. and HENDERSON, D. (1969) 'Social class differences in the relevance of language to socialization', *Sociology*, **3**, pp. 1–20.

BERRUETA–CLEMENT, J.R., SCHWEINHART, L.J., BARNETT, W.S., EPSTEIN, A.S. and WEIKERT, D.P. (1984) *Changed Lives: The Effects of the Perry Preschool Program on Youths Through the Age 19*, Ypsilanti, MI: High/Score Press.

BLOOM, B.S., DAVIS, A. and HESS, R.D. (1965) *Compensatory Education for Cultural De-privation*, New York: Holt, Rinehart & Winston.

BLOOM, H. (1994) *The Western Canon: The Books and the School of the Ages*, New York: Harcourt Brace.

BOURDIEU, P. (1984) *Distinction: A Social Critique of the Judgment of Taste*, London: Routledge.

BOURDIEU, P. and DE SAINT MARTIN, M. (1974) 'Scholastic excellence and the values of the educational system', in EGGLESTON, J. (Ed) *Contemporary Research in the Sociology of Education*, London: Methuen, pp. 338–71.

BOURDIEU, P. and PASSERON, J.C. (1977) *Reproduction in Education, Society and Culture*, London: Sage.

BOWLES, S. and GINTIS, H. (1976) *Schooling in Capitalist America: Educational Reform and the Contradictions of Economic Life*, New York: Basic Books.

CALIFORNIA DEPARTMENT OF EDUCATION (1994) *On Alert! Gang Prevention*, Sacramento, CA: Sales Unit, California Department of Education, PO Box 271.

CARTER, W.T. (1977) 'The Career Opportunities Program: A summing up', in GARTNER, A., RIESSMAN, F. and CARTER-JACKSON, V. (Eds) *Paraprofessionals Today*, New York: Human Services Press, pp. 183–221.

CHILMAN, C. (1966) *Growing up Poor*, Washington, DC: US Department of Health, Education, and Welfare, US Government Printing Office.

CHOROVER, S.L. (1979) *From Genesis to Genocide: The Meaning of Human Nature and the Power of Behavior Control*, Cambridge, MA: The Massachusetts Institute of Technology Press.

CLARK, K.B. and CLARK, M.P. (1947) 'Racial identification and preference in Negro children', in NEWCOMB, T.M. and HARTLEY, E. (Eds) *Readings in Social Psychology*, New York: Holt, pp. 169–78.

DEUTSCH, M. (1967) *The Disadvantaged Child*, New York: Basic Books.

DEUTSCH, M. and BROWN, B. (1964) 'Social influences in Negro–white intelligence differences', *Journal of Social Issues*, **20**, pp. 24–35.

D'SOUZA, D. (1991) *Illiberal Education: The Politics of Race and Sex on Campus*, New York: Free Press.

DURKHEIM, E. (1933) *The Division of Labor in Society* (2nd ed.) (SIMPSON, G. Trans.), Glencoe, IL: Free Press. (Original work published 1893).

EAGLETON, T. (1987) 'Awakening from modernity', *London Times Literary Supplement*, p. 194.

EDMONDS, R. (1979) 'Effective schools for the urban poor', *Educational Leadership*, **37**, pp. 57–62.

EDMONDS, R. (1984) 'School effects and teacher effects', *Social Policy*, **15**, pp. 37–40.

ERIKSON, E.H. (1959) 'Identity and the life cycle', *Psychological Issues*, **1**, pp. 1–171.

ERIKSON, E.H. (1963) *Childhood and Society* (2nd ed.) New York: W.W. Norton.

ERIKSON, E.H. (1964) *Insight and Responsibility*, New York: W.W. Norton.

ERIKSON, E.H. (1968) *Identity: Youth and Crisis*, New York: W.W. Norton.

FROST, J.L. and HAWKES, G.R. (Eds) (1966) *The Disadvantaged Child: Issues and Innovations*, New York: Houghton Mifflin.

GARRETT, H.E. (1961) 'The equalitarian dogma', *Mankind Quarterly*, **1**, pp. 253–7.

GILLIGAN, C. (1982) *In a Different Voice: Psychological Theory and Women's Development*, Cambridge, MA: Harvard University Press.

GLADWIN, T. (1961) 'The anthropologist's view of poverty', in the *Social Work Forum*, New York: Columbia University Press, pp. 73–86.

GREENBERG, D. (1977) 'The correctional effects of corrections: A survey of evaluations', in GREENBERG, D. (Ed) *Corrections and Punishment*, Beverly Hills, CA: Sage.

HARPER, P.B. (1994) *Framing the Margins: The Social Logic of Postmodern Culture*, New York: Oxford University Press.

HARVEY, D. (1989) *The Condition of Postmodernity*, Cambridge, MA: Basil Blackwell.

HAYCOCK, K. and NAVARRO, S.M. (1988) *Unfinished Business: Fulfilling our Children's Promise*, Oakland, CA: The Achievement Council.

HELLMUTH, J. (Ed) (1967) *Disadvantaged Child*, **1**, New York: Brunner/Mazel.

HESS, R.D. and SHIPMAN, V. (1965) 'Early experience and the socialization of cognitive modes in children', *Child Development*, **36**, pp. 869–86.

HOLLINS, C.E. (1991) *It was Fun from the Beginning*, New York: Carlton Press.

hooks, b. (1990) *Yearning: Race, Gender and Cultural Politics*, Boston, MA: South End Press.

HUBBELL, R. (1983) *Head Start Evaluation, Synthesis and Utilization Project*, DHHS Publication No. OHDS 83–31184, Washington, DC: US Government Printing Office.

HUNT, J. McV. (1961) *Intelligence and Experience*, New York: Ronald Press.

JENSEN, A.R. (1969) 'How much can we boost IQ and scholastic achievement?', *Harvard Educational Review*, **37**, pp. 1–123.

KLINEBERG, O. (1935) *Negro Intelligence and Selective Migration*, New York: Columbia University Press.

KLINEBERG, O. (1940) *Social Psychology*, New York: Henry Holt.

KOHLBERG, L. (1963) 'Moral development and identity', in *National Society for the Study* of Education, 62nd Yearbook, Part 1, Child Psychology, Chicago, IL: University of Chicago Press.

KOHLBERG, L. (1973) 'The contribution of developmental psychology to education — examples from moral education', *Educational Psychologist*, **10**, pp. 2–14.

KOHLBERG, L. (1975) 'The cognitive-developmental approach to moral education', *Phi Delta Kappan*, **56**, pp. 670–7.

KOHLBERG, L. and GILLIGAN, C. (1971) 'The adolescent as a philosopher: The discovery of the self in a postconventional world', *Daedalus*, **100**, pp. 1051–86.

KOZOL, J. (1991) *Savage Inequalities: Children in America's Schools*, New York: Crown.

LABOV, W. (1970) 'The logic of nonstandard English', in WILLIAMS, F. (Ed) *Language and Poverty*, Chicago, IL: Markham Press, pp. 153–87.

LEWIS, O. (1961) *The Children of Sanchez*, New York: Random House.

LEWIS, O. (1966a) *La Vida: A Puerto Rican Family in the Culture of Poverty — San Juan and New York*, New York: Random House.

LEWIS, O. (1966b) 'The culture of poverty', *Scientific American*, **215**, pp. 19–25.

LYOTARD, J.F. (1984) *The Postmodern Condition*, Minneapolis, MN: University of Minnesota Press.

MARTINSON, R.M. (1974) 'What works? Questions and answers about prison reform', *In The Public Interest*, **35**, pp. 22–54.

MASLOW, A. (1970) *Motivation and Personality* (2nd ed.), New York: Harper & Row.

MASLOW, A. with DIAZ-GUERRERO, R. (1971) *The Farther Reaches of Human Nature*, New York: The Viking Press.

MEIER, D. (1995) *The Power of their Ideas*, Boston, MA: Beacon Press.

MILLER, W.B. (1958) 'Lower class culture as a generating milieu of gang delinquency', *Journal of Social Issues*, **14**, pp. 5–19.

MOYNIHAN, D.P. (1965) *The Negro Family: The Case for National Action*, Washington, DC: US Department of Labor, US Government Printing Office.

PAI, Y. (1990) *Cultural Foundations of Education*, Columbus, OH: Merrill.

PATEMAN, C. (1985) 'Feminism and democracy', in DUNCAN, G. (Ed) *Democratic Theory and Practice*, Cambridge, MA: Cambridge University Press, pp. 204–17.

PEARL, A. (1972) *The Atrocity of Education*, New York: Dutton.

PEARL, A. (1991) 'Systemic and institutional factors in Chicano school failure', in VALENCIA, R.R. (Ed) *Chicano School Failure and Success: Research and Policy Agendas for the 1990s*, London: Falmer Press, pp. 273–320.

PEARL, A. and RIESSMAN, F. (1965) *New Careers for the Poor*, New York: Macmillan.

PETTIGREW, T.F. (1964) *A Profile of the Negro American*, Princeton, NJ: Van Nostrand.

RIESSMAN, F. (1962) *The Culturally Deprived Child*, New York: Harper & Row.

RIESSMAN, F. and HOLLOWITZ, E. (1965) *Neighborhood Service Centers Program*, A report to the US Office of Economic Opportunity on the South Bronx neighborhood service center.

RYAN, W. (1971) *Blaming the Victim*, New York: Random House.

SECHREST, L., WHITE, S. and BROWN, E. (1979) *The Rehabilitation of Criminal Offenders: Problems and Prospects*, Washington, DC: The National Academy of Sciences.

SOWELL, T. (1995, December 8) 'Ghetto blacks are hanging on to a destructive (and white) legacy', *San Jose Mercury News*, p. 8.

SWARTZ, D. (1990) 'Pierre Bourdieu, culture, education and social inequality', in DOUGHERTY, K.J. and HAMMACK, F.M. (Eds) *Education and Society: A Reader*, New York: Harcourt Brace Jovanovich, pp. 70–80.

WEST, C. (1993) *Race Matters*, Boston, MA: Beacon Press.

WHITE, J.L. and PARHAM, T.A. (1990) *The Psychology of Blacks: An African American Perspective* (2nd ed.), Englewood Cliffs, NJ: Prentice Hall.

WILSON, J.Q. (1975) *Thinking about Crime*, New York: Basic Books.

YANKELOVICH, D. (1981) 'New rules in American life: Searching for self-fulfillment in a world turned upside down', *Psychology Today*, April, pp. 35–78.

Chapter 6

Contemporary Deficit Thinking

Richard R. Valencia and *Daniel G. Solórzano*

Although the deficit thinking model has been rebuked by a number of scholars for many decades and is held in disrepute by many current behavioral and social scientists, it nevertheless manifests, in varying degrees, in contemporary educational thought and practice. Furthermore, not only does deficit thinking demonstrate an adherence to current social thought and educational practice, but by all indicators it continues to gain ground as we approach the twenty-first century. Our goal in this chapter is to examine how modern day deficit thinking gets expressed in theory and practice.

It is difficult to place the contemporary displays of deficit thinking under a rubric as was done for the three previously discussed variants (i.e., genetic pathology; culture of poverty; cultural and accumulated environmental deficits). The reason for being unable to apply a single, clear marker for the modern period is that contemporary deficit thinking is characterized by an assortment of the three models. As such, we discuss deficit thinking developments in the following contexts: First, there is current deficit thinking that uses genetic bases as explanations of human behavior, particularly racial/ethnic differences in intelligence. These genetic pathology perspectives come under our section, 'Inferior Genes, Inferior Intelligence: Neohereditarianism'. Second, there are contemporary deficit thinking views that draw from the culture of poverty paradigm (discussed in the section, 'Blaming the Victim, Blaming the Poor: The Underclass'). Third, the theses of cultural and accumulated environmental deficits continue to be embraced by some modern day deficit thinkers (covered in the section, '"Inadequate" Parents, Home, and Child: Current Families, 1960s Style'). In our analysis of these contemporary deficit thinking expressions, we need, at times, to go beyond educational thought and practice in that such perspectives have worked their way into the broader context of American social thought regarding race, ethnic, gender, and class relations.

Inferior Genes, Inferior Intelligence: Neohereditarianism

Audrey M. Shuey

We daresay that most scholars familiar with the evolution of hereditarian thought would agree that the modern version of the genetic pathology model was launched with Arthur Jensen's 1969 disputatious treatise in which he conjectured that the lower performance of black children — compared to whites — on intelligence tests was mostly due to genetic influences. Although Jensen (1969) is often cited as the source that rekindled the coals leading to a revival of modern day hereditarianism, we believe it is necessary to go back a decade further to get a better sense of the development of neohereditarianism.

In 1958, Audrey Shuey published her controversial book on *The Testing of Negro Intelligence*. Her second edition, which we shall use as our source of discussion, was published in 1966. Shuey's massive review (578 pages) spanned 50 years of research and included 380 original investigations of Negro intelligence (singularly studied or in direct comparison to white participants). The review included research studies in which more than 81,000 Negro school children (primarily grades 1–8) and 48,200 Negro high school and college students were tested on intelligence measures. Furthermore, military officers, enlisted men, veterans and other adults, such as criminals, homeless men, were also subjects in some of the reviewed studies. In all, 80 different intelligence tests (excluding different test editions or forms) were employed in the various investigations.

Of Shuey's (1966) numerous conclusions, the ones most germane to our discussion are:

1 There was a striking consistency in intelligence test results. Combining all studies, blacks performed about 1 standard deviation (15 IQ points) below whites.

2 Small average differences (1 to 6 points) were found between the IQs of northern-born black children and southern-born black children (favoring the former group) living in the same northern cities and attending the same public schools. Shuey concluded 'about half of this difference may be accounted for by environmental factors and half by selective migration' (p. 495).

3 There was a 'tendency for racial hybrids to score higher than those groups described as, or inferred to be, unmixed Negro . . .' (p. 521).

4 Generally, when SES was controlled, the observed black–white differences in IQ were still present.

5 Blacks, compared to whites, did better on intelligence test items requiring concrete and practical solutions and poorer on those items demanding logical analysis and abstract reasoning.

Regarding her major explanation for the differences in intellectual performance between blacks and whites, Shuey (1966) was silent throughout her lengthy review. Her conclusion did appear, however, in the final sentence on the final page. Atavistically, Shuey posited a genetic hypothesis reminiscent of 1920s hereditarian thought: '[the test results] all taken together, *inevitably point to the presence of native differences between Negroes and whites as determined by intelligence tests* [emphasis added]' (p. 521).

Suffice it to say, Shuey's (1966) alleged hereditarian conclusion of black intellectual inferiority did not go unchallenged. A number of investigators (see Bond, 1958; Klineberg, 1963; Pettigrew, 1964; Hicks and Pellegrini, 1966) offered sharp critiques.[1] Horace Mann Bond — whom the reader will recognize as one of the very early critics of intelligence testing research that alleged black children were mentally inferior — presented, for example, the following criticisms of Shuey's work:

1   She failed to distinguish the comments and conclusions of the authors she reviewed, from her own inferences. Bond (1958) cited examples of authors who concluded the observed lower IQ scores of blacks were largely due to environmental factors. Yet, Shuey apparently lumped together the results of a large number of such studies and concluded the differences were largely due to heredity.

2   Bond (1958) took Shuey to task for not fully discussing her reporting that white southerners invariably scored lower on IQ tests than white northerners. With respect to this major, well-known finding, Bond explained:

> Southern whites *do* score below northern whites; but this is due to the circumstances of historic and contemporary educational, cultural, and social disadvantages, to which residents of this section have been immemorially exposed, as compared to northern whites. (p. 523)

Regarding Shuey's (1966) observation that the lower scores of blacks (in comparison to whites) were found not only in the rural and urban South but also in northern cities, Otto Klineberg (1963) — now 64 years old and who we recall did some of the original work in intelligence testing of black children living in northern cities — explained:

> When my students and I indicated (Klineberg, 1935) that test scores of Southern Negro children improved in proportion to their length of residence in New York City, we were perfectly aware that they still did not reach the white norms, and we pointed that out. Could anyone have expected them to do so under Harlem living conditions, and in the Harlem schools as they were at that time? Could anyone possibly suggest that in New York or in Philadelphia ... there is *no* discrimination against Negroes. There was improvement, however, because there was *less* discrimination than where they came from. (p. 200)

Thomas Pettigrew (1964), a noted expert on race relations, offered these assessments of Shuey's (1966) analysis:

1   Shuey cited a number of studies in which she claimed blacks still scored significantly lower even when environmental factors were 'equated'. Pettigrew found fault with Shuey's analyses, however, critiquing her failure to

read carefully the qualifications of the authors, (such as the assumption of socioeconomic status equality of blacks and whites was not entirely valid).

2   Pettigrew (1964) reprehended Shuey's work in terms of a definitional issue of race:

> Other fundamental problems complicate the scene. The very con-
> cept of 'race' raises special issues. Since Negro Americans do not
> even approach the status of a genetically pure 'race', they are a
> singularly inappropriate group upon which to test racist theories
> of inherent intellectual inferiority of the Negroid subspecies . . . To
> find that many descriptive investigations using intelligence tests
> elicit differences between the races does not necessarily mean
> that these differences result from race. (p. 7)

The criticism presented by Hicks and Pellegrini (1966) is a novel, yet signi-ficant, rebuke of Shuey's book in that it deals with the *meaningfulness* of racial differences regarding *policy*. That is, can any policy implications stemming from race studies in intelligence be empirically substantiated? For example, Henry Garrett (1962) argued that blacks were so constitutionally inferior that miscegenation and school integration should be prohibited. Hicks and Pellegrini (1966), arguing that almost any study could be made to show significant differences if enough subjects were used regardless of how nonsensical the variables might be, criticized Garrett for misconstruing the meaning of 'statistical significance' and erroneously equating it with 'practical significance'. Hicks and Pellegrini reexamined 40 studies by 26 investigators that Shuey reviewed in her 1958 book (first edition) and computed an estimated ω^2 (omega square) from the t value in each case.[2] The estimated ω^2s ranged from .000 to .383; the median value was .061 (i.e., 6 per cent explained variance). Of the 40 studies, 24 had estimated ω^2s of less than .10, 11 were between .100 and .199, 3 between .200 and .299, and 2 between .300 and .383. One study that Hicks and Pellegrini listed had an astronomical t of 149.05, but 93,955 whites and 23,596 blacks were subjects; the est. ω^2 was .159.

Hicks and Pellegrini (1966), in sum, argued that there is no established objec-tive basis for Shuey's (1966) conclusion of innate intellectual inferiority of blacks and any policy recommendation resultant of such a conclusion, such as Garrett's (1962) call for the school segregation of black children. Rebuking both Shuey and Garrett, the authors commented:

> The results of this study [Shuey's book] reflect directly on the conflicting
> interpretations of racial differences in IQ.
>   The median est. ω^2, .061, is thought to best represent the strength of
> association between skin color and intelligence. Six per cent represents
> only a small reduction in uncertainty. When Garrett [1962: 2] claims that
> the differences in Negro and white IQ 'are real and highly useful in guid-
> ance and prediction', he has greatly exaggerated the strength of the rela-
> tionship between skin color and IQ.

It is concluded that studies of racial intelligence have failed to establish the existence of meaningful ethnic differences in intelligence. Therefore any interpretation of racial IQ data that stipulates differential treatment of Negroes and whites is unwarranted. (1966: 45)

Henry E. Garrett

It is difficult to fathom why Shuey in 1966 — a time which the Civil Rights Movement was gaining ground and white America was being sensitized to the plight of African Americans and other people of color — would proffer a genetic interpretation of the black–white gap in measured intelligence. After all, hereditarianism as a form of social thought had been silenced for over three decades. We speculate that Shuey's deficit thinking was influenced, in part, by her mentor — Professor Henry E. Garrett.

Garrett received his PhD from Columbia University and subsequently chaired Columbia's Department of Psychology (1940–1956). It appears that during his career his colleagues held him in high esteem, as he was elected as president of the Eastern Psychological Association, the American Psychological Association and the Psychometric Society. In addition, he was a fellow of the American Association for the Advancement of Science and a member of the National Research Council.

One would think that in light of his prestigious appointments and leadership roles in a number of learned societies, Garrett would have been a man with an open mind and whose scholarly endeavors would have been guided by the basic principle of objectivity. Well, in the area of racial comparisons we know that Garrett approached his research with the vigor of a pseudoscientist. He was biased, dishonest and frequently a proselytizer of his racial views about the alleged inferiority of blacks and the alleged superiority of whites. Although Garrett made some of his racial pronouncements in respectable scholarly journals (see Garrett, 1962), his most egregious racial animus was voiced in a series of self-serving, pseudoscientific, non-peer reviewed pamphlets. For example, in *Breeding Down* (Garrett, nd, circa mid 1960s; cited in Chorover, 1979) Garrett, a strident anti-miscegenationist, offered justification for race segregation on the grounds that blacks were mentally inferior:

You can no more mix the two races and maintain the standards of white civilization than you can add 80 (the average IQ of Negroes) and 100 (the average IQ of whites), divide by two and get 100. What you would get would be a race of 90s, and it is that 10 per cent differential that spells the difference between a spire and a mud hut; 10 per cent — or less — is the margin of civilization's 'profit'; it is the difference between a cultured society and savagery. Therefore, it follows, if miscegenation would be bad for white people, it would be bad for Negroes as well. For, if leadership is destroyed, all is destroyed. (quoted in Chorover, p. 47)

Garrett's racist views on race mixing through intermarriage also included a staunch posture against school desegregation. Such race mixing of blacks and whites in schools must be opposed, he argued, because desegregation would likely lead to friendships, and subsequently, intermarriage. It appears that his anti-miscegenationist and anti-desegregationist convictions were so fervently articulated that other racist ideologues embraced them with vigor. 'During the 1960's 500,000 copies of Henry Garrett's pamphlets on the evils of miscegenation were distributed free of charge to American teachers by opponents of integrated education' (Chorover, 1979: 48).

As late as the 1970s, Garrett was still spewing his racist diatribe. In 1975, during the middle of the emotionally charged school busing debate in Boston, an advertisement appeared in the *Boston Globe*, announcing the publication of Garrett's 1973 'book' (actually a 57-page pamphlet) entitled *IQ and Racial Differences* (Chorover, 1979). Written, it appears, for an educated layperson, Garrett is not reticent about his views concerning the heritage, intelligence and schooling of the American Negro. Note the following quotes:

- In recent years it has become fashionable to depict in glowing terms the achievement of the Negro over the past 5000 years, although the truth is that the history of the black African is largely a blank (pp. 1–2).
- The roster of Negro achievements has been greatly distorted and is mostly fictitious . . . All in all, it would seem that, if an exception is made for jazz, the contribution of the Negro in American life has not been great (pp. 4–5).
- Since most Negroes [after the Civil War] were in a prehistoric state of civilization, the South resorted to segregation as a self-protective device . . . Segregation was a unique institution and in many ways worked quite well (pp. 5–6).
- Egalitarianism makes a bow to heredity, but argues that almost all of the undeniable differences among mankind arise from environmental pressures, many of which are under man's control . . . The author [Garrett] of this study holds to the thesis that egalitarianism is dead wrong. Black and white children do *not* have the same potential. They do *not* learn at the same rate (pp. 10–11).
- the American Negro is aided [intellectually] by his racial admixture with the American white (p. 11).
- The case for genetic differences in [Negro–white] intelligence is a solid one (p. 47).
- Since environmental theory has wrought havoc, why not try a 'new' set of premises based on genetic theory? For example . . . institute separate and equally well-equipped schools for Negroes and whites, wherever feasible (p. 51).
- It is clear there cannot be complete desegregation of our classrooms on the one hand and first-rate education on the other. Under such conditions there would only be second-rate education for the children of both races (p. 53).

In the final analysis, it appears likely that Audrey Shuey (1966) in her genetic hypothesis of black–white differences in IQ was influenced by the racial views of her mentor, Henry Garrett. Our conjecture is further supported by examination of the foreword, written by Garrett, of Shuey's *The Testing of Negro Intelligence*. Several points he makes are noteworthy. First, on the subject of ethics, he comments: 'The honest psychologist, like any true scientist, should have no preconceived racial bias' (p. viii). Apparently, Garrett felt he was above this principle. Keep in mind that at the same time he made this statement he was voicing, in his pamphlets, his repugnant, biased opinions about blacks. Second, on the environmental hypothesis of racial differences in intelligence, he argues: 'the American Negro is generally below the white in social and economic status and his work opportunities are more limited. Many of these inequalities have been exaggerated' (p. viii). Notwithstanding all the empirical evidence that black–white differences are best accounted for by environmental and socioeconomic status (SES) factors, he shrugs off this body of data. Finally, with respect to Garrett's interpretation of the cause of black–white differences in intelligence, he posits — as does Shuey 527 pages later — a genetic hypothesis:

> It [Shuey's book] is a careful and accurate survey which should command the attention of all serious students of the subject. Dr Shuey finds that at each age level and under a variety of conditions, Negroes regularly score below whites [on intelligence tests] . . . We are forced to conclude that the regularity and consistency of *these results strongly suggest a genetic basis for the differences* [italics added]. I believe that the weight of evidence (biological, historical and social) supports this judgment. (p. viii)

Arthur R. Jensen

The title of Jensen's (1969) highly controversial monograph — 'How much can we boost IQ and scholastic achievement?' — cleverly encapsulates his prescriptive views about the educability of black and poor children. The wording of Jensen's monograph title is actually a double-barreled query. He asks two questions regarding black and poor children: 1) How much can their IQ be raised? 2) How much can their school achievement be raised? To the first question his conclusion is: very little. The second: somewhat — but in a very prescribed manner.

Thus, as did genetic pathology theorists before him (see Terman, 1916), Jensen (1969) also offered recommendations for schooling. In his Level I–Level II theory of learning (which basically is a theory of educability), he suggested that curriculum for low-SES and black children should concentrate on lower-level skills development (Level I) in that they are unable to master the higher-level cognitive skills (Level II). Jensen came to this pedagogical recommendation via the following reasons:

1 Compensatory education for 'disadvantaged' children has been tried, and it has failed to increase their IQ scores for any significant period of time.

2   The heritability coefficient of intelligence is about .80 for within groups (i.e., US and European whites).

3   Study after study have shown that US blacks — compared to whites — perform about one standard deviation below the normative mean on IQ tests.

4   In that the heritability coefficient for blacks *may* also be of the same magnitude for US whites, Jensen hypothesized that the observed differences between US blacks and whites may be attributed to genetic influences.

5   Finally, Jensen argued that educational attempts to boost disadvantaged children's IQs have been misdirected, and therefore the schools should focus on teaching concrete and specific skills (i.e., Level I learning). The reader can readily observe that Jensen's instructional recommendation in 1969 was very reminiscent to what Terman (1916) suggested for American Indian, Mexican American, and black children over a half a century previously.

Blum (1978) raises critical points about the timing (1969) of Jensen's monograph with respect to the sociopolitical climate of the late 1960s and how educational psychologists were responding to the educational plight of black youth. Blum notes that during the late 1960s, 'the liberal response to the civil rights movement had been to view the educational system as the major vehicle for achieving racial equality' (p. 114). How did educational psychologists respond? Some, Blum suggests, took the approach that schooling inequalities could best be examined by understanding the broader context of institutionalized racism. This strategy, however, was difficult for the majority of these scholars 'who preferred not to drift too far outside of the national political mainstream' (p. 114). The obvious rival approach, Blum notes, 'was to resurrect a modernized version of Galton's theory by contending that the programs [preschool compensatory education] had failed because many black youths were innately ineducable' (p. 114). Jensen's monograph fit this need. To be sure, Jensen's genetic pathology thesis and his pedagogical recommendations set off a flurry of responses, both in the media and in academia. As Blum comments:

Once published, the article [Jensen, 1969] was destined to attract considerable attention. It clearly offended the liberal biases of many academics and thereby aroused a storm of criticism. On the other hand, it justified inequality and seemed to provide a justification for conservative policymakers wishing to eliminate programs like compensatory education. The fact that its publication in winter 1969 coincided with the inauguration of a conservative president [Richard Nixon] intent on dismantling such programs guaranteed that the article would receive widespread publicity, both favorable and unfavorable. (p. 115)

It is well beyond the scope of this chapter to review the many criticisms leveled against Jensen's (1969) monograph.[3] We shall, however, briefly comment on some of these assessments by focusing on the five major conclusions Jensen presented in his article as described above.

1   Jensen's conclusion that preschool compensatory education was ineffective in increasing the intellectual performance (as measured by IQ) of disadvantaged children was based, in part, on the massive Westinghouse–Ohio National Evaluation of Head Start study (Cicirelli, Evans and Schiller, 1969).[4] This investigation, which was based on a national sample of 102 Head Start Centers and nearly 4000 children, concluded that Head Start failed to produce any significant and lasting cognitive and effective gains in the children. Smith and Bissel (1970), in a major critique of the Westinghouse–Ohio study, contended there were serious methodological problems: the use of random rather than stratified sampling; the final sample was unrepresentative in that more than half of the target centers refused to participate; the Head Start and non-Head Start children (controls) were not equated adequately.

2   Regarding Jensen's contention that the heritability coefficient of intelligence is about .80 within groups for Caucasians (Europeans and US whites), several scholars have raised criticisms. For example: the sample sizes in kinship/heritability of intelligence studies of twins and siblings reared together have been limited (Crow, 1969); Jensen has chosen the higher heritability coefficient although a range of coefficients has been found in human populations (Lewontin, 1973); the original work on the heritability of intelligence by Sir Cyril Burt, a noted English psychologist, is suspect of being fraudulent (Wade, 1976).

3   For his conclusion that study after study has shown US blacks, as a group, perform about one standard deviation lower than US whites on IQ tests, Jensen relied heavily on Shuey's (1966) review — a work that was previously brought into question in this chapter.

4   Jensen has been criticized for making an unwarranted leap from within-group to between-group variance regarding the estimated .80 heritability coefficient of intelligence. As Mercer and Brown point out:

> All of these [heritability] studies were conducted on Caucasian samples using similar socio-cultural environments . . . Because similar 'heritability' studies have not been done on black and Mexican-American samples, we do not know if similar 'heritability' coefficients would occur in these ethnic groups. There is [sic] no data. (1973: 85)

5   Jensen's schooling recommendation — that educational attempts to boost disadvantaged children's IQ have been misdirected, and therefore schools should focus on teaching specific skills, for example, Level I learning, has come under fire by several scholars. The major criticism has been directed towards Jensen's claim that his Level I–Level II theory is a hierarchical

model of learning (i.e., Level I precedes Level II). Jensen viewed his two levels as being genetically and independently determined (factorially distinct). Phillips and Kelly (1975) have pointed out, however, that Jensen made an assumption that confused his claim and contradicted his assertion that Level I–Level II abilities are independent. Phillips and Kelly, on this point, stated:

> If Jensen is correct here, and a cursory analysis of his other Level I–Level II tasks such as forward and backward digit span seems to support his argument, then what is involved are not two separate types of ability, Level I (e.g., ability A) and Level II (e.g., ability C). Rather, the situation is that there is Level I (ability A) and Level II (abilities A+B=ability C). This being the case, it would not be at all surprising to find that subjects who do well on tests at Level II (A+B) also do well on tests at Level I (A), although the reverse need not be true: Level I is necessary for Level II but not vice-versa. (p. 363)[5]

In sum, Jensen's (1969) account of the existence of black–white racial differences leads us to conclude that he offers little that is new. Jensen's monograph of 1969 was an anachronism. Although he had the benefits of modern day statistical tools and an advanced knowledge base of human genetics, the core of Jensen's analysis followed the tradition of the 1920s genetic pathology model. Close inspection of his treatise indicated a near alignment with several tenets of 50 years past: 1) Intelligence is innately acquired; 2) IQ tests measure innate intelligence; 3) black–white differences in measured intelligence are largely explained by genetic differences, and environmental factors such as SES, culture, inequality are not important, for the most part, to consider; 4) schooling for blacks should consist of concrete, practical instruction.

It is difficult to assess the overall impact Jensen's (1969) monograph had on social thought and educational practice. Our conjecture is that it probably had some influence in both *reinforcing* existing deficit thinking beliefs held by some individuals and in *shaping* a new wave of hereditarianism. On the former, for example, it is likely that Jensen's Level I–Level II theory gave some support to educators who had already been implementing what he advocated. Bereiter, who has done extensive work with black school children stated, '*We were not trying to teach academic skills directly in ways that did not demand of the children abilities they demonstrably did not possess*' [emphasis added] (1969: 315). Regarding the revivalism of hereditarianism, such scholars (referred to as 'restorationists' by Blum, 1978), found, we daresay, a convenient foundation in Jensen (1969) to push ahead with research and policy studies concerning racial differences in intelligence, alleged dysgenics trends in national intelligence and governmental programs aimed at the poor. Such issues became focal points in the early 1970s, later went into a lull, and then resurfaced in the late 1980s and mid-1990s.

The Evolution of Deficit Thinking

Lloyd M. Dunn

The genetic pathology model, with respect to racial/ethnic differences in intelligence, reappeared in 1987 in a research monograph entitled *Bilingual Hispanic Children on the US Mainland: A Review of Research on Their Cognitive, Linguistic, and Scholastic Development.*[6] The monograph, published by American Guidance Service (a well known test publisher), was authored by Lloyd M. Dunn, the senior author of the *Peabody Picture Vocabulary Test* (PPVT) series.[7]

Dunn's (1987) monograph, it appears, was a shock in particular to Latino scholars in that his treatise was the *first* research report (88 pages) ever published in which Latinos (Mexican American and Puerto Rican children) were the *prime focus* of a genetic interpretation (in part) regarding Latino–white differences in intelligence. As we have seen in this chapter (and likewise discussed by Valencia, Chapter 3) historical and contemporary studies of genetically-driven explanations of group differences in intelligence have predominantly targeted black–white comparisons (such studies of Mexican American children were fairly much confined to the 1920s; see Valencia, Chapter 3). Thus, it was to the dismay of many Mexican American and Puerto Rican behavioral and social scientists when Dunn — after reviewing Latino/white studies of intellectual performance, with emphasis on English/Spanish language versions of the PPVT-Revised — concluded in a neohereditarian fashion:

> While many people are willing to blame the low scores of Puerto Rican and Mexican-American on their poor environmental conditions, few are prepared to face the probability that inherited genetic material is a contributing factor. Yet, in making a scholarly, comprehensive examination of this issue, this factor must be included. (1987: 63)

Dunn continued, referencing the work of Vernon and Jensen who have studied the nature–nurture issue:

> It is argued that it would be simplistic and irresponsible to contend that the 10- to 12-point IQ differential is due exclusively, or even to all environmental influences combined, including cultural incompatibility. Such naive contentions continue to abound, showing a complete lack of knowledge of the scholarly works of Vernon (1979) and Jensen (1981), among others, who have presented strong cases for the important role of heredity. (1987: 64)

Finally, Dunn provides an estimated heritability of .50 for Latino children: 'Therefore . . . my best tentative estimate is that about half of the IQ difference between Puerto Rican or Mexican [American] school children and Anglos is due to genes that influence scholastic aptitude, the other half to environment' (p. 64).

Suffice it to say, Dunn's (1987) monograph resulted in a swift response by concerned scholars. A distinguished panel of experts, both Latino and white, participated in a symposium at the 1988 meeting of the American Educational Research Association (AERA). Furthermore, the papers presented at that AERA panel were published as critiques later in the year in a special issue of the *Hispanic Journal of Behavioral Sciences* (*HJBS*) (see Fernandez, 1988a, 'Achievement Testing: Science v. Ideology'). Time and space do not allow a detailed review of these critiques of Dunn's publication (see Berliner, 1988; Cummins, 1988; Prewitt Diaz, 1988; Fernandez, 1988b; Mercer, 1988; Trueba, 1988; Willig, 1988). What we present here is a brief list of representative criticisms:

1 Dunn, though citing Jensen's (1981) hereditarian interpretations about black–white differences in intelligence, fails 'to explain or to defend Jensen's genetic conclusions. He [Dunn] does not review any of the voluminous literature which has criticized Jensen's methods and his conclusions . . .' (Mercer, 1988: 200).[8]

2 In his discussion of comparison of vocabulary scores (as measured by the PPVT-R) across Spanish, Puerto Rican and Mexican American children, Dunn fails to control for SES (Willig, 1988).

3 'The Spanish version of the PPVT-R was a poor translation, and is not appropriate to measure receptive language in Puerto Rican and Mexican children in the United States' (Prewitt Diaz, 1988: 249).

4 Dunn's assertions that Latino pupils 'are inadequate bilinguals' (p. 49) and 'do not have the scholastic aptitude or linguistic ability to master two languages well, or to handle the switching from one to the other, at school, as the language of instruction' (p. 7) are unsubstantiated and contrary to existing research (Prewitt Diaz, 1988; Willig, 1988).

5 In his contentions that schools are exculpatory in creating inferior education for Puerto Rican and Mexican American students, he ignores the perspective that structural forces in schools have, indeed, been implicated in creating inequitable learning climates for Latinos (Fernandez, 1988b).

6 A criticism we offer of Dunn (1987), which was not presented in the *HJBS* critiques, has to do with the measure of 'intelligence' emphasized in Dunn's analysis — the *Peabody Picture Vocabulary Test* series (PPVT and PPVT-R). In the development of the PPVT, Dunn (1959) conceptualized his instrument as an intelligence test, in that raw scores were converted into an IQ. This practice was abandoned in the revision (PPVT-R; Dunn and Dunn, 1981). Yet, raw scores are still converted into standard scores (or age equivalent scores) with a standardization mean of 100 and a standard deviation of 15 (similar to conventional scales of intelligence). Was the PPVT and is the PPVT-R a general measure of the construct of intelligence? Experts in testing say 'no'. Note the following:

   • Salvia and Ysseldyke (1988) on the nature of picture vocabulary tests, in general, caution test consumers: 'it is important to state what these devices measure. The tests are *not* measures of intelligence per se; *they measure only one aspect of intelligence, receptive vocabulary* [emphasis added] (p. 179).

- Cohen, Swerdlik, and Smith (1992) — noting that the practice of using IQ scores on the PPVT was misleading — say this of the new version: '*the PPVT-R is not an intelligence test* [emphasis added] but rather one that measures one facet of cognitive ability — receptive (hearing) vocabulary for standard American English' (p. 370). Cohen, *et al.* also make the observation that concurrent validity research in which the PPVT-R has been compared with conventional intelligence measures, such as *Stanford–Binet; Wechsler Intelligence Scale for Children-Revised,* has yielded correlation coefficients of low to moderate magnitudes. As such, 'These types of correlations should be expected once it is acknowledged that, unlike some of the tests to which it has been compared, *the PPVT-R is not a test of general intelligence* [emphasis added] (1992: 371).
- Anastasi's (1988) comment has clear implications for the assessment of linguistically and culturally diverse children, such as Puerto Rican and Mexican American children: 'Scores on the PPVT-R reflect in part the respondents' degree of cultural assimilation and exposure to Standard American English' (p. 296).
- Sattler's (1992) warning about the PPVT-R is directed specifically to the assessment of Hispanics: 'The Peabody Picture Vocabulary Test-Revised should *never* be used to obtain an estimate of young Hispanic-American children's general intelligence' (1992: 586).[9]

Even Dunn and Dunn, in the prepublication copy of the PPVT-R manual, offer caveats about what the test is purported and not purported to measure:

> The PPVT-R is designed primarily to measure a subject's receptive (hearing) vocabulary for Standard American English. In this sense, it is an achievement test, since it shows the extent of English vocabulary acquisition.
>
> Another function is to provide a quick estimate of one major aspect of verbal ability for subjects who have grown up in a standard English-speaking environment. In this sense, it is a scholastic aptitude test. It is not, however, a comprehensive test of general intelligence. Instead, it measures only one important facet of general intelligence: vocabulary. (quoted in Salvia and Ysseldyke, 1988, p. 182)

It appears, then, that because the PPVT series does not measure general intelligence, any conclusions about general intellectual or cognitive differences Dunn (1987) has raised about Latino–Anglo comparisons cannot be supported. At the very best, the PPVT series measures a very small sliver of the construct of intelligence — that being *receptive vocabulary*. That lexicon, in general, is very culturally bound, and for Dunn to draw any genetic conclusions based on the administration of a 15-minute test in which children point to plates containing vocabulary words of Standard American English is psychometrically indefensible and professionally irresponsible.[10]

Fortunately, for the sake of discourse, Dunn was invited to present a rejoinder to his *HJBS* critics. In some of his comments, he was recalcitrant in addressing criticisms raised by the scholars who found fault in his monograph. For example, Dunn: 1) continued to press his argument that bilingual education for Puerto Rican and Mexican American children does 'more harm than good . . . and . . . most such children will have great difficulty even learning to speak Standard English well . . .' (1988: 319); 2) held to his assertion that the educational problems and the low social and economic conditions Latinos endure are, for the most part, due to their own limitations. (Later in this chapter, we will discuss this aspect of his deficit thinking). Regarding the heavy criticism directed toward his suggestion that genetic factors are partially implicated in explaining the poor performance of US Puerto Ricans and Mexican Americans on standardized scholastic aptitude tests, Dunn announced a shift in his thinking:

> Thanks to such critiques as have been presented in this journal, and further study and additional research on my part, I now view my monograph as only a 'working paper' that is badly in need of extensive revision. It is now clear that many people were offended by certain of my comments, especially those suggesting that the poor performance of impoverished Hispanic children may be due, in part, to genetic factors. Now I see that the insertion of this element into my discussion was a tactical error and a distraction. From my point-of-view, it is not a central issue. Since it has aroused such strong reactions, I will downplay this point of discussion or eliminate it from any rewrite, so that the main body of my report may get more attention. Therefore, I wish to retract my statements in this area. Both AGS and I now recognize that we showed lack of sensitivity toward Mexican Americans and Puerto Ricans in introducing this point of contention. We apologize. I cannot resist saying, however, that none of us is consistently correct, and that all of us end up with egg on our faces from time to time. (1988: 302–3)

It appears that Dunn's response on the genetic issue is more of an apology for offending people, rather than a recantation of making scientifically unjustifiable conclusions about Latino–white differences in intelligence. In any event, the damage has been done. Dunn's monograph is an angry, self-righteous, pseudoscientific treatise fueled by deficit thinking. Regarding his totally unfounded heritability estimate of .50 that he believes partially accounts for the IQ difference between Puerto Ricans/Mexican Americans and Anglos on scholastic aptitude tests, Mercer's conclusion in her critique of Dunn captures our sentiment:

> It is distressing to find Dunn reviving the old myths about racial differences in inherited 'intelligence' and especially distressing that he is now applying those myths not only to black but to Hispanic populations. He

has no new evidence. He does not even bother to make the case for his position using the old arguments. The fact that the mean scores on tests of learned behavior are different for different populations tells us nothing whatsoever about the sources of those differences. His monograph obscures rather than enlightens and is a disservice to school psychologists who are laboring to conduct fair and accurate assessments in a multicultural society, to bilingual education and to special education. (1988: 217)

Richard J. Herrnstein and Charles Murray

In the fall of 1994, *The Bell Curve: Intelligence and Class Structure in American Life* was published and immediately set off a maelstrom of disputation. The authors are the late Richard Herrnstein (PhD from Harvard University; psychology professor at Harvard from 1958 to 1994) and Charles Murray (PhD from MIT; currently a Bradley Fellow at the conservative research group in Washington, DC, the American Enterprise Institute). Although Herrnstein and Murray sought to shed new light on the complex relations between social class, race, heredity and intelligence, the two authors *have never published* any peer-reviewed scientific journal articles on the genetic basis of intelligence and its relation to race or poverty (Dorfman, 1995).

The Bell Curve, in our opinion, ranks as one of the most sustained treatises on genetic pathology deficit thinking ever published. Herrnstein and Murray claim that cognitive differentiation among Americans (within- and between-racial/ethnic groups) has resulted in a bifurcated society at the extreme levels of the IQ continuum — the emergence of a *cognitive elite* (top 5 per cent, IQ of 120 or higher) and the *very dull* (bottom 5 per cent, IQ of 75 or lower).[11] In some cases, Herrnstein and Murray include the *dull* (IQs from 75 to 89) as part of the *cognitive underclass*. The authors contend that such 'cognitive partitioning' is strongly linked to 'socially desirable behaviors' (i.e., high schooling attainment; prestigious occupational status; high income level) as well as 'socially undesirable behaviors' (i.e., poverty; high school dropouts; unemployment; divorce; illegitimate births; welfare dependency; malparenting; crime; poor civility and citizenship).

Thus, Herrnstein and Murray's (1994) cognitive partitioning thesis contends that 1) having a high IQ greatly improves one's life chances of social mobility and possessing desirable behaviors and 2) having a low IQ places one at substantial risk for possessing undesirable behaviors. The authors derive their thesis and larger model of social stratification as follows:

1 High IQ is an invaluable raw material for social and economic success in American society.
2 Intelligence is endowed unequally within the white population and between groups (i.e., white–black and white–Latino comparisons; about 40 to 80 per cent of intelligence, Herrnstein and Murray claim, is due to genetic influences).[12]

3 The cognitive elite, through concentrated social pools and self-selection (i.e., assortative mating) has emerged. Members of this class (which are disproportionately white) have become the controllers of power, privilege and status, 'restructuring the rules of society so that it becomes harder and harder for them to lose' (1994: 509).

4 Concomitant with the increasing isolation of the cognitive elite and its growing influence over the control of America, is the growth and perpetuation of the cognitive underclass and its accompanying intractable social problems. Furthermore, there is an alleged dysgenics effect presently occurring in which the 'intellectually disadvantaged' (disproportionately Latinos and blacks, according to Herrnstein and Murray) are having the highest fertility rates.

5 In that the cognitive underclass is a) allegedly deficient in intellectual endowments and abilities and b) attempts to raise the IQ of members of this class are not available, a national policy agenda needs to be set in motion.

6 Such policy considerations that should be considered, for example, include: a) evaluation of the immigrant situation (*legal* and *illegal*) in that 'Immigration does indeed make a difference to the future of the national distribution of intelligence' (1994: 358); this is particularly seen in the cases of 'Latino and black immigrants [who] are, in least in the short run, putting downward pressure on the distribution of intelligence' (1994: 360–1); b) society's approach to handling crime should be simplified, meaning what constitutes 'crime' should be easily understood (i.e., a transgression is clear cut) and swiftly enforced; c) in that 'a person of low cognitive ability [finds it difficult] to figure out why marriage is a good thing . . .' (p. 544), a policy prescription 'is to return marriage to its formerly legal status . . . [meaning] you take on obligations' (p. 545). If you are not married and have children, you have no rights and obligations regarding your offspring. For example, an unmarried mother has no legal foundation to demand child support from the father, and the father has no right to see the child; d) an end to welfare payments and other government subsidies to low-IQ unmarried women. In that these women are 'disproportionately at the low end of the intelligence distribution . . . the extensive network of cash and services for low-income women who have babies [should] be ended' (1994: 548).

7 Regarding policy directed toward educational reform, Herrnstein and Murray tangentially mention the use of 'national achievement tests, national curricula, school choice, vouchers, tuition tax credits, apprenticeship programs, restoration of the neighborhood school, minimum competency tests, ability grouping . . .' (1994: 435).[13] One reform suggestion, however, that they discuss in some detail is a need for more attention and funding for the gifted — whom they claim — were 'out' when economically disadvantaged became 'in.'[14] To meet the needs of neglected gifted, Herrnstein and Murray advocate that the federal government '*reallocate some portion of existing elementary and secondary school federal aid from programs for the disadvantaged to programs for the gifted*' (1994: 441–2).

8   Finally, Herrnstein and Murray, in *The Bell Curve*'s penultimate chapter, offer a speculation of the future impact of cognitive stratification on American life and the workings of the government. Their prediction of the future — which can be best described as resembling a horrendous caste system — is frightening and has a calamitous tone for those people who will occupy the bottom rungs of the cognitive ability continuum. The authors comment, 'Like other apocalyptic visions, this one is pessimistic, perhaps too much so. On the other hand, there is much to be pessimistic about' (1994: 509).

Herrnstein and Murray contend that this deplorable future scenario, if realized, will be shaped by three tendencies currently in motion: a) a cognitive elite that is increasing in its isolation; b) a fusing of the cognitive elite with the affluent sector of society; c) a worsening of the quality of life for the cognitive underclass. The authors assert that the merging of the cognitive elite and the affluent will eventually reach such a level of wealth that 'the haves [will] begin to feel sympathy toward, if not guilt about, the condition of the have-nots' (1994: 523). What will result, Herrnstein and Murray speculate, is the development and implementation of an 'expanded welfare state'. By expanded, the authors suggest that this will be a welfare state in which the cognitive elite's motives are guided by sympathy *and* fear and hostility toward the underclass recipients. In that the new coalition of cognitive and affluent elites will have grown weary of spending money on 'remedial social programs' that do little to advance the underclass, coupled with the elites' enmity toward the have-nots, the social program of choice will be the *custodial state.*[15]

Herrnstein and Murray comment that the coming of the custodial state will be influenced, over the next two decades, by a growing acceptance of the belief that the underclass are in dire conditions 'through no fault of their own but because *of inherent shortcomings* [emphasis added] about which little can be done' (1994: 523). As such, there will be more open discussion among politicians and intellectuals that members of the underclass cannot, for example, fend for themselves from such things as violence, child abuse and drug addiction and be trusted to spend cash appropriately (thus, the custodial state will rely more on services, than cash for the underclass).

What specific features and consequences of the custodial state do Herrnstein and Murray envision? Some are:

- 'Child care in the inner city will become primarily the responsibility of the state' (p. 523). Meaning, there will be comprehensive care facilities for infants, preschoolers, and school-age children in which state staff will provide training in hygiene, sexual socialization and preparation for the work force 'and other functions that the parents are deemed incapable of providing' (p. 523).
- 'The homeless will vanish' (p. 524). That is, the homeless (largely the mentally incompetent) will be required to reside in elaborately equipped

shelters. There will be a reassertion of control over public sectors. 'Police will be returned their authority to roust people and enforce laws prohibiting disorderly conduct' (p. 524).

- 'Strict policing and custodial responses to crime will become more acceptable and widespread' (p. 524). This will likely result in the comeback of the old police practice of 'stop-and-frisk', increased police surveillance, the use of electronic bracelets for criminals under house arrest, a national system of ex-convict identification cards, and so on.

- 'The underclass will become even more concentrated spatially than it is today' (p. 524). In that services provided to the underclass, such as day care centers and public housing, will be situated in the poverty pockets of cities, people who desire such services will need to reside there. As such, the segregation of the underclass and the rest of society will intensify, such as school segregation.

Herrnstein and Murray offer this conclusion about the custodial state:

> In short, by *custodial state*, we have in mind a high-tech and more lavish version of the Indian reservation for some substantial minority of the nation's population, while the rest of America tries to go about its business. In its less benign forms, the solutions will become more and more totalitarian. Benign or otherwise, 'going about its business' in the old sense will not be possible. It is difficult to imagine the United States preserving its heritage of individualism, equal rights before the law, free people running their own lives, once it is accepted that a significant part of the population must be made permanent wards of the state. (p. 526)

Predictably so, the publication of *The Bell Curve* — designed to provoke — was followed by a flurry of reactions (negative and positive) and a variety of contexts for such reactions, in radio and television talk shows, newspapers, magazines, and scholarly publications. Regarding the latter, responses to *The Bell Curve* in academia were overwhelmingly adverse, a few favorable. Thomas Bouchard's book review (1995) in *Contemporary Psychology* ('Breaking the Last Taboo') is quite glowing.[16] Apparently agreeing with the thesis of Herrnstein and Murray, Bouchard comments, '*The Bell Curve* carefully documents in table after table, graph after graph, that cognitive ability has become a more important determiner of social status than social class of origin' (p. 416). He also notes, 'This is a superbly written and exceedingly well-documented book' (p. 418). Juxtaposed to Bouchard's 1995 review in *Contemporary Psychology* is the evaluation of *The Bell Curve* by Donald Dorfman ('Soft science with a neoconservative agenda', 1995). Dorfman criticizes *The Bell Curve* along a number of lines, for not being scientific, but rather having a political agenda; for omitting important historical facts that would hurt the case of Herrnstein and Murray (failure to discuss the Sir Cyril Burt fraud on the heritability estimate); for making a fundamental error, that is 'inferring between-race heritability in IQ from within-race heritability in IQ' (Dorfman, 1995: 420)[17].

To date, the most negative and sustained reactions to *The Bell Curve* are presented in an edited book by Steven Fraser — *The Bell Curve Wars: Race, Intelligence, and the Future of America* (1995).[18] For our abridged presentation of these critiques, we have arranged them around several categories we believe best capture their essence. Also, we provide samples of direct quotes in order to preserve the actual points the authors are attempting to convey. Here is our analysis:

On what is new in *The Bell Curve*:

- *The Bell Curve*, with its claims and supposed documentation that race and class differences are largely caused by genetic factors and are therefore essentially immutable, contains no new arguments and presents no new compelling data to support its anachronistic social Darwinism . . . (Gould, 1995: 11)
- The science in the book was questionable when it was proposed a century ago, and it has now been completely supplanted by the development of the cognitive sciences and neurosciences. (Gardner, 1995: 23)
- The science reflected in the book is that of old-fashioned psychometrics and an almost equally outdated behavior genetics that operate in hermetic isolation from recent findings [for example, biology of behavior; cultural evolution] (Nisbett, 1995: 54).
- The book is simply the most recent in a long line of efforts to prove the congenital inferiority of poor people in general, and (in this country) black people in particular. (Jones, 1995: 80)

On the sources used in *The Bell Curve*:

- By scrutinizing the footnotes and bibliography in *The Bell Curve*, readers can more easily recognize the project for what it really is: a chilly synthesis of the work of disreputable race theorists and eccentric eugenicists . . . even a superficial examination of the primary sources suggests that some of Murray and Herrnstein's substantive arguments rely on questionable data and hotly contested scholarship, produced by academics whose ideological biases are pronounced. To this extent, important portions of the book must be treated with skepticism. (Rosen and Lane, 1995: 58)[19]

On statistical data presented in *The Bell Curve*:

- almost all their relationships are weak: very little of the variation in social factors is explained by either independent variable [IQ and SES] . . . their own data indicate that IQ is not a major factor in determining variation in nearly all the social behaviors they study — and so their conclusions collapse . . . most of Herrnstein and Murray's correlations are very weak — often in the 0.2 to 0.4 range. (Gould, 1995: 19–20)[20]

- Nearly all the reported correlations between measured intelligence and societal outcomes explain at most 20 per cent of the variance. In other words, over 80 per cent (and perhaps over 90 per cent) of the factors contributing to socioeconomic status lie beyond measured intelligence. (Gardner, 1995: 26–7)
- Perhaps the most troubling aspect of *The Bell Curve* from an intellectual standpoint is the authors' uncritical approach to statistical correlations. One of the first things taught in introductory statistics is that correlation is not causality. It is also one of the first things forgotten and one of the most widely ignored facts in public policy research. (Sowell, 1995: 77)

On the political nature of *The Bell Curve*:

- *The Bell Curve* is scarcely an academic treatise in social theory and population genetics. It is a manifesto of conservative ideology; the book's inadequate and biased treatment of data displays its primary purpose — advocacy. (Gould, 1995: 20–21)
- Perhaps the most troubling aspect of the book is its rhetorical stance. This is one of the most stylistically divisive books that I have ever read. Despite occasional avowals of regret and the few utopian pages at the end, Herrnstein and Murray set up an us–them dichotomy that eventually culminates in an us–*against*–them opposition. (Gardner, 1995: 33)
- Herrnstein and Murray must deny history, and replace it with mythology, in order to justify a social structure that will keep black people disproportionately relegated to the jobs of nursing aides, orderlies and attendants, cleaners and servants, maids and horsemen . . . *The Bell Curve* amounts to hate literature with footnotes. (Jones, 1995: 92–3)
- *The Bell Curve* is a *Communist Manifesto* for the mind — a stirring, but portentous, announcement of a new world order recently come into being . . . Because there is no such evidence, scenarios about a 'custodial state' in which the smart and rich will do everything to protect themselves from the dumb and poor are more the projections of political pundits than they are the conclusions of disinterested social scientists. (Wolfe, 1995: 109, 123)

The reader can clearly observe that *The Bell Curve* has been heavily criticized. As we have catalogued, the criticisms tend to fall in four categories: 1) a reliance on the old, now thoroughly debunked, pseudoscientific hereditarianism of the 1920s; 2) a reliance, in part, on disreputable neohereditarianists; 3) an improper, misleading use of statistics; and 4) the biased, strongly political nature of the book. In our reading of *The Bell Curve*, we contend that the litany of unfavorable assessments seen in *The Bell Curve Wars* and elsewhere have merit and deserve to be considered in one's overall evaluation of Herrnstein and Murray's treatise.

Of the numerous criticisms directed toward *The Bell Curve*, the one we find particularly germane to the present book's focus on the evolution of deficit thinking

is Herrnstein and Murray's *foundation* for cognitive stratification and policy formation — that is, their reliance on 1920s hereditarianism. As some critics have voiced,
The Bell Curve offers little new in understanding contemporary social stratification
in the US. Valencia (Genetic Pathology Model of Deficit Thinking, Chapter 3, this
book) has identified a number of ideological and 'scientific' streams that helped to
shape 1920 hereditarianism and are pertinent to our present analysis. The major
forces were: 1) Galton's belief that one's social status was genetically predeter-
mined, as were socially desirable and undesirable behaviors; 2) Terman's (and
others') view that intelligence was largely innately based and it predicted, fairly
accurately, one's eventual social, economic, and occupational status; 3) McDougall's
perspective of a society that can and should be divided between the 'haves' and
'have nots', where the former are more deserving to reap societal benefits, should
control the latter, and need to reproduce at greater levels than the latter. A close
examination of *The Bell Curve* reveals that Herrnstein and Murray have incorporated — in whole or part — these pseudoscientific, historically refuted ideas into
their work. Interestingly, the fundamental question that Herrnstein and Murray pose
is remarkably similar to what McDougall (1921) posed 76 years ago in *Is America
Safe for Democracy?* 'Does the social stratification of society correspond to, is
it correlated with, a stratification of intellectual capacity?' (McDougall, p. 62). In
sum, if one is to reject 1920s hereditarianism as bad science and policy, then *The
Bell Curve* must be rejected on the same basis.

Regarding the deficit thinking nature of *The Bell Curve*, this book is a 'hard
read'. We are not speaking of the length (845 pages, including references), but
rather of the tone and mood of the book. Gloom and doom fill the pages of *The Bell
Curve* with fatalistic, pessimistic, totalitarian visions of the future. Nowhere is there
hope for the oppressed (or as Herrnstein and Murray prefer to label them, the
underclass). Gardner (1995) indeed is right: *The Bell Curve* is designed to provoke
by its divisiveness in setting up an 'us–against–them' portrait of current social
relations and an apocalyptic future. IQ controls all. Cognitive partitioning — where
the cognitive elite control and oppress the cognitive underclass — is America's
destiny. The final words of Herrnstein and Murray in *The Bell Curve* speak directly
to their perverse vision of America:

> Much of public policy toward the disadvantaged starts from the premise
> that interventions can make up for genetic or environmental disadvan-
> tages, and that premise is overly optimistic. Part of our answer has been
> positive: Much can and should be done to improve education, especially
> for those who have the greatest potential . . . *Cognitive partitioning will
> continue. It cannot be stopped* [emphasis added] . . . Inequality of endow-
> ments, including intelligence, is a reality. Trying to pretend that inequality
> does not really exist has led to disaster. . . . *It is time for America once
> again to try living with inequality, as life is lived* [italics added] . . . (1994:
> 550–1)

It would be remiss on our part to end our discussion of *The Bell Curve* on such
a cynical note. To be sure, there are a number of scholars and policymakers who

have disdain for the tenebrific societal views held by Herrnstein and Murray. For example, Randall Kennedy (1995), Professor of Law at Harvard Law School and the editor of *Reconstruction* magazine, reminds us that not only have leftists and liberals presented pointed critiques of *The Bell Curve*, but so have a substantial number of conservatives and centrists joined the renunciations. As such, Kennedy contends, the obviously powerful 'cultural–political–social network' that embraces and supports 'The Bell Curve ethos is by no means ascendant' (1995: 186). He asserts that this development is largely due 'to effective efforts undertaken by a wide range of people to uproot the racist beliefs, intuitions, and practices that are buried so deeply throughout this culture' (1995: 186).

As we have seen, some of the criticism directed at contemporary hereditarian thought lay in questioning the basic assumptions of the construct of intelligence and its measurement — a strategy effectively deployed by a number of critics of hereditarianism of the 1920s. In closing we wish to examine, more closely, the historical and current anti-hereditarian perspective that in order to conclude intellectual differences between racial/ethnic groups are genetically influenced, *the assumption has to be met that members of the groups compared need to have had very similar linguistic, cultural, developmental and educational experiences.* Critics of the hereditarian position would argue that this fundamental assumption is *never met.* Thus, if a basic assumption of a theory is not valid, then the framework is scientifically indefensible. The theory collapses from within — it implodes. Let us inspect the views of two anti-hereditarian scholars — remotely separated in time, but closely connected in their analyses — to see how they question the underlying assumption of hereditarianism.

William C. Bagley (1922), in a scrutiny of 'the basic assumption that underlies the whole theory of mental measurement . . .' (p. 376), commented that even an hereditarianist individual would agree that innate intelligence is never measured. Such 'inborn intelligence', Bagley argued, was inferred from 'acquired intelligence'. This influence, he continued, was made on the assumption that people being compared in intelligence had common experiences. Bagley concluded that such an assumption is extremely questionable and never truly met. Note the following:

> The validity of mental measurements and of every influence that is drawn from the alleged facts that the measurements have disclosed is based upon the assumption *that with respect to the materials of the tests*, the environment, the experience, the education the stimulation and the inspiration of those compared have been identical. (1922: 376)

Nearly seven decades later, Jane R. Mercer (1989) offered a similar, but more detailed, argument. Her points can be summarized as follows:

1   From a construct point of view, intelligence and achievement 'cannot be distinguished operationally. They are not separate dimensions' (1989: 294).
2   The WISC-R, an achievement test as a case in point, can measure what a person has learned about the language and cultural content presented in the

test. The scores derived from such a test can be used to compare individuals' knowledge. Such comparisons, Mercer states, are *first-order* inferences, and these inferences 'can be drawn that a person with an appreciably higher score on the test has *learned* more than a person with a lower score. There is no controversy about such first-order inferences' (294).

3　What is controversial, Mercer states, is a *second-order* inference — which is an inference about *intelligence*. She contends that the traditional IQ paradigm rests on the basic assumption that intelligence tests measure *g*, a general factor accounting for about 50 per cent of the variance in the test items, (such as Stanford-Binet). Furthermore, she observes that 'The universal appearance of the *g* factor is interpreted as evidence of some type of organic, genetic substrata for *g*' (p. 293). Second-order inferences are contentious because they 'infer that person A *is more intelligent* than person B because person A has learned more than person B' (p. 294).

4　Finally, Mercer points out that the major problem with the traditional IQ paradigm is that it is remiss in distinguishing between first- and second-order inferences. She argues, as did Bagley in 1922, that the IQ paradigm's central assumption — equivalent or comparable experiences and backgrounds of individuals — with respect to drawing second-order inferences cannot be met.

> An achievement test can be used to make second-order inferences about intelligence *if* the persons being compared have had the same opportunity to learn what is in the test, have been similarly motivated to learn what is in the test, have comparable learning strategies, and have no sensory disabilities that might interfere with learning. *If all the factors that affect learning other than intelligence are held constant and if one person has learned significantly more than another, then a second-order inference is possible* [italics added]. It can be inferred that the person who has learned more is more intelligent than the person who has learned less. In short, when all the factors other than intelligence that influence learning have been held constant, then any residual difference in scores is attributed to differences in intelligence. If all factors that can affect learning, other than intelligence, are *not* controlled, then second-order inferences are not possible. In such circumstances, it is not legitimate to attribute all residual differences in learning to differences in intelligence, and no inferences about intelligence are possible. (p. 295)

It appears to us that critics of the contemporary genetic pathology model, which by all indications is experiencing a small revival, need to be more cognizant about the questionable and unsound assumptions hereditarianism rests on — especially the assumption of equivalent or comparable experiences and backgrounds of test takers. This key assumption is so tenuous that any critical analysis of the

IQ paradigm and resultant theorizing about racial/ethnic innate differences in intelligence would be ineffective without a focused, informed criticism of the assumption.

Blaming the Victim, Blaming the Poor: The Underclass

Another major form of contemporary deficit thinking involves the construct of the *underclass,* a notion that draws heavily from the *culture of poverty* model — a deficit thinking framework discussed by Douglas Foley in Chapter 4 of this book. The culture of poverty model has been retooled and reemerged in the early 1980s (and still vogue in the 1990s) under the rubric of the *cultural underclass* (see Baca Zinn, 1989; Singh, 1994; Steinberg, 1989). As were those individuals who were trapped in the culture of poverty, people currently mired in the depths of poverty — the underclass — also are believed to constitute a 'self-sustaining culture' (Lemann, 1986). The original concept of the underclass began in the academic community and focused on those segments of the population that remain at the bottom rungs of the socioeconomic ladder during periods of both economic growth and downturn (Myrdal, 1944). In the early 1980s, however, the concept of the under-class entered the popular press, and eventually the political presidential campaigns in 1988, focusing on the attitudinal and behavioral aspects of the underclass that allegedly were at odds with mainstream values and behaviors (Auletta, 1982).

In this section we examine several questions about the underclass debate. Who are, or what constitutes, the underclass? What are some of the criticisms of the underclass model? What might serve as a non-deficit thinking public policy approach to the underclass issue?

The Nature of the Underclass

There are at least three related ways that we can define this group or location called the underclass. They are persistence-based, location-based, and behavioral-based definitions (Mincy, Sawhill and Wolf, 1990; Rickets and Sawhill, 1988).

Persistence-based definitions focus on those persons who remain in poverty for longer than a certain number of years (usually 5 to 8 years). These models identify the underclass population with an eye toward examining their size and growth. Moreover, using the persistence-based definition, one can establish an empirical baseline of the persistence of poverty among individuals and communities. Empirically-based persistence definitions of the underclass focus more on the description and tenacious nature of poverty among certain groups and communities and less on individual and group deficits.

Location-based definitions examine those places that have certain negative characteristics. For instance, the location-based underclass model identifies census tracts that have certain criteria such as high proportions of school dropouts, unemployment, welfare recipients, female heads of households and poverty (see Herrnstein and Murray, 1994; Ricketts and Sawhill, 1988; Mincy *et al.*, 1990). In fact, Wilson

(1987) developed an operational definition of the underclass by identifying the per cent of persons in a census tract living below the poverty line. He developed three different types of poverty areas. The first, or *poverty tract*, had 20 to 29 per cent of its residents living in poverty; *high poverty tracts* ranged from 30 to 39 per cent, and *extreme poverty tracts* (i.e., the underclass), had 40 per cent or more of community members living in poverty. Wacquant and Wilson found that in 1980 'fully 38 per cent of all poor blacks in the 10 largest American cities lived in extreme poverty tracts, compared to 22 per cent a decade before, and with only 6 per cent of poor non-Hispanic whites' (1989: 10). Clearly, Wacquant and Wilson have identified communities where extreme poverty, or the underclass, is rampant and the residents of these communities appear to be African American. It also appears that locational trends of extreme poverty are also acute for Puerto Ricans in the northeast (Massey and Eggers, 1990).

Behavioral-based definitions zero in on those people who do not behave in accordance with so-called social norms as measured by such variables as crime rates, welfare dependency, joblessness, teenage pregnancy and child abuse. For instance, using some of these criteria, Herrnstein and Murray (1994) in *The Bell Curve* developed a 'Middle-Class Values Index' that consists of four items for males. A man would receive a 'yes' (and thus have middle-class values), if 'he had obtained a high school degree (or more), been in the labor force throughout 1989, never been interviewed in jail, and was still married to his first wife' (1994: 263). A female would receive a 'yes' if 'she had obtained a high school degree, had never given birth to a baby out of wedlock, had never been interviewed in jail, and was still married to her first husband' (1994: 263). Persons who failed any one of the above conditions were scored 'no' and did not possess middle-class values, while those who succeeded in all of the conditions were scored 'yes' and did possess middle-class values, which Herrnstein and Murray contend 'are related to civility' (p. 263). This definition is in part consistent with the work of Rickets and Sawhill (1988) in identifying the behavioral characteristics associated with people who live in poverty or are not in the so-called middle class.

Suffice it to say, it is here — in the behavioral-based conceptions of the underclass — that deficit thinking is most likely to arise. The ideologically conservative explanation of the underclass phenomenon (see Lemann, 1986; Mead, 1989; Murray, 1984) lay in the life-style and allegedly self-sustaining culture of this socially and economically isolated group. Regarding the black underclass and the conservative thesis, Singh comments:

> the value system of this group [the underclass] has been fostered and, indeed, reinforced by programs originally conceived to help abate existing racial and class disparities . . . Conservatives insist the black underclass is a product of unique cultural attributes which generally encourage dependency, and that generous, liberal-inspired welfare programs have contributed to the persistence of this dependency . . . The distinctiveness of culture is reflected in the black underclass not valuing mobility, education, work, marriage or economic progress. (1994: 61)

Critiques of the Underclass Model

Many of the critiques of the underclass model argue against its salience for understanding people in poverty because of the failure to take into consideration the impact of four interrelated areas: 1) perpetuation of the myth that behavior is equated with values; 2) downplaying the impact of economic restructuring; 3) ignorance of the role of racism; 4) perpetuation of the myth of the passive poor.

The first critique of underclass theorizing — and the one most central to our analysis of deficit thinking — is the perpetuation of the long-standing myth that the poor, because of their value system, behave the way they do. William McDougall, a well-known social psychologist, seventy-five years ago implied that the alleged submissive behavior observed among Negroes was due to their value hierarchy, as a race:

> in the Negro the submissive impulse is strong . . . [this] point may be illustrated by a true story of a Negro maid, whose Northern mistress, after treating her with forbearance for a time, in spite of shortcomings, turned upon her and scolded her vigorously. The maid showed no resentment, but rather showed signs of a new satisfaction, and explained: 'Lor', Missus, you do make me feel so good'. Is this not a typical and significant incident? I will even venture to suggest that, in the great strength of this instinct of submission, we have the main key to the history of the Negro race. (1921: 118–19)

McDougall, deficit thinker, failed to discuss a more plausible reason for the maid's deference — fear of being punished or fired by her clearly dominant white mistress.

The behavior-based conceptions of the underclass (described earlier) certainly carry with them the dangers of erroneously equating behavior with values. Such analyses are not only fundamentally illogical in explaining the complexities of human behavior (regarding antecedent–consequent links), they are problematic from a measurement perspective. Allen's criticism of the culture of poverty concept still carries weight today in the underclass debate and is useful in communicating the above two points:

> behavior cannot be equated with values. In other words, simply because a person behaves in a certain way does not mean he desires to do so because of his beliefs or values. Another problem is that the concept is tautological: values inferred from behavior are used to explain behavior. To be useful for explaining behavior, values should be measured independently of the behavior to be explained, or no advantage can be claimed for the gratuitous labeling of behavior. (1970: 372–3)

The second criticism of the underclass model focuses on that aspect of the theory that ignores and/or downplays the impact of economic restructuring on poor communities generally, and communities of poor people of color in particular.

Also, the underclass model fails to examine the structural inequalities in the workplace, housing and education and their relations to people in poverty. As Wilson (1994) has stated, 'A history of discrimination and oppression created a huge black underclass, and the technological and economic revolutions have combined to insure it a permanent status' (1994: 529).

Moreover, Moore (1989) has argued that if there is a 'ghetto-specific' culture of the underclass resulting from the 'social isolation and concentration effects' of the middle and working class leaving the ghetto, then these behaviors will change only when structural constraints and job opportunities change in the ghetto. Moore's critique of the underclass model stresses that in the 1970s and 1980s the manufacturing economy of the United States declined and the service and information economies grew. The service and information jobs available for racial/ethnic minority workers were mainly in the secondary labor market and at the low end of the salary distribution, and thus their job prospects leading to a decent job in the primary labor force were not good. Moore argues that when the ladder that bridges these two sectors (i.e., secondary and primary) disappear, then poorly educated workers are trapped for a lifetime. Steinberg (1989), in a related vein, takes the position that the labor force experience of the minority community differs significantly from the earlier European American workplace history because this occupational bridge from the secondary to the primary sector was intact. One result of the lack of opportunities in the primary labor market is a disproportionate number of working poor people in the informal labor market, such as street vendors, day labors and home workers (Moore, 1989).

The third critique of the underclass model is that it fails to understand the role of race and racism in the production and maintenance of the underclass. For instance, underclass theorizing tends to ignore or downplay the role of institutional racism in the creation, maintenance and domination of the racial/ethnic minority urban underclass. This leads to the question: Does the dominance of a racial group need a rationalizing ideology? One could answer this question by arguing that dominant groups legitimize their interests and privilege through an ideology. If racism is the ideology that justifies the dominance of one race over another, how then do we define racism and what role does underclass theorizing play in that process? For our purpose, Lorde might have the most concise definition of racism as, 'the belief in the inherent superiority of one race over all others and thereby the right to dominance' (1992: 496). Moreover, Marable also defined racism as 'a system of ignorance, exploitation, and power used to oppress African Americans, Latinos, Asians, Pacific Americans, American Indians and other people on the basis of ethnicity, culture, mannerisms, and color' (1992: 5). Embedded in the Lorde and Marable definitions of racism are at least two important points: 1) one group believes itself to be superior; and 2) the group that believes itself to be superior has the power to carry out the racist behavior. Racism is about institutional power, and people of color in the United States have never possessed this form of authority and might. This fact seems to have gone unnoticed by underclass theorists.

A good case in point in which underclass theory fails to address the role of institutional racism is how social prejudice and discrimination in the housing market and resultant residential segregation and increased poverty help to produce the underclass. Massey, in a provocative and empirically-based study, presents a thesis that due to racism in the housing market, poor blacks and Puerto Ricans become even more spatially segregated *and* poorer, thus 'racial segregation is crucial to explaining the emergence of the urban underclass during the 1970s' (1990: 329). Massey contends, through his data analysis, that when poverty concentration increases, the socioeconomic character of neighborhoods dramatically transform, leading to high crime rates, poor schools, physical deterioration of buildings and closing of some businesses. Massey's theoretical argument is as such:

> Thus, residential segregation plays a very important role in creating the 'tangle of pathology' long identified with the ghetto and more recently with the underclass (see Clark, 1965; Wilson, 1987). *Racial segregation is the structural condition imposed on blacks that makes intensely deprived communities possible, even likely* [emphasis added]. When racial segregation occurs in the class-segregated environment of the typical American city, it concentrates income deprivation within a small number of poor black areas and generates social and economic conditions of intense disadvantage. These conditions are mutually reinforcing and cumulative, leading directly to the creation of underclass communities typified by high rates of family disruption, welfare dependence, crime, mortality, and educational failure. Segregation creates the structural niche within which a self-perpetuating cycle of minority poverty and deprivation can survive and flourish. (1990: 350)

A final point Massey raises that is especially germane to this book's analysis of deficit thinking is his idea that the segregation of poor blacks in isolated neighborhoods — and the resultant conditions of increased poverty, such as high crime rates, family disruption and poor schools — helps to reinforce in the minds of economically advantaged whites the connections (hence stereotypes) between *behavior* and *being poor*. Such stereotypic thinking, Massey contends, helps to set in motion '*a structural version of "blaming the victim" . . . thereby hardening prejudice, making discrimination more likely, and maintaining the motivation for segregation* [emphasis added]' (1990: 353). In short, 'Whites benefit from segregation because it isolates higher rates of black poverty within black neighborhoods' (p. 353).

The underclass model also fails to examine the interlocking nature of race, class and gender in lives of those in extreme and persistent poverty. As Wacquant and Wilson have stated:

> It is the cumulative structural entrapment and forcible socioeconomic marginalization resulting from the historically evolving interplay of class, race, and gender domination, together with sea changes in the organization of American capitalism and failed urban and social policies, not a 'welfare ethos', that explain the plight of today's ghetto blacks. Thus, if the concept

of the underclass is used, it must be a structural concept; it must denote a new sociospatial patterning of class and racial domination, recognizable by the unprecedented concentration of the most socially excluded and economically marginal members of the dominated racial and economic group. It should not be used as a label to designate a new breed of individuals molded freely by a mythical and all-powerful culture of poverty. (1989: 25)

The fourth critique of underclass theorizing rests in its portrayal of a people that are unable and unwilling to do anything for themselves. The racial/ethnic minority urban underclass is shown as passively allowing individuals and institutions to exploit them with little or no response or resistance. Both an historical and contemporary examination of poor communities generally, and black and Mexican American communities specifically, show that this is not the case (Acuna, 1988; Barrera, 1979; Gates, 1991; James and Farmer, 1993; Takaki, 1987). Not only do members of these communities persist against all odds, but they do so in creative and empowering ways that go unrecognized by underclass theorists (see Swadener and Lubeck, 1995a). Indeed, an examination of minority social networks, organizations, and modes of resistance are testaments to their tenacity and creativity.

A Non-Deficit Thinking Public Policy Approach to the Underclass Issue

In summary, it can be stated that the conservative explanation for the existence and growth of the underclass constitutes a contemporary form of deficit thinking. The construct of the underclass (i.e., extreme poverty) within this perspective is a reinvented notion of the culture of poverty model — a deficit thinking framework that contends the poor are autonomous, self-sustaining cultures who are responsible for creating their own problems. The other competing explanation for the causes of the underclass is structural in nature — involving the impact of economic restructuring of society and institutional racism, for the most part.

Regarding the issue of public policy debate over the underclass sector, we expect that the conservative deficit thinking camp will likely continue to mount a successful campaign. Such tactics as severe cutbacks in welfare aid, for example, make no economic sense. Funicello (1993) cleverly captures this nonsense in the oxymoronic title of her book, *The Tyranny of Kindness: Dismantling the Welfare System to End Poverty in America.*

We contend that any humane and nondiscriminatory public policy approach to assisting the extremely poor must rest on, at least, two premises. First, we are in agreement with Massey that the issue for public policy should not be located in whether race *or* class is responsible for the present plight of the underclass, 'but how race *and* class interact to undermine the well-being of this group' (1990: 354). Certainly, recent Census data reflect this intersection. For example, *nearly 1 in 2 Puerto Rican children under 18 years of age lived in poverty in 1990* (Chapa and

Valencia, 1993). Thus, the role of racial/ethnic *and* class discrimination is integral to any policy discussion germane to the underclass. We must add, however, that sexism is also an important form of discrimination to consider, as it is well known, single mothers and their children are the most likely to be found living in poverty (Swadener and Lubeck, 1995b).

Second, the question of who the underclass is remains unresolved — both quantitatively and qualitatively. On-going academic discourse on theorizing and policy implications pertinent to the underclass and education needs to do the following:

Identify and then quantitatively and qualitatively describe the extreme poverty census tracts. Recent ethnographic research in poor communities has already begun to explode negative myths about severely economically disadvantaged families (see Arnold, 1995; Cook and Fine, 1995; Hauser and Thompson, 1995).

Examine and compare the schools in these tracts with schools in less impoverished tracts on a number of different educational conditions, outcomes, and community resources. The assumption is that racial/ethnic minority urban underclass students attend the same quality schools as more economically privileged students. This assumption is not supported by available research on the topic (see Solórzano and Solórzano, 1995). Also, the assumptions that schools need limited change and are economically uniform are faulty premises (see Reyes and Valencia, 1993).

This approach also places the schools within the context of a particular community and focuses more on structural issues inside and outside the school and less on individual or group attitudinal and behavioral deficits. Indeed, many of the 1960s War on Poverty compensatory education programs failed because they were aimed at correcting superficial inequities or at compensating for some alleged cultural disadvantage, rather than addressing the ingrained societal factors that maintain such inequities.

Finally, research in minority urban underclass communities must start from the premise that these students and their parents are and should be active participants in their education. They should also acknowledge that these students come to school with cultural strengths and these strengths should be recognized and utilized by the schools (see Henry Levin's *Accelerated Schools* Program — Hopfenburg and Levin, 1993; Hopfenberg, Levin, Meister and Rodgers, 1990; Levin, 1987).

In summary, if we are to challenge the current deficit thinking embedded in the underclass model, we must focus on the roles of racism, sexism and class discrimination, as well as economic restructuring on the lives of poor and minority communities.

'Inadequate' Parents, Home and Child: Current Families, 1960s Style

Although current deficit thinking with respect to allegations that some poor and low-SES parents (typically of color) provide inferior cognitive socialization and child-rearing practices is not as invective and pervasive as it was in the 1960s (see

Pearl, Chapter 5, this volume), such views still exist. In this section, we will provide an analysis of samples of these contemporary perspectives (1980s and 1990s), focusing on schooling implications for low-SES children of color. Contemporary deficit thinking in this area cannot be as neatly boxed for discussion as seen for the literature in the 1960s. We have, however, identified three facets for analysis: 1) parental value of and involvement in education; 2) cognitive socialization and competence; 3) the construct of the at-risk child and family.

Parental Value of and Involvement in Education

One aspect of deficit thinking that fails to die is the major myth that low-income parents of color typically do not value the importance of education, fail to inculcate such a value in their children, and seldom participate — through parental involvement activities — in the education of their offspring. This allegation cannot be taken lightly, as there is mounting evidence that 'When parents are involved in their youth's schooling, children do better in school . . .' (Marburger, 1990: 82).

How have these deficit thinking views about low-SES racial/ethnic minority parents not valuing and participating in their children's schooling been communicated? Let us examine, as a case in point, Latino parents:

- Thomas Sowell, author of *Ethnic America* (in the US), in his chapter on The Mexicans rewrote history with this sweeping, totally decontextualized statement, 'The goals and values of Mexican Americans have never centered on education' (1981: 266).
- Lloyd Dunn, while acknowledging the schools have in part been implicated in not serving Hispanic pupils, largely places the blame on parents who do not care about education. '. . . it would be more correct to point out that these Hispanic pupils and their parents have also failed the schools and society, because *they have not been motivated and dedicated enough* [emphasis added] to make the system work for them' (1987: 78). Dunn, in the absence of any supportive data, asserts, '*It* [valuing education] *is a tradition that Hispanics in general do not appear to have*' [emphasis added] (1987: 80).
- Lauro Cavazos, former United States Secretary of Education and the top-ranking Latino in President Bush's administration, commented in 1990 that Latino parents deserve much of the blame for the high dropout rate among their children because, 'Hispanics have always valued education . . . but somewhere along the line we've lost that. I really believe today, there is not that emphasis' (Snider, 1990: 1).

With respect to Sowell's (1981) indiscriminate comment that Mexican Americans *have never* had education as a goal nor valued it, this is far from the truth. Had Sowell, a historian, done his research he would have found that Mexican Americans have rallied around education for many decades. An excellent starting point for this historical analysis is Arnoldo De Leon's (1974) article, 'Blowout 1910 style: A Chicano school boycott in west Texas', in which he reconstructs the lengthy struggle of Mexican American parents in seeking equal education in San Angelo, Texas, 87 years ago. Had Sowell researched the history of Mexican American education, he would have concluded that Mexican American's goals and values *did* center on education.[21] This history, and contemporary developments of the Mexican American community's quest for equal educational opportunity and participation in their children's schooling is so rich that the first author of this chapter (Valencia) is able to teach a course on the topic. His course, Chicano Educational Struggles, is an analysis of how Chicanos struggled for better education via five historical and contemporary processes: 1) litigation (for example, *Méndez v Westminster*, 1946); 2) advocacy organizations (such as, League of United Latin American Citizens, LULAC; Márquez, 1993); 3) individual activists (e.g., George I. Sánchez; Romo, 1986); 4) political demonstrations (for example, East Los Angeles high school blow-outs [walkouts] of 1968; Rosen, 1974); 5) legislation (such as, Senate Bill 477, bilingual education law of Texas, 1981; San Miguel, 1987).

The above statements by Dunn (1987) and Cavazos (Snider, 1990), have at least two things in common. First, these men are either unaware or disregard the available literature that documents Mexican American parents do value and/or get involved in their children's education (see Delgado-Gaitan, 1992; Goldenberg, 1988, 1989; Solórzano & Solórzano, 1995; Valencia, 1984).[22] For example, in an analysis of Mexican American parental involvement in a California community, Valencia (1984) observed that parents participated in a variety of school involvement activities, such as: the Parent Teacher Association, parent–teacher conferences, classroom volunteer, field trips, school programs, bilingual education advisory meeting and school board meetings. Second, Dunn and Cavazos evoke the long-standing deficit thinking tactic of shifting the blame from structural problems in schools, (such as financial inequities, curriculum differentiation and segregation), to the backs and shoulders of Latino parents who are expected to carry the exclusive burden of school success for their children.

On a final note, it needs to be mentioned that although there are ways and programs in which schools and parents can come together as equal partners in working toward school success for children (see Chavkin, 1989; Jennings, 1989; Williams and Chavkin, 1989), much of so-called parental involvement strategies still are compensatory or deficit thinking in philosophy and design. As Fine comments:

> With some important exception . . . little is being said or done by policy-makers or educators that truly incites parental participation, empowerment, and critique . . . To the extent that parent involvement is noted as 'essential' to school improvement, the strategy is typically one in which parents are trained as homework monitors or 'better parents' — not as collaborators, sources of critical information, innovators or critics. Even many one-time liberals have given up on 'those parents' (perhaps now that 'those parents' in cities are disproportionately African American, Latino, and low-income). Unless this power differential that marks the relations

between schools and low-income communities is addressed as controversial and inside public policy, the relationship will continue to be educationally bankrupt. (1995: 86–87)

Cognitive Socialization and Competence

As Pearl informed us (Chapter 5), the 1960s gushed with scholarly literature on the 'culturally deprived' or 'culturally disadvantaged' family, home, and child (see Frost and Hawkes, 1966; Hellmuth, 1967). The targeted populations of 1960s deficit thinking are all too familiar: 'the disadvantaged refer to Whites, Negroes, Puerto Ricans, Mexicans, and all others of the poverty group who basically share a common design for living' (Marans and Lourie, 1967: 20). As well, the carrier of the deficit was frequently identified as an inadequacy of the parents who 'seem to perpetuate their own conditions in their children through their child-rearing patterns . . .'[23] and who '. . . produce a disproportionate incidence of academic failures and of lower socioeconomic memberships among their full-grown offspring' (Marans and Lourie, 1967: 21). With an eye closer to the home problem, it was not uncommon for deficit thinkers three decades past to comment, 'very frequently the unique environment of a given subculture may not provide the prerequisite learnings or general acculturation essential to school success or to optimal life development' (Edwards, 1967: 164). Most important, what was the favored intervention? What was trumpeted as the magic pill for such social pathology and deprivation, or as J. McVicker Hunt noted in a 1964 article, the 'antidote for cultural deprivation'? The consensus solution, as we have seen, was early intervention and compensatory education, operationalized in public policy such as Operation Head Start (see Hellmuth, 1968).

One would surmise that given the debunking of 1960s deficit thinking literature plus post-60s major research advancements in identifying and understanding the rich, varied and stimulating experiences that often occur in linguistically and culturally diverse low-income homes, current references to inferior and deprived cognitive socialization and competence among *present* familial situations would not be warranted. This, however, is not the case. For example, Robert Slavin (1986), in his *Educational Psychology: Theory into Practice* (a textbook formerly used in teacher training programs), has this to say about social-class differences:

> Hess and Shipman's (1970) findings suggest that lower-class children received an upbringing less consistent with what they will be expected to do in school than do middle-class children. By the time they enter school, middle-class children are likely to be masters at following directions, explaining and understanding reasons, and comprehending and using complex language, *while lower-class children will probably have less experience in all these areas* [emphasis added].
> *Another important difference between middle-class and lower-class families is in the kinds of activities parents do with their children* [emphasis

added]. Middle-class parents are likely to express high expectations for their children, and to reward them for intellectual development. They are likely to provide good models for language use, to talk and read to their children frequently, and to encourage an interest in reading and other learning activities. They are particularly apt to provide all sorts of learning opportunities for children at home, such as books, encyclopedias, records, puzzles, and increasingly, home computers. These parents expose their children to learning experiences outside the home, such as museums, concerts, and zoos (see Bloom, 1964). *In fact, middle-class children are constantly engaged in learning activities* [emphasis added]. (1986: 494)

Clearly, Slavin (1986) has relied on deficit thinking literature published during the era of the cultural and accumulated environmental deficit models to discuss *current* social class differences among children. This is inexcusable. Slavin's references to Hess and Shipman (1970) and Bloom (1964) could easily have been contextualized as being biased, flawed and inconclusive research during the height of 1960s deficit thinking. Better yet, he could have juxtaposed (for comparison purposes), or even substituted, more recent and credible research on social class differences and similarities. For example, the ethnographic work of Heath (1982) argues that black linguistic behavior in lower-class homes is not deficient, but that the congruence between verbal behavior, such as questioning at home and school is not as tight as seen in white middle-class communities (also, see Brown, Palinscar and Purcell, 1986).

Another example of a study that speaks to the strengths of low-income children of color — and which was available for Slavin's (1986) consideration for inclusion — is the research investigation by Valencia, Henderson, and Rankin (1985).[24] These researchers, using a proximal measure of home intellectual climate sensitive enough to reveal what typically goes concealed about young Mexican American children's cognitive competence, reported two important findings. First, based on parental reports via home interviews, the Mexican American mothers (low-SES) reported many dyadic experiences that Slavin (in the above quote) implies are confined to *only* middle-class homes. For example, many of the Mexican American mothers frequently reported high educational aspirations for their children, provided positive reinforcement for intellectual behavior, read regularly to their offspring, and exposed their children to a variety of learning experiences outside the home. Second, Valencia *et al.* found that their measure of the intellectual environment of the home (Henderson Environmental Learning Process Scale, HELPS; Henderson, Bergan, and Hurt, 1972) was the best predictor (compared to distal variables of language/schooling, SES, and family size) of the children's cognitive performance as measured by the *McCarthy Scales of Children's Abilities* (McCarthy, 1972). The major contribution of the investigation by Valencia *et al.* is that in studies of low-income children's intellectual performance in which only distal independent variables are used (SES gradations; schooling attainment level; family size), cognitive competence can often be masked. Thus, it is important to use proximal variables that represents the learning experiences provided in the home or are under the family's direction. In short, the intellectual performance of poor and low-SES children, particularly of color, when examined in the 1960s and early 1970s was seldom detected due to methodological shortcomings. As Ginsburg (1986) notes, 'The research techniques employed were not sensitive enough to uncover the true extent of poor children's performance' (p. 172). Furthermore, Valencia *et al.* comment:

> Data on proximal processes may also prove more practical than informa-tion on status characteristics. Socioeconomic status indices, for example, are summarizing variables that predict performance on intellectual meas-ures with some consistency, but otherwise tend to conceal the considerable range of variation that exists among the specific classes of experiences that families provide for their children within a given SES level. (Valencia *et al.*, 1985: 325)

In sum, that which goes *concealed* in the intellectual climates of low-SES homes can be *revealed* with sensitive instruments.

In addition to the work mentioned above (see Heath, 1981; Valencia *et al.*, 1985), Slavin (1986) could have introduced the reader to the writings of Herbert Ginsburg, especially his book on *The Myth of the Deprived Child: Poor Children's Intellect and Education* (1972) in which he presents a critique, as well as an analy-sis of available research on the intellect and education of poor children. What we find most distressing, however, about Slavin's coverage of social-class differences in *Educational Psychology: Theory into Practice* is that it is directed to impression-able, future teachers. It is a shame that tomorrow's teachers have to be subjected to deficit thinking research and discussion in a textbook that is designed to prepare them, in part, to teach children from diverse backgrounds. (In all due fairness to Slavin, he does show in his most recent edition of his book [Slavin, 1997] a more sensitive and accurate assessment of the strengths in low-SES homes.)

Other examples of current deficit thinking perspectives that blame parents for their children's lack of school success are seen in the previously discussed works of Dunn (1987) and Herrnstein and Murray (1994). Dunn, arguing that Hispanic (meaning Puerto Rican and Mexican American) parents have failed the schools, lays out a set of recommendations these mothers and fathers need to consider in improving the school performance of their children. To wit, Hispanic parents need to: 1) value education as a top priority; 2) monitor and enforce homework; 3) uphold strict discipline; 4) instill a work ethic. Dunn, in a foreboding manner, concludes:

> The more I examined the evidence, the more convinced I became that the major source for overcoming the lack of school success of Hispanics rests squarely with the people themselves, and more specifically, with the parents. *In my view, none of my suggested strategies or any others, for that matter, will succeed unless there are dramatic changes in the child-rearing practices of Hispanic mothers and fathers* [emphasis added]. (1987: 80)

As we have introduced, Herrnstein and Murray (1994) in *The Bell Curve* also single out economically disadvantaged parents as inadequate in raising their children. Particularly targeted are 'single women of low intelligence' (p. 519) who, of course, according to the authors produce 'the child of low intelligence' (p. 519). Such children, plagued by the alleged victimizations of cruel parents, will live lives in which 'inadequate nutrition, physical abuse, emotional neglect, lack of intellectual stimulation [and] a chaotic home environment...' (p. 519) are normative experiences. Although Herrnstein and Murray are not explicit on the issue, we assume that these unfortunate children will become school failures.

In both the writings of Dunn (1987) and the Herrnstein and Murray (1994) team, we consistently see the evocation of 'blaming the victim'. In Dunn, for example, we see analyses that 'blame the parents, change the parents' and not 'blame the schools, change the schools'. In both treatises, the authors fail to discuss any structural problems concerning schools. Absent is any analysis, for example, of: 1) the detrimental connections between school segregation of low-income children of color and schooling outcomes (see Donato, Menchaca and Valencia, 1991); 2) the 'savage inequalities' brought on by an unequal distribution of school financing dollars (see Kozol, 1991); and 3) the academic inequalities stemming from curriculum differentiation in our nation's schools (see Bennett and Le Compte, 1990; Oakes, 1985). Perhaps a reason scholars such as Dunn, Herrnstein, and Murray avoid such discussions is that if a discourse of structural inequalities arose, their theoretical positions and policy ideas would be highly threatened, perhaps even languish into a state of balderdash.

The Construct of the At-Risk Child and Family[25]

A major strategy utilized by legislators and policymakers in their attempts to understand and solve the secondary school dropout problem — particularly among low-income racial/ethnic minority students — is to identify characteristics of students who are predisposed to dropping out, for example, overage for grade; failing grades. The key construct employed in this predictive scheme is the notion of 'at risk'. First popularized in educational policy circles as a reaction to the notion of *excellence* in the early 1980s, the label *at risk* is now entrenched in the educational literature as well as in the talk of educators and policymakers. Since 1989, a literature review informs us that over 2500 articles and conference papers have dealt with the at-risk construct (Swadener and Lubeck, 1995a). There are also general introductory books being written on the topic (see *Students at Risk* [1995] by Manning and Baruth; *Hope at Last for At-Risk Youth* [1995] by Barr and Parrett). Furthermore, there are institutes and centers on the at-risk population, for example the Institute for the Study of At-Risk Students, College of Education, University of Maine; Center for Research on the Education of Students Placed At Risk, Johns Hopkins University. There is even a journal, *Journal of Education for Students Placed At Risk*, recently launched by faculty at Johns Hopkins University.

Margonis (1992) explains that the term at risk was first used by critics of the 'excellence' movement (also see Gitlin, Margonis and Brunjes, 1993). These critics sought to move educators and policymakers away from 'the belief that educational success and failure hinge primarily on individual effort' (Margonis, 1992: 343), a view popularized by excellence reforms in the American educational system in the 1980s. Critics contended that school failure was largely systemically based. Margonis further argues that the term was coopted by the proponents of the excellence movement that it was first used to challenge. He claims that cooptation of the at-risk notion has done the reverse of what critics of the excellence movement intended. That is, critics sought to use the term at risk to demonstrate the short-sightedness of the movement, arguing that standardization in curricula (tracking) and testing — coupled with large workloads of teachers — created insensitive and impersonal school environments and thus placed students in jeopardy (i.e., at risk) for school failure. Nevertheless, excellence proponents won the semantic war over the terminology. As Margonis notes, 'The educational goals embodied in the ideas of excellence became the standard, and students who could not reach these goals came to be at risk' (p. 344).

In light of the analysis of the nature of deficit thinking by Valencia (Chapter 1), a strong case can be made that the notion of at risk denotes a form of deficit thinking (also, see Fine, 1991; Richardson, Casanova, Placier and Guilfoyle, 1989). Part of the problem with the concept of at risk is that it tends to overlook any strengths and promise of the student so-labeled, while drawing attention to the presumed shortcomings of the individual. Students continue to be defined at risk based on 'personal and familial characteristics' (Donmoyer and Kos, 1993: 9). As such, at risk has become a person-centered explanation of school failure. The construct of at risk is preoccupied with describing 'deficiencies' in students, particularly alleged shortcomings rooted in familial and economic backgrounds of students. Finally, at risk qualifies to be under the rubric of deficit thinking in that the notion pays little, if any, attention to how schools are institutionally implicated in ways that exclude students from learning. In sum, the idea of at risk blames the victim, as does the notion of deficit thinking. The deficit model turns students into burdens and trades potential for risk.

Our contention that the construct of at risk constitutes a popular form of contemporary deficit thinking is given considerable support by the 1995 publication of Betty Blue Swadener and Sally Lubeck's book, *Children and Families 'at Promise': Deconstructing the Discourse of Risk* (1995b). This edited volume represents the most comprehensive and sustained analysis and critique of the at-risk notion to date. Swadener and Lubeck's purposes in *Children and Families 'at Promise'* are twofold:

1   to deconstruct the 'at risk' label through an analysis of historical and contextual issues, and discussions of contemporary critiques and to include voices and perspectives which have been largely absent from the discussion, and
2   to suggest that we begin to utilize the construct 'children and families at promise' to convey the potential *all* children hold . . . (1995b: 4).

It is beyond the scope of this chapter to offer an extended discussion of Swadener and Lubeck's (1995b) book. We can, however, provide the reader with several points that are most germane to our present discussion:

1   The new term, *at risk*, is a resurrected metaphor of the *cultural deprivation* and *culturally disadvantaged* terms used with great frequency in the 1960s (Sleeter, 1995, foreword). As such, the construct of at risk is a 'retooled [social construction] for the 1990s, placing yet another *repressive label* [emphasis added] on an even widening group of young people and their families . . .' (Swadener, 1995: 19).
2   The at-risk notion, as does deficit thinking, holds structural inequalities absolved in creating problems for the so-called at-risk child and family. Sleeter comments:

> Like the discourse of 'cultural deprivation' and 'disadvantage' of the 1960s . . . the discourse of 'children at risk' deflects attention away from injustices perpetrated and institutionalized by the dominant society and again frames oppressed communities and homes as lacking in the cultural and moral resources for advancement. (1995: x)

3   Similar to the bandwagon effect of instant, pejorative labeling, such as 'culturally deprived' of poor children during the 1960s deficit thinking period, 'Scholars, practitioners, and activists [today] have been quick to name, identify, and ossify those who presumably suffer at the mercy of "risk factors"' (Fine, 1995: 76).
4   As does the general notion of deficit thinking, terms such as *the urban underclass* and *at risk* owe in part their popularity to the influence of politics. Some scholars 'have attributed the popularity of such concepts to the shift to the right during the late 1970s and 1980s in terms of policies and public debate about social welfare and education policy' (Swadener and Lubeck, 1995a: 3).
5   As it is in the case of deficit thinking in general, the notion of at risk fails to acknowledge the strengths, competencies and promise of low-income children and parents (see Arnold, 1995; Cook and Fine, 1995; Hauser and Thompson, 1995; Quintero and Rummel, 1995; White, 1995).

On a final note about the at-risk notion, we wish to share with the reader an account of a disastrous public relations incident that recently occurred in a Texas community. According to the *Austin American-Statesman* in late January and early February of 1994, the Austin Independent School District (AISD) — attempting to comply with state regulations that require parents be notified if they have an at-risk student — sent home *33,450* notices informing parents their children were prime dropout candidates (Lott, 1994a). The 33,000 plus notices, which were sent to 17,000 elementary and 16,450 secondary school students, comprised *46 per cent* of the total 72,000 AISD student enrollment!

Swiftly, many angry parents mounted a protest. Their criticisms of the notices centered on two points. First, 'Although the letters were intended for parents, many students read the letters themselves and were confused and hurt . . .' (Lott, 1994a: A1, A7). The at-risk notification and report card, *sent home with the elementary school-age child*, should have been mailed, according to the AISD spokesman. In a sweeping generalization, the at-risk notification letter told 'parents that it is their responsibility to guarantee that their children are loved and cared for and that they study and attend school regularly' (Lott, 1994a: A7). Second, a number of parents were upset and angry over the at-risk notices in that they mischaracterized their children. For example, a fifth-grade girl who was a straight-A student was labeled at-risk for dropping out of high school 'because she has an August birthday and her parents held her back a year before kindergarten. So she is a year older than most of her classmates and statistics show overage students are more likely to drop out' (Lott and Vargas, 1994: A1).

Suffice it to say, the way the AISD handled the at-risk notification did not set well with some parents. On February 10, 1994, a group of parents of Metz Elementary School (approximately a 95 per cent Mexican American school) organized and held a meeting at a community center in East Austin (overwhelmingly a Mexican American and African American sector of Austin).[26] Present were 100 parents and interim Superintendent Terry Bishop. In this emotionally charged meeting, Bishop apologized to the parents, saying 'I am sorry this happened . . . I apologize. I think it was a mistake to send those letters out. We probably won't do that again' (Vargas, 1994: B1).[27] But —

> For some parents, the damage has already been done.
>
> Griselda Martinez said two of her children received the letter saying they were at-risk. She said both her children, who attend Porter Middle School, are honor-roll students.
>
> 'They're upset about it still', Martinez said. 'They said what's the use of doing hard work if the school isn't going to support them or believe in them.'
>
> One parent was even brought to tears over the issue.
>
> 'What you did was a mistake?' she asked Bishop. 'What you did was put all these children down. You make them feel low.' (Vargas, p. B5)

The unfortunate incident in Austin represents how the deficit thinking nature of the at-risk construct of pathology, blame and stereotypes can generate into the *reductio ad absurdum* of the at-risk discourse.

In sum, deficit thinking is alive and well in the contemporary period. A strong case can be made that the genetic pathology thesis, the culture of poverty model, and the cultural and accumulated environmental deficit models have, and are, growing in currency. What is most disturbing, we feel, is the apparent pervasiveness among the general public of such beliefs held towards minority groups. Results from a 1990 national survey conducted by the National Opinion Research Center at the University of Chicago showed there is strong evidence that a substantial proportion of white Americans still cling to racial stereotypes of a deficit nature.

'A majority of whites questioned in the nationwide survey said they believe blacks and Hispanics are likely to prefer welfare to hard work and tend to be lazier than whites, more prone to violence, less intelligent and less patriotic' (Duke, 1991: A1).

Even the highest ranking public servant in the nation, President Clinton, is not immune to deficit thinking. In October, 1995, at The University of Texas at Austin, Clinton delivered a major speech on race relations. Earl Ofari Hutchinson, in a special article to the *Los Angeles Times* and published in the *Austin American-Statesman* (October 30, 1995), commented: 'instead of dispelling them [myths and stereotypes], Clinton repeated the worst of them' (Hutchinson, p. A11). For example, Clinton stated in his address, 'Violence for white people too often comes with a black face' (Hutchinson, p. A11). Hutchinson notes, however, that based on 1990/1991 FBI data, '70 per cent of violent crimes against whites were committed by other whites. In 1991, white males made up 70 per cent of the juveniles arrested for criminal offenses' (p. A11). Clinton, on the subject of drug abuse, commented, 'It isn't racist for whites to say they don't understand why people put up . . . with drugs being sold in the schools or in the open' (Hutchinson, p. A11). Referring to a 1991 National Household Survey on Drug Abuse by the University of Michigan, Hutchinson countered: ' [the survey] revealed that 8.7 million whites used drugs in a given month vs. 1.6 million blacks. And white high school seniors were far more likely to use drugs than black high school seniors' (p. A11). On welfare, Clinton informed his audience: 'It's not racist for whites to assert that the culture of welfare dependency . . . cannot be broken . . . unless there is first more personal responsibility' (Hutchinson, p. A11). Hutchinson responded: 'Nationally, nearly two out of three welfare recipients are white . . . More than 80 per cent of 1200 black welfare recipients in a 1987 University of Chicago survey said that if jobs were available, they'd take them if the pay and medical coverage were the same as that provided by welfare' (p. A11). Hutchinson concluded his news article as such: 'Clinton wants badly to heal the racial divide. We all should. *But blaming and scapegoating blacks for America's social problems will only deepen that divide*' [emphasis added] (p. A11).

It is our conclusion that current deficit thinkers have little knowledge and understanding of the many problems the poor and certain racial/ethnic minority groups have in attaining equitable and useful schooling. To blame the poor and minority person is to blame the victim. Deficit thinkers should look for solutions not scapegoats. Given the high likelihood that deficit thinkers will not develop workable school success programs for low-SES minority students, the responsibility will indubitably rest with those who espouse anti-deficit thinking views. To this effect, we turn to Arthur Pearl's chapter, Democratic Education as an Alternative to Deficit Thinking.

Notes

1   These criticisms are in reference to Shuey's (1958) first edition of *The Testing of Negro Intelligence*. Her genetic hypothesis of racial differences in intelligence was presented in both the 1958 and 1966 editions.

2 Est. ω^2 is a measure of the association between the independent and dependent variable, calculated after a statistical test of significance is run. Est. ω^2 has the element of *practical significance*, that is it estimates the proportion of variance in the dependent variable that can be accounted for by specifying the independent variable. As such, est. ω^2 is more meaningful, compared to statistical significance, because it can be used to inform decisions about practical matters.

3 See, for example, *The Harvard Educational Review* (1969, **39**) for a number of critiques of Jensen (1969). For examples of scholars who favored Jensen's views see Eysenck (1971) and Herrnstein (1973).

4 Although Jensen (1969) does not cite the Westinghouse–Ohio study, it appears that he was referring to the preliminary report by Cicirelli, Evans and Schiller, 1969.

5 There is one study that presents strong empirical evidence that questions the assumed invariance of Jensen's (1969) Level I–Level II theory. See the Taylor and Skanes (1976) investigation with Canadian Inuit Indian and White Canadian children.

6 The subtitle of the monograph is: *Emphasizing Studies Involving the English-and Spanish-Language Versions of the Peabody Picture Vocabulary Test-Revised.*

7 Dunn (1988) contends that American Guidance Service (AGS) 'did not *publish* my monograph and did not *sell* it. They only reproduced and mailed it, upon request, as a free service . . .' (p. 302). It appears Dunn has attempted to clarify matters in that some critics of Dunn's piece advocated the blacklisting of AGS. While it may be true Dunn had such an agreement with AGS, the title page of the monograph does read 'published by AGS'.

8 Mercer's (1988) contention is that Dunn (1987) generalizes from Jensen's conjecture of black intellectual inferiority to Latino intellectual inferiority. She refers to Dunn's reference to Latinos as 'dark-skinned' people as the basis for her assertion:

> Most Mexican immigrants to the US are brown-skinned people, a mix of American Indian and Spanish blood, while many Puerto Ricans are dark-skinned, a mix of Spanish, black, and some Indian. Blacks and American Indians have repeatedly scored about 15 IQ points behind Anglos and Orientals on individual tests of intelligence. (1988: 64)

9 Notwithstanding the consensus that the PPVT series are not general measures of intelligence, the PPVT-R is still listed under 'assessment of intelligence' in texts on testing (see Anastasi, 1988; Cohen *et al.*, 1992; Salvia and Ysseldyke, 1988). In our opinion, for authors to do such listings is not only misleading but this practice helps to perpetuate the misconception that the PPVT-R is an appropriate measure of intelligence. We believe the test best fits under the 'assessment of language'.

10 Dunn (1988), in his rejoinder to Berliner (1988), asserted: 'I did not say that the PPVT/TVIP [Spanish version of the Peabody] should be used as a measure of verbal intelligence/scholastic aptitude for immigrant Hispanic youth . . . for such children, the [tests], are only achievement tests of vocabulary for single words spoken in isolation' (p. 315). Yet, in his monograph, Dunn (1987) relies on data from two sources to draw his heritability estimate. The first source includes studies with 'instruments other than the Peabody tests', such as WISC-R, and the second cluster includes research involving the original PPVT (which used an IQ index) and the PPVT-R. Thus, his response to Berliner makes little sense, based on the approach he took in reviewing studies germane to his genetic interpretation.

11 Herrnstein and Murray (1994), based on the normal distribution of IQ scores, break the continuum into five 'cognitive classes'. The classes, names given, IQ intervals, and

percentage of cases are, respectively: Class I (very bright; 125 and above; 5 per cent); Class II (bright; 110 to 124; 20 per cent); Class III (normal; 90 to 109; 50 per cent); Class IV (dull; 75 to 89; 20 per cent); Class V (very dull; 74 and below; 5 per cent). These classification by IQ are very similar to the interval breaks testing specialists have used since the time of Lewis Terman. Herrnstein and Murray note, however, that they substituted more 'neutral' terms ('very dull') for 'less damning terms' ('retarded').

12   Two points are worthy here. First, the discussion of intelligence being substantially inherited and linked with cognitive ability and social behaviors and outcomes (poverty, dropouts, etc. seen in Chapters 5 through 12) focus *exclusively on whites* (see page 125 and note 11 of Part II introduction of *The Bell Curve*). Second, discussion on black–white and Latino–white differences in cognitive ability is confined to Chapter 13. Regarding the role of genetics in explaining the higher IQ performance of whites, compared to blacks and Latinos, Judis (1995) comments: 'The authors [Herrnstein and Murray] . . . claim agnosticism on the question of whether genes or environment cause low IQ scores, but their analysis is heavily weighted toward genetic causes' (p. 128).

13   These reform ideas are not really new. For the most part, these ideas stem from discourse beginning in the early 1980s and are viewed, by critics, as agenda items of the conservative school reform movement.

14   Herrnstein and Murray argue that the funding priority for the gifted and the economically disadvantaged 'turned 180 degrees' with the passage of the Elementary and Secondary Education Act of 1965, a federal program designed to serve the educational needs of students in low-income areas.

15   For an earlier discussion of the argument for the custodial state, see Murray (1988).

16   *Contemporary Psychology*, a periodical of the American Psychological Association, is the leading journal of critical reviews of books in the broad field of psychology. All reviews are invited by the editor.

17   This basic error is sometimes referred to as 'Jensen's error', a mistake well known by experts on human genetics. The error was first clearly articulated and coined by Milkman (1978; cited in Dorfman, 1995). In the present chapter, we have alluded to this fundamental error in discussing the work of Jensen (1969) and Dunn (1987).

18   With the exception of two chapters (Jones; Patterson), all chapters in Fraser (1995) are expanded versions of articles that first appeared in *The New Republic* (October 31, 1994).

19   The two disreputable scholars that Rosen and Lane (1995) refer to, as examples, are Richard Lynn and Phillipe Rushton. Lynn, of the University of Ulster (in Ireland), has published frequently in:

> *Mankind Quarterly*, a journal of racialist anthropology, founded by the Scottish white supremacist Robert Gayre. *Mankind Quarterly* has a long history of publishing pseudoscientific accounts of black inferiority. Lynn and others have used its pages to ventilate their view that society should foster the reproduction of the genetically superior, and discourage that of the genetically inferior. (Rosen and Lane, 1995: 58–9)

An examination of the bibliography in *The Bell Curve* shows Herrnstein and Murray list 23 studies authored or co-authored by Richard Lynn.

Rushton, a Canadian developmental psychologist at the University of Ontario, for a decade has been advancing a theory that the three races he has studied have evolved to different levels of intellectual development. According to Rushton, *Mongoloids* are the most advanced, *Caucasoids* are intermediate, and *Negroids* are least advanced. In that such an ordering of the races stems from an evolutionary basis, the engine must be genetics, he asserts. Suffice it to say, Rushton's work has been frequently criticized (see Cain and Vanderwolf, 1990; Lynn, 1989; Zuckerman and Brody, 1988). Curiously, Herrnstein and Murray introduce the reader to Rushton in what Rosen and Lane (1995) refer to as a 'two-page gratuitous appendix' (p. 60). Herrnstein and Murray describe his thesis, followed by only a passing word on Rushton's critics. Herrnstein and Murray conclude: 'Rushton's work is not that of a crackpot or bigot, as many of his critics are given to charging. As science, there is nothing wrong with Rushton's work in principle; we expect that time will tell whether it is right or wrong in fact' (1994: 643).

20　As Gould notes, a correlation of .4 yields an R^2 of only .16. R^2, a statistic known as the coefficient of determination, is the square of the observed correlation coefficient and is useful in explaining how much of the variance in the dependent variable, for example, dropping out of high school can be accounted for by the independent variable, such as IQ. Gould comments that the values of R^2 presented in Appendix 4 of *The Bell Curve* are very low.

21　An excellent example of a sustained analysis of this topic is San Miguel's (1987) book on Mexican American's campaign for educational equality in Texas from 1910 to 1981.

22　For examples of other research on racial/ethnic minority parental valuation of and/or involvement in education see: Boyd-Franklin (1989); Chavkin (1989); Chavkin and Williams (1988); Manns (1988); Scanzoni (1985); Solórzano, 1992a, 1992b; Tabachnick and Bloch (1995); White (1995).

23　Although Marans and Lourie (1967) do acknowledge that 'the issue of the effects of malnutrition, inadequate prenatal care and the like, on the physical constitution of the children is an extremely important one' (p. 21), such concerns were typically secondary. The onus for deprivation was primarily placed on the parents and the home environment.

24　For a review of research on the cognitive socialization and competence of Mexican American children, see Laosa and Henderson (1991).

25　The first three paragraphs of this section on the at-risk construct is excerpted (with minor revisions) from a previous publication (Ronda and Valencia, 1994: 364, 366) co-written by Valencia.

26　Politically, it was not unexpected that minority parents would register the most vocal criticisms concerning the at-risk notices, in that their children were more likely to receive such notifications. Although no data are provided in the newspaper article regarding racial/ethnic breakdown of who received the at-risk notifications, we surmise that Mexican American and African American students — who comprised the majority of the AISD enrollment — disproportionately received more notices. This conjecture is based, in part, on data that show racial/ethnic minority students in the AISD (and throughout Texas) perform considerably poorer on one of the key at-risk criteria — the state-mandated Texas Assessment of Academic Skills test (Valencia and Guadarrama, 1996).

27　The AISD, in May, 1994, began to consider alternative ways to inform parents if their children were being identified at risk, such as individualized (not form) letter; phone calls; in person; see Lott, 1994b.

References

Acuna, R. (1988) *Occupied America: A History of Chicanos* (3rd ed.), New York: Harper & Row.

ALLEN, V.L. (1970) 'The psychology of poverty: Problems and prospects', in ALLEN, V.L. (Ed) *Psychological Factors in Poverty*, Chicago, IL: Markham, pp. 367–83.

ANASTASI, A. (1988) *Psychological Testing* (6th ed.), New York: Macmillan.

ARNOLD, M.S. (1995) 'Exploding the myths: African American families at Promise', in SWADENER, B.B. and LUBECK, S. (Eds) *Children and Families 'at promise': Deconstructing the Discourse of Risk*, Albany, NY: State University of New York Press, pp. 143–62.

AULETTA, K. (1982) *The Underclass*, New York: Random House.

BACA ZINN, M. (1989) 'Family, race and poverty in the eighties', *Signs: Journal of Women in Culture and Society*, **14**, pp. 856–74.

BAGLEY, W.C. (1922) 'Educational determinism: or democracy and the IQ', *School and Society*, **15**, pp. 373–84.

BARR, R.D. and PARRETT, W.H. (1995) *Hope at Last for At-risk Youth*, Boston, MA: Allyn & Bacon.

BARRERA, M. (1979) *Race and Class in the Southwest: A Theory of Racial Inequality*, Notre Dame, IN: University of Notre Dame Press.

BENNETT, K.P. and LeCOMPTE, M.D. (1990) *The Way Schools Work: A Sociological Analysis of Education*, New York: Longman.

BEREITER, C. (1969) 'The future of individual differences', *Harvard Educational Review*, **39**, pp. 310–18.

BERLINER, D.C. (1988) 'Meta-comments: A discussion of critiques of L.M. Dunn's monograph *Bilingual Hispanic Children on the US Mainland*', *Hispanic Journal of Behavioral Sciences*, **10**, pp. 273–99.

BLOOM, B.S. (1964) *Stability and Change in Human Characteristics*, New York: Wiley.

BLUM, J. (1978) *Pseudoscience and Mental Ability: The Origins and Fallacies of the IQ Controversy*, New York: Monthly Review Press.

BOND, H.M. (1958) 'Cat on a hot tin roof', *Journal of Negro Education*, **27**, pp. 519–25.

BOUCHARD, T.J., JR. (1995) 'Breaking the last taboo' [Review of the book *The Bell Curve: Intelligence and Class Structure in American Life*], *Contemporary Psychology*, **40**, pp. 415–18.

BOYD-FRANKLIN, N. (1989) 'Five key factors in the treatment of black families', *Journal of Psychotherapy and the Family*, **6**, pp. 53–69.

BROWN, A.L., PALINSCAR, A.S. and PURCELL, L. (1986) 'Teach, don't label', in NEISSER, U. (Ed) *The School Achievement of Minority Children: New Perspectives*, Hillsdale, NJ: Erlbaum, pp. 105–43.

CAIN, D.P. and VANDERWOLF, C.H. (1990) 'A critique of Rushton on race, brain size and intelligence', *Personality and Individual Differences*, **11**, pp. 777–84.

CHAPA, J. and VALENCIA, R.R. (1993) 'Latino population growth, demographic characteristics, and educational stagnation: An examination of recent trends', *Hispanic Journal of Behavioral Sciences*, **15**, pp. 165–87.

CHAVKIN, N.F. (1989) 'Debunking the myth about minority parents', *Educational Horizons*, **7**, pp. 119–23.

CHAVKIN, N.F. and WILLIAMS, D.L. (1988) 'Critical issues in teacher training for parental involvement', *Educational Horizons*, **6**, pp. 87–9.

CHOROVER, S.L. (1979) *From Genesis to Genocide: The Meaning of Human Nature and the Power of Behavior Control*, Cambridge, MA: The Massachusetts Institute of Technology Press.

CICIRELLI, V., EVANS, J.W. and SCHILLER, J.S. (1969) *The Impact of Head Start: An Evaluation of the Effects of Head Start on Children's Cognitive and Affective Development*, report of a study undertaken by Westinghouse Learning Corporation and Ohio University under contract B89–4536 dated June 20, 1968 with the Office of Economic Opportunity. The preliminary report was issued in April, 1969.

CLARK, K.B. (1965) *Dark Ghetto: Dilemmas of Social Power*, New York: Harper & Row.

COHEN, R.J., SWERDLIK, M.E. and SMITH, D.K. (1992) *Psychological Testing and Assessment: An Introduction to Tests and Measurement* (2nd ed), Mountain View, CA: Mayfield.

COOK, D.A. and FINE, M. (1995) ' "Mother-wit": Childrearing lessons from African American mothers of low income', in SWADENER, B.B. and LUBECK, S. (Eds) *Children and Families 'at Promise': Deconstructing the Discourse at Risk*, Albany, NY: State University of New York Press, pp. 118–42.

CROW, J.F. (1969) 'Genetic theories and influences: Comments on the value of diversity', *Harvard Educational Review*, **39**, pp. 338–47.

CUMMINS, J. (1988) ' "Teachers are not miracle workers": Lloyd Dunn's call for Hispanic activism', *Hispanic Journal of Behavioral Sciences*, **10**, pp. 263–72.

DE LEON, A. (1974) 'Blowout 1910 style: A Chicano school boycott in west Texas', *Texana*, **12**, pp. 125–40.

DELGADO-GAITAN, C. (1992) 'School matters in the Mexican American home', *American Educational Research Journal*, **29**, pp. 495–513.

DONATO, R., MENCHACA, M. and VALENCIA, R.R. (1991) 'Segregation, desegregation and integration of Chicano students', in VALENCIA, R.R. (Ed) *Chicano School Failure and Success: Research and Policy Agendas for the 1990s*, The Stanford Series on Education and Public Policy. London: Falmer Press, pp. 27–63.

DONMOYER, R. and KOS, R. (Eds) (1993) *At-risk Students: Portraits, Policies, Programs and Practices*, Albany, NY: State University of New York Press.

DORFMAN, D.D. (1995) 'Soft science with a neoconservative agenda' [Review of the book *The Bell Curve: Intelligence and Class Structure in American Life*], *Contemporary Psychology*, **40**, pp. 418–21.

DUKE, L. (1991, January 9) 'Racial stereotypes found to persist among whites', *Austin American-Statesman*, pp. A1, A6.

DUNN, L.M. (1959) *Peabody Picture Vocabulary Test*, Minneapolis, MN: American Guidance Service.

DUNN, L.M. (1987) *Bilingual Hispanic Children on the US Mainland: A Review of Research on Their Cognitive, Linguistic and Scholastic Development*, Circle Pines, MN: American Guidance Service.

DUNN, L.M. (1988) 'Has Dunn's monograph been shot down in flames — Author reactions to the preceding critiques of it', *Hispanic Journal of Behavioral Sciences*, **10**, pp. 301–23.

DUNN, L.M. and DUNN, L.M. (1981) *Peabody Picture Vocabulary Test-Revised*, Circle Pines, MN: American Guidance Service.

EDWARDS, T.J. (1967) 'Pedagogical and psycho-social adjustment problems in cultural deprivation', in HELLMUTH, J. (Ed) *Disadvantaged Child*, **1**, New York: Brunner/Mazel, pp. 161–71.

EYSENCK, H. (1971) *The IQ Argument*, New York: Library Press.

FERNANDEZ, R.R. (Ed) (1988a) 'Achievement testing: Science vs ideology' [Special issue], *Hispanic Journal of Behavioral Sciences*, **10**(3).

FERNANDEZ, R.R. (1988b) 'Introduction', *Hispanic Journal of Behavioral Sciences*, **20**, pp. 179–98.

FINE, M. (1991) *Framing Dropouts: Notes on the Politics of an Urban Public High School*, Albany, NY: State University of New York Press.

FINE, M. (1995) 'The politics of who is "at risk", in SWADENER, B.B. and LUBECK, S. (Eds) *Children and Families 'at Promise': Deconstructing the Discourse of Risk*, Albany, NY: State University of New York Press, pp. 76–94.

FRASER, S. (Ed) (1995) *The Bell Curve Wars: Race, Intelligence, and the Future of America*, New York: Basic Books.

FROST, J.L. and HAWKES, G.R. (Eds) (1966) *The Disadvantaged Child: Issues and Innovations*, New York: Houghton Mifflin.

FUNICELLO, T. (1993) *The Tyranny of Kindness: Dismantling the Welfare System to End Poverty in America*, New York: Atlantic Monthly Press.

GARDNER, H. (1995) 'Cracking open the IQ Box', in FRASER, S. (Ed) *The Bell Curve Wars: Race, Intelligence, and the Future of America*, New York: Basic Books, pp. 23–35.

GARRETT, H.E. (1962) 'Rejoinder by Garrett', *SPSSI Newsletter*, May, 1–2.

GARRETT, H.E. (1973) *IQ and Racial Differences* [pamphlet], Cape Canaveral, FL: Howard Allen.

GARRETT, H.E. (nd) *Breeding Down* [pamphlet], Richmond, VA: Patrick Henry Press.

GATES, H. (Ed) (1991) *Bearing Witness: Selections from African-American Autobiography in the Twentieth Century*, New York: Pantheon Books.

GINSBURG, H. (1972) *The Myth of the Deprived Child: Poor Children's Intellect and Education*, Englewood Cliffs, NJ: Prentice-Hall.

GINSBURG, H. (1986) 'The myth of the deprived child: New thoughts on poor children', in NEISSER, U. (Ed) *The School Achievement of Minority Children: New Perspectives*, Hillsdale, NJ: Erlbaum, pp. 169–89.

GITLIN, A., MARGONIS, F. and BRUNJES, H. (1993) 'In the shadow of the excellence reports: School restructuring for at-risk students', in DONMOYER, R. and KOS, R. (Eds) *At-risk Students: Portraits, Policies, Programs and Practices*, Albany, NY: State University of New York Press, pp. 265–90.

GOLDENBERG, C.N. (1988) 'Methods, early literacy and home–school compatibilities: A response to Sledge *et al.*, *Anthropology and Education Quarterly*, **19**, pp. 425–32.

GOLDENBERG, C.N. (1989) 'Parents' effects on academic grouping for reading: Three case studies', *American Education Research Journal*, **26**, pp. 329–52.

GOULD, S.J. (1995) 'Curveball', in FRASER, S. (Ed) *The Bell Curve Wars: Race, Intelligence, and the Future of America*, New York: Basic Books, pp. 11–22.

HAUSER, M.E. and THOMPSON, C. (1995) 'Creating a classroom culture of promise: Lessons from a first grade', in SWADENER, B.B. and LUBECK, S. (Eds) *Children and Families 'at Promise': Deconstructing the Discourse of Risk*, Albany: State University of New York Press, pp. 210–23.

HEATH, S.B. (1982) 'Questioning at home and at school: A comparative study', in SPINDLER, G. (Ed) *Doing Ethnography of Schooling: Educational Anthropology in Action*, New York: Holt, Rinehart, & Winston, pp. 102–31.

HELLMUTH, J. (Ed) (1967) *Disadvantaged Child*, **1**, New York: Brunner/Mazel.

HELLMUTH, J. (Ed) (1968) *Disadvantaged Child: Head Start and Early Intervention*, **2**, New York: Brunner/Mazel.

HENDERSON, R.W., BERGAN, J.R. and HURT, M. (1972) 'Development and validation of the Henderson Environmental Learning Process Scale', *Journal of Social Psychology*, **88**, pp. 185–96.

HERRNSTEIN, R.J. (1973) *IQ in the Meritocracy*, Boston, MA: Little, Brown.

HERRNSTEIN, R.J. and MURRAY, C. (1994) *The Bell Curve: Intelligence and Class Structure in American Life*, New York: Free Press.

HESS, R.D. and SHIPMAN, V.C. (1970) 'Early experiences and the socialization of cognitive modes in children', in MILES, M.W. and CHARTERS, JR. W.W. (Eds) *Learning in Social Settings*, Boston, MA: Allyn & Bacon, pp. 170–88.

HICKS, R.B. and PELLEGRINI, R.J. (1966) 'The meaningfulness of Negro–white differences in intelligence test performance', *Psychological Record*, **16**, pp. 43–6.

HOPFENBERG, W. and LEVIN, H. (1993) *The Accelerated Schools Resource Guide*, San Francisco, CA: Jossey-Bass.

HOPFENBERG, W., LEVIN, H., MEISTER, G. and RODGERS, J. (1990) *Accelerated Schools*, Stanford, CA: Center for Educational Research at Stanford.

HUNT, J. McV. (1964) 'The psychological basis for using preschool enrichment as an antidote for cultural deprivation', *The Merrill-Palmer Quarterly of Behavior and Development*, **10**, pp. 249–64.

HUTCHINSON, E.O. (1995, October 30) 'Clinton speech reinforced white fears by perpetuating black racial myths', *Austin American-Statesman*, p. A11.

JAMES, J. and FARMER, R. (Eds) (1993) *Spirit, Space and Survival: African American Women in (white) Academe*, New York: Routledge.

JENNINGS, W.B. (1989) 'How to organize successful parent advisory committees', *Educational Leadership*, **47**, pp. 42–5.

JENSEN, A.R. (1969) 'How much can we boost IQ and scholastic achievement?', *Harvard Educational Review*, **39**, pp. 1–123.

JENSEN, A.R. (1981) *Straight Talk about Mental Tests*, New York: Free Press.

JONES, J. (1995) 'Back to the future with *The Bell Curve*: Jim Crow, slavery and *G.*', in FRASER, S. (Ed) *The Bell Curve Wars: Race, Intelligence, and the Future of America*, New York: Basic Books, pp. 80–93.

JUDIS, J.B. (1995) 'Hearts of darkness', in FRASER, S. (Ed) *The Bell Curve Wars: Race, Intelligence, and the Future of America*, New York: Basic Books, pp. 124–9.

KENNEDY, R. (1995) 'The phony war', in FRASER, S. (Ed) *The Bell Curve Wars: Race, Intelligence, and the Future of America*, New York: Basic Books, 179–86.

KLINEBERG, O. (1935) *Negro Intelligence and Selective Migration*, New York: Columbia University Press.

KLINEBERG, O. (1963) 'Negro–white differences in intelligence test performance: A new look at an old problem', *American Psychologist*, **18**, pp. 198–203.

KOZOL, J. (1991) *Savage Inequalities: Children in America's Schools*, New York: Crown.

LAOSA, L.M. and HENDERSON, R.W. (1991) 'Cognitive socialization and competence: The academic development of Chicanos', in VALENCIA, R.R. (Ed) *Chicano School Failure and Success: Research and Policy Agendas for the 1990s*, London: Falmer Press, pp. 164–99.

LEMANN, N. (1986) 'The origins of the underclass', *The Atlantic Monthly*, September, pp. 31–55.

LEVIN, H. (1987) 'New schools for the disadvantaged', *Teacher Education Quarterly*, **14**, pp. 60–83.

LEWONTIN, R.C. (1973) 'Race and intelligence', in SENNA, C. (Ed) *The Fallacy of IQ*, New York: Joseph Okpatu, pp. 1–17.

LORDE, A. (1992) 'Age, race, class, and sex: Women redefining difference', in ANDERSEN, M. and HILL COLLINS, P. (Eds) *Race, Class, and Gender: An Anthology*, Belmont, CA: Wadsworth, pp. 495–502.

LOTT, T. (1994a, February 8) '33,000 Austin students "at-risk"', *Austin American-Statesman*, pp. A1, A7.

LOTT, T. (1994b, May 9) 'Austin school board to consider new at-risk policy', *Austin American-Statesman*, p. B2.

LOTT, T. and VARGAS, D.J. (1994, February 9) 'Parents, students angry over "at-risk" notices', *Austin American-Statesman*, pp. A1, A5.

LYNN, M. (1989) 'Criticisms of an evolutionary hypothesis about race differences: A rebuttal to Rushton's reply', *Journal of Research in Personality*, **23**, pp. 21–34.

McCARTHY, D. (1972) *McCarthy Scales of Children's Abilities*, New York: The Psychological Corp.

McDOUGALL, W. (1921) *Is America Safe for Democracy?*, New York: Charles Scribner's Sons.

MANNING, M.L. and BARUTH, L.G. (1995) *Students at Risk*, Boston, MA: Allyn and Bacon.

MANNS, W. (1988) 'Supportive roles of significant others to black families', in McADOO, H.P. (Ed) *Black Families*, Beverly Hills, CA: Sage, pp. 270–83.

MARABLE, M. (1992) *Black America*, Westfield, NJ: Open Media.

MARANS, A.E. and LOURIE, R. (1967) 'Hypotheses regarding the effects of child-rearing patterns on the disadvantaged child', in HELLMUTH, J. (Ed) *Disadvantaged Child*, **1**, New York: Brunner/Mazel, pp. 17–41.

MARBURGER, C.L. (1990) 'The school site level: Involving parents in reform', in BACHARACH, S.B. (Ed) *Education Reform: Making Sense of it All*, Boston, MA: Allyn and Bacon, pp. 82–91.

MARGONIS, F. (1992) 'The cooptation of "at-risk": Paradoxes of policy criticism', *Teachers College Record*, **94**, pp. 343–64.

MÁRQUEZ, B. (1993) *LULAC: The Evolution of a Mexican American Political Organization*, Austin, TX: University of Texas Press.

MASSEY, D.S. (1990) 'American apartheid: Segregation and the making of the underclass', *American Journal of Sociology*, **96**, pp. 329–57.

MASSEY, D.S. and EGGERS, M.L. (1990) 'The ecology of inequality: Minorities and the concentration of poverty, 1970–1980', *American Journal of Sociology*, **95**, pp. 1153–88.

MEAD, L.M. (1989) 'The logic of workforce: The underclass and work policy', *Annals of the American Academy of Political and Social Science*, **501**, pp. 157–69.

Méndez v. Westminster School District (1946) 64 F. Supp 544 (SD Cal 1946), 161 F. 2d 774 (9th Cir 1947).

MERCER, J.R. (1988) 'Ethnic differences in IQ scores: What do they mean?' (A response to Lloyd Dunn), *Hispanic Journal of Behavioral Sciences*, **10**, pp. 199–218.

MERCER, J.R. (1989) 'Alternative paradigms for assessment in a pluralistic society', in BANKS, J. and McKEE BANKS, C.A. (Eds) *Multicultural Education: Issues and Perspectives*, Boston, MA: Allyn and Bacon, pp. 289–304.

MERCER, J.R. and BROWN, W.C. (1973) 'Racial differences in IQ: Fact or fiction?', in SENNA, C. (Ed) *The Fallacy of IQ*, New York: Joseph Okpatu, pp. 56–113.

MILKMAN, R. (1978) 'A simple exposition of Jensen's error', *Journal of Educational Statistics*, **3**, pp. 203–8.

MINCY, R., SAWHILL, I. and WOLF, D. (1990) 'The underclass: Definition and measurement', *Science*, **248**, pp. 450–3.

MOORE, J. (1989) 'Is there a Hispanic underclass?', *Social Science Quarterly*, **70**, pp. 265–84.

MURRAY, C. (1984) *Losing Ground: American Social Policy, 1950–1980*, New York: Basic Books.

MURRAY, C. (1988) 'The coming of custodial democracy', *Commentary*, **86**, pp. 9–14.

MYRDAL, G. (1944) *An American Dilemma: The Negro Problem and Modern Democracy*, New York: Harper & Row.

NISBETT, R. (1995) 'Race, IQ, and scientism', in FRASER, S. (Ed) *The Bell Curve Wars: Race, Intelligence, and the Future of America*, New York: Basic Books, pp. 36–57.

OAKES, J. (1985) *Keeping Track: How Schools Structure Inequality*, New Haven, CT: Yale University Press.

PETTIGREW, T.F. (1964) 'Negro American intelligence: A new look at an old controversy', *Journal of Negro Education*, **33**, pp. 6–25.

PHILLIPS, D.C. and KELLY, M.C. (1975) 'Hierarchical theories of development in education and psychology', *Harvard Educational Review*, **45**, pp. 351–75.

PREWITT DIAZ, J.O. (1988) 'Assessment of Puerto Rican children in bilingual education programs in the United States: A critique of Lloyd M. Dunn's monograph', *Hispanic Journal of Behavioral Sciences*, **10**, pp. 237–52.

QUINTERO, E. and RUMMEL, M.K. (1995) 'Voice unaltered: Marginalized young writers speak', in SWADENER, B.B. and LUBECK, S. (Eds) *Children and Families 'at Promise': Deconstructing the Discourse at Risk*, Albany, NY: State University of New York Press, pp. 97–117.

REYES, P. and VALENCIA, R.R. (1993) 'Educational policy and the growing Latino student population: Problems and prospects', *Hispanic Journal of Behavioral Sciences*, **15**, pp. 258–83.

RICHARDSON, V., CASANOVA, U., PLACIER, P. and GUILFOYLE, K. (1989) *School Children at Risk: Schools as Communities of Support*, London: Falmer Press.

RICKETS, E. and SAWHILL, I. (1988) 'Defining and measuring the underclass', *Journal of Policy Analysis and Management*, **7**, pp. 316–25.

ROMO, R. (1986) 'George I. Sánchez and the civil rights movement: 1940 to 1960', *La Raza Law Journal*, **1**, pp. 342–62.

RONDA, M.A. and VALENCIA, R.R. (1994) '"At-risk" Chicano students: The institutionalized and communicative life of a category', *Hispanic Journal of Behavioral Sciences*, **16**, pp. 363–95.

ROSEN, G. (1974) 'The development of the Chicano movement in Los Angeles from 1967 to 1969', *Aztlán*, **4**, pp. 155–83.

ROSEN, J. and LANE, C. (1995) 'The sources of *The Bell Curve*', in FRASER, S. (Ed) *The Bell Curve Wars: Race, Intelligence, and the Future of America*, New York: Basic Books, pp. 58–61.

SALVIA, J. and YSSELDYKE, J.E. (1988) *Assessment in Special and Remedial Education* (4th ed.) Boston, MA: Houghton Mifflin.

SAN MIGUEL, G., JR. (1987) *'Let All of Them Take Heed': Mexican Americans and the Campaign for Educational Equality in Texas, 1910–1981*, Austin, TX: University of Texas Press.

SATTLER, J.M. (1992) *Assessment of Children* (3rd ed.) San Diego, CA: Jerome M. Sattler.

SCANZONI, J. (1985) 'Black parental values and expectations of children's occupation and educational success: Theoretical implications', in McADOO, H.P. and McADOO, J.L. (Eds) *Black Children*, Beverly Hills, CA: Sage, pp. 113–22.

SHUEY, A.M. (1966) *The Testing of Negro Intelligence* (2nd ed.), New York: Social Science Press.

SINGH, V.P. (1994) 'The underclass in the United States: Some correlates of economic change', in KRETOVICS, J. and NUSSEL, E.J. (Eds) *Transforming Urban Education*, Boston, MA: Allyn and Bacon, pp. 57–72.

SLAVIN, R.E. (1986) *Educational Psychology: Theory into Practice*, Englewood Cliffs, NJ: Prentice Hall.

SLAVIN, R.E. (1997) *Educational Psychology: Theory into Practice* (5th ed.), Boston, MA: Allyn and Bacon.

SLEETER, C.E. (1995) 'Foreword', in SWADENER, B.B. and LUBECK, S. (Eds) *Children and*

Families 'at Promise': Deconstructing the Discourse of Risk, Albany, NY: State University of New York Press, pp. ix–xi.

SMITH, M.S. and BISSELL, J.S. (1970) 'Report analysis: The impact of Head Start', *Harvard Educational Review*, **14**, pp. 51–104.

SNIDER, W. (1990, April 18) 'Outcry follows Cavazos comments on the values of Hispanic parents', *Education Week*, p. 1.

SOLÓRZANO, D.G. (1992a) 'Chicano mobility aspirations: A theoretical and empirical note', *Latino Studies Journal*, **3**, pp. 48–66.

SOLÓRZANO, D.G. (1992b) 'An exploratory analysis of the effects of race, class and gender on student and parent mobility aspirations', *Journal of Negro Education*, **61**, pp. 30–44.

SOLÓRZANO, D.G. and SOLÓRZANO, R. (1995) 'The Chicano educational experience: A proposed framework for effective schools in Chicano communities', *Educational Policy*, **9**, pp. 293–314.

SOWELL, T. (1981) *Ethnic America: A History*, New York: Basic Books.

SOWELL, T. (1995) 'Ethnicity and IQ', in FRASER, S. (Ed) *The Bell Curve Wars: Race, Intelligence and the Future of America*, New York: Basic Books, pp. 70–9.

STEINBERG, S. (1989) *The Ethnic Myth*, New York: Random House.

SWADENER, B.B. (1995) 'Children and families "at promise": Deconstructing the discourse at risk', in SWADENER, B.B. and LUBECK, S. (Eds) *Children and Families 'at Promise': Deconstructing the Discourse of Risk*, Albany, NY: State University of New York Press, pp. 17–49.

SWADENER, B.B. and LUBECK, S. (1995a) 'The social construction of children and families "at risk": An introduction', in SWADENER, B.B. and LUBECK, S. (Eds) *Children and Families 'at Promise': Deconstructing the Discourse of Risk*, Albany, NY: State University of New York Press, pp. 1–14.

SWADENER, B.B. and LUBECK, S. (Eds) (1995b) *Children and Families 'at Promise': Deconstructing the Discourse of Risk*, Albany, NY: State University of New York Press.

TABACHNICK, B.R. and BLOCH, M.N. (1995) 'Learning in and out of school: Critical perspectives on the theory of cultural compatibility', SWADENER, B.B. and LUBECK, S. (Eds) *Children and Families 'at Promise': Deconstructing the Discourse of Risk*, Albany, NY: State University of New York Press, pp. 187–209.

TAKAKI, R. (Ed) (1987) *From Distant Shores: Perspectives on Race and Ethnicity in America*, New York: Oxford University Press.

TAYLOR, L.J. and SKANES, G.R. (1976) 'Level I and Level II intelligence in Inuit and white children from similar environments', *Journal of Cross-Cultural Psychology*, **7**, pp. 157–68.

TERMAN, L.M. (1916) *The Measurement of Intelligence*, Boston, MA: Houghton Mifflin.

TRUEBA, H.T. (1988) 'Comments on L.M. Dunn's *Bilingual Hispanic Children on the US Mainland: A Review of Research on Their Cognitive, Linguistic and Scholastic Development*', *Hispanic Journal of Behavioral Sciences*, **10**, pp. 253–62.

VALENCIA, R.R. (1984) 'The school closure issue and the Chicano community: A follow-up study of the *Angeles* case', *The Urban Review*, **16**, pp. 145–63.

VALENCIA, R.R. and GUADARRAMA, I.N. (1996) 'High-stakes testing and its impact on social and ethnic minority students', in SUZUKI, L.A., MELLER, P.J. and PONTEROTTO, J.G. (Eds) *Multicultural Assessment: Clinical, Psychological and Educational Applications*, San Francisco, CA: Jossey-Bass, pp. 561–610.

VALENCIA, R.R., HENDERSON, R.W. and RANKIN, R.J. (1985) 'Family status, family constellation and home environmental variables as predictors of cognitive performance of Mexican American children', *Journal of Educational Psychology*, **77**, pp. 323–31.

VARGAS, D.J. (1994, February 10) 'AISD official apologizes to parents for notices', *Austin American-Statesman*, pp. B1, B5.

VERNON, P.E. (1979) *Intelligence, Heredity and Environment*, San Francisco, CA: W.H. Freeman.

WACQUANT, L. and WILSON, W. (1989) 'The cost of racial and class exclusion in the inner city', *Annals of the American Academy of Political and Social Sciences*, **501**, pp. 8–25.

WADE, N. (1976) 'IQ and heredity: Suspicion of fraud beclouds classic experiment', *Science*, **194**, pp. 916–19.

WHITE, C.J. (1995) 'Native Americans at promise: Travel in borderlands', in SWADENER, B.B. and LUBECK, S. (Eds) *Children and Families 'at Promise': Deconstructing the Discourse of Risk*, Albany, NY: State University of New York Press, pp. 163–84.

WILLIAMS, D.L. and CHAVKIN, N.F. (1989) 'Essential elements of strong parent involvement programs', *Educational Leadership*, **47**, pp. 18–20.

WILLIG, A.C. (1988) 'A case of blaming the victim: The Dunn monograph on bilingual Hispanic children on the US mainland', *Hispanic Journal of Behavioral Sciences*, **10**, pp. 219–36.

WILSON, W. (1987) *The Truly Disadvantaged: The Inner City, the Underclass and Public Policy*, Chicago, IL: The University of Chicago Press.

WILSON, W. (1994) 'The declining significance of race: Blacks and changing American institutions', in GRUSKY, D. (Ed) *Social Stratification: Class, Race and Gender in Sociological Perspective*, Boulder, CO: Westview Press, pp. 520–31.

WOLFE, A. (1995) 'Has there been a cognitive revolution in America? The flawed sociology of *The Bell Curve*', in FRASER, S. (Ed) *The Bell Curve Wars: Race, Intelligence, and the Future of America*, New York: Basic Books, pp. 109–23.

ZUCKERMAN, M. and BRODY, N. (1988) 'Oysters, rabbits and people: A critique of "Race differences in behaviour" by J.P. RUSHTON', *Personality and Individual Differences*, **9**, pp. 1025–33.

Chapter 7

Democratic Education as an Alternative to Deficit Thinking

Arthur Pearl

In this chapter we present an alternative to deficit thinking — *democratic educa-tion.* We briefly indicate the features and requirements of democratic education and then summarize the results of experiments in democratic education that indicate the enormous potential in educational improvements if it would replace deficit thinking in educational practice and policy. Such transformation, however, will not come easily.

Deficit thinking is deeply embedded in every aspect of modern American life. It is so much a part of the landscape that it is difficult to recognize, let alone address. Because it is so ubiquitous and so much of everyday experience, and because it saturates the entire political spectrum, what are advertised as campaigns against deficit thinking become instead substitutions of different forms of deficit thinking. Deficit thinking constitutes a fundamental canon of conservative thought. It is part of the natural order of the cream rising to the top. One of the distinguish-ing features of conservative thought, according to one of its most distinguished spokespersons, Russell Kirk, is the

> conviction that civilized society requires orders and classes, as against the notion of a 'classless society'. With reason, conservatives often have been called 'the party of order'. If natural distinctions are effaced among men, oligarchs fill the vacuum. Ultimate equality in the judgment of God, and equality before courts of law, are recognized by conservatives; but equal-ity of condition, they think, means equality in servitude and boredom. (Kirk, 1986: 8–9)

The essence of the conservative thinking on this subject is that natural order has withstood the test of time (another conservative canon) and is not to be tinkered with. Predisposed to believing that there is natural inferiority and superiority, and never the twain shall meet, it does not take much evidence to reinforce an already well-lodged opinion.

Conservative support of deficit thinking is to be expected. What adds to the difficulty is that liberal and radical thinkers and policymakers have created their own manifestations of deficit thinking. In attempting to eliminate deficit thinking we literally are walking into an intellectual battle field confronting canons to the left and canons to the right.

How could it be otherwise. With the founding fathers, deficit thinking spawned their distrust of democracy and led them to build in so many safeguards against public participation in public policy, such as justification for slavery, limiting the vote to white males with property, and prohibiting the direct election of the president or senators.

A nation that sanctions slavery, and limits suffrage, needs justification for such policies (for a solid analysis of early racist discourses and the rooting of deficit thinking, see Menchaca, Chapter 2). Instructive is the extent to which Thomas Jefferson — the primary author of the Declaration of Independence, and denounced by the conservatives of his time as a dangerous radical and largely recognized as a strong advocate for 'democracy' — would go to convince himself that black people lacked the intellectual capacity to participate as equals in the fledgling democracy. Early in his career he came to the 'scientific' conclusion on the capacities of African-Americans:

They secrete less by the kidneys and more by the glands of the skin, which gives them a very strong and disagreeable odor. They seem to require less sleep . . . They are more ardent after their female: but love seems with them to be eager desire, than a tender delicate mixture of sentiment and sensation. Their griefs are transient. In general their existence appears to participate more of sensation than reflection. To this must be ascribed their disposition to sleep when abstracted from their diversions, and unemployed in labor. An animal whose body is at rest, and who does not reflect, must be disposed to sleep of course. Comparing them by their faculties of memory, reason and imagination, it appears to me, that in memory they are equal to whites; in reason, much inferior, as I think one could scarcely be found capable of tracing and comprehending the investigations of Euclid; and that in imagination they are dull, tasteless and anomalous . . . The Indians will astonish you with strokes of the most sublime oratory; such as prove their reason and sentiment strong, and their imagination glowing and elevated. But never yet could I find that a black had uttered a thought above the level of plain narration . . .

In music, they are generally more gifted than the whites with accurate ears for tune and time . . . I believe that disposition to theft with which they have been branded, must be ascribed to their situation, and not any depravity of the moral sense. The man, in whose favor no laws of property exist, probably feels himself less bound to respect those made in the favor of others . . . Notwithstanding these considerations which must weaken their respect for the laws of property, we find among them numerous instances of the most rigid integrity, and as many as among their better instructed masters, of benevolence, gratitude and unshaken fidelity. The opinion that they are inferior in the faculties of reason and imagination must be hazarded with great diffidence. To justify a general conclusion, requires many observations . . . where our conclusions would degrade a whole race of men from the rank in the scale of beings which their Creator may perhaps have given them. *Notes from Virginia*, 1781–85, quoted in Wallechinsky and Wallace, *The People's Almanac*. (1978: 173–74)

Jefferson, a child of The Enlightenment, worked hard to divest himself of deficit thinking (Padover, 1939), and while he could admit that there were exceptions to his conclusion that black people were inferior to whites (as do most people saddled with deficit thinking) he never was able to believe as he had once written that 'all men [*sic*] are created equal'. Jefferson's 'democracy' was a meritocracy — a 'natural', as distinct from a privileged 'artificial', 'aristocracy' (Padover, 1939: 82–3). He was opposed to the notion of privilege, but he accepted the idea that there were clear differences in intellectual ability and that these differences were influenced by race. In comparison to Jefferson, the thinking of others who molded the society and developed the frames of intellectual reference that have guided us for more than two centuries, deficit thinking was more readily accepted and the actions that were informed by such thinking provoked very little reflection. To Jefferson's credit, he questioned his own beliefs, something very few of our leaders did then or now.

The insistence on deficit thinking was not purely expedient, nor was it limited to slaveholders or to the slave states. Alexis de Tocqueville, who more than any other person in the mid-nineteenth century explained the United States to itself as well as to Europe, observed:

Race prejudice seems stronger in those states that have abolished slavery than in those where it still exists, and nowhere is it more intolerant than in those where slavery was never known. *Democracy in America*. (1850 ed., p. 343)

Karl Marx, as virulent a critic he was of oppression, developed nonetheless a model of deficit thinking that became embodied in movements and governments that followed his thinking. Marx dismissed democracy and the importance of rights. He called for a 'vanguard party' to care for the interests of the proletariat that was too corrupted by 'bourgeois' thinking to be entrusted to rule itself (Marx, 1875). It was such thinking that justified a 'Dictatorship of the Proletariat' and the need for caretakers until such time that oppression ended and the state would wither (Lenin, 1919). The state guided by this form of deficit thinking did wither (disintegrated would be more accurate), but not in the ways envisioned by those who fathered this type of thinking.

The deficit thinking of the extreme right and extreme left are easy targets and give smugness to those who maintain the mainstream middle-of-the-road deficit thinking that dominates school practices and policies. It is the *differential encouragements* maintained by statute, enacted by policy and informally practiced by classroom teachers and administrators that help to perpetuate deficit thinking. In turn, these educators and administrators have been abetted by the academics who trained and provided them with a philosophy that either defended such practices or buried them in a verbiage that unwittingly camouflaged inequities.

Uncontaminated, deficit thinking is justification for the denial of what those without deficits receive. For example, it is right and proper to deny a person with an allegedly limited intelligence to take a course that he or she will surely fail. Right, because the afflicted are spared from the pain of defeat and the humiliation of failure. Right, because the capable are not held back by those who are unable to learn. Deficit thinking thus results in a justified *unlevel* playing field. In recent years, because of increased anxiety brought on by the uncertainty of the opportunity structure, deficit thinking has been adulterated with the efforts made to gain a competitive advantage. The 'competitive advantage thinking' reinforces the justification of 'denial thinking'. It is the other side of the deficit thinking coin. The deficit in competitive advantage is denial of the advantage. In either instance, the results are the same. Students are denied equal encouragement.

Competitive advantage is a particularly difficult form of deficit thinking to combat. There is little effort made to justify competitive advantage. It is *not* the Jeffersonian ideal meritocracy that assumes a wide range of differences in talent and capabilities of a natural hierarchy would spring, with the 'best and the brightest' emerging as a 'natural aristoi' (Jefferson letter to John Adams, 1815 quoted in Padover, 1939: 82), after everyone has been given equal encouragement. Competitive advantage is a denial of equal encouragement. It can take many forms. It is a major advertisement for 'vouchers'. In times of declining resources, competitive advantage is a better resourced school (Kozol, 1991). Traditional deficit thinking and the notion of competitive advantage reinforce each other.

Strong Democracy as the Alternative to Deficit Thinking

It is a strange and somewhat remarkable attribute of United States citizens that they can be fierce advocates of democracy without ever bothering to understand what it is that they support. It is only when democracy becomes an operational concept capable of informing policy and practice that inadequacies and cruelties of deficit thinking (and its analogue, competitive advantage) can be exposed and alternatives found. Without such a standard it is difficult to consider other possibilities.

Deficit thinking, I contend, is inevitable unless there exists an informing general theory that does not require some form of imputed deficits to explain inequity in a society. 'Strong democracy' provides such an alternative.

> Strong democracy [formally defined] as politics in the participatory mode where conflict is resolved in the absence of an independent ground through a participatory process of ongoing, proximate self-legislation and the creation of a political community capable of transforming dependent, private individuals into free citizens and partial and private interests into public goods. (Barber, 1984: 132)

> Since the objective [of strong democracy] is to find working maxims rather than fixed truths and shared consciousness rather than immutable principles, what is needed is a common language and a mode of common seeing that will facilitate legitimate political judgments. (Barber, 1984: 170)

Sadly, there has been little attention given to examining education from a democratic perspective. John Dewey made a heroic effort in the first half of the twentieth century (Dewey, 1916; 1938a, 1938b) to reconcile education with democracy. For a variety of reasons Dewey's ideas never became a significant part of mainstream education. However, even if Dewey's ideas of democracy had informed American education it would not have had much impact on deficit thinking. He did not fully comprehend how deep were the roots of racism, classism, ethnocentrism and sexism in American culture and institutions. Nor did he address democratic practice with specific reference to deficit thinking.

Strong democracy must begin with schools because it cannot begin anywhere else. No other agency can introduce democracy. People need to be educated for it. That has been one of the paradoxes of American life: a desire for a democratic life without providing an agency to prepare for democratic citizenship.

The call for democratic schools is not a harking back to George Counts and his now generally ridiculed *Dare Schools Build a New Social Order?* (Counts, 1932). The primary purpose of a democratic school is to prepare students to be competent citizens. There is no requirement that they change society, only that they be prepared to function as citizens in it. Citizenship is what all students share. They will not go forth from schools and have identical work futures. They will not think the same, have the same tastes, read the same books, watch the same television programs, have the same number of children, etc. But, they will all have equal and identical status as citizens. Each will have one vote. The school has the responsibility that they will use that vote wisely. Not only do schools fail to produce informed citizens, they are one of the major institutions that have helped turn students off to politics.

In the midst of an anti-democratic populist uprising there has been a reawakened interest in democratic education (Apple and Beane, 1995; Barber, 1992; Meier, 1995; Wood, 1992). In this chapter, we add our understanding of democracy and direct it specifically to deficit thinking.

It is right and proper that deficit thinking be solidly entrenched as a way of thinking. The efforts to combat it were top-down and were contaminated by other forms of deficit thinking — doing for people that which they were unable to do for themselves. A democratic education is not only a philosophical and theoretical alternative to deficit thinking, it is the means by which a constituency can be organized to overcome it. By using deficit thinking to combat deficit thinking we have reaped what we have sowed.

It is our contention that unless schooling can meet the requirements of democratic education, deficit thinking will continue to exist and if anything, grow. We propose four requirements of democratic education: 1) providing that kind of knowledge that will enable *every* student to engage *equally* in an informed debate on every generally recognized important social and personal issue; 2) guaranteeing *everyone equally* the particular rights of:

a freedom of expression, (which includes the right to express unpopular political beliefs, and to disagree with constituted authority, including the teacher);
b specified rights of privacy;
c due process that includes presumption of innocence, trial by independent tribunal and protection from cruel and unusual punishment; and
d freedom of movement;

3) providing *everyone* the opportunity and the skill to participate with *equal power* in all the decisions that effect one's life; 4) providing *everyone equal encouragement* in all of society's legitimate activities (Pearl, 1990).

Each of these four requirements of democratic education (knowledge; rights; participation; encouragement) has specific relevance to different aspects of deficit thinking. Let us examine them more closely.

Knowledge and Deficit Thinking

The issue of knowledge addresses curriculum. The single most important question in any meaningful discussion of curriculum is: What constitutes important knowledge? *This is the debate that education has not had.* Reforms are made with conclusions drawn about important knowledge, for example, 'the basics', 'the classics' and 'bilingual/multicultural' education in the absence of anything resembling serious debate. Decisions are made using a top-down approach that students must be taught this or that. These decisions are surrounded with inflated rhetoric and are transmogrified into standards. To a large extent, students are labeled as deficient because of their failure to meet arbitrarily defined standards. Deficit thinking here takes one form by dismissing from consideration those individuals who have not been persuaded that what is taught in school is important. Bear in mind that it is not only the students with labels of deficiency that are unpersuaded about the importance of school based learning. In general, very few students believe that what they learn is important. They suffer through perceived irrelevance because they are encouraged to believe that school is an obstacle course that they can survive; once the course is over, they will be given a visa into a well-paying and otherwise desirable future. Students with 'deficits' are not encouraged to survive the obstacle course, as they see no reason to invest in schools. I discuss the logical consequence of lack of encouragement later in this chapter.

The lament about the curricular subject of history provides a valuable lesson (one which commentators about history, Diane Ravitch among them, persistently refuse to learn; Ravitch, 1989). Students resist a prescribed history, no matter how packaged. Note the following:

To test whether students had a secure command of the 'foundations of literacy', the National Assessment of Educational Progress (NAEP) administered the first national assessment of history and literature in the spring of 1986. One object of the test was to ascertain whether students had ready command of essential background knowledge about American history.

The results were not reassuring ... we found it disturbing that two-thirds of the sample did not know that the Civil War occurred between 1850 and 1900; that nearly 40 per cent did not know that the Brown decision held school segregation unconstitutional, that 40 per cent did not know that the East Coast of the United States was explored and settled mainly by England and that the Southwest was explored and settled mainly by Spain, that 70 per cent did not know that the purpose of Jim Crow laws was to enforce racial segregation, and that 30 per cent could not find Great Britain on a map of Europe. (Ravitch, 1989: 52)

Although considerable attention was directed against historical ignorance and efforts were made to remediate the situation, no improvements were apparent nearly a decade later (Lapham, 1996). Nor would it have been reasonable to expect that interest in history would be reawakened even if the teaching of it had been dramatically improved. It is impossible to teach history effectively without a sense of mission. What is it that we expect to be accomplished through the investment of time and energy in its study? Ravitch and others, whose essays appear in the Bradley Commission volume on Historical Literacy (Gagnon, 1989), call for enlivening its teaching and convincing students that they have much to learn from the past. If history is to be enlivened, however, it must be debated, and crucial to that debate is the issue of justice. For that debate to have meaning and generate interest in specifics, and become generally perceived as having relevance, *it is imperative that the excluded be included and that the undiscussible be discussed.* It is impossible to teach history if the prevailing attitude eschews debate and if efforts to identify specific acts of inequity are traduced with charges of 'political correctness'. History cannot be properly taught because there is an unwillingness to examine the history of deficit thinking and how such thinking has distorted education and contorted debate.

For historical knowledge to be important, its lessons must provide the widest spectrum of students with the skills and knowledge that will enable all students to become informed citizens capable of solving important problems. While those who would reform the teaching of history insist historical literacy is essential to good citizenship, nowhere do they identify the problems that good citizenship would be required to solve, or, specifically how the study of history can be used to solve those problems.

The history that is taught is designed for those who would perpetuate the system, not dramatically alter it. It is a history that accepts deficit thinking, without opening it up for examination. There has been recognition that textbooks have distorted history, that students have received a glossed over, sugarcoated, carefully expurgated version of the past. To remedy that, the historically excluded get referenced and *prior* injustices are acknowledged with a self-congratulatory insistence that we do not do those things anymore. The history served up to students is a too thin gruel to give much intellectual nourishment and only further alienates those already alienated.

Deficit thinking certainly enters the history curriculum in the answering of the question of 'whose history?' To avoid a serious tackling of a difficult question, the compromises made satisfy no one. The inclusion of bits and snippets of African American History, Chicano History, Puerto Rican History, Native American History, and Asian American History are rightfully criticized by traditionalists as adulteration, and the persons to whom crumbs are thrown, rightfully dismiss the changes as tokenistic window-dressing. What has occurred has been concessions in the absence of debate.

Elitism is a logical consequence of deficit thinking. Elites make important decisions because others are decreed to be incapable of important decisionmaking. Elite decisions, however, exact a heavy price. The mess that is history curriculum derives from elitist decisions. Students are left in the dark about the reasons for change and the result is a lot of unhappiness and finger pointing. White students often react with anger to the suggestions that they are guilty of transgressions about which they knew nothing. Furthermore, they are not certain that they are receiving a more accurate accounting of what happened than was provided in the old histories. What they hear in class does not square with what they are told at home or at church. Some get caught in the frenzy of uninformed statements concluding that less qualified women and minorities have taken over everywhere; these statements emanate from such well situated women and minorities as Rush Limbaugh, the Governor of the State of California (Pete Wilson), and the minority and women who dominate the United States Senate.

Women and ethnic minority students are not placated by multicultural curriculum, as currently conceived. They are as mystified by it as the white male students. It does nothing for them. It provides no beacons, opens no doors, illuminates no passageways.

History will become an exciting topic when it deals substantially with pressing problems; when it is organized to solve present problems; when it is understood to be an ongoing debate; and when all students' understanding of history is given equal respect and opportunity for expression. Although the efforts at the reform of the history curriculum and the intent of historical literacy is to prepare students to be informed citizens capable of functioning in a democratic society, the reform effort is fatally flawed by its elitism. There can be no democratic result in the absence of a democratic method.

One of the most important history lessons that students need to learn is the history of deficit thinking and how that thinking has impacted, and continues to impact their lives. Such a lesson *cannot be delivered* to students; it must be *discovered* by them. To learn about deficit thinking, students cannot be consumers of knowledge. They cannot have information handed to them by historians; they must become historians.

In addition to elitism, a second form of deficit thinking is curriculum that reinforces belief in deficits. The lack of meaningful sustained debate of history and the lack of focus on problem solving are not the only ways in which deficit thinking affects the curriculum. Deficit thinking creeps into the curriculum both overtly and subtly. The emphasis on leaders tends to minimize the accomplishments of those who really made history. Lincoln did not free the slaves. And, although some students may know about Lincoln's ambivalence toward abolition of slavery and *his* acceptance of deficit thinking, very few know about the long, arduous battle that courageous men and women abolitionists, black and white, conducted to raise consciousness and build opposition to slavery in the North, and of the death-defying activities of the underground railroad maintained and conducted by both black and white, in the antebellum South.

Deficit thinking in curriculum is not restricted to history, it intrudes into every subject taught in schools. It can be found in the great works. Shakespeare engages in deficit thinking in his treatment of Othello. Iago becomes totally unbelievable unless Othello is invested with deficiencies that are attributable to black people. It can be found in Twain. In what many consider to be Twain's masterpiece, the *Adventures of Huckleberry Finn*, Jim is saddled with stereotypic deficits (Smiley, 1996). Deficit thinking intrudes into mathematics and science curriculum in very intricate ways that lend support to the unequal encouragements to master those subjects (we discuss unequal encouragements later in this chapter).

Third, and perhaps the most devastating form of deficit thinking in the curriculum, is *omission* — that which should be taught, but is not taught. There is nothing in the current curriculum that brings people together. A recent survey provided not only powerful data indicating how different in perceptions America was by race and ethnicity, but how ignorant all groups were of simple and undeniable facts. As an example, 46 per cent of whites said blacks on average held jobs equal to those of whites, 6 per cent said blacks had jobs that were a little better and another 6 per cent said 'a lot better' (Morin, 1995: 6).

> A majority of white Americans have fundamental misconceptions about the economic circumstances of black Americans, according to a new national survey, with most saying that the average black is faring as well or better than the average white in such specific areas as jobs, education and health care.
>
> That's not true. Government statistics show that whites on average, earn 60 per cent more than blacks, are far more likely to have medical insurance and more than twice as likely to graduate from college. (Morin, 1995: 6)

Obviously, when whites believe that blacks are doing as well as them, it is impossible to justify affirmative action and this is one of the reasons given in the survey for opposition to affirmative action (Morin, 1995: 7)

There is similar abysmal ignorance about the composition of the United States population. Whites believe that almost one-quarter (23.8 per cent) of the United States population is black. Blacks believe that more than a quarter (25.9 per cent) of the United States is black. Asians and Latinos believe that more than 20 per cent of the US is black (Gladwell, 1995). According to the 1990 United States Census data, 11.9 per cent of the United States is black. Similarly, all groups overestimate Latinos and Asians in the population with Latinos overestimating themselves the most (20.7 per cent estimate versus 9.5 per cent Census count) (Gladwell, 1995). The Census figures may and should be disputed and that is something that is worthy of classroom discussion. The overestimation of black academic and economic status can also be challenged — best so in an atmosphere where there is instruction and curriculum that emphasizes persuasion through the development of logic and evidence, and not who can yell the loudest and make the nastiest comment. The logical consequence of a white population overestimating minorities is the perception of being overrun, and that fuels anti-immigration sentiments and influences vote. If education cannot deal with ignorance, what can it do?

> White Americans always think racism is a feeling, and they reject it or they embrace it. To most Americans, it seems more honorable and nicer to reject it, so they do, but they almost invariably fail to understand that how they feel means very little to black Americans, who understand racism as a way of structuring American culture, American politics, and the American economy. (Smiley, 1996: 63)

In a democratic society with freedom of investigation and expression it would be expected that there would be widely different attitudes and proposed directions in social policy. It is inexcusable, however, that there not be a common base from which all can begin. Students should no more be allowed to fabricate population and income figures than they should be allowed to fabricate answers to simple arithmetic problems. Two plus two is not five just because a majority believes it to be true, nor is the economic condition of blacks and Latinos equal to whites just because the majority believes it. If students appear to be unable to solve simple arithmetic problems, there is considerable upset followed by condemnation of the schools. There is no such outcry when students are permitted to express their ignorance on facts from which racial and ethnic attitudes are developed. Widespread support of deficit thinking develops from ignorance.

The failure to deal seriously with serious issues has given birth to the travesty of 'political correctness'. Political correctness is a term generated by atavists to deflect attention away from matters that urgently need to be debated. The walls of an institution that had maintained itself as exclusionary and immune from criticism for centuries has come crashing down. It, like Humpty Dumpty (that it so much resembles), cannot be put back together again. It needs to be reconstructed, not deconstructed. Rather than a sober, meticulous and extensive examination of the changing mission of the university in a rapidly changing society, the public's mind, to use Disraeli's phrase, has been 'guanoed' with a spate of deficit oriented publications — for example, Allan Bloom's (1987) *The Closing of the American Mind.*

So, in sum, what might be a democratic or non-deficit approach to knowledge in the curriculum? The major thrust of a democratic curriculum is to prepare the student to be an informed citizen capable of functioning in a democratic society.

Preparation of a democratic citizen can only take place in a school-created democratic multicultural curriculum. Democratic multicultural education provides an alternative to the traditional canon (Bloom, 1994), or its 'liberal' reintroduction in just as coercive form (Lind, 1995). It is also an alternative to the series of disconnected celebrations of difference that has made what passes for multicultural education both so contentious and so unproductive in improving the conditions of the those at the bottom of the social ladder. Such an approach does nothing to improve the understandings of those who perceive themselves to be part of the dominant culture (for an excellent critique of conventional approaches, and meaningful alternatives to multiethnic curriculum, see Banks, 1989).

A democratic multicultural education starts with a shared common understanding from which different cultures emerge as spokes. The democratic multicultural curriculum equips all students with the capacity to be informed, competent citizens in a society with diverse populations and diverse interests. This means that unless there is a shared center that attracts all cultures, it will be impossible for there to be the discourse necessary and the concerted action required to solve any significant problem in the United States. The sole justification of a *public* school system, in contrast to *private* school systems, is that a public school has the potential to draw the widest ranges of people together. It can prepare the future citizen in a crucible of reality. Splintering into sealed off enclaves precludes problem solving. In that sense, the replacement of deficit thinking with a centripetal democratic education is more than a moral issue of fairness to people who have been systematically treated unfairly, it can be a matter of national survival.

Rights and Deficit Thinking

Rights, which have become increasingly imperiled, have to be seen as the foundation on which democracy rests. There can be no antidote to deficit thinking without a shared recognition of what does constitute and what does not constitute a right. We limit our rights to the four that have withstood the test of time (expression; privacy; due process; movement). We restrict our discussion to these rights because it is the way these rights are interpreted and respected that deficit thinking intrudes. Deficit thinking translates into rationing of rights — some get them and some do not. The attribution of deficits is a critical determining factor in deciding who will be afforded rights.

Because rights have been stretched and distorted, it is essential that we make clear our understanding of a *right*. We define a right as an unabridged activity that does not restrict the activity or make special demands of others. One person's freedom of expression does not prevent another from also expressing himself or herself. Respecting one person's privacy does not invade another's privacy. Due process for one does not come at the expense of the due process of another. Granting freedom of movement to one person does not cause another's to be restricted.

Defining what is *not* a right is as important as defining the existence of a right. This is particularly true today when a new right is enunciated by one group or another almost daily. Part of a democratic education is to evaluate whether a claim for a right meets an agreed upon definition. Deciding what is and what is not a right is should be included as an important part of the curriculum.

For example, does an individual have the *right* of freedom from sexual harassment, assault, or even murder? No, not by our definition of rights. *But*, any civil society has the *responsibility* to protect its citizens against attacks on person and property, and, to remove from society those who engage in such abuses. Rights, like all of democracy, are not simple. The few that are recognized must be fully understood and scrupulously exercised. To complicate matters, each of these rights have fuzzy boundaries and can be rescinded in states of emergency. The gray areas and conditions of emergency are important areas of knowledge. Students should ponder whether a responsible and democratic society can restrict expressions that offend others and may even provoke violence. If the answer is 'yes', what precisely can be restricted and under what circumstances? These are issues that need to be debated and analyzed in democratic classrooms.

Deficit thinking intrudes into rights in two related ways. One concerns defining the nature of the relationship between rights and responsibilities and the other in the differential ways in which rights are granted. If the argument that responsibility precedes rights prevails, then deficit thinking is used to preclude those who have never been given the opportunity to be responsible. In the later instance, reputation is used to deny people basic elemental rights. The denial of rights often precludes those denied the opportunity to engage in the deliberations that established the grounds for the denial of the rights. Thus, those with 'deficits' have their Catch 22: they are denied rights because they have deficits, and because they have deficits they are not permitted to engage in the discussions on who should have rights.

1) *Rights of expression* are those that have been defined in the First Amendment to the United States Constitution. Rights of expression did not come easily to this republic. Before rights of expression were accepted, people had to endure centuries of torture and even death for the expression of unacceptable beliefs.

The struggle for acceptance of freedom of expression did not end with the Bill of Rights. Some citizens have consistently been protected, while others have been excluded. African slaves had no First Amendment rights, nor, for most of our history, did women. Political radicals and trade union organizers found that the First Amendment was a 'now you see, now you don't' proposition. More than any other group, *school children* were denied the freedom of expression. It was not until 1965, after 13-year-old Mary Beth Tinker decided to protest the Vietnam war by wearing to school a black band on her arm, and only after she was suspended and only after a series of appeals, did the Supreme Court in *Tinker v. Des Moines Independent School District* (1969) establish freedom of expression for students. Mary Beth Tinker had a lot more going for her than do students with 'deficits'.

Freedom of expression is not a settled matter in public schools, nor is it a settled matter in any aspect of public life. Still unresolved are student rights to express orally unpopular opinions in class or elsewhere on school grounds, the right to symbolically express an opinion through dress, the right to criticize adult authority in student newspapers, and the right to peacefully assemble to express dissent. Freedom of expression largely rides, however, on the status of the student. Celebrated or advantaged students have those rights and rarely do they find their rights to expression challenged by school authorities.

In contrast, students who have been labeled with moral, character or intellectual deficits are actively discouraged from expressing their opinions (especially if those opinions challenge the authority that has decreed that the student has a deficit). Gang membership serves as an excellent example. In many schools, students are forbidden to wear gang colors. The justification for this action is that suspending the right of expression is necessary to maintain security and safety in the school. We recognize the importance of a safe school; an unsafe school cannot be a democratic school. We believe that school authorities have the responsibility to insure a safe school, and we recognize that gangs sometimes represent a threat to public safety. We are concerned, however, that authorities rush to suspend rights without sufficiently examining whether school safety requires truly such a suspension — or whether the suspension of rights actually works to further endanger the school. The primary reason that so little attention is given to attempting to insure safety while also respecting rights is that those affected are deemed to have deficits. It is to be noted that restriction of rights has not produced more safe schools.

As important as it is to define and defend student rights as a necessary ingredient of a democratic school, it is equally important to be able to define where those rights end. The right of expression has never included libel, slander or the use of expression to deliberately endanger others. The boundaries of permissible expression are not easily or immutably established. That boundary will be more defensibly established when students debate and reflect on all the arguments. Democracy is not served when adult authority arbitrarily determines what is permissible student expression and what is not.

Is conversing in a language other than English covered by rights of expression? Of course! The language a person uses does more than communicate information to others. Language also expresses identity and loyalty. All oppressed people develop secret codes that they use to communicate to kindred others without revealing matters believed to be reserved for sharing in private only with trusted others. To be democratic, teachers and other officials need to find persuasive reasons for students to become fluent in English without requiring them to surrender fluency in their mother tongue. If students resist learning English, school officials should examine how deficit thinking has promoted such resistance.

2) *Right of privacy* does not appear in the Constitution, but it is nonetheless a widely recognized value in society at large and among school children. Justice Louis Brandeis had no difficulty recognizing privacy as a right. He defines it as 'the right to be let alone' and asserts that it is 'the most comprehensive and the most valued by civilized men' (dissenting opinion in *Olmstead v. United States*, 1928). In *Roe v. Wade*, the critical decision of abortion, the modern definition of right of privacy was established. The decision provided an understanding that there existed an area of private life into which government cannot pry.

It must be remembered that the Constitution was created by men devoted to liberty, but opposed to equality. They believed humans to be selfish and untrustworthy and who needed to be controlled. The Constitution they created was intended to be an instrument of control, not emancipation. In fact, the idea of democracy is consciously not part of their thinking. It was not until the Civil War ended and the 13th, 14th and 15th amendments were ratified that the nation moved to recognize the importance of equality. As suffrage was extended, so too was the concern for privacy. Privacy was an important protection for the emerging labor movement, populism, feminism, and is important for the still very vulnerable minorities, labor unionists, and political radicals and — perhaps most important — students.

Students have never had much legal guarantee of privacy. In recent years, the Supreme Court has ruled that school principals can search student lockers without the same warrants required of police officers. As school safety becomes an ever increasing concern and fear of violence and crime grows, the concern for student privacy diminishes. As with rights of expression, privacy is far more denied those who are deemed threats to the system than denied to those who are afforded first-class citizenship. A logical consequence of being labeled deficit is the denial of rights of privacy.

In a democratic classroom, privacy is an important consideration and there is much more respect for it than is currently the case. It is a subject ripe for discussion in class, organized appropriately by levels of development. By the 5th or 6th grade, students should be able to engage in debate on the subject and defend their arguments with logic and evidence. Such issues as the connection of the early (founding fathers') concern for rights of person and the current concern for the rights of privacy should be explored in considerable depth. Important in that debate would be consideration of the conditions when abrogation of the rights of privacy could be approved. It is also important that if it is deemed necessary to restrict rights of privacy, such restriction should be equally applied to all students.

3) *Right of due process* is a major emphasis in the Bill of Rights. The 4th through 8th amendments were designed to reduce the power of established authority in the area of criminal justice. The colonists had been forced to suffer under uncontrolled police power and they did not like it. In the Bill of Rights they did something about it. In five amendments they provided: protection against search and seizure (4th Amendment, also important as a right of privacy); prevention of a trial unless there was a reasonable charge, prevention of double jeopardy through retrial after an acquittal, protection against being forced to testify against oneself (5th Amendment, also important for privacy); a speedy public trial, an impartial jury, access to knowledge about the charges, and the right to counsel (6th Amendment); further protection during the trial (7th Amendment); protection against cruel or unusual punishments (8th Amendment).

All of these amendments are designed for one goal: the establishment of a system of fairness. While the founding fathers were not much for equality in general, there was one area where equality was very important to them and that was equal treatment before the law. Distrustful as they were of democracy and universal suffrage, and as committed as they were to class hierarchy, they were also firm believers in fairness in the administration of justice. Equality to them was equal rights of defense when brought before the bar.

It is the lack of perceived fairness in the treatment of transgressions that is the cause of so much alienation and anger in schools. In an informal disciplinary action, deficits take priority over due process rights. Only when faced with expulsion do students have access to a clearly defined due process system, and then it is far too late. Students have long before been turned off to school in their encounters with a justice system that comes under the general rubric of discipline.

In the absence of a compelling curriculum — one which students find interesting and important — teachers serve primarily as policepersons. They try to coerce students into obedience. They spend hours, and schools thousands of dollars, in learning new and more effective discipline techniques. These techniques are not bound by Bill of Rights logic. None of these efforts seem to have changed the public impression that discipline and problems that need to be disciplined, such as drug use continue to be a major problem for schools.

In an authoritarian system the student's sole function is to obey. The teacher is an unchallengeable authority. If the teacher accuses the student of a transgression the student has no recourse. There is no assumption of innocence. To the contrary, the student is guilty if the teacher says so. It is worse than that if the teacher makes a mistake (and teachers have been known to make mistakes) and identifies the wrong person, or, as is often the case, a student pushes back at the student who shoved first, and is the one who is caught and disciplined. When the student who has been caught tries to explain, he or she is charged with a second infraction for his or her protestations (insubordination or disruptive behavior). Again, such miscarriage of justice is much more likely to happen to those with 'deficits' than those who are believed to be superior students. It is almost impossible for such a system to be fair. Students with bad reputations are going to be identified as disrupters when the teacher is unsure, and with 20 or more students in the class, it is very difficult to be certain.

In an authoritarian system, where the authorities make the laws, the very least that must be guaranteed to make such a system tolerable is fairness. Fairness would require presumption of innocence, the right to counsel, a trial before an independent tribunal, and protection against cruel and unusual punishment. Displaying a name on the board for all the class and every visitor to see is the modern equivalent of the medieval stocks. Public humiliation is cruel. Deficit thinking serves to undermine due process. Not much effort is made to encourage these students who teachers and other authorities believe are disruptive and incapable of learning.

Due process is not limited to disciplinary actions, it also extends to the grades that students receive. Grades are not, as some would insist, purely a reflection of what a student has learned in particular subjects. Grades are yet another way that teachers control student behavior.

4) *Right not to be a captive audience* does not appear in the Bill of Rights. How could it, in that slavery was permissible in the new nation, as was indentured service. Furthermore, because women had neither voting rights or access to the workplace, they too often were, in effect, imprisoned. It was not until the nation was almost 100 years old that the right not to be held captive was established.

School remains a (or perhaps, the) place where there has been no trend to emancipation. Long after slaves were freed from captivity, compulsory education laws were passed. By 1918 every state had a compulsory education law. Now, the only place where someone can be sentenced without first committing a crime is school.

Compulsory education is, by its very nature, coercive. There is a solid reason for students to be required to be in school. Uninformed citizens cannot make reasoned choices on critical social issues. Democracy requires an informed citizenry, and it follows that only through education can the citizen be well informed. However, to *compel* a student to become well educated is undemocratic. We have here, a large-sized dilemma. How do we resolve it? With compulsory education, respecting the right not to be a captive will take imagination. If compulsory education is a necessary requirement for informed citizenship, then it is absolutely essential that the classroom be an acceptable place for *all* students. The right not to be a captive requires an examination of policies that punish for tardiness and absenteeism. In a democratic school, it is far more important to determine why students are unable or unwilling to participate in a class activity and act to change those ungratifying conditions, than it is to try to bludgeon them back to the classroom. In fact, tardiness and absenteeism only become problems if they impede acquisition of important knowledge. If the school cannot make a persuasive case that what is being taught is worth learning, it is difficult to defend that idea that students must be in a classroom. Asserting that important material is being discussed in class does not make it so.

One reasonable approach to democratizing compulsory education is to increase the number of choices that students have in school. No student should be required to remain in a situation that she or he does not find gratifying. Students should be able to exercise choice over teachers, classes and schools. Students' claims of unfair treatment have to be taken seriously. Choice can be very difficult for schools. Some classes, schools and teachers will be much more popular than others. But difficult is not impossible. If increased choice leads to undersubscription in some classes and some schools (i.e., very few students want to be there), it is incumbent on the school system to take necessary action to either change the class or do something with the teacher. Those classes and schools have to be made more attractive — be places where students *want to attend*. Make no mistake, for a school to be universally gratifying an examination of activities that students do not find gratifying is mandatory, and that examination must be followed by actions to alter those ungratifying conditions.

Being a captive is particularly painful for those who have been relegated to deficit status. Students so vilified are forced to be where teachers do not want them, do not respect them and do not encourage them. The problem of compulsory attendance is lessened when all students are made equally welcome in the classroom.

There is a necessary relationship between rights and responsibilities. Without responsibilities there can be no rights. But what should be the nature of that relationship? The conservative position is that rights are bestowed with clear understanding that duties are attached. Theirs is a conclusion drawn from natural law and established tradition. It is that tradition that is used to deny those with alleged deficits their rights. I hold that rights come first, and then come responsibilities. My position is that tradition works in opposition to strong democracy. If neither natural law or tradition can guarantee rights (which they cannot), then rights can be bestowed only by a responsible community operating with a commonly respected system of laws and procedures. And if rights can come only from a responsible community, how can we propose that rights precede responsibilities? Rights precede because they are easier to define than responsibilities. That would not be true if we were indeed, 'one nation indivisible, under God, with liberty and justice for all'. We are not such a nation, nor have we ever been. Our pledge must be perceived as a commitment to a goal yet to be reached. From the very beginning of our nation we have struggled with a dilemma to develop strength from our diversity; however, diversity continues to be an obstacle to shared understanding. The only way that we can possibly generate a defensible and credible set of responsibilities under conditions of differing values is to first establish the ground rules for debate. A necessary component of those ground rules must be individual rights. It is only after everyone's rights are guaranteed that there can be a debate to define responsibilities. Responsibilities will continue to change. Rights remain a constant.

Rights precede responsibilities because democratic education is founded in tradition, not mired in it. Tradition supports a hierarchical society. Rights are necessary to protect powerless minorities. Rights are important, because as a society, we are always as vulnerable as our most despised minority. Rights are imperative for those defined as possessing deficits, because without those rights they will never be able to demonstrate the capacity to be responsible.

Participation and Deficit Thinking

Participation is a critical element of democracy. To many, participation is the *sine qua non* of democracy (Pateman, 1970). Underlying all deficit thinking theories is justification for exclusion (i.e., denying opportunity for participation). Limiting participation in democracy has been the most serious challenge to American democracy. Deficits were the basis for exclusion. Slaves were only three-fifths of a human (as stated by Article 1, Section 3 of the US Constitution). This fractionated characterization of blacks would be long-standing, as seen, for example, in the early intelligence testing research on black–white groups (Guthrie, 1976). For example, Pyle (1915), after testing 408 black children attending Missouri public schools and then comparing the scores to white children in the same locale concluded: '*In general the marks indicated mental ability of the Negro are about two-thirds of the whites*' [italics added] (quoted in Guthrie, 1976: 56).

Women were meant for private, not public life participation (Pateman, 1989). Deficits are the basis for exclusion from higher education and thus for entrance into the higher rungs of the economic ladder. Exclusion begets exclusion. It is the exclusionary practices in the early years of school that logically lead to exclusion in the later years. It is assignment to low-ability groups in elementary school that limits participation in full range of educational activities that leads to assignment to lower tracks in high school and limited opportunities to participate in intellectual and advanced academic activities (Oakes, 1985, 1992).

There are marked differences in class participation between high-performing and low-performing students (those with deficits). The high performers have their hands up, are called on frequently, sit in the front rows and are active participants. The low performers sit on their hands, rarely are called on, sit in the back, and rarely participate (see, for example, the classic study by Rist, 1970). The differences in participation are not limited to the classroom. Assigned deficits preclude participation in a variety of extracurricular school activities and has some effect on exclusion from community activities.

One of the most difficult forms of exclusion to understand is the practice that suspends those who have attributed deficits from school when they are having difficulty in school, such as suspending students for missing class when the most logical effort should be to find ways to encourage precisely those students to attend class. The practice of suspension means that students who are already behind find themselves further behind and that plays into further exclusion. A democratic class would encourage everyone to participate equally in all school sanctioned activities and would look to change school practices when there are wide discrepancies in student participation.

Benjamin Barber (1984), an advocate of strong democracy, insists that democratic education requires all students to participate in community service as a requirement for graduation (Barber, 1992). There is abundant evidence that when students normally denigrated as slothful (or with other deficits) are encouraged to participate, they will (see Edmonds, 1984; Hollins, 1991; Meier, 1995; Wood, 1992).

Encouragement and Deficit Thinking

Deficit thinking intrudes the most where it should be least welcome, and that is in discussion of equality. Neither conservative definitions of equality, 'treating all the same' (Kirk, 1986), or liberal definitions, 'equal result' (Rawls, 1971) are adequate. Both are predicated on deficits. Treating everyone identically is not an adequate definition of equality. No one would seriously argue that the blind should be given the same books to read that those with sight receive, or that the hearing impaired should be denied access to sign language on the grounds that such provision constitutes unequal, that is, unidentical treatment.

Jonathan Rawls (1971) accepts the notion of deficits in his fairness thesis when he argues for a sharing of benefits. He assumes that what exists is a meritocracy and that fairness requires that the gifted share with those less endowed than them, those with attributed deficits. Rawlsian notions of fairness are hardly in political ascendance, but political unpopularity is not the basis of our concern. We do not think an equal result is fair because it assumes what has not been proven. It assumes that the deficits, rather than unequal treatment, explain social and economic hierarchies.

We believe social hierarchy can be explained by unequal encouragement.

Some of these unequal encouragements — inequality in participating in the determination of important knowledge, unequal exercise of rights, unequal opportunities to participate in societal functions, and unequal encouragement to succeed in school and other life activities — we have already discussed. Some of the inequalities are obvious and have been documented. There is an enormous discrepancy in the amount of money spent on educating the affluent who are very rarely perceived to have deficits, than there is on the poor, who are alleged to have a near monopoly on deficits (Kozol, 1991).

Equalizing money spent on schools is not synonymous with equalizing encouragement. The most important inequalities take place in classrooms where ostensibly the same amount of money is spent on each student. It is only when gratifications in the classroom are equalized, is it likely that deficits will disappear.

In the intense effort to define and celebrate differences, similarity in humans has been largely overlooked. Yet, in many ways all human beings strive for similar fulfillments. These fulfillments have not been made equally available. In the following paragraphs we briefly discuss nine universal desires, indicate how they have been unequally made available, and conclude with some indications of what happens when effort is made to encourage students, equally, in these areas.

1. *Security*. No one disputes the importance of security to the individual and to the society. It is the primary justification for government spending — three hundred billion dollars for national security, about the same for social security. Security in the work world is the guarantee of income today and at times when one is unable to work. Security is also safety and non-threatening relationships on the job. Because of the importance of income security, work is a key element in a life action plan. Security is also important in school. In school, security, in addition to providing a safe environment, means willingness to take risks.

Equal encouragement is equally encouraging all students to take risks, to make mistakes and learn from them. Very early in school life, those who have attributed deficits learn that they should not take risks, that the costs far outweigh the benefits. Not risking to the non-achiever is not making a mistake. And yet, it is only from mistakes that students grow. Willingness to risk distinguishes the achiever from the non-achiever. We believe that willingness to risk is less a personality attribute than it is part of the social environment. Teachers, very early in a school career, communicate very clearly who will be punished for risking and who will be given encouragement to risk. A democratic classroom encourages *all* students equally to take chances. When differences in risk-taking become apparent, rather than jumping to the conclusions that risking is a quality of the person, one needs to look to classroom practices, differential encouragements and discouragements in the operation of the classroom that are producing the differences in behavior. Students who have been fearful and insecure can blossom when encouraged to take risks (Hollins, 1991; Meier, 1995).

2. *Comfort (relief from unnecessary pain)*. Comfort has been vulgarized in recent years. People go to absurd lengths to immerse themselves in comfort. They pump themselves full of psychoactive agents and close their minds to unpleasantness.

They become encapsulated and inert, indifferent to the plight of others. Such pursuit is doomed to fail. What is possible is *relief from unnecessary pain.* Viktor Frankl, in analyzing his own experience as an inmate in a Nazi concentration camp argues that human suffering is essential in human nature, but only that suffering that is absolutely necessary. He claims that much unhappiness is the result of being unable to accept necessary unhappiness and he further postulates that the infatuation with happiness robs people of the gratification that comes with 'accepting the challenge to suffer bravely' (Frankl, 1962: 116).

In school, unnecessary pain takes the form of humiliation, boredom and loneliness. Virtually no student is spared from some unnecessary pain, but for the deficit pupils, humiliation, boredom and loneliness typify their school days. They are assigned to less stimulating classes (Oakes, 1985, 1992) and are routinely embarrassed publicly and isolated. The inflicted pain from deficit labels, such as, at-risk, explains the internalization of hopelessness, believing one is bad or dumb, far more parsimoniously than attributed deficits (see, for example, Ronda and Valencia, 1994).

Teachers and administrators are not the only ones who inflict unnecessary pain. Students do it to each other. Bullying, harassment, and name-calling are all part of the existing school culture. However, students inflicting pain on students does not absolve the teacher from altering that situation. Drawing attention to the process, generating projects that address the situation, actively engaging in team building, individual counseling, continuously consulting with students and keeping a record of put-downs, etc., all help develop a new culture. Students do abuse students; if that condition is to change, it must begin with teachers serving as models. A democratic classroom strives to eliminate unnecessary pain and strives to ensure that necessary pain is distributed equally.

3. *Competence.* Robert White (1959) constructed a theory of personality based on the human need to be competent. It is a theory that passes the test of common sense — people do those things that they do well and try to avoid activities where they feel incompetent. A society dominated by a handful of experts is one which has its dismal side, a huge number of incompetents. In every arena of life we are quick to attach the label 'incompetent' on great numbers of people and then we are surprised when they lose interest in their assigned responsibilities. Denying people the opportunity to be competent, for example, at work, politics, school and in health does not end the matter. If people are unable to be competent in actions approved by legitimate authority, then they will find places and activities where their competence is recognized. Burglars brag of their ability to pick locks, drug dealers of their ability to elude police and school clowns on their talent to irritate teachers.

Competence in school is measured by evaluated performance — that is, grades. Students very quickly learn who are considered competent and who are dismissed as incompetents (and in between there are the semi-competents). It is through this system of grading that a meritocracy is supposedly established. But grades are far less a measure of competence, than a means to encourage and discourage. Students rapidly learn who are encouraged to be competent and who are discouraged from competence. They know that grades are as much a willingness to be submissive as they are a measure of academic accomplishment. The connection between the 'hidden' or 'unofficial' curriculum (e.g., conformity behavior) and the 'official' curriculum (e.g., reading; mathematics) has been aptly described (see, e.g., Jackson, 1968).

Competence will be universally attained when all students are encouraged equally to be competent, when competence is equally recognized, and when students who are having difficulty are encouraged to build on the competencies they have, rather than be discouraged by the emphasis on failure. In school, competence is attached to relevance. It is difficult to encourage students to be competent in matters that they believe are insignificant. Students will strive to be competent when the knowledge and skills they are developing is organized for important problem solving. Students with alleged deficits when encouraged to become competent, respond accordingly (Edmonds, 1984; Hollins, 1991; Meier, 1995).

4. *Belonging.* Ours is a society that systematically includes and excludes. Wealth, race, and gender have been long-standing qualifying conditions for employment. Every arena of life has been subjugated to some form of segregation. The system that existed in the past provided opportunity for belonging not only for those who benefited from the exclusionary practices, but even for those who were oppressed. The exclusion made it possible for a banding together in intimate and supporting bodies during times of conflict (see, for example, Menchaca, 1989, for an analysis of how Mexican Americans mobilized a united front against Anglo dominance in a California town). In the past, family, neighborhood, union, church and fraternal order provided psychological centering and opportunity for psychological investment. People were able to play gratifying roles. They had identities. They knew they were not alone. Much of that is lost. The existential vacuum noticed by so many is partially the result of technological takeover of community. Passive reception has replaced active participation. So much of life is centrifugal — and impersonal. It has become a society of people sitting passively before televisions and belonging is measured by the channel they are watching.

Belonging is a vital human need. Humans hunger for companionship. They are terrified in isolation. If denied belonging in formal institutions, they will struggle frantically to fabricate informal systems, such as gangs, cliques, etc. These efforts can be destructive. They can maintain illegal ventures. They can serve to alienate people from work, politics and culture. Failure to find a supportive group, in extreme instances, can mean mental breakdown and suicide.

In school, belonging is active participation. Schools have always included and excluded. Exclusion from welcomed membership in school does not terminate student desire for belonging. Students with 'deficits' will search for belonging outside of school-sanctioned activities. They will join cliques, gangs, and clubs for identity, and they will demonstrate their affiliation by dress, music, language, designation of turf, identifying behavior, shared values, and other indicators of a common culture (Willis, 1990). These groups become references for acceptable and unacceptable behavior, and in time, rob established authority of its legitimacy. In contrast, in a democratic classroom, all students are made equally welcome and effort is made to make the classroom an inclusive community.

5. *Meaning.* 'Meaning' is insufficiently understood in our society. Despite the gobbledygook of an information society, meaning is rarely considered in school or in life. Viktor Frankl insists that the human need to understand what is happening to himself/herself is vital to mental health (*Man's Search for Meaning*, 1962). I agree with Frankl on the importance of meaning; I disagree with him on how that meaning is attained. Frankl, as I, rejects self-actualization and insists that meaning is external to the person. He nonetheless takes the position that meaning is detected and rejects teaching and preaching and logical reasoning (p. 99) as factors involved in the development of meaning. I believe that meaning can be derived from teaching and logical reasoning, and I accept (with Frankl) the existence of a widespread existential vacuum leading to great numbers of people lamenting the lack of meaning in their lives. It is my contention that meaninglessness is the result of a denial of vital information, a technology racing faster than people can understand it and a confusion of messages.

Meaning in school is the demystification of process and goals. Reading and mathematics have suffered because they have been made unnecessarily mysterious. Educators speak in weird languages. They pride themselves on a vocabulary that neither parents nor students can understand. Often the teacher and the administrator in a school site cannot explain because they themselves do not understand. They use curriculum developed by high-powered research teams in the employ of publishing houses and are not privy to either the theory used or the logic of the lessons. Teachers are losing control over evaluation of student competence as testing has become a business captured by remote corporations, adding yet another foreign dimension to the process. As a result, students are so confused that they are no longer able to ascertain for themselves what they know. They have lost ownership of their intelligence and are thus unable to evaluate if they can or cannot read, multiply, or analyze a historical situation. Who are they to argue with the Educational Testing Service? For there to be meaning in schooling there must be demystification, discussion and negotiation. True evaluation is sharing and is not the imposition of an arbitrary outside authority that uses rules and criteria not mutually accepted and if seriously analyzed, would be found acceptable by the majority of those concerned.

Meaning in culture is active participation. As with so much of modern life, culture, too, is dominated by 'experts', often self-anointed. Furthermore, these experts are gatekeepers of culture. They determine what books will be published, whose art will be subsidized, and who makes it as a guest to the Jay Leno or the David Letterman shows. Culture will not become meaningful until it is decentralized and freed from the grip of corporate or governmental bureaucratic control.

Meaning in leisure activities are guides, coaches and informed support. It is those services that make it possible for everyone to enjoy the wilderness, catch fish in a mountain stream, and enjoy an afternoon in a downtown park while allowing others also to do the same. Those with 'deficits' tend to be denied both meanings of meaning — purpose of the lesson and what is to be done. A democratic class explains and demystifies equally to all students.

6. *Usefulness.* A human is unfulfilled if he or she is a mere recipient. Uselessness is a dreaded condition. Enforced uselessness is cruel punishment. The unemployed find uselessness as excruciating as the loss of income. In a good society, usefulness is not differentially made available by race, gender or class. Usefulness is choice in providing a service and choice in accepting it. Usefulness is meaningful problem-solving in school, rather than mindless drill and alleged preparation for a dubious and murky future without participating in useful activities in the present.

For those saddled with alleged deficits, school offers little in the way of usefulness. There is no place where they feel less useful. They rarely are allowed to be useful to others in school — gratifications the achieving students get when they are tutors, or when they represent the school, for example, in an academic decathlon. The student with deficits is denied the gratification of seeing future utility in school. He or she is not encouraged to perceive the school as a way station to some future good place. In a democratic classroom, all students are given equal opportunities to be useful.

7. *Hope.* A few decades ago, at least in the United States, it would have been unnecessary to include hope as a human need. It sprang eternal; it was the essence of our national character and was manifest everywhere. We largely believed with Franklin Roosevelt that 'the only thing we had to fear was fear itself'. Hopelessness comes at us from many sources.

Pessimism is reflected in opinion polls and loss of confidence in one's ability to influence one's future. Pessimism is reflected in youths' fears about their future. Pessimism is reflected in the ultimate expression of hopelessness — statistics on suicide. The suicide rate for the general population is climbing and the suicide rate of young people is growing faster than the rate for the general population.

Hope in a good society is more than rhetoric. Hope is more than quick fixes and magic shows. Hope is a realistic life plan for the future. Students who have been designated with deficits have little to be hopeful about. In a democratic classroom all students are provided reasons to be hopeful. There is a continuous dialogue. Problems are organized with possible solutions in mind. Students are encouraged to be problem solvers, rather than to be overwhelmed by the problems they have. Labeling a student as deficient is saddling that student with an unnecessary and insoluble problem. If a teacher cannot provide a plausible reason for a student to be hopeful, the very least that teacher can do is not become an additional problem for the student to solve.

8. *Excitement.* Excitement is a legitimate hunger. We believe it is an important determinant of crime and other mischief making. Presently constructed, society not only limits excitement but makes it more and more spurious. Excitement is found, such that it is, in the behaviors of others — for example, watching professionals play football. That excitement is insufficiently gratifying. Drug abuse, gang life and other illicit doings maintain much of their allure because in these activities — and

very rarely elsewhere — excitement is to be found. We believe that excitement can be found in legal endeavors.

Classrooms can be exciting if students are encouraged to participate in activities where they generate knowledge and make important discoveries. The opportunity for such excitement needs to be extended to those now denied — those with 'deficits.'

9. *Creativity.* Humans are, by nature, a creative species. Each generation creates a new world. School officials arbitrarily establish limits on creativity, insisting that only a privileged few have the capacity to be creative. Special programs are created for the creative, for example, Gifted and Talented Education [GATE] programs provide incentives and resources for a few students. Students enjoy these programs and they provide a sharp distinction from the tedium that those with alleged deficits are forced to endure.

Creativity is, in a certain sense, undefinable. There are no acceptable criteria for creativity and often it goes unrecognized. Creativity should not be defined solely by school recognized accomplishment, or by an even more capricious criterion, assessed capacity to be creative. Both standards for creativity are powerfully correlated with race, ethnicity and parental economic condition. Creativity is not parceled out by class, race, gender or ethnicity. It is not a province of the gifted. Creativity exists for all, or it is likely to be extinguished in everyone. The way that schools are currently constructed creativity is constricted for all students, and by so doing, the adult authority decides who can be creative and how that creativity is to be expressed. Those who are characterized as limited by deficits are not permitted outlets for creativity, or the perceptions of them are so overpowering, their creativity goes unrecognized.

Those with 'deficits' are not uncreative. Unfortunately, when the creativity of those with labeled deficits are not allowed in school sanctioned activities, the denied often find creative fulfillment in proscribed activities. They are creative in ways in which they torment teachers, do graffiti, and get involved in complex illegal activities. In a democratic class, all students are encouraged to be constructively creative and to use creativity in community building, that is, to make the class a far more interesting, exciting and creative place than is currently the case; and, far more interesting, exciting and creative than any of the proposed highly advertised reforms.

Feasibility and Desirability of Democratic Education

There is powerful evidence that democratic education is possible, and that when tried, deficits largely disappear. It is not at all clear that such an approach would be considered universally desirable. A democratic education means the abandonment of an education based on competitive edge. The gist of this chapter is that the postulation of deficits serves as a conscious or unconscious justification for an unfair system that is based on unequal encouragement. What is not at all clear is whether beneficiaries of the unequal encouragement are willing to surrender that advantage for a more equitable system. What would they gain from opening up the system? The building of a constituency for democracy requires more than demonstrating the inequity of the current approach. It would require a willingness to examine the logical consequences of a society with deeper and deeper racial and class schisms, with increased violence, and with more and more of the society's energy invested in keeping those down who have been denied equal opportunity. We believe a persuasive case can be made for an equal encouragement society, but that is beyond the scope of this chapter. We limit our discussion here to the feasibility of democratic education as an alternative to deficit thinking.

Deborah Meier has produced remarkable results with her Central Park South Secondary School (Meier, 1995). Note the following accomplishments:

> The data on the Central Park East [CPE] elementary and secondary schools is not in dispute. The CPE population is roughly equivalent to a cross sampling of New York City. The majority of students are African-American and Latino, most are low-income or poor, and they experience a full range of academic strengths and handicaps.
>
> Of the first seven graduating classes of CPE elementary school (1977–1984), 85 per cent received regular diplomas and another 11 per cent got GEDs. This compares to roughly 50 per cent citywide. Furthermore, two thirds of those who graduated from high school prior to the opening of our own secondary school had gone on to college. And the statistics held across race and class lines. In 1991, the Central Park East Secondary School [CPESS] topped this impressive showing. While some students moved and a few transferred, fewer than 5 per cent of those who started with us in ninth grade dropped out along the way. And not only did the rest graduate with regular diplomas, but 90 per cent went directly on to college and stayed there. These figures for 1991 have held up for each subsequent graduating class. And the graduates of 1994 outstripped their predecessors in quality of work achieved and colleges attended. We've gotten better and so have they. (Meier, 1995: 16)

What made CPESS special? Why did the those with 'deficits' succeed there, when they fail so dismally nearly everywhere else? The reasons for CPESS are not crystal clear. Many factors came together to make the school successful. Democracy is an important factor in CPESS's success. CPESS consciously organized itself to be a democratic school. The CPESS definition of democracy is softer than ours, but it is nonetheless a very important aspect of the school. Democracy to CPESS meant meaningful participation of teachers, parents and to some extent students, in decisions that affected the student's life.

> We also saw schools as examples of the possibilities of democratic community, and what we meant by this was continuously under debate and review. It wasn't simply a question of governance structures, and certainly

not a matter of extending the vote to four-year-olds. Although classroom life could certainly include more participation by children in decisions than traditional schools allowed, we saw it as even more critical that the school life of adults be democratic. It seemed unlikely that we could foster values of community in our classrooms unless the adults in the school had significant rights over their own workplace. For us, democracy implied that people should have a voice not only in their own individual work, but in the work of others as well. Finally, we saw collaboration and mutual respect among staff, parents, students and the larger community as a part of what we meant by calling our experiment democratic. (Meier, 1995: 22)

In CPESS, democracy also meant preparing students for democratic citizenship. It is the understanding of democracy that leads Meier to be a strong believer in choice in *public schools* and an opponent of privatization. But the strongest components of CPESS, and what distinguishes it, is the encouragement given all students to succeed. CPESS worked because Meier and her staff expected it to work, and the expectation of success was clearly communicated to all students. Expectation is not enough. But expectation *coupled* with specific encouragements and accompanied by developing competence will go a long way to overcome the impediments of a deficit label.

Competence is an important element in CPESS, and CPESS probably is the exemplar of authentic assessment (see Wiggins, 1989).

When they enter the last phase — our Senior Institute — students take on the task of completing fourteen portfolios full of work, including seven major presentations in such areas as math, science, literature, history, the arts, community service and apprenticeship, and autobiography. These 'presentations,' made to a graduation committee consisting of at least two faculty members, an adult of the student's choice, and another student, are carried out with enormous seriousness and zeal. They are the primary record — transcript — of a student's success at CPESS, and the basis for receiving the diploma. (Meier, 1995: 6)

CPESS was also special in its departure from traditional approaches to curriculum. Mastering topics was important in CPESS, but more important as educational goals were 'habits of mind', which required students to learn how to answer the following questions:

'How do we know what we know?'; the question of viewpoint in all its multiplicity, or 'Who's speaking?'; the search for connections and patterns, or 'What causes what?'; supposition, or 'How might things have been different?'; and finally, why any of it matters, or 'Who cares?'. (Meier, 1995: 50)

A somewhat different approach with a quite different history and historical experience, took place in the Upward Bound program at the University of Oregon in the late 1960s. Upward Bound was a 'poverty' program instituted in the 1960s for low-income high school students. In Upward Bound, low-income students were brought to a university or college campus for two summers for enriched educational experiences. Some of those students went on to enroll in institutions of higher education. The percentages varied by different programs. A great many colleges and universities had Upward Bound programs, and it is one of the 1960s' War on Poverty programs that has survived the onslaught on social programs.

The University of Oregon program was unique in many ways. Unlike any other Upward Bound programs, *all* participants were guaranteed admission to the University of Oregon. The logic for this was to test whether students had deficits or whether the system had failed to encourage them. It is well known that a large number of admitted students to public universities fail to graduate; this is well established. These students are false positives. The criteria for admission was met, but the criteria was not foolproof. It had errors. It logically follows that an inexact admission criteria also had a large number of false negatives, inadmissible students, who if they had been admitted would have succeeded. The number or percent of false negatives is not known since there are so few of them, and those that exist came to higher education under special circumstances, i.e., affirmative action. One goal of the Upward Bound program was to determine whether false positives were significant enough to warrant a reconsideration of admission policies.

The Oregon Upward Bound program was unique in that it grew out of a series of successful experiments that had challenged deficit thinking (Grant, 1967; Pearl, 1965; Riessman and Hollowitz, 1965). The Oregon Upward Bound was distinctive in yet another way: It brought to the campus those students *least likely* to succeed, that is, those with the most severe 'deficits.' The Upward Bound program administrators recruited from Oregon's six most difficult institutions for delinquents. The same request was made of a job corps program administered by the University of Oregon. The students assembled for the experiment were extraordinarily diverse — African American, Chicano, Native American, and poor white in near equal proportions — at a time when race relations in the United States were extremely volatile. The achievements of the Upward Bound students rivaled the achievements of the admissible students. More than half graduated in four years. Many went on to distinguished careers. An incorrigible delinquent became a medical doctor (her achievements were portrayed in a CBS made for television movie, *Love Mary*, 1987); a teen-age prostitute went on to become an influential administrator and lawyer; a street-wise delinquent earned a PhD and is now on the faculty of a state university; and dozens of others found that alleged deficits did not prevent them from attaining postgraduate degrees and professional status. One of those designated a troublemaker at the job corps was able to become an administrator in a private college in Southern California. That troublemaker wrote a book about the Oregon Upward Bound. He described the experiences and chronicled the successes of many of the program participants (Hollins, 1991). The Upward Bound stressed equal encouragement with specific emphasis on feelings of belongingness, competence and usefulness. Charles Hollins identified the opportunity for students to be significant participants in the administration of the program and the application of the New Career approach as vital factors in its success (Hollins, 1991).

New Careers (Pearl and Riessman, 1965) was an attempt to democratize the professions. In a credential society, such that ours has become, many years of formal education are required before one can enter a profession. The educational requirement culls out the unqualified on arbitrary criteria. There is no established correlation between success in school and success in a profession. Raising education requirements are advertised as raising standards. These standards may in reality be impediments to progress. With New Careers, a career ladder was established that led from an entering position that had no education, skill or experience requirements through a series of negotiable steps of which the upper rung was the terminal professional status.

In the book *New Careers for the Poor* (Pearl and Riessman, 1965) a four-step ladder was proposed. The initial rung (an aide) had no prerequisites; the next rung up (an assistant) called for the equivalent of 2 years of higher education; the third rung (an associate) called for the equivalent of 4 years of higher education; the top of the ladder was the existing professional with the existing prerequisites. Pearl and Riessman proposed that the credits for advancement be earned from a combination of credits earned for performance on the job, from special courses delivered to the work site, and from the existing courses offered at the college or university.

The Oregon Upward Bound created a career ladder within its own administrative structure. Students in the program were employed as aides and promoted up the administrative ladder when vacancies occurred. Three of the original students became directors of the program; one of the three was Charles Hollins, the author of *It Was Fun from the Beginning* (1991) (for more information on how the career ladder functioned in Upward Bound, see Hollins, 1991).

Many New Career programs were established in the late 1960s. Almost all of the participants in New Careers were people with 'deficits'. These 'New Careerists' when given an opportunity to demonstrate competence were able to overcome alleged deficits (Gartner, 1969). The largest of the New Career programs was the Career Opportunity Program (COP) for teachers that existed in 132 sites with 18,000 participants in 3000 schools enrolled in 272 colleges and universities. The participants were 88 per cent female, 100 per cent poor, and more than two-thirds minority (54 per cent African American; 14 per cent Hispanic; 4 per cent Native American) (Carter, 1977). In the short history of the COP (it was eliminated with the election of Richard Nixon in 1972), much was accomplished. Many under-represented minorities became professional teachers. 'Of the 142 degree-earning COP participants in the Chicago project, 118 became teachers in "target area" schools, that is, in schools populated by children of low-income, minority (black and Hispanic) background' (Carter, 1977: 204).

Students in the COP project did extremely well in higher education. Typical of the performances is that reported in the evaluation of four COP projects in Pennsylvania. Carter notes:

> people who normally would have been rejected in a standard (college) admissions review . . . less than four per cent of all COP participants were dropped from the program for academic problems . . . in Philadelphia 85

per cent had a C average or better and 46 per cent had an average of B or higher . . . (in Philadelphia 27 students had graduated with grade point average 3.5 or higher and been named Presidential Scholars). (Carter, 1977: 188)

The impact of a New Career program can be seen after two decades. The University of Minnesota, in conjunction with many social agencies, had a New Career program, which included the COP; 20 years after its inception, efforts were made to evaluate its success. Like other such efforts, the program participants had been poor, predominantly black, single parents, women on welfare. Virtually none had completed high school. Twenty years later, of the 207 persons who had been in the program, at least one had earned a doctorate, dozens had master degrees and about half on whom information was found had graduated from the university. New Careerists reported that the program had changed their lives from seemingly hopeless poverty to much more comfortable and stable existences (Amram, Flax, Hamermesh, and Marty, 1988). Moreover, New Careerists were on every measurable component at least as competent as the traditionally prepared teacher (Carter, 1977). There is reawakened interest in the New Career strategy. The State of California has 15 pilot projects in which paraprofessionals are to become teachers through the negotiation of a career ladder.

There are other dramatic examples of programs, and even more of individual teachers, that provide powerful evidence that deficits are more a function of lack of equal encouragement than attributes of the individual. There are many, many examples of individuals who have overcome the handicap of a deficit label. However, the prevalence of deficit thinking, unfortunately, has limited both the number of experiments and has tended to minimize the accomplishments of those who have overcome the handicap of labeled deficits.

Deficit thinking dominates current educational policy and practice. Unfortunately, when opposed, it is replaced with another form of deficit thinking. A comprehensive democratic approach is presented in this chapter as the logical alternative to deficit thinking. A democratic education requires changes in curriculum, participation, rights and understandings of equality. When a comprehensive democratic education is attempted, there is evidence that alleged deficits disappear. The fundamental issue is not whether deficits can be overcome with equal encouragement, but whether, when we pledge allegiance to 'freedom and justice for all', we mean it.

References

AMRAM, F., FLAX, S., HAMERMESH, M. and MARTY, G. (1988) *New Careers: The Dream that Worked*, Minneapolis, MN: University of Minnesota.

APPLE, M.W. and BEANE, J.A. (Eds) (1995) *Democratic Schools*, Alexandria, VA: ASCD.

BANKS, J.A. (1989) 'Integrating the curriculum with ethnic content: Approaches and guidelines', in BANKS, J.A. and MCGEE BANKS, C.A. (Eds) *Multicultural Education: Issues and Perspectives*, Boston, MA: Allyn and Bacon, pp. 189–207.

BARBER, B. (1984) *Strong Democracy: Participatory Politics for a New Age*, Berkeley, CA: University of California Press.

BARBER, B. (1992) *An Aristocracy of Everyone*, New York: Oxford University Press.

BLOOM, A. (1987) *The Closing of the American Mind: How Higher Education has Failed Democracy and Impoverished the Souls of Today's Students*, New York: Simon & Schuster.

BLOOM, H. (1994) *The Western Canon: The Books and the School of the Ages*, New York: Harcourt Brace.

CARTER, W.T. (1977) 'The Career Opportunities Program: A summing up', in GARTNER, A., RIESSMAN, F. and CARTER-JACKSON, V. (Eds) *Paraprofessionals Today*, New York: Human Services Press, pp. 183–221.

COUNTS, G.S. (1932) *Dare the School Build a New Social Order?*, New York: John Day.

DE TOCQUEVILLE, A. (1850) *Democracy in America* (translated by LAWRENCE, G. edited by MAYER, J.P. based on de Tocqueville's 13th edition), New York: Harper and Row.

DEWEY, J. (1916) *Democracy and Education*, New York: Macmillan.

DEWEY, J. (1938a) *Experience and Education*, New York: Macmillan.

DEWEY, J. (1938b) *Art and Education*, Merion, PA: The Barnes Foundation Press.

EDMONDS, R. (1984) 'School effects and teacher effects', *Social Policy*, **15**, pp. 37–40.

FRANKL, V. (1962) *Man's Search for Meaning*, New York: Simon & Schuster.

GAGNON, P. (Ed) (1989) *Historical Literacy: The Case for History in American Education*, The Bradley Commission for History in American Education, Boston, MA: Houghton-Mifflin.

GARTNER, A. (1969) *Do Paraprofessionals Improve Human Services?: A First Critical Appraisal of the Data*, New York: New Careers Development Center.

GLADWELL, M. (1995) 'Fundamental ignorance about the numbers', *Washington Post National Weekly Edition*, October 16–22, p. 7.

GRANT, J.D. (1967) *New Careers Development Project, Final Report*, National Institute of Mental Health project OM-01616.

GUTHRIE, R.V. (1976) *Even the Rat was White: A Historical View of Psychology*, New York: Harper and Row.

HOLLINS, C.E. (1991) *It was Fun from the Beginning*, New York: Carlton Press.

JACKSON, P. (1968) *Life in Classrooms*, New York: Holt, Rinehart and Winston.

KIRK, R. (1986) *The Conservative Mind* (7th ed.) Chicago, IL: Regency Books.

KOZOL, J. (1991) *Savage inequalities: Children in America's Schools*, New York: Crown.

LAPHAM, L.H. (1996) 'Time lines', *Harpers Magazine*, January, pp. 7–9.

LENIN, V.I. (1919) *State and Revolution*, London: George Allen & Unwin, Ltd. (included in *The Essential Left: Marx * Engels * Lenin, The Essential Left* (1961) New York: Barnes & Noble, pp. 147–255.)

LIND, M. (1995) *The Next American Nation: The New Nationalism and the Fourth American Revolution*, New York: Free Press.

MARX, K. (1875) *Critique of the Gotha Program*, (Reprinted in SAUL K. PADOVER (Ed and Trans.), *Karl Marx, on Revolution* (1971) New York: McGraw-Hill, pp. 488–506.

MEIER, D. (1995) *The Power of their Ideas*, Boston, MA: Beacon Press.

MENCHACA, M. (1989) 'Chicano–Mexican cultural assimilation and Anglo–Saxon cultural dominance', *Hispanic Journal of Behavioral Sciences*, **11**, pp. 203–31.

MORIN, R. (1995) 'Across the racial divide', *Washington Post Weekly Edition*, October 16–22, pp. 6–10.

OAKES, J. (1985) *Keeping Track: How Schools Structure Inequality*, New Haven, CT: Yale University Press.

OAKES, J. (1992) *Educational Matchmaking: Academic and Vocational Tracking in Comprehensive High Schools*, Santa Monica, CA: Rand Corporation.

Olmstead v. United States (1928) US 437.

PADOVER, S.K. (1939) *Thomas Jefferson on Democracy*, New York: D. Appleton-Century.

PATEMAN, C. (1970) *Participation and Democratic Theory*, Cambridge, MA: Cambridge University Press.

PATEMAN, C. (1989) *The Disorder of Women: Democracy, Feminism and Political Theory*, Cambridge, England: Polity Press in association with Basil Blackwell.

PEARL, A. (1990) 'The requirements of a democratic education', in SLEE, R. (Ed) *Discipline and Schools*, Melbourne, Australia: Macmillian of Australia, pp. 225–43.

PEARL, A. (1965) 'Youth in low income settings', in SHERIF, M. and SHERIF, C. (Eds) *Problems of Youth*, Chicago, IL: Aldine Publishing, Co, pp. 89–109.

PEARL, A. and RIESSMAN, F. (1965) *New Careers for the Poor*, New York: Macmillan.

PYLE, W.H. (1915) 'The mind of the negro child', *School and Society*, **1**, pp. 357–60.

RAVITCH, D. (1989) 'The plight of history in American schools', in GAGNON, P. (Ed) *Historical Literacy: The Case for History in American Education, The Bradley Commission on History in the Schools*, Boston: Houghton Mifflin, pp. 51–68.

RAWLS, J. (1971) *A Theory of Justice*, Cambridge, MA: Harvard University Press.

RIESSMAN, F. and HOLLOWITZ, E. (1965) *Neighborhood Service Centers Program: A Report to the US Office of Economic Opportunity on the South Bronx Neighborhood Service Center*.

RIST, R.C. (1970) 'Student social class and teacher expectations: The self-fulfilling prophecy in ghetto education', *Harvard Educational Review*, **40**, pp. 411–51.

RONDA, M.A. and VALENCIA, R.R. (1994) ' "At-risk" Chicano students: The institutional and communicative life of a category', *Hispanic Journal of Behavioral Sciences*, **16**, pp. 363–95.

SMILEY, J. (1996) 'Say it ain't so, Huck: Second thoughts on Mark Twain's "masterpiece" ', *Harpers Magazine*, pp. 61–7.

Tinker v. Des Moines Independent Schools District (1969) 393 US 503.

WALLECHINSKY, D. and WALLACE, I. (1978) *The People's Almanac*, New York: Bantam Books.

WHITE, R. (1959) 'Motivation reconsidered: The concept of competence', *Psychological Review*, **66**, pp. 279–333.

WIGGINS, G. (1989) 'A true test: Toward more authentic and equitable assessment', *Phi Delta Kappan*, **70**, pp. 703–13.

WILLIS, P. with JONES, S., CANAAN, J. and HURD, G. (1990) *Common Culture: Symbolic Work at Play in the Everyday Cultures of the Young*, Buckingham, England: Open University Press.

WOOD, G. (1992) *Schools that Work: America's Most Innovative Public Education Programs*, New York: Dutton.

Chapter 8

Epilogue: The Future of Deficit Thinking in Educational Thought and Practice

Richard R. Valencia and Arthur Pearl

This book has attempted to present some understanding of the evolution of deficit thinking in educational thought and practice, and by necessity, some sense of the protean nature of the wider American social thought on deficit thinking, such as attitudes towards and beliefs about the behavior of the poor. The contributors have provided, in a collective manner, an analysis of deficit thinking spanning a time frame from the early 1600s to the present, the mid-1990s. To be sure, this has been no easy task. Much remains to be examined that was not detected or was not covered because of space and time limitations. We trust that scholars who have interest in the intersection of deficit thinking and education will find *The Evolution of Deficit Thinking: Educational Thought and Practice* a foundation on which to pursue further research on the topic.

In that 'evolution' denotes a process of change over time, an unfolding, what does the future hold in store for deficit thinking, particularly in the area of education? As America approaches and then enters the twenty-first century — mere years ahead — how will deficit thinking manifest itself? Will the genetic pathology model and neohereditarianism continue to gain currency? Will the poor and the 'underclass' continue to be the scapegoats for the 'cognitive elite'? Will Herrnstein and Murray's (1994) apocalyptic vision of a 'custodial state' be realized? Given the long-standing critiques of deficit thinking, is a denouement of this discourse around the corner? And, also important in our eyes, is the central query: What dangers does deficit thinking hold for democracy in America, especially in the mission of providing equal educational opportunity (for example, access and equity) and democratic education (for example, equal participation and encouragement; useful knowledge) for poor, working-class, and racial/ethnic minority students?

It is beyond the scope in this final chapter to address each of these questions. We shall, however, use them collectively as the substantive core to share with the reader our thoughts on the future of deficit thinking. By design, we need to be prognosticatory — that is, providing some sense of future developments by keeping in mind historical and contemporary signs and symptoms. Our analysis will cover four aspects: 1) current sociodemographic realities and trends; 2) the demise of school desegregation; 3) the economy, politics, and education; 4) the growing anti-deficit thinking discourse.

242

Current Sociodemographic Realities and Trends

Based on 1990 census data (and related reports), a body of recent sociodemographic analyses of America's population have identified a number of significant transformations occurring (see Bouvier, 1991; Pallas, Natriello and McDill, 1989; Valencia and Chapa, 1993). Two trends that are especially germane to our discussion involve: the dramatic growth of racial/ethnic minority populations, and the increase in the number of poor adults, youth, and children — particularly among people of color.

Regarding the general population, the growth rate in the US from 1980 to 1990 was 9.8 per cent (226.6 to 248.7 million people; Macías, 1993). Disaggregated by race/ethnicity, however, the national growth reveals dramatic group comparisons. For this last decade, the white general population increased only 4.4 per cent, while all racial/ethnic minority populations outstripped the white growth — in some cases remarkably so. In descending order the growth rates were: Asian/Pacific Islanders (107.8 per cent), Latino (53.0 per cent), Amerindians (37.9 per cent), and blacks (13.2 per cent) (Macías).[1]

In 1990, the white general population comprised 75.6 per cent of the total US population. This majority status will gradually decline, however, over the next half century. By 2050 — a year in which the US population is expected to reach 392 million — it is projected that the nation's population will be nearly evenly divided between whites and racial/ethnic minority populations (Bovee, 1993).[2] Whites will lose their numerical majority status even earlier in some sections of the nation. In California, the state currently having the largest population, projections are that whites will dip under 50 per cent as early as the year 2000 (high scenario) or 2005 (low scenario).[3] Demographer Leon Bouvier, who calculated these projections, notes: 'California is on the verge of becoming a truly multi-racial society where no single group will predominate' (1991: 25). In Texas, the nation's second largest state in population, the white population is projected to lose its numerical majority status sometime between 2009 (high scenario) and 2026 (low scenario) (Eskenazi, 1994).

Young children and school-age populations projections are even more dramatic regarding racial/ethnic minority increases. Using a baseline year of 1982, it is projected that the national youth population (defined as newborns through 17 years of age) will increase from 63 million (in 1982) to 73 million in 2020 (Pallas *et al.*, 1989). Disaggregating this growth by race/ethnicity shows white growth will decline by 6 million, blacks and 'others' will increase by 2.6 million and 1.2 million respectively, and Hispanic youth will grow by a huge 12.7 million.[4] The growth of the combined racial/ethnic minority school-age population (kindergarten through grade 12 [K–12]) is so rapid that the white school-age population in California dropped under 50 per cent in 1988 (Watson, 1988) and in Texas it dipped under the majority mark in 1991 (The Tomás Rivera Center, 1992). The inescapable fact is that presently in California and Texas, *no single racial/ethnic group constitutes a numerical majority* in the total K–12 school population.

The 1990 census data are also revealing in the identification of family income differences across racial/ethnic groups. The annual mean income of white families with young children was $29,400, considerably higher than the $15,800 and $15,400 reported for Hispanics and blacks, respectively (Chapa and Valencia, 1993). Furthermore, Hispanic and black families with young children have the greatest concentration in the lowest-income category (under $10,000). Blacks have the highest percentage (46 per cent), followed by Hispanics (38 per cent); only 12 per cent of white families are concentrated at the lowest level. The skewed distribution of minority families falling in the bottom end of the continuum is further illustrated by examining the lowest two income categories (under $10,000 and $10,000–$14,999). The *majority* of black (59 per cent) and Hispanic (57 per cent) families with young children — compared to 21 per cent of whites — were concentrated in the lowest two levels (Chapa and Valencia).

One of the most tragic outcomes of the 1980s, and reported in the 1990 Census data, was the increase of children living in poverty in the US.[5] Peréz and De La Rosa Salazar (1993), examining trend data between 1980 and 1990, make this observation about the persistence of poverty:

> In the early part of the decade [1980s], poverty rates increased slightly for both whites and blacks but rose sharply for Hispanics. During the mid-1980s, as the nation began the process of economic recovery from the recession, both whites and blacks began to experience decreases in poverty; for Hispanics, however, the poverty rate increased between 1983 and 1985. By 1987, after the rate for Hispanics had fallen slightly, it increased again — as it did for blacks — although the white poverty rate continued to decrease. (1993: 214)

A particularly unfortunate feature of poverty has been its impact on children (under 18 years of age). A sad outcome of the 1980s was, 'About a million Latino children were added to the ranks of the poor, plunging 36.2 per cent of them into poverty, compared with 43.7 per cent of blacks and 11.5 per cent of whites' (Puente, 1991: 1). In terms of percentage increases from 1979 to 1989, poor Latino children rose from 1.5 million in 1979 to 2.6 million in 1989 — a 73.3 per cent increase. Poor black children increased from 3.8 million to 4.4 million (15.8 per cent), and poor white children climbed from 6.2 million to 7.6 million (22.6 per cent; Puente). Latino child poverty has had disparate impact on the Latino subgroups. About 1 in 2 Puerto Rican children live in poverty, while nearly 2 in 5 Mexican-origin children are poor. For Cuban and Central/South American children, about 1 in 4 live in poverty (Chapa and Valencia, 1993). For the nation as a whole, the number of children living in poverty will increase sharply. In 1984, the number of children in poverty was 14.7 million. By 2020, the number is projected to be 20.1 million — a 37 per cent increase (Pallas *et al.*, 1989).

As far as the demographer's eye can see, the US — in both its general and public school-age populations — is becoming increasingly comprised of people of color. Low-income African Americans, Mexican Americans and Puerto Ricans, who are typically the targets of current deficit thinking, collectively are growing in much greater rates than their white peers (economically advantaged and disadvantaged). Adults and children of color continue to be overrepresented in the ranks of poverty. Projections are that such concentrations will increase. What is the future of deficit thinking in educational thought and practice in light of these current sociodemographic realities and trends? Based on the present state of affairs, we assert (with regret) that deficit thinking is likely to gain momentum and currency. This appears to be a reasonable assessment given that scholars and 'experts' of the 'at-risk' assuredly will see their general targeted population increase in size. After all, the social construction of at-risk, scholarly work on the topic, and subsequent educational policy are all tightly linked to the sociodemographic realities of the nation. Polakow captures this point well:

> The language of pathology, therefore, constructs another world of otherness — of definers and the defined; of programs and outcomes and assessments; of technologies and methodologies of risk; of cost-benefit analyses related to funding and maintenance; of risk factor remediation. In short, *the risk industry rests heavily on the poverty industry* [emphasis added], which Funiciello claims has become, 'a veritable fifth estate' (1993: xvii) in which countless middle-class people in the human service professions have built their careers as the direct beneficiaries of poverty. So too, as we trace the formation of deficit images actively perpetuated in the college classrooms of teacher training institutions, disseminated through educational institutes and research associations such as the American Educational Research Association, and funded by major grant organizations, we see that diagnosis and remediation are the essential ingredients of a proliferating deficit/pathology business, nuanced by color and class codes. (1995: 268)

The Demise of School Desegregation

America has turned its back to school desegregation. The court orders of the 42-year-old *Brown v. Board of Education* (1954) decision, which struck down the then 58-year-old *Plessy v. Ferguson* (1896) 'separate but equal' doctrine, are now shattered visions. Notwithstanding the scattered attempts in recent decades to desegregate our country's public schools, there has been only a smidgen of reduction of racial/ ethnic isolation. Why? Orfield, Monfort, and George (1987) contend that much of the failure in desegregation struggles is related to opposition at the national political level since the early 1970s:

> Three of the four Administrations since 1968 were openly hostile to urban desegregation efforts and the Carter Administration took few initiatives in the field. There have been no important policy initiatives supporting desegregation from any branch of government since 1971. (1987: 1)

Although the Clinton administration has demonstrated advocacy for school desegregation by either serving as a plaintiff, intervenor or filing a brief in 513 court orders, there is a rising tide of anti-desegregation politics in the 1990s (Applebome, 1995):

> More than two decades after the high tide of court-ordered school deseg-regation, critics of school busing around the country are mounting re-newed campaigns to end federal desegregation mandates and the busing plans that come with them.
>
> Encouraged by conservative electoral successes and Supreme Court decisions limiting the responsibilities of schools to foster desegregation, Denver, Minneapolis, Cleveland, Pittsburgh, Seattle, Wilmington, Del., and Indianapolis are among the cities revisiting the emotional debate over school busing. Norfolk, Va., and Oklahoma City already have eliminated mandatory busing for the purposes of desegregation. (Applebome, 1995: A2)

Meanwhile, in the midst of the current desegregation battle, millions of Latino and African American students enrolled in segregated schools suffer by being denied equal educational opportunity. Since the early 1970s, nationally the deseg-regation of African American students has remained essentially unchanged, but the isolation of Latinos has increased substantially.[6] In states that have had long-standing segregation, the isolation of racial/ethnic minority (and white) students continues to rise. In Texas, for example, in the 1993–94 school year 58.4 per cent of all school-age minority students attended schools in which 70 per cent or more of its pupils are minority; only 6.9 per cent of white students attended such schools. Furthermore, given the tight connection between minority status and low-income background, these segregated minority students in Texas are clustering in schools where many pupils are poor: More than four of ten students of low-income back-ground statewide were enrolled in schools in 1993–94 where more than 70 per cent of students are poor (Brooks and South, 1995).

How is the future of deficit thinking and the school segregation of African American and Latino students linked? First, there is strong evidence that the seg-regation of minority students is statistically associated with indices of school fail-ure, such as low reading achievement levels and increased dropout rates (see Donato, Menchaca and Valencia, 1991; Espinosa and Ochoa, 1986; Jaeger, 1987; Rumberger and Willms, 1992; Valencia, 1984). Such schools, then, are targeted sites for the deficit thinking research and policy interventions of the at-risk profession. Second, segregated schools have become symbols, images among some deficit thinkers that students attending these institutions *are not even worthy of attention* — a modern form of Moynihan's (1965) notion of 'benign neglect'. To write off, devalue and think undeserving of education for some students are the most vicious forms of deficit thinking that can be perpetrated against the poor and children of color. Such utter disregard for segregated schools and poor students is seen in Kozol's *Savage Inequalities* in his interview with the chief executive officer of Citicorp Savings of Illinois who commented: 'You don't dump a lot of money into guys who haven't done well with the money they got in the past . . . You don't rearrange the deck chairs on the *Titanic*' (1991: 80).

In sum, unless school desegregation and 'true integration' (i.e., cultural plu-ralism; high expectations of students; positive interethnic/interracial contact; equal status; avoidance of curricular resegregation; see Donato *et al.*, 1991) are vigor-ously approached and successfully implemented, deficit thinking is likely to in-crease. A further backing off — and the worst case scenario, a total dismantling of desegregation — will allow deficit thinking to fester in its manifestations of blaming the child and his/her parents for school failure (the at-risk discourse) and neglecting the needs of economically/racially isolated schools (the 'Titanic syndrome').

The Economy, Politics and Education

There are very clear impacts on education by both the existing economy and by the perception of the impending economy. Education is an integral part of the political process and is influenced by the prevailing political philosophy. The existing situ-ation in which we find ourselves reinforces deficit thinking and militates against changes that would provide more opportunities for those suffering from educational oppression. It is truly 'the best of times and the worst of times', although not as Charles Dickens meant it. It is the best of time for the wealthy. The economy is humming along, the Dow-Jones index has broken the 5000 barrier, and never has there been so much enthusiasm about the future among those who have never had it so good

> Here is the great paradox of the new American economy: The very forces that have restored the nation's industries to competitive health also are widening the gap between the economy's winners and losers, concentrat-ing incomes and economic power in fewer and fewer hands ...
>
> Average workers feel the pinch of winner-take-all in paychecks that are growing slowly, or not at all. Meanwhile, the richest 5 per cent of households saw their share of national income grow by about one-quarter over the past two decades, to 21.2 per cent last year from 16.8 per cent in 1978. (Pearlstein, 1995: 6)

In this winner-take-all mentality there is little concern for others than self. It is not a time for altruism. It is 'sink or swim' and every 'man' for himself. It is also a time of deep resentment. As income for most decline and prospects for the future look dim, the idea that others are given special privilege rankles. Affirmative action is one of those special privileges that stick in the craw of those whose futures look increasingly bleak. That very little affirmation action has occurred, that the thrust for it peaked in the early 1980s, and that the supposed beneficiaries of special privilege fall farther and farther behind, is immaterial. It is what people *believe* that matters, and that is what is being reflected in the political transformation that is occurring in the United States.

There is very good reason to feel pessimistic if you are not among the top fifth in income. The top fifth has done very well. Individual incomes in this level have soared in the past two decades, rising from a median of $80,000 a year in 1994 dollars to over $100,000 a year in 1994 dollars. The upper-fifth of the income population earns slightly less than half (49 per cent) of all income in the United States (Pearlstein, 1995: 6; derived from Economic Policy Institute based on Current Population Survey). It is the upper fifth that are being favored with proposed tax cuts. Helping them is a major piece of the Contract with America that became the thrust of the Republican party when they gained control over Congress in 1994.

The middle fifth did not fare as well in the 20 years between 1975 and 1995. Their incomes remained constant over that period, averaging about $35,000, peaking slightly in 1989–90, and declining since then. That segment of the population earns 15 per cent of the national income (Pearlstein, 1995: 6; derived from Economic Policy Institute based on Current Population Survey).

The bottom fifth, where the victims of deficit thinking are overwhelmingly to be found, had a median income of less than $10,000 and the income of this group has been slowly and steadily declining over the past 20 years. In 1995, the lower fifth earned 4 per cent of the national income (Pearlstein, 1995: 6; derived from Economic Policy Institute based on Current Population Survey).

Schooling attainment continues to be a critical statistical predictor for economic success. There is a payoff in education and the differences between the income of college graduates and high school graduates has grown slightly larger over the years. It is not so much that college graduation is the guaranteed stairway to economic success; it is much more that having no more than a high school degree is a guaranteed path to economic disaster. In 1975, the college graduate's average hourly wage was $17.50; the average high school graduate's hourly income was $12. Twenty years later the average college graduate earned $16.50; whereas the high school graduate's income had fallen to $10 an hour (all in 1994 dollars) (Pearlstein, 1995, p. 6; derived from Economic Policy Institute based on Current Population Survey). The loss in earnings for high school graduates makes the slogan 'stay in school and get a good job' ring hollow for the nearly half of the population for whom higher education is not in the picture and for the 70 per cent who never graduate from a university or college. Furthermore, the payoff of receiving a high school diploma and a college degree (four years) becomes more revealing when disaggregated by race/ethnicity. Median annual income (1988) for whites with a high school diploma was $28,032; for Hispanics and blacks with four years of high school, median annual earnings were $26,282 and $19,784, respectively. Median annual incomes for whites with four years of college was $46,350 in 1988. In contrast, Hispanics and Blacks with four years of college had median incomes of $38,140 and $32,960, respectively (Pérez and De La Rosa Salazar, 1993).

Complicating the matter further is that a college education not only has lost some of its earning power, it is not uniformly beneficial. For some, the payoff from college is very large, others are no better off than if they would have been had they discontinued education after high school. In 1975, college graduates in the upper tenth of income earned just under $30 an hour (1994 dollars); in 1995, the upper tenth of college graduates in income earned $28 an hour. Over the same period, those in the lower tenth of college graduate income declined from $9 an hour to $8 an hour.

The economic reality has influenced attitude. There is little optimism for the future. Although blacks and whites see things very differently in many, many areas, they agree on one point: Both are fearful about the future (Morin, 1995: 7).

When whites envision an insecure future for themselves and believe that minorities have already caught up, if not surpassed them, there is limited support for affirmative action (Morin, 1995). With the current mind-set, even if public opinion would coincide with the factual world, there would be little interest in equalizing opportunity. In 'an every "man" for himself' world, the emphasis is on getting an edge, not in leveling the playing field.

The current political agenda is for more of the same. There is virtually no one of stature in either political party that advocates democratic education. Calls for equalizing opportunity are dismissed as remnants of discredited liberal past. With the demise of the Soviet Union, liberals have become the demons of the current political war and they are traduced daily in 'search and destroy' missions on increasingly influential talk shows, and by a well organized fundamentalist Christian political machine that has both supported the Republican agenda and independently and effectively militated against democratizing the school. Even when defeated, the Christian fundamentalists have become such a focus that other issues have lost priority.

More important than the fundamentalist effort to take over schools has been the corporate effort to dictate the conditions of educational reform. Beginning with the *Nation at Risk* (National Commission on Excellence in Education, 1983) the report published by President Reagan's appointed National Commission, schools have been pressured to accept as their overriding mission the preparation of a skilled work force. In *Nation at Risk*, schools were blamed for the failure of the United States to remain competitive in the world economy. The results of what amounted to an unrelenting barrage against schools has led people across the entire ethnic spectrum to believe that schools are not as good as they used to be (Morin, 1995). Schools became a major concern of legislatures. Democrats tried to prove that they were as draconian as Republicans in forcing schools to toe the mark. Thus, a spate of standards and conditions were imposed on schools, all of which served to limit debate and to force into the background issues of justice and equity. Through this national, top-down, elitist, remote control strategy of school reform, omnibus reform packages were passed by many state legislatures. Given the deficit thinking paradigm of such reform efforts, it was inevitable that low-socioeconomic status minority schools would be hit the hardest — particularly the reforms implemented in testing (see Valencia and Guadarrama, 1996).

The search for a competitive edge supplants equal opportunity as the overriding emphasis of parents. When the future looks bleak, equity appears to be a luxury that cannot be afforded. Such attitude coincides neatly with the campaign for privatizing schools. Privatization is viewed as a means of salvation from schools burdened by bureaucracy and made inefficient by teacher unions that are portrayed as greedy wastrels and protectors of the incompetent.

The Evolution of Deficit Thinking

Add yet another dimension — the importance of crime and violence in people's political thinking. Crime has become the single largest issue in political life. Increasingly victimized, but importantly inflamed by media sensationalism that associates crime and race, a public has been mobilized to seek vengeance, not justice.

At the present time, much of what were described as social programs are being dismantled. Schools have lost their way. If the trend continues, the prospects are that the poor will be left to fend for themselves; an increasingly high proportion of public monies will be invested in prisons; a disproportionately large number of prisoners will be black and Latino; and schools will be deployed as independent enclaves, catering to differences and struggling to remain alive as free enterprises in an ever more bitter and ruthless competitive market. The gulf between racial/ethnic will grow, with the dialogue between them reduced to shrill and angry diatribe. Racial violence and hate crimes will likely increase. The future we face has been graphically presented to us as 'The Coming Anarchy' (Kaplan, 1994). It is not a consummation devoutly to be wished.

The Growing Anti-Deficit Thinking Discourse

In our analysis thus far, the portrait of the future of deficit thinking has been painted with hues of pessimism. This depiction is based on the premise that deficit thinking will go unchallenged. This, of course, is *not* the case. Many scholars, past and present, have called into question the validity of the deficit thinking construct. Thus, our portrait's canvas must share its space with hues of optimism.

In this book, the contributors have documented not only the unfolding of deficit thinking, but also the dissent that has accompanied its evolution. For about a century, numerous scholars from many disciplines (notably anthropology, psychology, sociology and educational psychology) have been critiquing deficit thinking in educational thought and practice. Such criticisms have ranged from mild, guarded disagreements from within an academic field (psychology) to outright, severe rebukes from an outsider perspective (anthropology contra psychology). In some points in history (hereditarianism in the 1920s), deficit thinking *was* the orthodoxy. Thus, it was necessary for intellectuals to mount a full-blown heterodoxy.

Current anti-deficit thinking discourse is an extension of decades of dissent. Contemporary challenges to deficit thinking, like the 'at-risk' debate, which have in common the shifting of blame from endogenous to exogenous bases, follow the early trails laid down by the likes of Franz Boas, W.E.B. DuBois, Ada Arlitt, Otto Klineberg, William Bagley, Martha MacLear, Horace Mann Bond, E. Franklin Frazier, Howard H. Long, Martin Jenkins, George I. Sánchez, and many others (see Valencia, Chapter 3). More recently, in the early 1970s and spanning through the mid-1990s, there has been considerable discourse in which deficit thinking has been criticized and, in some cases, we have seen the advancement of competing and more valid explanations for school failure and/or the plight of the poor (just to name a small number of critics and innovators — Fine, 1990, 1995; Foley, 1990;

Funicello, 1993; Ginsburg, 1972, 1986; Kozol, 1991; Lubeck and Garrett, 1990; Neisser, 1986; Pearl, 1970, 1972, 1991; Reed, 1992; Ronda and Valencia, 1994; Ryan, 1971; Swadener, 1990; Swadener and Lubeck, 1995; Valencia, 1991). We are pleased that the present book joins these ranks.

In the final analysis, it appears that deficit thinking is resurging. We do think, however, that its momentum can be substantially slowed down. This will not be easy. Although current deficit thinking in educational thought and practice — and in the negative views held towards the poor, in general — are held in disrepute by many scholars, we still live in troubled times. The neoconservatism in national and state politics is quick to blame the victim. Neohereditarianism, à la *The Bell Curve*, appears to be mounting. The at-risk construct, albeit attempts to deconstruct it, is gradually driving its taproot deeper into the academic soil. Lo and behold, even white hate groups, spewing their racist diatribe, have found a home in cyberspace via the Internet (Sheppard, 1995).

As veterans of the deficit thinking discourse, we can say with an historical perspective, that current deficit thinking, if left to go unchallenged, will grow in such magnitude in education policy implications that the first decade of the forth-coming twenty-first century will rival the 1960s deficit thinking in social import. As such, full-scale war must be declared on current deficit thinking. On-going dissent, deconstruction of deficit notions, alternative and credible interpretations of school failure, and models of democratic, equitable education must continue to be advanced. Much is at stake. In sum, deficit thinking *vis-à-vis* any deconstruction of the notion remains an intellectual war over the more credible theory of school failure and school reform. To this effect, we are reminded by the words of Stephan Chorover who wrote in *From Genesis to Genocide*:

> Theories of human nature and programs of behavior control are inherently controversial because they are socially constructed. No amount of special pleading on behalf of the alleged moral and ethical neutrality of 'behavior science' should be allowed to obscure the fact that the conceptual and material products of scholarship are not value-free. To the contrary, they have long been used (and still are being used) as social weapons. (1979: 210)

And, we cannot forget the role of human agency in any anti-deficit thinking discourse. To be sure, deficit thinking is a brutal form of oppression as it thwarts human development. For those who have been victimized by deficit thinking, there must be counterattacks driven by a rage to win. For if not, one's liberation from the grip of deficit thinking's impact will be difficult to attain. To this effect, we find some comfort in the words of John Amos Comenius, Czech theologian and educator (1592–1670), who over three and a half centuries ago advocated for public and universal education, a league of nations to discuss politics and government, and universal peace. Although he was 'Driven from country to country by tyranny and inquisition . . .' (Ulich, 1945: 199), Comenius still had faith in achieving his goals. In 1657 he wrote in his *Via Lucis* (*The Way of Light*; Comenius, 1657/1939):

For there is inborn in human nature a love of liberty — for liberty man's mind is convinced that it was made — and this love can by no means be driven out: so that, wherever and by whatever means it feels that it is being hemmed in and impeded, it cannot but seek a way out and declare its own liberty. (1657: 18)

Notes

1   As the data show, contrary to widespread belief, *Latinos* were *not* the fastest growing ethnic group in the US from 1980 to 1990. Asian/Pacific Islanders were increasing at a rate twice that of Latinos. This comparison needs to be tempered with caution, however, when growth in absolute numbers is the referent point. As Macías underscores, 'One should keep in mind . . . that the numerical growth of Latinos was almost as large as that for blacks, Amerindians, and Asian/Pacific Islanders *combined*, and was equal to about 68 per cent of the growth of whites' (1993: 237).

2   Major population shifts are also expected to occur among racial/ethnic minority groups. The projection is that Hispanics will eclipse blacks in the year 2010 to become the nation's largest minority group (Bovee, 1993).

3   California is another example of where the unprecedented growth of the Latino population is occurring. Using the medium projection scenario, Bouvier (1991) estimates Hispanics (at 40 per cent) will be the *largest* ethnic group in California by 2020 (Anglos are projected to be 35.9 per cent, Asians, 17.4 per cent, and blacks 6.7 per cent).

4   And still yet another example of the phenomenal growth in the Hispanic population (in this case, the youth sector) is that the Pallas, *et al.* (1989) projections translate into this observation by these authors: The Hispanic youth population will account '. . . *for most of the overall* [youth] *population growth* [emphasis added] expected between 1982 and 2020' (p. 19). Stated more specifically in percentage growth, it is projected that Hispanic youth will account for 77 per cent of the total, national youth growth between 1982 and 2020.

5   The official poverty line in 1989 was $9855 per year for a family of three and $12,675 for four (Puente, 1991).

6   Historically, and to a large extent currently, school segregation is frequently viewed only as a black–white issue. However, 'The notion that school desegregation and integration is only a concern relating to one minority group [black] is false. With the nation's Hispanic and Asian populations increasing, the segregation of students from those groups is also a concern' (Orfield and Monfort, 1992: i; also, see Donato, Menchaca and Valencia, 1991). The isolation of Hispanic students has been so remarkable in recent years that Hispanic students enrolled in California and Texas schools experience greater segregation than do blacks in Alabama and Mississippi (Orfield and Monfort 1992).

References

APPLEBOME, P. (1995, September 26) 'School busing battle lines being drawn', *Austin American-Statesman*, p. A2.

BOUVIER, L.F. (1991) *Fifty Million Californians?*, Washington, DC: Center for Immigration Studies.

BOVEE, T. (1993, September 9) 'Hispanics to become largest US minority', *Austin American-Statesman*, pp. A1, A11.

BROOKS, A.P. and SOUTH, J. (1995, April 9) 'School-choice plans worry resegregation critics', *Austin American-Statesman*, pp. A1, A18–19.

Brown v. Board of Education of Topeka (1954) 347 US 483, at 494.

CHAPA, J. and VALENCIA, R.R. (1993) 'Latino population growth, demographic characteristics and educational stagnation. An examination of recent trends', *Hispanic Journal of Behavioral Sciences*, **15**, pp. 165–87.

CHOROVER, S.L. (1979) *From Genesis to Genocide: The Meaning of Human Nature and the Power of Behavior Control*, Cambridge, MA: The Massachusetts Institute of Technology Press.

COMENIUS, J.A. (1939) *The Way of Light* (E.T. Campagnac, trans.), Liverpool, England: University Press of Liverpool. (Original work published 1657.)

DONATO, R., MENCHACA, M. and VALENCIA, R.R. (1991) 'Segregation, desegregation, and integration of Chicano students: Problems and prospects', in VALENCIA, R.R. (Ed) *Chicano School Failure and Success: Research and Policy Agendas for the 1990s*, London: Falmer Press, pp. 27–63.

ESPINOSA, R. and OCHOA, A. (1986) 'Concentration of California Hispanic students in schools with low achievement: A research note', *American Journal of Education*, **95**, pp. 77–95.

ESKENAZI, S. (1994, January 25) 'Minority groups are growing share of Texas population', *Austin American-Statesman*, pp. A1, A5.

FINE, M. (1990) 'Making controversy: Who's "at-risk"?', *Journal of Cultural Studies*, **1**, pp. 55–68.

FINE, M. (1995) 'The politics of who's "at-risk"', in SWADENER, B.B. and LUBECK, S. (Eds) *Children and Families 'at Promise': Deconstructing the Discourse of Risk*, Albany: State University of New York Press, pp. 76–94.

FOLEY, D.E. (1990) *Learning Capitalist Culture: Deep in the Heart of Tejas*, Philadelphia, PA: University of Pennsylvania Press.

FUNICELLO, T. (1993) *The Tyranny of Kindness: Dismantling the Welfare System to End Poverty in America*, New York: Atlantic Monthly Press.

GINSBURG, H. (1972) *The Myth of the Deprived Child: Poor Children's Intellect and Education*, Englewood Cliffs, NJ: Prentice-Hall.

GINSBURG, H.P. (1986) 'The myth of the deprived child: New thoughts on poor children', in NEISSER, U. (Ed) *The School Achievement of Minority Children: New Perspectives*, Hillsdale, NJ: Erlbaum, pp. 169–89.

HERRNSTEIN, R.J. and MURRAY, C. (1994) *The Bell Curve: Intelligence and Class Structure in American Life*, New York: Free Press.

JAEGER, C. (1987) *Minority and Low Income High Schools: Evidence of Education Inequality in Metro Los Angeles* (Report No. 8), Chicago, IL: University of Chicago, Metropolitan Opportunity Project.

KAPLAN, R.D. (1994) 'The coming anarchy', Atlantic Monthly, **233**, pp. 44–76.

KOZOL, J. (1991) *Savage Inequalities: Children in America's Schools*, New York: Crown.

LUBECK, S. and GARRETT, P. (1990) 'The social construction of the "at-risk" child', *British Journal of Sociology of Education*, **11**, pp. 327–40.

MACÍAS, R.F. (1993) 'Language and ethnic classification of language minorities: Chicano and Latino students in the 1990's', *Hispanic Journal of Behavioral Sciences*, **15**, pp. 230–57.

MORIN, R. (1995) 'Across the racial divide: A new survey reveals the depths of our differences', *Washington Post Weekly Edition*, October 16–22, pp. 6–10.

MOYNIHAN, D. (1965) *The Negro Family: The Case for National Action*, Washington, DC: Office of Planning and Research, US Department of Labor.

NATIONAL COMMISSION ON EXCELLENCE IN EDUCATION (1983) *A Nation at Risk: The Imperatives for Educational Reform*, Washington, DC: US Government Printing Office.

NEISSER, U. (Ed) (1986) *The School Achievement of Minority Children: New Perspectives*, Hillsdale, NJ: Erlbaum.

ORFIELD, G. and MONFORT, F. (1992) *Status of School Desegregation: The Next Generation*, Report to the National School Boards Association, Alexandria, VA: Council of Urban Boards of Education.

ORFIELD, G., MONFORT, F. and GEORGE, R. (1987) *School Segregation in the 1980s: Trends in the States and Metropolitan Areas*, Chicago, IL: University of Chicago, National School Desegregation Project, report to the Joint Center for Political Studies.

PALLAS, A.M., NATRIELLO, G. and McDILL, E.L. (1989) 'The changing nature of the disadvantaged population: Current dimensions and future trends', *Educational Researcher*, **18**, pp. 16–22.

PEARL, A. (1970) 'The poverty of psychology — an indictment', in ALLEN, V.L. (Ed) *Psychological Factors in Poverty*, Chicago, IL: Markham, pp. 348–64.

PEARL, A. (1972) *The Atrocity of Education*, New York: Dutton.

PEARL, A. (1991) 'Systemic and institutional factors in Chicano school failure' in VALENCIA, R.R. (Ed) *Chicano School Failure and Success: Research and Policy Agendas for the 1990s*, The Stanford Series on Education and Public Policy, London: Falmer Press, pp. 273–320.

PEARLSTEIN, S. (1995) 'The winners are taking all: In the new economy more and more of us qualify as "losers"', *Washington Post Weekly Edition*, December 11–17, pp. 6–8.

PÉREZ, S.M. and DE LA ROSA SALAZAR, D. (1993) 'Economic, labor force and social implications of Latino educational and population trends', *Hispanic Journal of Behavioral Sciences*, **15**, pp. 188–229.

Plessy v. Ferguson (1896) 163 US, pp. 537–64.

POLAKOW, V. (1995) 'Epilogue: Naming and blaming: Beyond a pedagogy of the poor', in SWADENER, B.B. and LUBECK, S. (Eds) *Children and Families 'at Promise': Deconstructing the Discourse of Risk*, Albany, NY: State University of New York Press, pp. 263–70.

PUENTE, T. (1991, September 2) 'Latino child poverty ranks swell', *Hispanic Weekly Report*, **9**, pp. 1–2.

REED, A., JR. (1992) 'The underclass as myth and symbol: The poverty of discourse about poverty', *Radical America*, **24**, pp. 21–40.

RONDA, M.A. and VALENCIA, R.R. (1994) ' "At-risk" Chicano students: The institutional and communicative life of a category', *Hispanic Journal of Behavioral Sciences*, **16**, pp. 363–95.

RUMBERGER, R.W. and WILLMS, J.D. (1992) 'The impact of racial and ethnic segregation on the achievement gap in California high schools', *Educational Evaluation and Policy Analysis*, **14**, pp. 377–96.

RYAN, W. (1971) *Blaming the Victim*, New York: Random House.

SHEPPARD, G., JR. (1995, December 23) 'Hate groups find a home in cyberspace', *Austin American-Statesman*, pp. A1, A13.

SWADENER, E.B. (1990) 'Children and families "at-risk": Etiology, critique and alternative paradigms', *Educational Foundations*, **4**, pp. 17–39.

SWADENER, B.B. and LUBECK, S. (Eds) (1995) *Children and Families 'at Promise': Deconstructing the Discourse of Risk*, Albany, NY: State University of New York Press.

THE TOMÁS RIVERA CENTER (1992) *Latinos in Texas: A Brief Profile*, Claremont, CA: Author.

ULICH, R. (1945) *History of Educational Thought*, New York: American Book Company.

VALENCIA, R.R. (1984) *Understanding School Closures: Discriminatory Impact on Chicano and Black Students* (Policy Monograph Series, No. 1). Stanford, CA: Stanford University, Stanford Center for Chicano Research.

VALENCIA, R.R. (Ed) (1991) *Chicano School Failure and Success: Research and Policy Agendas for the 1990s*, The Stanford Series on Education and Public Policy, London: Falmer Press.

VALENCIA, R.R. and CHAPA, J. (Eds) (1993) 'Latino population growth and demographic trends: Implications for education' [Special issue], *Hispanic Journal of Behavioral Sciences*, **15**(2).

VALENCIA, R.R. and GUADARRAMA, I.N. (1996) 'High-stakes testing and its impact on racial/ethnic minority students', in SUZUKI, L.A., MELLER, P.J. and PONTEROTTO, J.G. (Eds) *Multicultural Assessment: Clinical, Psychological and Educational Applications*, San Francisco, CA: Jossey-Bass, pp. 561–610.

WATSON, A. (1988, May 15) 'Changing classes: States' minority students to make a majority next fall', *San Jose Mercury News*, pp. 1A, 12A.

Notes on Contributors

Douglas E. Foley is Professor of Education and of Anthropology at The University of Texas at Austin. He specializes in ethnic and race relations and the schooling of ethnic minorities. Dr Foley has written numerous articles and several recent books: *The Heartland Chronicles* (University of Pennsylvania Press, 1995); *Learning Capitalist Culture: Deep in the Heart of Tejas* (University of Pennsylvania Press, 1990); *From Peones to Politicos: Class and Ethnicity in a South Texas Town, 1900–1987* (University of Texas Press, 1988).

Martha Menchaca is Associate Professor of Anthropology at the University of Texas at Austin. Her research explores issues of race and ethnicity in the United States, with a specific focus on the reconstruction of racial minority group histories. Dr Menchaca has published on topics dealing with ideology, school segregation, Chicano–Mexican group conflict, the racial heritage of the Chicanos and legal theory. Her recent book, *Mexican Outsiders: A Community History of Marginalization and Discrimination in California* (University of Texas Press, 1995) reconstructs a community history and examines the social evolution of Anglo American racism in an apparently peaceful town.

Arthur Pearl is Professor Emeritus of Education, University of California, Santa Cruz. He has published widely in the areas of the political economy of education and school reform. Dr Pearl's most recent publications include 'Theoretical trends in youth research' in *International Social Science Journal* (1985); 'Characteristics of a democratic school' in *Disruptive Behavior and Effective Schooling* (edited by R. Slee, 1988); 'Systemic and institutional factors in Chicano school failure' in *Chicano School Failure and Success* (edited by R.R. Valencia, Falmer Press, 1991).

Daniel G. Solórzano is an Associate Professor in Social Sciences and Comparative Education at the Graduate School of Education and Information Studies, University of California, Los Angeles. His current teaching and research interests include the study of minority doctorate production and their career paths, and the application of Critical Race Theory to the educational experience of Chicana and Chicano students. Dr Solórzano's most recent publications on these topics can be found in issues of the *Hispanic Journal of Behavioral Sciences*, *Journal of Negro Education*, *Journal of Women and Minorities in Science and Engineering*, and *Emerging Issues in the Sociology of Education: Comparative Perspectives* (with O. Villalpando), edited by C. Torres, SUNY Press.

Richard R. Valencia is Associate Professor of Educational Psychology at The University of Texas at Austin. His major field of specialization is racial/ethnic minority education (psychological and social aspects), with an emphasis on Mexican American students. He has published extensively on test validity/test bias issues regarding Chicano students. As well, Dr Valencia has published on minority cognitive development, school closures, school segregation, high-stakes testing and Latino demographic trends and educational implications. His 1991 edited book, *Chicano School Failure and Success: Research and Policy Agendas for the 1990s* (Falmer Press), received one of CHOICE's Outstanding Academic Book awards in 1993. From 1984 to 1995, Dr Valencia served in capacities as Editorial Board member and Associate Editor of the *Journal of Educational Psychology*. He currently serves on the editorial Boards of the *Hispanic Journal of Behavioral Sciences*, the *Educational Psychologist*, and the Sage Book Series on *Racial and Ethnic Minority Psychology*.

Author Index

Subject Index

ability 2, 8, 59–61, 68, 72–3, 91, 95, 213, 227
abuse 153–4, 176, 199, 222, 233
access 132, 137, 139, 144, 146, 153, 242
accumulated environmental deficit models 7, 132–55, 193, 198
achievement 53–4, 149, 165, 172, 181–2, 246, 248
  academic 1, 66, 70, 74, 93, 95, 133–4, 140, 237
affirmative action 117, 153, 219, 237, 247, 249
African Americans
  behavior 185
  colonization 17
  culture 122–4, 136
  curriculum 81, 218
  delinquency 146
  deprivation 149
  educability 166
  education 1, 24, 37
  family 119, 133, 143–4
  income 244, 248
  intelligence 43, 84–6, 88, 91, 94, 175
  intelligence testing 55–7, 61–2, 67–71, 161–4, 168, 227
  Jefferson and 212–13
  language 119
  miscegenation 50
  networks 118
  origins 27–9
  perceptions of 199
  population trend 243
  poverty 184
  racism 25–6, 220
  research 83
  rights 21–3, 222
  segregation 4–5, 82, 246
  status 166
  success 139
  support networks 188
animal/human origins 18–19, 24–5, 27–9, 33
anthropological theory of culture 113–26
anthropology 44, 86, 132, 134–5, 250
Army intelligence testing 54–6, 65, 67, 86–7, 91, 93
Asian Americans 37, 56, 87, 124, 218, 220, 243
assimilation 22–3, 114, 119, 124, 137, 143, 172
at-risk concept 190, 195–9, 230, 245–7, 250–1

behavior 2, 7, 42, 44, 52–3, 59, 62, 134, 143–5, 174, 178, 180, 185–7, 225, 231, 233, 251
Bell Curve, The (Herrnstein and Murray) 60, 174–83, 184, 195, 251
belonging 150, 231–2, 237
bilingualism 87, 95–6, 137–9, 171, 173–4
Binet-Simon test 38, 43, 53, 60

capitalism 14, 66, 81, 116, 120, 123, 187
Chicanos 118–19, 122–4, 191, 218
citizenship 21, 32, 37, 146, 215, 217–18, 220–1, 224, 226, 236
civil rights 32, 96, 118, 132, 135, 152, 164, 167
class
  achievement 134
  anthropological concept 122–3
  bias 141
  creativity 234
  culture 136, 148
  culture of poverty 120–2

CPSIA information can be obtained
at www.ICGtesting.com
Printed in the USA
LVHW081257241219
641598LV00007B/328/P